W9-AYJ-918

Discourses of Sexuality

# RATIO
## INSTITUTE FOR THE HUMANITIES

Edited by Tobin Siebers

To take the measure of things and their mismeasure,
to reason unto unreason, to suffer to count and to be
accountable—such is the ratio of that form of life
called the human.

*Discourses of Sexuality: From Aristotle to AIDS*
   Edited by Donna C. Stanton

# DISCOURSES OF SEXUALITY

## *From Aristotle to AIDS*

Edited by Domna C. Stanton

*Ann Arbor*

THE UNIVERSITY OF MICHIGAN PRESS

Copyright © by the University of Michigan 1992
All rights reserved
Published in the United States of America by
The University of Michigan Press
Manufactured in the United States of America

1995   1994   1993   1992     4   3   2   1

*A CIP catalogue record for this book is available from the
British Library.*

## Permissions

"Portraits of People with AIDS" by Douglas Crimp is reprinted from *Cultural Studies*, edited by Lawrence Grossberg, Cary Nelson, and Paula Treichler and published in 1992 by Routledge, Chapman and Hall.

"Toni Morrison's *Beloved:* Re-Membering the Body as Historical Text" by Mae G. Henderson is reprinted from *Comparative American Identities*, edited by Hortense Spillers and published in 1991 by Routledge, Chapman and Hall.

"Does Sexuality Have a History" by Catharine A. MacKinnon first appeared (without the discussion section) in *Michigan Quarterly Review* 30 (Winter 1991): 1-11.

The original version of "The Work of Gender and Sexuality in the Elizabethan Discourse of Discovery" by Louis Montrose appeared in *Representations* 13 (Winter 1991) (copyright 1991, The Regents of the University of California).

"Invented Moralities" by Jeffrey Weeks first appeared in *History Workshop* 32, and is reprinted here in an abridged and revised form with the kind permission of Oxford University Press.

## Acknowledgments

Like most volumes, this one represents a collective enterprise. Most obvious, *Discourses of Sexuality* would not exist without the work that its fourteen authors generously contributed; editing their texts has been pleasurable labor. Less visible but no less important are those who brought production to completion—Eliza Woodford for her indispensable assistance throughout the process, from contacting authors to creating a camera ready copy; Peg Lourie for her skillful and patient copyediting; and James Han for his meticulous conversion of text to disk. To Colin Day and Joyce Harrison of the University of Michigan Press my appreciation for their keen interest in the project and their support. Above all, my thanks to Tobin Siebers, the editor of *RATIO*, the Institute's book series with the University of Michigan Press; knowledgeable and flexible, responsive and efficient, he has been an exemplary collaborator. This volume is the end product of an immensely rewarding year I spent directing the University of Michigan's Institute for the Humanities. My thanks to Mary Beecher Price, the Institute's rock and memory, for her always generous help in guiding me through that year's complexities. And special thanks to James Winn, the permanent Director of the Institute, for committing an entire year to the "Histories of Sexuality" and for enthusiastically supporting the programs we devised. These thanks to all who were part of this enterprise do not cancel debts; they simply register them with gratitude.

—Domna C. Stanton

# Contents

# INTRODUCTION: THE SUBJECT OF SEXUALITY

## Domna C. Stanton

"Sex, the explanation for everything, our master key." So Michel Foucault noted critically in the first of his influential volumes on *The History of Sexuality* as he described the "immense verbosity . . . our civilization has required and organized" around sex.[1] The will to knowledge embodied in the proliferation of discourses about sex in the West, Foucault insisted, nonetheless masked a fundamental will to ignorance about its "political economy"—the conditions of the emergence and operation of its deployment (1:73). The need to expose this unknowledge and to analyze the apparatus of sexuality implicitly justified Foucault's undertaking but did not dispel the irony of his position: he made a voluminous contribution to studies of sexuality while condemning "perpetual discourse" on sex (1:33); he placed sex at the center of an analysis while striving to demystify its cultural significance. To be sure, such irony did not escape Foucault, who observed that the West had invented "the specific pleasure of true discourse on pleasure . . . the formidable 'pleasure of analysis'"(1:71). Still, Foucault waxed more utopic than ironic when he urged "us" "to consider the possibility that one day, perhaps in a different economy of bodies and pleasures, people will no longer quite understand how the uses of sexuality, and the power that sustains its organization, were able to subject us to that austere monarchy of sex, so that we became dedicated to the endless task of forcing its secret" (1:159).

The problematic position that Foucault exemplifies subtends the new studies of sexuality. The sexualism that permeates the pores of Western culture catalyzes the need for a critical analysis of its "excess of significance," to use Gayle Rubin's phrase, its

---

[1] Michel Foucault, *The History of Sexuality*, 3 vols., trans. Robert Hurley (New York: Vintage Books, 1990) 1:78, 33. The publication of volumes 2 and 3 (*The Use of Pleasure* and *The Care of the Self*) in 1984 coincided with his death from AIDS. This notion of "immense verbosity" initiates Foucault's famous challenge to the repressive hypothesis. Foucault does not discard this hypothesis, however: "The doubts I would like to oppose to the repressive hypothesis are aimed less at showing it to be mistaken than at putting it back within a general economy of discourse on sex in modern societies since the seventeenth century" (1:11).

1

sexual categories and practices both past and present, and their imbrication in cultural, political, and economic phenomena, even though this work may further legitimize the idea of "a master key." And yet, this problematic does not diminish the status of modern sexuality as "the most meaning intensive of human activities," in Eve Sedgwick's words, or reduce the importance of sex as "a sign, symbol, or reflection of nearly everything in our culture," to cite Stephen Jay Gould. Nor can this discursive dilemma be resolved by dismissing attention to sexuality as "a frivolous diversion from the more critical problems of poverty, war, disease, racism, famine or nuclear annihilation." As Rubin observes, conflicts over sexual values and conduct explode in the face of such problems; they "acquire immense symbolic weight" and become the "vehicles for displacing social anxieties" (267). Nor, finally, can a concern for the links between sexual and socio-political struggles simply (and simplistically) be classified as white, Western, middle-class obsessions. Underscoring the "centrality of sexuality and male domination to the political and national struggles in the Middle East," for instance, Evelyne Accad has warned that "unless a sexual revolution is incorporated into political revolution, there will be no real transformation of social relations."[2]

"As sex goes, so goes society," Jeffrey Weeks has written, though he would surely agree that "as sex goes, so goes subjectivity." Since the early nineteenth century, when the term first

---

[2]Gayle Rubin, "Thinking Sex: Notes for a Radical Theory of Politics of Sexuality," *Pleasure and Danger: Exploring Female Sexuality*, hereafter *PaD*, ed. Carol S. Vance (Boston: Routledge and Kegan Paul, 1984) 267, 279. For a critique of sexualism as the "new religion" that strives not to be anti-sex, see Stephen Heath, *The Sexual Fix* (New York: Schocken Books, 1984). Eve Kosofsky Sedgwick, *Epistemology of the Closet* (Berkeley: University of California Press, 1990) 5; hereafter, *Closet*. Stephen Jay Gould, "The Birth of the Two-Sexed World" (a review of Thomas Laqueur's *Making Sex: Body and Gender from the Greeks to Freud*), *New York Review of Books* (13 June 1991): 11. Evelyne Accad, "Sexuality and Sexual Politics: Conflicts and Contradictions for Contemporary Women in the Middle East," *Third World Women and the Politics of Feminism*, ed. Chandry Talpade Mohanty, Ann Russo, and Lourdes Torres (Bloomington: Indiana University Press, 1991) 237, 239. Writing on black women, Hortense Spillers dubs sexuality "the locus of great drama—perhaps the fundamental one" ("Interstices: A Small Drama of Words," *PaD* 74).

appears in the English dictionary, sexuality has been considered the "cause" of the natural, interior self, the site of the individual's truth: "it is up to sex to tell us our truth, since sex is what holds it in darkness," says Foucault, paraphrasing doxal thinking (1:77). Situated in the subject's physiology or psychology, and perhaps since Rousseau, believed to antedate the constraints of culture, sex has been defined as the natural, unchanging, essential core of the self. As Robert Padgug has written, in challenging the predominant twentieth-century view of sexuality as an autonomous sphere:

> Such a view necessitates the location of sexuality within the individual as a fixed essence, leading to a classic division of individual and society and to a variety of psychological determinisms, and, often enough, to a full-blown biological determinism as well. These in turn involve the enshrinement of contemporary sexual categories as universal, static, and permanent, suitable for the analysis of all human beings and all societies.[3]

More than one fixed essence, Padgug continues, sexuality is conceived as a group of analytically discrete essences—the male, the female, the homosexual, the lesbian, the fetishist, the sadomasochist, and so forth (8).

Calling this longstanding naturalism and essentialism into question, the new studies of sexuality are markedly historicist and culturalist. For Foucault, sexuality is "the name that can be given to a historical construct"(1:105); and any "answers" about sex will have "to come out of a historical inquiry" (1:72). Of course, Freud had already refuted the naturalness of sexuality at the dawn of the twentieth century, when he showed, for instance, the decisive influence of familial configurations and interrelations on individual sexuality. But as his universal oedipal complex suggests, Freud rejected or ignored the historicity of sexual practices and categories as well as their cultural

---

[3]Jeffrey Weeks, "Sexuality and History Revisited," *State, Private Life and Political Change*, ed. L. Jamieson and H. Corr (London: Macmillan, 1990) 37, 40. The OED lists 1800 as the earliest date for the term *sexuality*, though the adjective, *sexual*, appears as early as the 1650s. Robert A. Padgug, "Sexual Matters: On Conceptualizing Sexuality in History," *Radical History Review* 20 (1979): 16.

specificity, which Mary Douglas has underscored: "nothing is more essentially transmitted by a social process of learning than sexual behavior." Citing Douglas, Padgug rejects the Marxist relegation of sex to the superstructural on the grounds that the history of sexuality is "the history of social relations," and thus that its contents and meanings are in constant change and flux (11). In a crosscultural perspective, this view points to the existence of a myriad of histories of sexuality, and to "sexuality" itself as an unstable category. As David Halperin observes: "To the extent . . . that histories of 'sexuality' succeed in concerning themselves with sexuality, to just that extent are they doomed to fail as histories . . . unless they also include as an essential part of their proper enterprise the task of demonstrating the historicity, conditions of emergence, modes of construction, and ideological contingencies of the very categories of analysis that undergird their own practice."[4]

No category has been put under greater scrutiny in the new studies of sexuality than subjectivity—the history of its changing conceptions, the differences among subject positions at specific historical moments, and even more controversial, the precise degree to which it is culturally constructed. Indeed, the historicization (and thus the denaturalization) of sexuality can be viewed as part and parcel of the deconstruction of an essential subjectivity that has marked modernity, and more specifically, postmodernity. The new studies of sexuality reflect and reinforce the demise of the transcendental "Cartesian" subject, whose identity is the compendium of a universal, unchanging set of traits. Heralded by Freud's division of the self into the conscious/ unconscious, this subject is no longer unified, master of—and present to—itself, in Derridean terms; it is an alienated and divided subject with a contingent, unstable, incoherent, and perhaps fictitious identity. Haunted by the specter of non-identity, for Lacan, the "I" becomes an effect of language as a symbolic system; or then, for Foucault, the product of a historically specific system that speaks it, of discourses that construct it. Not surprisingly, then, in the seminal introduction to *The Use of*

[4]Mary Douglas, *Natural Symbols: Explorations in Cosmology* (New York: Vintage, 1973) 93. This volume should be titled *Discourses of Sexualities*, were it not for the awkward, comic ring of those pluralities in our singularly tuned ears. David Halperin, "Is There a History of Sexuality?" *History and Theory* 28 (1989): 273.

*Pleasure*, the second volume of his *History of Sexuality*, Foucault redefined his project as a study of the modes according to which individuals in "modern Western societies came to recognize themselves as subjects of a 'sexuality,'" in short, as "the history of desiring man" (2:4, 6).

In the process of reconceptualizing subjectivity, sexual identity becomes fundamentally problematic. "What can 'identity,' even 'sexual identity' mean in a new theoretical and scientific space where the very notion of identity is challenged?" asks Julia Kristeva. Accordingly, the rigid distinctions between heterosexual and homosexual identities, which grounded the system of sexuality and which Freud had already blurred, are consistently and concretely subverted in the new work on sexuality. This includes scholarship that shows the meaninglessness of the modern categories of hetero/homosexual for the classical and early-Christian periods; the proliferation of studies of crossdressing, which display both the performative nature of sexual gender and the ambiguity of hetero/homosexual desire for—and in—the transvestite; the debate surrounding Adrienne Rich's influential "lesbian continuum," which encompasses both hetero- and homosexual women; and Eve Sedgwick's widely used notion of "the homosocial bond" as determinant in the heterosexual object choice of male desire.[5]

Inevitably, assumptions of an unchanging "homosexual" essence have been challenged within gay and lesbian studies in ways that emblematize the debates over the construction of sexual subjectivity.[6] As scholars have examined changing attitudes

---

[5]Julia Kristeva, "Women's Time," *Signs: Journal of Women in Culture and Society* 7 (1981): 33–34. On the breakdown of these categories, see Marjorie Garber's *Vested Interests: Cross-Dressing and Cultural Anxiety* (New York: Routledge, 1992); Adrienne Rich, "Compulsory Heterosexuality and Lesbian Existence," *Signs* 5 (1980): 631–60 ; Eve Sedgwick, *Between Men: English Literature and Male Homosocial Desire* (New York: Columbia University Press, 1985). This distinction between hetero/homosexuality is already undermined in Caroll Smith-Rosenberg's study of the erotic rhetoric in eighteenth-and nineteenth-century women's friendships, in *Signs* 1 (1975): 1–29.

[6]I am using the homosexual and the lesbian here to represent the horizon and limit of subjectivity. Extending this idea, Sedgwick shows "how a whole cluster of the most crucial sites for the contestation of meaning in twentieth-century Western culture are . . . quite indelibly marked with the historical specificity of homosocial/homosexual definition . . . from around

toward homosexuals in different cultures and eras, changing definitions of sexual categories and thus of the practices those categories purportedly denoted, they have often concluded that the differences are so profound and rooted in yet other cultural differences that, as Sedgwick states, "there may be no continuous defining essence of 'homosexuality' to *be* known" (*Closet* 44). Moreover, "the homosexual," as a unified category, has been undermined by the study of differences *between* gays and lesbians; Diane Fuss, for instance, considers those differences to be so radical and adversarial that they constitute "a gay/lesbian binarism within homosexual theory and politics." Enumerating some differences, George Chauncey, Martin Duberman, and Martha Vicinus distinguish lesbian from gay social networks, but especially, the centrality ascribed to genital sexuality in gay studies, as compared to the importance of romantic or idealized female friendships in lesbian studies; but this characterization of women's eroticism has been strongly contested by some lesbian theorists. At bottom, Fuss finds that gay male theory espouses different notions of subjectivity from lesbian theory. Lesbian theory has been

> less willing to question or to part with the idea of a "lesbian essence" and an identity politics based on this shared essence. Gay male theorists, on the other hand, following the lead of Foucault have been quick . . . to develop more detailed analyses of the historical construction of sexualities. That lesbian scholarship tends, on the whole, to be more essentialist than gay male scholarship is *not* to imply that lesbian theory is unsophisticated or reactionary; it . . . may well indicate that lesbians inhabit a more precarious and less secure subject position than gay men. Lesbians, in other words, simply may have

the turn of the century" (*Closet* 43–44). Within gay studies, the notion of a transhistorical homosexual identity has been defended by John Boswell, in *Christianity, Social Tolerance and Homosexuality: Gay People in Western Europe from the Beginning of the Christian Era to the Fourteenth Century*, 1980 (Chicago: University of Chicago Press, 1980), the constructionist position by Weeks, Jonathan Dollimore, in *Sexual Dissidence: Augustine to Wilde, Freud to Foucault* (New York: Oxford University Press, 1991), and by David Halperin. Halperin observes, however, that even if homosexuality is learned, it can't

more to lose by failing to subscribe to an essentialist philosophy. (98–99)[7]

Such resistance to the de-essentialization of subjectivity and to the culturalist (or constructionist) notion of sexuality dramatizes the stakes involved in the politics of identity for sexual minorities. As with feminist studies two decades ago and African-American, postcolonial, and ethnic studies in the 1980s, the subversion of the concept of subjectivity that guaranteed the authority of one gender, race, and class in the West seems to coincide suspiciously, for some lesbian and gay critics, with the emergence of minority discourse ("Queer Theory"), on the one hand, and heightened backlash (homophobia), on the other. Julia Epstein and Kristina Straub thus wonder whether identity is a trap from which a fluid (or "ambiguous") subjectivity "can liberate us," or whether this fluidity is "a seductive but dangerous illusion in political struggles with a right wing which is all too comfortable with its beliefs in 'essentials' . . . ?" To "give up" identity or ontology may entail the loss of the community that empowered this minority discourse, and thus of the political and psychic basis for combatting oppression. Acknowledging the "political imperative . . . to rally and represent an oppressed political constituency," and to use some sign of identity now, Judith Butler asks how it can be used "in such a way that its futural significations are not *foreclosed*?"[8]

---

necessarily be unlearned. See his *One Hundred Years of Homosexuality and Other Essays on Greek Love* (New York: Routledge, 1990) 29–52.

[7]Diana Fuss, *Essentially Speaking: Feminism, Nature and Difference* (New York: Routledge, 1989) 110, hereafter, *ES*. On the tensions between gays and lesbians over identity, see Sedgwick, *Closet* 36ff. See also George Chauncey, Jr., Martin Duberman, and Martha Vicinus "Introduction," *Hidden from History: Reclaiming the Gay and Lesbian Past* (New York: Meridian, 1989) 5–8. Exceptions to Fuss' view of lesbian theory as essentialist are numerous, including Rubin, "Thinking Sex" 275–77 and Judith Butler (see n. 8).

[8]Julia Epstein and Kristina Straub, "Introduction: The Guarded Body," *Body Guards: The Cultural Politics of Gender Ambiguity* (New York: Routledge, 1991) 9. The political efficacy of gender "ambiguity" is questionable, Epstein and Straub continue, because of the degree to which it has been successfully marketed; they ask, do ambiguous bodies subvert dominant structures or do they create a safety valve that reinforces them? (10, 25). Judith

Invoking a psychoanalytic "Other" incorporated in the self, which vitiates the possibility of any self-identity, Butler believes it should be "permanently unclear" what the sign, *lesbian*, signifies, since "identity categories" are for her, as for Foucault, "instruments of regulatory regimes, whether as the normalizing categories of oppressive structures or as the rallying points for a liberatory contestation of that oppression" (quoted in Fuss, *I/O* 13–14). Like Butler, Fuss criticizes the constructionist view of sexual subjectivity for eliding the psychic and the unconscious, and thus jettisoning "psychoanalysis along with essentialism" (*ES* 108–9). Critical, moreover, of the idea of "multiple identities" for still failing to challenge identity as unity, Fuss favors the idea of transitory, provisional identity that is continually assumed and immediately called into question, and that highlights differences within as well (103–4). In my view, this fractured, fluid, mobile, and divided sexual subject would still allow for single or multiple, brief or longlasting affiliations or identifications without being entrapped in the identity categories of the institutional discourses of sexuality.

The vexed issue of sexual identity may not only be impossible to adjudicate, as Sedgwick suggests (*Closet* 44), it may be counterproductive to do so. Within a culture, different communities with different needs, histories, and traditions may require, from a pragmatic perspective, the simultaneous existence of different conceptions of sexual identity. At the very least, this would now include the deconstructed (male) subject, propounded by postmodern master thinkers, which, at its most radical, is only an effect of language, and a fluid, deferred identity that favors multiple provisional identifications. In addition, however, some communities need to affirm identity as a phase in the process of empowerment, what Gayatri Spivak calls "the *strategic* use of a positivist essentialism in a scrupulously visible political interest." Indeed, the effort to (re)think essentialism as a historically situated (utopian) project spells yet another project for reconceptualizing subjectivity.[9] More than simply pluralistic, the

Butler, "Imitation and Gender Insubordination," *Inside/Out: Lesbian Theories, Gay Theories,* ed. Diana Fuss (New York: Routledge, 1991) 19; hereafter, *I/O.*

[9]Like Spivak's concept of "strategic essentialism," presented in *In Other Worlds: Essays in Cultural Politics* (New York: Methuen, 1987) 205, Leslie Rabine's view that essentialism is the only means available for

new studies of sexuality delineate what I would call "a subjectivity continuum" along which a subject may identify through his/her agency at one—and, in all probability, more than one—point depending on the practice, institutional context, or moment.

*I*

It is difficult to determine the political implications of the various positions in the essentialism/constructionism debates, which have been critical both to work on sexual subjectivity and, more broadly, to discussions within and between the humanities and social sciences in the last decade. The willingness to "take the risk of essentialism," for instance, may represent a necessary "minority" strategy to combat powerful, conservative forces and/or an imitation of conservative foundationalism. Analogously, whereas the new studies of sexuality have clearly emerged "along with" the rise of the New Right, it is unclear, to frame a complex question reductively, whether this field is the academic arm of "the sexual liberation" of the 1960s and early 1970s, which catalyzed a conservative onslaught, or whether it developed in opposition to a revived puritanism and fundamentalism that spread from the Bible Belt to the White House. More than a linear sequence of actions and reactions, causes and effects, the history of sexuality ("sexualities") after the Second World War involves the coexistence of "repressive" and "progressive" trends at any particular time, on the understand-

speaking against the dominant ideology of gender in certain contexts, and that essentialism and anti-essentialism are unstable, interdependent terms in a heterogeneous feminist strategy, is elaborated in an issue on "The Essential Difference," in *differences* 2, n. 1 (Summer, 1989). See also Teresa de Lauretis, "Upping the Anti (*sic*) in Feminist Theory," *Conflicts in Feminism*, ed. Marianne Hirsch and Evelyn Fox Keller (New York: Routledge, 1990) 256–58. Linda Alcoff argues for a third way, beyond essentialism and constructionism, based on historical positionality in "Cultural Feminism vs. Poststructuralism: The Identity Crisis in Feminist Theory," *Signs* 13, n. 3 (Spring 1988) especially 429ff. Eve Sedgwick has tried to recast the debate through the notion of minoritizing vs. universalizing arguments (*Closet* 82–86).

ing that those terms have meaning only in a relational sense informed by my own partial perspective. I also understand the difficulty of pinpointing the demarcations between the resistance of sexual movements and their complicity with regulatory regimes.

In the 1950s, for instance, the cold war abroad seems to have paralleled conservative sexual trends at home, even as homosexual activity or visibility grew.[10] Just as Alfred Kinsey was attacked for weakening America's moral fiber and making it more vulnerable to communism, communists and homosexuals were the objects of witch hunts to eliminate their "menace" to national and familial stability. A possible reaction to the increase of homosexual associations (the Mattachine Society and the Daughters of Bilitis were founded in 1950s, the first by gay men associated with the communist party), institutions (the gay bar), and discourses, and to expanded opportunities for non-conjugal sex during World War II, this sexual conservatism did not disappear during the 1960s. It focused on the battle—largely successful judging by the formation of hundreds of organizations—to keep sex education out of the classroom, an attitude still rampant today. The "sexual liberation" of the Woodstock decade, which witnessed a marked increase of sexual activity among the young (the "swinging singles"), along with the countercultural rejection of the monogamous, matrimonial nuclear family, was fueled by the needs of consumer capitalism. This produced what John D'Emilio and Estelle Freedman call an unprecedented "commercialization of sex and . . . sexualization of commerce" (358), exemplified by the dramatic rise of the pornographic and advertising industries. As the burgeoning movement of second-wave feminism saw it, females were still sexual objects in mainstream culture; "(hetero)sexual freedom" seemed to be the cover for freer male access to female bodies, and it maintained—even reinforced—inequalities between the genders. Spurred by their experience in New Left politics and the civil rights movement, feminists succeeded, through the passage of

---

[10]The rapid survey of developments in the politics of sexuality that follows is indebted to John D'Emilio and Estelle B. Freedman, *A History of Sexuality in America* (New York: Harper and Row, 1988) especially 275–360. See also, John D'Emilio, "The Homosexual Menace: The Politics of Sexuality in Cold War America," *Passion and Power*, ed. Kathy Peiss and Christina Simmons (Philadelphia: Temple University Press, 1989) 226–40.

Roe vs. Wade in 1973, in ensuring a woman's right to reproductive choice, and thus to (some) control over her body. In turn, these three movements mobilized homosexuals—notably after the 1969 Stonewall Inn confrontation proclaiming "gay power"—and resulted in the elimination of sodomy statutes from the penal codes of half the states and of strictures against the employment of gays and lesbians in the Civil Service, as well as the passage of several city ordinances for their civil rights.

By the mid 1970s, however, a crisis over sexuality had crystallized, and it pitted these sexual activists against a new coalition of conservative forces. Already in 1976, reproductive rights had been severely curtailed when the use of federal dollars to fund abortions was prohibited; this encouraged the new pro-life movement to engage in a campaign abortion-as- murder, which would include bombings against abortion clinics. Beyond their determination to abrogate reproductive rights, the right-wing organizations that proliferated in the 1970s and the Protestant fundamentalist sects that disseminated their moral crusades through televangelism aimed to bring about the moral "rejuvenating of a nation," as Jerry Falwell of the Moral Majority stated (D'Emilio and Freedman 348). Once again, "immoral" sexual behavior was linked to putative declines in American power and, as neo-conservative Norman Podhoretz claimed, the inability to stand up to the Russians (Rubin 273). Spearheaded by Anita Bryant's successful crusade in Dade County in 1977, gay rights ordinances were repealed in numerous cities and counties. Opposed to homosexuality, pornography, abortion, sex education, and premarital sex, the right-wing coalition of political conservatives and religious fundamentalists were to capture "the center" of American thought with the landslide victory of Ronald Reagan in 1980. The "sexual counter-revolution" of the 1980s[11] was intent on restoring sexuality to the "safe" haven of reproduction within the "traditional" family and on bringing about an era of abstinence, of "just-say-no" to all non-conjugal practices.

In 1981, the crisis over sexuality assumed the traits of a moral panic with the AIDS epidemic, targeting gay men, intravenous drug users and, what was at first not known or disseminated, heterosexuals in Africa. As the New Right proclaimed the

[11]Paul Robinson, *The Modernization of Sex: Havelock Ellis, Alfred Kinsey, William Masters and Virginia Johnson* (New York: Harper and Row, 1976) viii–ix.

disease a just retribution from God—"AIDS is God's way of weeding his garden," intoned evangelist Pat Robertson (*Closet* 129)—and succeeded in constructing the face of AIDS in the mainstream media, the Reagan Supreme Court in 1986 sustained the constitutionality of sodomy laws directed against homosexuals. Proposals to impose mandatory testing and to quarantine carriers and high risk groups, matched by the slowness to commit resources to combat the plague and alleviate the devastation, provoked terror within the gay community and raised the specter of "gay genocide" (128). As AIDS spread to the heterosexual population in the West—heterosexual women are the fastest-growing AIDS demographic group in the United States today—this phantasm was tantamount to "omnicide" (130). Concurrently, however, AIDS provoked an upsurge of organization and activism from groups—such as the Gay Men's Health Crisis and ACT UP—to care for the sick and dying, raise money for education and research, and engage in demonstrations to combat indifference, ignorance, and discrimination. Much less successful, however, has been the ability of progressive forces to construct a sexual discourse to combat the dominance of the Right.

Despite the global implications of the AIDS epidemic, or more probably, because of them, assaults against sexual freedoms have intensified in recent years. Thus reproductive rights were attacked in the 1984 Republican platform and, subsequently, in a series of Supreme Court decisions that makes the demise of Roe vs. Wade a near certainty. More broadly, the New Right has waged "culture wars" in the name of traditional moral values to control what is said, depicted, and taught. It has prosecuted works of art (by Mapplethorpe and Serrano, for instance) as obscene, withdrawn federal support from art that might be offensive to some, and brought about the resignation of NEA's Executive Director in 1992, leaving the agency's future in serious doubt. Even a mainstream sitcom's depiction of single motherhood as a choice is denounced by the Vice President as mocking traditional values. Despite their campaign of censorship, neoconservatives have vilified "tenured radicals" as Stalinists who brook no disagreement with what they deem "politically correct," are hostile to the canon of great works of Western literature, and brainwash students with left ideologies, immoral values, and prurient interests through deconstructive, postcolonial, feminist, and now "queer" readings of unknown, third-rate, subversive texts.

To be sure, sexuality has been imbricated in political and cultural controversies since the emergence of the concept in the early nineteenth century. Still, the degree to which sexuality has been politicized and certain sexual issues bitterly contested in recent years seems to outdo even the previous *fin de siècle*.[12] The virulence of the crisis in the U.S. must be related to the particularities of this historical conjuncture: among these are a need to account for the decline of America's economic preeminence by associating excessive sexual preoccupations with the destruction of the work ethic and other "American values"; the search for enemies within now that the cold war is over; and radical demographic changes that have altered the color of America, and that generate nostalgic obsessions to return—sexually and in other ways—to a mythic purity that never was.

To cast this sexuo-political crisis simply as a battle between right and left, conservative and liberal or radical, the powerful and the powerless would be not only inaccurate but largely self-serving. "Repressive" and "progressive" sexual trends or phenomena are both enmeshed in networks and relations of power and, to (sometimes radically) different degrees, are complicitous with dominant forces. Thus, the feminist activism that led to the redefinition of pornography as violence against women c. 1975, rather than the "liberal" view of healthy sexual expression against a puritanical society, influenced and gained support from the 1986 Meese commission conclusion that pornography is and causes violence.  Some feminists—notably Women Against Pornography—formed an alliance with the New Right to ban sexually explicit materials: the ordinance written by Andrea Dworkin and Catharine A. MacKinnon, though subsequently overturned, declared pornography a violation of women's civil rights.  While it aimed to combat misogyny, this alliance also supported broad conservative goals of imposing stringent limitations on sexual practices and discourses.[13]

---

[12]On the sexual parallels between the two *fins de siècle*, see Elaine Showalter, *Sexual Anarchy: Gender and Culture at the Fin de Siecle* (New York: Viking, 1990).

[13]For a critique of the Meese commission hearings and report, see Carol Vance, "The Pleasures of Looking: The Attorney General's Commission on Pornography versus Visual Images," *The Critical Image: Essays on Contemporary Photography*, ed. Carol Squiers (Seattle: Bay Press, 1990) 38–58.  On this conflict among feminists, see Daphne Read, "(De)Con-

As this mode of resistance against the sexual oppression of women demonstrates, analytical discourse that strives to produce "new" knowledge about sexual histories, categories, and practices   does not occur against—or outside of—power relations. "We must not think that by saying yes to sex, one says no to power," Foucault emphasizes, nor that one who speaks about sex "places [him/herself] to a certain extent outside the reach of power; . . . upsets established law; . . . somehow anticipates the coming freedom"(1:157, 6). Clearly, "new" knowledge or interpretations can only be tracked "along the course laid out by the general deployment of sexuality," along its mechanisms of power-knowledge in different institutions, and by those discourses dating back to the nineteenth century, which "did not multiply apart from or against power, but in the very space and as the means of its exercise" (1:157, 32). It could even be argued, with Foucault, that "if sexuality was constituted as an area of investigation, this was only because relations of power had established it as a possible object" (1:98). This idea may be easier to accept for past eras than for "our" own embattled times. Still, the deafening noise of "our" sexual culture and the general deployment of sexuality it reinforces undeniably determine the parameters of any analysis, indeed, may make it impossible to think outside of those parameters.

This does not mean that resistance—as theory or praxis—is impossible, however. For although "resistance is never in a position of exteriority in relation to power," as Foucault observes, the many types of resistance—spontaneous, solitary, concerted, compromising, violent, sacrificial, etc.—are not merely "a reaction or rebound," an underside to "the basic domination . . . always doomed to perpetual defeat" or betrayal (1:95–96). Spread

---

structing Pornography: Feminisms in Conflict," *Passion and Power* 277–92. Among the many texts criticizing the WAP position by what came to be loosely known as "anticensorship feminists," see Ellen Willis, "Feminism, Moralism and Pornography," *Powers of Desire: The Politics of Sexuality*, ed. Ann Snitow, Christine Stansell, and Sharon Thompson (New York: Monthly Review Press, 1982) 460–67; and essays in *PaD*, which I discuss below in connection with the feminist "sex wars." This is not to deny the crucial work that WAP feminists did—and continue to do—in combatting rape, incest, and sexual harassment, and in leading the fight for their criminalization. The WAP position is best presented in Andrea Dworkin's *Pornography: Men Possessing Women* (1981) and Susan Griffin's *Pornography and Silence* (1981).

over times and spaces at varying densities, mobilizing groups or individuals or certain types of behavior, they constitute, writes Foucault, "mobile and transitory points of resistance, producing cleavages in a society that shift about, fracturing unities and effecting regroupings, furrowing across individuals themselves, cutting them up and remolding them . . . the swarm of points of resistance traverses social stratifications and individual unities" (95).[14]

Like oppositional practices to "basic domination," however imprecise Foucault's term may be, analytical discourses about sexuality can constitute points of resistance within existing relations of power, most especially in the midst of a crisis, such as the current one, in which changes in notions of sexual subjectivity, its categories, and practices are combatted by repressive efforts to recreate an illusory past. As Rubin notes, comparing the 1980s with the 1950s: "All the signs indicate that the present era is another of those watersheds in the politics of sex. . . . It is therefore imperative to understand what is going on and what is at stake . . ." (274). Looking toward the resolution of this crisis, prematurely perhaps, Rubin concludes, "In one sense, what is now occurring is the emergence of a new sexual movement, aware of new issues and seeking a new theoretical basis. The sex wars out on the streets have been partly responsible for provoking a new intellectual focus on sexuality. The sexual system is shifting once again, and we are seeing many symptoms of its change" (310). More than a result of these "sex wars" or a superstructural consequence, the new studies of sexuality constitute a practice that has its own impact on the streets. Notwithstanding the paradox of their discursive position in our sexual culture, these studies are informed by—and participate in—a sexual crisis that points to the construction of other subjects of sexuality.

---

[14]These resistances help to counter the apparent ubiquitousness of Foucaultian power relations that has frequently been criticized, among others, by Edward Said in *The World, the Text, and the Critic* (Cambridge: Harvard University Press, 1983) 222–46.

## II

Aside from its complex interrelations with contemporary political movements, the new studies of sexuality are closely linked to developments in the academy since the 1970s, most especially in emerging (and often contested) areas of the humanities—in disciplinary subfields within history and literary studies, for instance, interdisciplinary areas such as women's studies, film studies, gay studies, and cultural studies, and various poststructuralist or postmodern theories and methodologies. Among these discourses, however, it was women's studies that from the outset privileged notions fundamental to the new studies of sexuality: that sexual roles are a product of culture, not nature—"one is not born a woman, one becomes a woman," in de Beauvoir's famous formulation—that power inheres in sexuality, and thus that sexual relations (for example, heterosexuality under "patriarchy") can constitute a fundamental source of social and other inequalities.

Over the past twenty years, dramatic shifts within women's studies have necessarily inflected work on sexuality. Roughly (or reductively), these include the shift from woman/sex to gender, from differences from men to differences within woman/women (a move spurred by strong and productive critiques from lesbians and women of color), and most recently, a focus on the body and sexuality informed by poststructuralist theory and cultural studies. Within this complex configuration, the earliest and still most consistent work on sexuality in women's studies has been the analysis of male sexual violence—rape, wife and child abuse, incest, sexual harassment—and the examination of androcentric imperatives underlying the construction and representations of "feminine" sexuality. More "gynocentric," but at times in my view essentialistic, the imperative to "unearth" the female body, to "rediscover" or "derepress" the silenced female subject of desire overdetermined the production of a variety of discourses in the 1970s in the U.S. Lesbian texts—confessional, novelistic, analytic, self-help, informational—proliferated; these include, beyond Rich's "Compulsory Heterosexuality and Lesbian Existence" (1976), Audrey Lorde's "Uses of the Erotic: The Erotic as Power" (1978), and Pat Califa's *Saphistry: The Book of Lesbian Sexuality* (1980). At the same time, translations of work by Julia Kristeva, Hélène Cixous, and Luce Irigaray, beginning with the first issue of *Signs* in 1975, brought U.S. feminist scholars reluctantly and resistingly into contact with "French theory." That body of texts combined a rigorous philosophical-linguistic-psychoanalytic critique of twentieth-century "masters" with a lyrical "writing of the body" that affirmed the subversive power of female sexuality as the return of the repressed in the phallocratic order, and the radical difference of unbounded, polymorphous female *jouissance*. In speaking to overcome women's centuries-old silence and absence, to displace what Irigaray called the "indifference" of male sexuality, feminists equated more sexual discourse with more freedom and empowerment. Across the Franco-American divide, their poetic, utopian sexual discourse focused (obsessively, in my view) on maternal erotics, a mythography of the preoedipal mother-daughter bond.[15]

In 1982, however, the "sex wars" that exploded at the Barnard College conference on The Politics of Sexuality— published as *Pleasure and Danger: Exploring Female Sexuality* in 1984—marked a watershed in women's studies.[16] Feminists were to be intensely divided, not only over the goals and methods of Women Against Pornography (WAP), which anti-censorship feminists (ACF) opposed, but also over sadomasochistic practices, which dramatized the question of "Politically Correct? Politically Incorrect?" sexuality, as Muriel Dimen ironically entitled her essay in *Pleasure and Danger*. Defining sexual pleasure as a

---

[15]Lorde's text is reprinted in *Sister Outsider* (New York: Out and Out Books, 1984) 53–59. For an analysis of the lesbian novel, see Catharine R. Stimpson, "Zero Degree Deviancy: The Lesbian Novel in English," *Critical Inquiry* 8 (Winter 1981): 363–79. I noted the resistance of Anglo-American feminists to French women theorists, but also the differences and similarities between them, in "The Franco-American Dis-connection," *The Future of Difference*, ed. Hester Eisenstein and Alice Jardine (New York: Columbia University Press, 1980) 73–87; the volume also contains articles by Jane Gallop and Carolyn Burke on the "new" work of French women. In the U.S., critical/lyrical writing on the mother found its first influential expression in Rich's *Of Woman Born* (1976). The first review of massive writing on mothers and daughters is Marianne Hirsch's review essay in *Signs* 7 (1982): 515–44.

[16]See also Ruby Rich's review essay, "Feminism and Sexuality in the 1980s," in *Feminist Studies* 12 (Fall 1986): 526. This is not to ignore the 1981 *Heresies* "Sex Issue," which features graphics and inscriptions of "personal experience."

fundamental right, Carol Vance denounced what she labeled the fear and guilt of WAP tactics, arguing that feminism must eliminate categories of "good" and "bad" sex and embrace self-defined, non-conformist practices (22–24). Widening Vance's attack on WAP to include what she called the lesbian and cultural feminist view of sexual pleasure solely as a reactionary male force, Alice Echols traced its idealization of female relationships to the Victorian model of the pure, unsexed mother (*PaD*, 50–66). Although both sides in these debates propounded arguments from culture ("we must reject patriarchal sexual ideologies of pain and degradation" [WAP] vs. "we must cast off bourgeois restraints on sexual practices" [ACF]), and more troubling, arguments from nature ("this is what Woman is" [WAP] vs. "this is who I am sexually" [ACF]), there was no common basis for discussion: each side defended its position in the name of a "new" feminist sexuality. So doing, both sides could claim to engage in what Foucault termed concerted resistance.

Even more radical for its epistemological implications was Gayle Rubin's essay in *Pleasure and Danger* which challenged the assumption that feminism, (narrowly) defined as the theory of gender oppression, should be the privileged site of work on sexuality. Insisting that "feminist thought simply lacks angles of vision which can encompass the social organization" and the "critical power relations" of sexuality, Rubin concluded, possibly under the influence of Foucault, that it was "essential to separate gender and sexuality analytically," though in the long run they could "enrich" or even "be incorporated into" each other (*PaD* 307–9). Although gender is often foregrounded in lieu (or in the name) of sexuality in women's studies (as in other contributing fields in the new studies of sexuality), Rubin's 1975 essay on "The Traffic in Women" had demonstrated the mutual benefits of their conjunction; instead, Rubin was now postulating a problematic nongendered subject of sexuality. Still, by the mid-1980s a growing dissatisfaction with the binarism of gender had led to a redefinition of this dominant category of feminist analysis or its displacement in favor of sex/uality. Thus Catharine A. MacKinnon privileged sexuality, instead of gender, as the "social process which creates, organizes, expresses, and directs desire, creating the social beings we know as women and men"; de Lauretis used Foucault's "technologies of sex" to elaborate the "technologies of gender" and to highlight differences among and within women; and Judith Butler argued that sex is as culturally constructed as gender, a concept she dissociated from binarism and identity, and redefined as a performative that allows for agency.[17]

In these moves from gender to sex/uality, feminist studies affirmed but by and large have not theorized or textualized the significance of racial/ethnic differences. For over a decade, feminist scholars of color decried this indifference to race and ethnicity, which, among other effects, invalidates propositions about "all women" or "woman" in feminist theory. By 1985, however, the work of women of color had produced a paradigm shift within women's studies, at least in theory, for it translated all too often as the "mantra" of gender, race, and class in white feminist texts. Nor did this shift break white and nonwhite silence about the sexuality of women of color. Reviewing work by white and African-American scholars in 1987, Hortense Spillers described black women as "the beached whales of the sexual universe, unvoiced, misseen, not doing, awaiting *their* verb."[18]  Where she

---

[17]Gayle Rubin, "The Traffic in Women: Notes on the Political Economy of Sex," *Toward an Anthropology of Women*, ed. Rayna Rapp (New York: Monthly Review, 1975) 157–210. See de Lauretis' critique of Rubin's nongendered notion of the sexual subject in "Sexual Indifference and Lesbian Representation," *Theatre Journal* 40 (May 1988): 162–63. Catharine A. MacKinnon, "Feminism, Marxism, Method and the State: An Agenda for Theory," *Signs* 7 (1982): 515–44; de Lauretis, *Technologies of Gender* (Bloomington: Indiana University Press, 1987) 1–28; Judith Butler, *Gender Trouble: Feminism and the Subversion of Identity* (New York: Routledge, 1990). For an excellent review of these shifting definitions of gender, see Donna Haraway, "'Gender' for a Marxist Dictionary: The Sexual Politics of a Word," *Simians, Cyborgs and Women: The Reinvention of Nature* (New York: Routledge, 1991) 127–48.

[18]For critiques of white feminist theory, see, for example, Angela Davis, *Women, Race and Class* (New York: Random House, 1981); Hazel Carby, "White Woman Listen! Black Feminism and the Boundaries of Sisterhood," *The Empire Strikes Back: Race and Racism in 70's Britain* (London: Hutchinson, 1982) 212–35; bell hooks, *Feminist Theory from Margin to Center* (Boston: South End Press, 1984); Chandra Mohanty, "Under Western Eyes: Feminist Scholarship and Colonial Discourse," *boundary* 2 (Spring/Fall 1984): 333–58; Gayatri Spivak, "Three Women's Texts and a Critique of Imperialism," *Race, Writing and Difference*, ed. Henry Louis Gates (Chicago: University of Chicago Press, 1986) 262–80. It is possible, of course, that the politics of identity discouraged a few white women from working on the sex-

does appear in critical discourse, according to Spillers, the black woman has usually been represented as either unsexed or whorish, in Patricia Hill Collins' terms, the nanny or the Jezebel. Beyond these stereotypes, writes Spillers, the historical enslavement of black women has constituted an "act of commodifying so thoroughgoing that the daughters labor even now under the outcome" (76); not surprisingly, then, scholarly work on black women's sexuality has most often focused on slavery and the Reconstruction. At the same time, and as Spillers recognizes, women of color in the U.S. have favored discursive forms other than scholarship to speak about sexuality—the blues, autobiography, life narratives, poetry, and novels—a kind of "first order naming" (87ff), which, I would argue, encompasses theory and might be called a hybrid critical-creative mode or a "theoretical fiction." Despite the often-noted (and exaggerated?) homophobia in African-American and Latino communities, the chief practitioners of these hybrid works have been lesbian women of color—Ann Allen Shockley, *Loving Her* (1974); Audre Lorde, *Zami* (1983); Cherrie Moraga, *Loving in the War Years* (1983); Cheryl Clarke, *Living as a Lesbian* (1986); Gloria Anzaldùa, *Borderlands/La Frontera* (1987); and Jewelle Gomez, *The Gilda Stories* (1991).[19] Paradoxically, this hybridity replicates the ef-

uality of women of color. In turn, women of color largely stayed out of the "sex wars," which they may have perceived as "white sex wars" (Ruby Rich 551). See also Hortense J. Spillers, "Interstices: A Small Drama of Words," *PaD* 74, although Spillers does not cite essays in Gloria T. Hull, Patricia Bell Scott, and Barbara Smith, eds., *All the Women Are White, All the Blacks Are Men, But Some of Us Are Brave: Black Women's Studies* (Old Westbury, New York: Feminist Press, 1982) and in Barbara Smith, ed., *Home Girls: A Black Feminist Anthology* (New York: Kitchen Table: Women of Color Press, 1983).

[19]Patricia Hill Collins, *Black Feminist Thought: Knowledge, Consciousness, and the Politics of Empowerment* (New York: Harper Collins, 1990) 77. On black women's sexuality under slavery see, for example, Angela Davis, "Rape, Racism and the Capitalist Setting," *Black Scholar* 9 (1981): 24–39; the articles of Jacqueline Dowd Hall, Rennie Simson, and Barbara Omolade in *Powers of Desire*; and Hazel Carby, "On the Threshold of Women's Era: Lynching, Empire and Sexuality in Black Feminist Theory," *Critical Inquiry* 12 (Autumn 1985): 262–77. On the importance of the blues as a discourse of black female sexuality see Carby, "'It Jus Be's Dat Way Sometimes': The Sexual Politics of Women's Blues," *Unequal Sisters: Multicultural Reader in*

forts to dissolve generic boundaries among poststructuralist French women theorists.

## III

Although the relations between women's studies and the new studies of sexuality will undoubtedly shift in the coming decade, as both continue to affect and be affected by developments in other humanistic sub/fields, Rubin's recommendation for a separation of the two has not occurred. On the contrary, feminism and Foucault constitute the principal theoretical discourses that have stimulated and shaped the new studies of sexuality, even by the tensions between them.[20] In each of the subfields that I examine briefly in the pages that follow—film studies, new historicism, history, gay and lesbian studies, and cultural studies—feminist or Foucaultian theory tends to dominate. And in keeping with broader epistemological trends in all

U.S. Women's History, ed. Ellen Carol Dubois and Vicky L. Ruiz (New York: Routledge, 1990) 238–49. Debora McDowell emphasizes the ways in which and the reasons why black women novelists treat sexuality with caution and reticence in her introduction to Nella Larsen, Quicksand and Passing (New Brunswick: Rutgers University Press, 1986) xiiiff. This is not to deny the role of novels by Toni Morrison, Gloria Naylor, Alice Walker, and others in forging a contemporary discourse about black women's sexuality. See also poetry by Hattie Gossett, Porter Grainger, and Cherrie Moraga in PaD. "Hybrid" anthologies by lesbian women of color combining essays with poetry, speeches with diary entries include Cherrie Moraga and Gloria Anzaldùa, eds., This Bridge Called My Back: Writings by Radical Women of Color (1981); C. Chung et al., eds., Between the Lines: An Anthology by Pacific/Asian Lesbians (1987); and Juanita Ramos, ed. Companeras: Latina Lesbians (1987). I take the term "theoretical fiction" from Nicole Brossard, cited in de Lauretis, "Sexual Indifference and Lesbian Representation" 165.

[20]On the problematic relation between feminism and Foucault and attempts to mediate them, see Isaac D. Balbus, "Disciplining Women: Michel Foucault and the Power of Feminist Discourse," Feminism as Critique, ed. Seyla Benhabib and Drucilla Cornell (Minneapolis: University of Minnesota Press, 1987) 110–27; see also Irene Diamond and Lee Quinby, eds., Feminism and Foucault: Reflections on Resistance (Boston: Northeastern University Press, 1988).

humanistic and social science disciplines, each displays a heightened concern for historicity and differences—for the positional specificity of the subject.

Fundamentally shaped by feminist studies in the Anglo-Saxon world, film studies, the theoretical avant garde of visual studies, has essentially ignored Foucault in favor of the Lacanian rewriting of Freud. Like most U.S. feminists, however, British film theorist Laura Mulvey was critical of Lacan's definition of the female subject as lack and his predication of sexual difference on the presence/absence of the Phallus; she aimed nonetheless to make "political use of psychoanalytic theory." In "Visual Pleasure and Narrative Cinema," an essay that set the terms of debates in film criticism after 1975, Mulvey insisted that (patriarchal) man possesses and controls the scopophilic look, which relegates the female to a passive erotic object. Because her lack or castration arouses male anxiety, and thus unpleasure, the female activates voyeuristic (sadistic) mechanisms to demystify, devalue, and/or punish her, or then, in a disavowal of the threat of castration, stimulates fetishistic mechanisms of overvaluation that reassure the spectator whose look is "sutured" with the male gaze.[21]

Mulvey's theorization of the female spectator as an absence, and her pleasure as a negative term that spells complicity with dominant (patriarchal) forces, has stimulated counter-efforts by de Lauretis, Gertrud Koch, and others to reconceptualize the sexual subjectivity of the female spectator in ways that undermined the psychoanalytic model. Linda Williams' *Hard Core: Power Pleasure and the "Frenzy of the Visible"* (1989) analyzes

---

[21]My thanks to Mary Ann Doane for discussing recent trends in film studies with me. Laura Mulvey, "Changes: Thoughts on Myth, Narrative and Historical Experience," *Visual and Other Pleasures* (Bloomington: Indiana University Press, 1989) 165, hereafter *VOP*; "Visual Pleasure and Narrative Cinema," *VOP* 14–26. The relevance of Lacan/psychoanalysis to cinema was perhaps first explored by Christian Metz, who was not interested in the sexual difference of the spectator, however; that was explored by Stephen Heath, Julia Lesage, and Mulvey in the pages of *Screen* in 1975. British film studies, emblematized by *Screen*, were also influenced by Brecht and by Althusser, who, significantly, did not cross the ocean along with Lacan. See E. A. Kaplan's analysis in "Introduction: From Plato's Cave to Freud's Screen," *Psychoanalysis and Cinema* (New York: Routledge, 1990) 8–9.

the heterosexual pornographic productions of Candida Royalle to gauge whether women's pleasure can be represented outside of the male gaze, and without identifying the penis with the phallus. Williams locates a new address to women, who now represent 40 percent of the consumers of the 2000 pornographic films and videos produced annually, an effort to depict "what they want," with attendant changes of style and tone, a more democratic give-and-take oriented toward the monogamous couple in search of better sexual performance. For Williams, this new trend is designed to make pornography's abiding misogyny and unaltered power relations more pleasurable to women and thus to viewing couples. Similarly, and in keeping with post-1985 trends in cultural studies and literary criticism that enlisted historical, ethnographical, and sociological methods, Deirdre Pribram's *Female Spectators* (1988) challenges decontextualized Lacanian subject positions with studies of female reception—as in Jacqueline Bobo's analysis of black women's reactions to Spielberg's *The Color Purple*—and highlights heterogeneous responses to the constant negotiations and accommodations of dominant ideology (1–8).[22]

The monolithic notion of a passive female spectator sutured to the male gaze has been fractured further by differences fore-

----

[22]On the reconceptualization of the female spectator, see Gertrud Koch, "Ex-changing the Gaze: Re-visioning Feminist Film Theory," *New German Critique* 34 (Winter 1985): 140ff; de Lauretis, "Aesthetic and Feminist Theory: Rethinking Women's Cinema," *New German Critique* 34 (Winter 1985): 161, 171. Compare with Mulvey's 1981 "Afterthoughts" on her 1975 essay, *VOP* 29–38. Williams, *Hard Core* (Berkeley: University of California Press, 1989) cites Foucault and object relations theory more often than Lacan. She notes that pornography represents a rare instance in which women are not punished for knowing and finding pleasure, indeed that S/M breaks down traditional masculine/feminine dichotomies, and that the new trends in "pornography, which view its sexual object more as exchange value in an endless play of substitution than as use value for possession," delineate "a more feminine economy of consumption" (273). Unfortunately, Williams excludes from her study gay/lesbian and bisexual pornography; see, however, Tom Waugh, "Men's Pornography: Gay versus Straight," *Jump Cut: A Journal of Contemporary Media* 30 (1985): 30–36 and Richard Dyer, *Now You See It: Studies on Lesbian and Gay Film* (New York: Routledge, 1990). Jacqueline Bobo, "*The Color Purple*: Black Women as Cultural Readers," *Female Spectators: Looking at Film and Television* (New York: Verson, 1988) 90–109.

grounded by critics both gay/lesbian and of color. Thus John D'Emilio exposes the heterosexism of a gaze theory predicated on a dominant male subject and a passive female object (*Powers of Desire* 117), while Jane Gaines and Patricia White both argue that the desire of the lesbian spectator to look at women does not cast her in the masculine position, but in fact disrupts it. Building upon Homi Bhabha's emphasis on the spectator's color, Gaines also shows the inherent racism of gaze theory from the position of black men who have been historically castrated *for* looking.[23]

Although film and literary theory are closely interrelated—a circulation of discourse facilitated by de Lauretis, Kaja Silverman, Bhabha, and Stephen Heath, for example, who write in both fields—literary studies of sexuality in the United States have been influenced by Foucault more than by Lacan.[24] New

[23]Patricia White, "Female Spectator: Lesbian Specter: *The Haunting*," *I/O* 142; Jane Gaines, "White Privilege and Looking Relations—Race and Gender in Feminist Film Theory," *Screen* 29, n. 4 (Autumn 1988): 12–27, special issue, ed. Isaac Julien and Kobena Mercer. This is not to suggest that gay/lesbian or African-American critics dispense with psychoanalysis (see for instance, D. A. Miller, "Anal Rope," *I/O* 119–41), but rather that the sexual/social positions of their subjects expose (some of) the problems of a psychoanalytic approach. See also in *Screen* 29, n. 4; Julien and Mercer's introduction, "De Margin and De Centre" 8; and Mantha Diawara, "Black Spectatorship: Problems of Identification and Resistance" 66–69. As Diawara does for black spectators, de Lauretis stresses the importance of not perpetuating "the presumption of a unified lesbian viewer/reader, gifted with undivided and non-contradictory subjectivity, and every bit as generalized and universal as the female spectator . . . [of] antipornography feminist performance art" ("Sexual Indifference and Lesbian Representation" 170). Homi K. Bhabha, "The Other Question," *Screen* 24, n. 6 (November-December 1983): 18–36. See also Diawara, ed., "Black Cinema," special issue of *Wide Angle* 13, n. 3/4 (July-October 1991).

[24]Psychoanalytic literary criticism, such as Shoshana Felman's *Literature and Psychoanalysis: The Question of Reading: Otherwise* (1977), has often privileged Lacan, but it has focused, as Peter Brooks urged, on the structure and rhetoric of literary texts, on the "erotics of form," rather than of human subjects; see his "The Idea of Psychoanalytic Literary Criticism," *The Trial(s) of Psychoanalysis* ed. Françoise Meltzer (Chicago: University of Chicago Press, 1987) 145–60. The influence of Foucault on literary studies of sexuality in the U.S. contrasts with the case of France, where Lacan dom-

historicists, who have stimulated a substantial body of literary work on sexuality—especially on Renaissance England but also on periods ranging from classical Greece to the late nineteenth century—have remained markedly uninterested in (suspicious of?) psychoanalytic categories, although their conception of the human subject is informed by Freud/Lacan. As they try to renegotiate "anew" the problematic relation between texts and history in the wake of poststructuralism, new historicist texts, following Foucault, feature the circulation of materials from one discursive sphere to another, synchronic coincidence instead of causality, a preeminent concern with the workings of power, and a focus on sexuality. As a metonymy, if not *the* metaphor for the modern subject, which emerged during the Renaissance along with the split between the private and the public/state, according to new historicism, sexuality serves as a powerful test case for its fundamental (and Foucaultian) culturalist/constructionist assumptions, as Louis Montrose has suggested.[25]

---

inated literary theory. Jane Gallop ("Reading the Mother Tongue: Psychoanalytic Feminist Criticism," in Meltzer 125–41) argues that Lacan may be less important to psychoanalytic feminist criticism in the U.S. than Derrida, and closer to home, than Nancy Chodorow's *The Reproduction of Mothering: Psychoanalysis and the Sociology of Gender* (Los Angeles: University of California Press, 1978), and object-relations theory.

[25]Of course, there is no agreement as to what new historicism is, but see H. Aram Veeser's introduction to his anthology, *The New Historicism*, hereafter, *TNH* (New York: Routledge, 1989) xiff and Jonathan Dollimore, "Introduction: Shakespeare, Cultural Materialism and the New Historicism," *Political Shakespeare: New Essays in Cultural Materialism*, ed. Dollimore and Alan Sinfield (Manchester: Manchester University Press, 1985) 2–17. "New historicism" was coined by Stephen Greenblatt in his introduction to *Genre* 15 (1982): 5, where he also stated, however, that he aimed to explore "the poetics of culture" (6), the term he chose for the title of his essay, "Toward a Poetics of Culture," in *TNH* 1–14. Foucault's role is emphasized in Frank Lentricchia's "Foucault's Legacy—A New Historicism," *TNT* 231–42. This is not to deny the importance of Marx, Pierre Macherey, Louis Althusser, Raymond Williams, Victor Turner, Clifford Geertz, and social and cultural historians such as Lawrence Stone. My brief comments on the etiology of sexuality in new historicist work are indebted to conversations with Louis Montrose. Marlon Ross regards this new historicist view of the Renaissance as one of its flaws; see his "Contingent Predilections: The Newest Historicisms and the Question of Method," *The Centennial Review* 34 (Fall

In its (Foucaultian) opposition to traditional historical "facts," the much-noted new historicist use of the anecdote has foregrounded the unofficial, "marginal," or bizarre aspects of Renaissance culture, the titillating fragments that sexualize readings of canonical texts. Greenblatt's emblematic "Fiction and Friction" (1988) begins with Montaigne's account of a case of hermaphroditism in 1580, when a woman was hanged for using "illicit devices to supply her defect of sex"; figures sixteenth-century notions of anatomical differences between the sexes as an "introverted homology," citing the different degrees of sexual heat thought necessary for conception and for the transformation of (superior) male into (inferior) female; and argues that this sexual discourse of friction not only shaped subjectivity but is figuratively represented in cultural productions, such as *Twelfth Night*, thus underscoring the reciprocal negotiation between "literary" and "non-literary" discourses.[26]

The hermaphrodite is only one type of "sexual deviant" featured in new historicist studies. The confusion of gender binarism that the reported plethora of hermaphrodites represents in the early-modern period finds its correlative in the "deviant" transvestite female, if not the crossdressed boy who "naturally" assumed women's roles on the Elizabethan stage. Admittedly, much of this work on crossdressing treats gender instead of—or more problematic, as synonymous with—sexuality, especially before 1986. Conversely, however, texts on early-modern homoerotic behavior, inspired in various degrees by new historicist

---

1990): 485–538. Links between the early-modern and the postmodern subject are explored in Dollimore's *Sexual Dissidence: Augustine to Wilde, Freud to Foucault* (New York: Oxford University Press, 1991) 23–23. Like Greenblatt, in *Renaissance Self-Fashioning* (Chicago: University of Chicago Press, 1980), Dollimore makes the Foucaultian argument that subversion may be "allowed" by dominant forces as a strategy of containment," a notion that undermines human agency and resistance and that prompted critiques of postmodern defeatism from Terry Eagleton, in "The Historian as Body Snatcher," *Times Literary Supplement* 18 January 1991: 7, and of a totalizing ideology of male power from Judith Lowder Newton, in "History as Usual? Feminism and the 'New Historicism,'" *Cultural Critique* (Spring 1988): 87–122.

[26] Greenblatt, "Fiction and Friction," *Shakespearean Negotiations: The Circulation of Social Energy in Renaissance England* (Berkeley: University of California Press, 1988).

approaches to Renaissance studies, such as Gregory W. Bred-beck's *Sodomy and Interpretation: Marlow to Milton* (1991) and Bruce R. Smith's *Homosexual Desire in Shakespeare's England: A Cultural Poetics* (1991), focus on male sexuality and ignore gender as a fundamental category of analysis, women and *tribades* in particular, despite the crucial connections between the representation of the sodomite, for example, and gender ideology. By contrast, Marjorie Garber's *Vested Interests* (1992) highlights the connection between gender and gay studies, showing that the history of transvestism and the history of homosexuality "constantly intersect and intertwine."[27]

As with women's studies, and perhaps in part because of developments in that field, new historicism has placed greater emphasis on sexuality since 1986, a shift dramatized by *Representations*—the journal now coedited by Greenblatt and Svetlana Alpers—beginning with the issue on *The Making of the Modern Body: Sexuality and Society in the Nineteenth Century* (1986). As

---

[27]See Dollimore's essay on "the sexual deviant," "Transgression and Surveillance in *Measure for Measure*," *Political Shakespeare* 72–87. On gender in crossdressing studies, see, for instance, Lisa Jardine, *Still Harping on Daughters: Women and Drama in the Age of Shakespeare* (Brighton, Sussex: Harvester Press, 1983), though her chapter on "Female Roles and Elizabethan Eroticism" focuses on sexuality, and Stephen Orgel, "Nobody's Perfect: or Why did the English Stage Take Boys for Women?" *South Atlantic Quarterly* 88 (Winter 1989): 7–29. Compare with Rudolf M. Dekker and Lotte C. van de Pol, *The Tradition of Female Transvestism in Early-Modern Europe* (Basingstoke, Hampshire: MacMillan Press, 1989). To be sure, tribadism is far less visible in the early-modern period than homoerotic relations between men and seems to have been disciplined and punished in the West later than "the homosexual." Bredbeck's book is published by Cornell University Press, Smith's by Chicago University Press, and Garber's by Routledge. Periods in which homoeroticism is visible, such as the English Renaissance, classical Greece, and the late nineteenth century, when "the homosexual" is constructed, have generated studies of sexuality, but with different assumptions and results than new historicism. As Marlon Ross observes, Eve Sedgwick has been more influential than Greenblatt on late nineteenth-century homosexuality studies, but her work is largely ahistorical. And historicist critics of early nineteenth-century literature, notably Marjorie Levinson and Jerome McGann, have been less influenced by Foucault than by Hegelian and Marxist conceptions of history, which are largely uninterested in sexuality" (personal communication).

*Representations* illustrates, new historicism is marked by Anglo-
American feminist theory and practices. And yet, as Judith
Newton rightly pointed out in 1988, genealogies of new historicism and analyses of its practices have rarely acknowledged
their debt to feminist studies, especially to women's history
(*TNH* 152-67). Instead, more "masterful" sources of self-legiti-
macy are cited, just as male figures dominate their texts, with
the notable exception of Elizabeth the First.[28] Exceptionally,
Montrose has stressed that "in Renaissance studies, as across
the discipline of criticism, feminist theory and practice have
called attention to the discursive construction of gender and of
social and domestic relations generally," and more broadly, have
"provided a model for the integration of intellectual, professional
and social commitments" (*TNH* 26). But this view tends to
"pedestalize" women's studies, rather than to integrate feminist
gender and sexual constructs in new historicist textual practices.

The historicism of new historicist and feminist analyses, like
that of other sub/fields in the new sexual studies, reflects and
inflects developments within history since the 1960s. Under the
influence of the *Annales* school, the center of "the queen of disciplines" shifted from political to social history in the 1960s
through the impact of sociological and other social scientific
methodologies, and displaced the focus on elites and events with
the lives of "ordinary people"—what came to be known as
"bottom up history." This radical shift provided a crucial stim-
ulus for the emergence of both women's history after 1969 and

---

[28]This issue of *Representations* 14 (Spring 1986) was edited by Catherine Gallagher and Thomas Laqueur. My thanks to Larry Norman (a graduate student at Columbia University), who took the time to confirm this shift
in *Representations*. See Maureen Quilligan's critique of the new historicist silence about women, in *The Allegory of Female Authority: Christine de Pisan's
"Cité des Dames"* (Ithaca: Cornell University Press, 1991), and Judith
Walkowitz, Myra Jehlen, and Bell Chevigny's on the new historicist failure
to note its debt to women's studies, in "Patrolling the Borders: Feminist
Historiography and the New Historicism," *Radical History Review* 43 (1989):
23-43. The indifference of new historicist texts to women and gender has
motivated feminist reworking of their materials; see, for example, Ann Rosalind Jones, *The Currency of Eros: Women's Love Lyric in Europe 1540–1620*
(Bloomington: Indiana University Press, 1990) and Constance Jordan *Renaissance Feminism: Literary Texts and Political Models* (Ithaca, NY: Cornell
University Press, 1990).

work on sexuality.    Although members of the *Annales* school such as J. L. Flandrin, British demographers, and historians of the family such as Lawrence Stone, Edward Shorter, and Randolph Trumbach had undertaken studies of fertility, illegitimacy, and disease in the 1970s, they were not concerned with sexuality as a concept, despite the fact that—or perhaps, because— women's history, to which they seemed indifferent or hostile, was evolving theories of gender and of sexuality.[29]    Indeed, in

---

[29]On the importance of the shift to social history for women's history see Mary S. Hartman and Lois Banner, eds., *Clio's Consciousness Raised: New Perspectives on the History of Women* (New York: Harper and Row, 1974) vii and Joan Scott, "Women's History," *New Perspectives on Historical Writing*, ed. Peter Burke (Cambridge: Polity Press, 1991) 53. The brief discussion that follows on shifts within history is indebted to Geoff Eley's "Is All the World a Text? From Social History to the History of Society Two Decades Later," Working Paper #55 of the Center for the Study of Social Transformation, University of Michigan (October 1990) 37pp. My thanks to Michigan historian Alice Echols and Princeton historian Laura Englestein for sharing their views on developments in history since the 1960s, notably in the study of sexuality. Scott's influential 1986 essay, which attempts to convince historians that "Gender [is] A Useful Category of Historical Analysis," is reprinted in her *Gender and the Politics of History* (New York: Columbia University Press, 1988) 28–50. Of course, the degree of acceptance/influence of women's history has varied considerably. In 1976, the founding issue of the *History Workshop Journal* contained an editorial on "Feminist History"; by 1982, it had been renamed *Journal of Socialist and Feminist Historians*. On this side of the Atlantic, Carl Degler in 1981 called for a new conception of history that included women in "What the Women's Movement Has Done to American History," *Soundings: An Interdisciplinary Journal* 64 (1981): 419. For some of this early work on sexuality see J. L. Flandrin, *Les Amours paysannes (XVIe–XIXe siècle)* (Paris: Gallimard, 1975) and *Familles: Parenté, maison, sexualité dans l'ancienne société* (Paris: Hachette, 1976); Emmanuel Le Roy Ladurie, *Montaillou: Village occitan de 1294 à 1423* (Paris: Gallimard, 1975); Edward Shorter, *The Making of the Modern Family* (New York: Basic Books, 1975); Lawrence Stone, *The Family, Sex and Marriage in England, 1500–1800* (New York: Harper and Row, 1977); and Randolph Trumbach, *The Rise of the Egalitarian Family: Aristocratic Kinship and Domestic Relations in Eighteenth-Century England* (New York: Academic Press, 1978). The absence of work on the *concept* of sexuality and the predominance of "ignorance" and "bias" in existing studies led Vern Bullough to entitle a 1972 essay "Sex in History: A Virgin Field" and to urge the creation of a "new new history"

early anthologies such as Martha Vicinus' *Suffer and Be Still*
(1972), Anne Koedt, Ellen Levine, and Anita Rapone's, *Radical
Feminism* (1973), Mary Hartman and Lois Banner's *Clio's Consciousness Raised* (1974), and in books such as Linda Gordon's
*Woman's Body, Woman's Right* (1976), women's historians,
working in "a separate sphere" from men, were investigating
(predominantly white women's hetero-) sexuality both as a function of their oppression and in relation to their sense of community and culture.[30]

Between 1975 and 1982, however, when it focused on the
historical construction of sexual (or gender) difference, women's
studies became one of the major forces that catalyzed "a dissolution . . . of 'History' as a . . . centered disciplinary project," according to Geoff Eley (2, 7), along with the rejection of classical
Marxism, Annalistic "total history," and quantitative methods;
the radical impact of the "linguistic turn" under the influence of
continental and Anglo-American literary theory; and the displacement of sociology by cultural anthropology as a model for
historical analysis. Indeed, according to Lynn Hunt, cultural anthropology, literary and feminist theories define the contours of
the new cultural history, which has not merely assumed the cat-
alytic role of social history but absorbed "the social" within "the
cultural." Hunt describes Foucault's influence on this new cul-

---

that would include the sexual behavior "of man"; see *The Journal of Sex Research* 8 (May 1972): 114. See also Stone's more recent work on "Sexuality,"
*Past and Present Revisited* (New York: Routledge, 1987) 344–82, which takes
copious note of the importance of women's historians.

[30]Martha Vicinus' anthology was published by Indiana University
Press; Hartman and Banner's by Harper and Row; *Radical Feminism* by
Quadrangle Books; Gordon's book by Grossman. The Victorian era was often
at the center of these early feminist historical studies of sexuality; see, for
instance, Nancy Cott, "Passionlessness: An Interpretation of Victorian Sex-
ual Ideology," *A Heritage of Her Own*, ed. Cott and Elizabeth Pleck (New
York: Simon and Shuster, 1979) 162–81; Judith Walkowitz, *Prostitution and
Victorian Society* (Cambridge: Harvard University Press, 1980); and Caroll
Smith-Rosenberg, *Disorderly Conduct: Visions of Gender in Victorian America*
(New York: Knopf, 1985). For a critique of the emphasis on commu-
nity/culture and sisterhood in the history of women's sexuality, and an in-
sistence instead on conflict and  discontinuities of race and class among
women, see Nancy A. Hewitt, "Beyond the Search for Sisterhood: American
Women's History in the 1980s," *Social History* 10 (October 1985): 299–321.

tural history as "undeniably tremendous" but his overall influence on history as limited, whereas Eley sees Foucault's influence on history less ambiguously as "pervasive" (8). Such views do not represent the range of responses—hostility, indifference, adulation—to Foucault's work, which is first cited by Anglo-American historians c. 1978–79, for instance, in Padgug's seminal "Sexual Matters: On Conceptualizing Sexuality in History" (1979) and in Jeffrey Weeks' advocacy of "Foucault for Historians" (1982).[31]

Not surprisingly, then, influential works on the history of sexuality, recently published in the United States, still reveal great disparities in the degree to which they integrate Foucaultian theory, though they confirm the impact of women's studies. Thomas Laqueur's *Making Sex: Body and Gender from the Greeks to Freud* (1990) is as informed by feminist gender analysis as by Foucaultian notions of sexuality when it examines the shift in medical discourses from a one-sex (male) body that considered the female's its interior, inferior, but nonetheless sexual, version to a two-sexed post-eighteenth-century body, which recognized difference and (thus) denied female sexual pleasure. By contrast, Freedman and D'Emilio's comprehensive survey, *Intimate Matters: A History of Sexuality in America* (1988), ascribes the "vast" new "field of sexual history" to the intellectual

---

[31]See Scott's apt notion of women's history as a *supplement*, at first in the literal sense of an addition to men's history, later, as a Derridean excess that forces reconceptualization of the core, in Peter Burke, ed., *New Perspectives*. Clifford Geertz has emphasized the importance of literary analysis in the social sciences, in fact, the need to probe the workings of metaphor, irony, paradox, etc., if those scientists are to understand "Ideology as a Cultural System"; see *The Interpretation of Culture* (New York: Basic Books, 1973) 208ff. See also Lynn Hunt, "Introduction: History, Culture, and Text," *The New Cultural History*, ed. Lynn Hunt (Berkeley: University of California Press, 1989) 4–22, hereafter *TNCH*. See Eley's concern about the potential disappearance of "the social" within the cultural (15–16), a trend he traces to Foucault. On Foucault's impact on historians, see Hunt, *TNCH* 7–9; and Patricia O'Brien, "Michel Foucault's History of Culture," *TNCH* 25–46. See Weeks, "Foucault for Historians," *History Workshop Journal* 14 (Autumn 1982): 106–19. An excessively hostile critic of Foucault, Roy Porter, according to Conference Reports, labeled "Foucault's revisionism . . . both stupid and reactionary . . . shallow"; see *Journal of the Society for the Social History of Medicine* 4 (1991): 196.

paradigms introduced by historians of the family and of women. But it hardly ever cites Foucault in analyzing changes in sexual meanings, sexual regulations, and sexual politics from puritanism to the present that reflect and reinforce dominant hierarchies—in particular, the shift from reproduction in the family to individual emotional intimacy and physical pleasure.[32]

A synthetic narrative that strives to be—and has been praised for being—inclusive about gender, class, race, ethnicity, region, and orientation, despite the acknowledged limits of knowledge about these differences in the field (xiv), *Intimate Matters* has nonetheless been sharply criticized by Ann Ducille in the new *Journal of the History of Sexuality*. While recognizing the advances it represents, Ducille maintains that this text "reconstructs the very racial/sexual hierarchy it critiques" because it centers on the sexual practices of the hegemonic white middle class. Morever, it fails to view black sexuality in the context of a culture of resistance and black Americans as subjects of discourse from what she problematically calls "the inside"—African-American primary and secondary sources (108, 110, 116).[33]

---

[32]Widely and favorably reviewed, Laqueur's book (Cambridge: Harvard University Press, 1990) has been criticized by Katharine Park and Robert A. Nye on the grounds that the one-sex, two-sex models have coexisted since the Greeks. Their review is marred by a condescension toward Laqueur's feminist analysis, which puts some of their other conclusions into question; see "Destiny is Anatomy," *The New Republic* 204 (18 February 1991): 53–57. On the twin influence of feminism and Foucault on history, see Eley 7–9, 12–14, 21–23; and on the new studies of sexuality, Halperin's *One Hundred Years of Homosexuality* 8. By contrast, Roy Porter's recent review essay on "The History of the Body" cites Foucault frequently, but "covers" the contributions of feminist theory to this field in one short paragraph (in Peter Burke, ed., *New Perspectives* 206–32).

[33]Ducille, "'Othered' Matters: Reconceptualizing Dominance and Difference in the History of Sexuality in America," *Journal of the History of Sexuality* 1 (1 July 1990): 108, 110, 116. D'Emilio and Freedman provide a brief "Commentary" on Ducille's essay in the same issue (128–30). A similar critique of women's history is voiced by Hewitt, "Beyond the Search." More recently, *Unequal Sister* includes important articles on sexuality inflected by gender, race, ethnicity, class, and sexual orientation, as does *Nationalisms and Sexualities*, ed. Andrew Parker, Mary Russo, Doris Sommer, and Patricia Yaeger (New York: Routledge, 1992). The notion that studies of "third-

As Ducille also suggests, homosexuality of color, indeed of all colors has been "Hidden from History," at least until very recently, despite the steady outpouring of historical work on homosexual behavior and identity since the mid-seventies—J. Steakley's *The Homosexual Emancipation Movement in Germany* (1975), Weeks' *Coming Out* (1977) in Britain, K. J. Dover's *Greek Homosexuality* (1978), and Jonathan Katz' *Gay American History: Lesbians and Gay Men in the U.S.A* (1976).[34]    Katz highlighted native Americans in his vast collection of primary sources from 1528 to 1976, and he included lesbians integrally in his work instead of making "a perfunctory gesture in the direction of lesbian or feminist studies," to cite de Lauretis' critique of gay studies.    To be sure, the relative invisibility of lesbians in gay history may derive in part, as Vicinus recognizes, from the difficulty of reconstructing lesbian history and defining what and who is a lesbian.    Still, the work of lesbian historians, such as Blanche Weisen Cook, Caroll Smith-Rosenberg, Lillian Fader-

world" peoples are no longer "ghettoized in marginal fields" but are now "constitutive of knowledge production in a number of disciplines" appears (optimistically) in Chandra Talpade Mohanty, Ann Russo, and Lourdes Torres' introduction to *Third World Women and the Politics of Feminism* (Bloomington: Indiana University Press, 1991) ix-x. On the problematical opposition between inside and outside, see Fuss, *I/O* 5-6.

[34]Martin Duberman, Martha Vicinus and George Chauncey, Jr.'s introduction to *Hidden from History* notes that little had been published in English about the histories of homosexuality in third-world societies before the four articles in their volume (3). Symptomatically, perhaps, Eley's scholarly and insightful essay never mentions the impressive body of work on gay and lesbian history, much less on homoeroticism of color. Scott comments on the absence of gay or lesbian history in the special forum on history and critical theory in *American Historical Review* 94 (June 1989), in Peter Burke, *New Perspectives* 66 n. 43. Steakley (New York: Arno Press); Weeks (London: Quartet Books); Dover (Cambridge: Harvard University Press, 1978); and Katz (New York: Crowell). Still, publications in gay and lesbian studies have increased by quantum leaps in the last five years; book series on this field exist now or are forthcoming at Chicago, Columbia, Duke, New York, and Oxford university presses. Although reports continue to circulate about texts that fail to find publishers because of their controversial content, it seems to be true that gay and lesbian studies has moved "From Margin to Mainstream," as *The Chronicle of Higher Education* entitled a recent article by Liz McMillen (22 July 1992): A8-9, A13.

man, and Vicinus, suggests that this invisibility may reflect and perpetuate the silencing of women in phallocentric discourses. So doing, gay historians emulate the absence of women in Foucault's own work.[35]

Along with Foucault, however, feminist (and lesbian) theory has visibly marked gay literary and visual theory, recently dubbed "queer theory." Inspired by Queer Nation, "queer" proclaims its antithesis to the "normal" rather than the merely heterosexual; by extension, observes Kevin Kopelson, all sexuality becomes "queer." For de Lauretis, the term affirms a transgressive, deviant, resistant subject, an agent for change in the social world, and no less "a crucial area of concern," changes within "queer theory" to deconstruct silences surrounding racial and lesbian specificities (iv–xi).[36]

---

[35]De Lauretis, "Introduction," special issue on "Queer Theory: Gay and Lesbian Sexualities," *differences* 3, n. 2 (Summer 1991): iv, vi–viii; she cites the essays by Tomas Almaguer and Earl Jackson, Jr. in this issue as exceptional for their engagement with lesbian studies (viii). Vicinus, " 'They Wonder to Which Sex I Belong': The Historical Roots of Modern Lesbian Identity," *Homosexuality, Which Homosexuality?*, ed. Theo van der Meer and Anja van Kooten Niekard (Amsterdam: An Dekker Schorer, 1989) 171–98. Duberman, Vicinus, and Chauncey comment on the imbalance in the historical research produced in lesbian vs. gay studies (2). On the invisibility of lesbianism from Freud to contemporary feminist theories, see Judith Roof, *A Lure of Knowledge: Lesbian Sexuality and Theory* (New York: Columbia University Press, 1991). Still, in recent months, Cook's "lesbian" biography of Eleanor Roosevelt (New York: Viking, 1992), and Faderman's *Odd Girls and Twilight Lovers: A History of Lesbian Life in Twentieth-Century America* (New York: Columbia University Press, 1992) have achieved enormous visibility. On Foucault's problematic stance toward women, see the articles of Dean-Jones, Hunt, and MacKinnon in Part I of *Discourses of Sexuality*, discussed below.

[36]Sedgwick seems anxious that the maternal feminist may engulf or overwhelm the gay son, and stresses the need to keep gay and feminist studies separate (*Closet* 32). By contrast, there is a productive conjunction of the two fields in Kaja Silverman's *Male Subjectivity at the Margins* (New York: Routledge, 1992), which examines the femininity (and masochism) in/of male subjectivity in general, the homosexual in particular. Queer Nation was founded in 1990, the year of the Santa Cruz conference on Queer Theory, which is the source of the issue of *differences* edited by de Lauretis; however, she claims the term bears no relation to the activist organization (see 3, n. 2,

That this emphasis on race, orientation, and other differences has recurred throughout this introduction not only reflects common concerns among the sub/fields in the new studies of sexuality; it reveals the inadequacy of disciplinary divisions for interdisciplinary analysis. To be sure, in gay, lesbian, feminist or, for that matter, new sexual studies, cross- or inter-disciplinary work largely remains an unrealized ideal, notwithstanding the important moves of literary studies toward history and anthropology, and vice versa. Even more likely than the realization of this ideal, however, is a rapprochement in the decade ahead between sexuality, literary and historical studies, on the one hand, and cultural studies, on the other. Symptomatically, Greenblatt points toward a "cultural poetics," and Lynn Hunt's anthology of historical, literary, and artistic essays on eighteenth-century eroticism and politics aims to "stimulate interest in the broader questions pertaining to the field of cultural studies" (*Eroticism* 4). Conversely, the thematic index of Lawrence Grossberg, Cary Nelson, and Paula Treichler's monumental anthology, *Cultural Studies* (1992), lists the largest number of articles on "Gender and Sexuality," although there is admittedly far more on the former than on the latter. Stuart Hall attributes this preoccupation with gender and sexuality to the "ruptural" impact of feminism, which "reorganized the field" in Britain, at the Birmingham Center for Contemporary Cultural Studies in particular, and provided a new understanding of (postmodern) subjectivity, "the personal," and, along with Foucault, "a radical expansion of the notion of power."[37]

---

xvii n. 2). Citing this issue of *differences*, as well as *How Do I Look?: Queer Film and Video*, the June 1992 issue of the *Village Voice Literary Supplement* (Michael Warner's "From Queer to Eternity" 18–19) extends "queer theory" to include the most influential texts in gay and lesbian literary and film theory.

[37]On the shift from literary to cultural studies, see Patrick Brantlinger, *Crusoe's Footprints: Cultural Studies in Britain and America* (New York: Routledge, 1990) 25. Terry Eagleton advocated this shift in *Literary Theory: An Introduction* (Minneapolis: University of Minnesota Press, 1983), as he pronounced the death of literature and urged the elimination of its departments (205–17). Cary Nelson emphasizes the links between new historicism and cultural studies in "Always Already Cultural Studies: Two Conferences and a Manifesto," *Journal of the Mid-West Modern Language Association* 24 (Spring 1991): 32–33, 41, hereafter *JMMLA*; see also *Cultural Studies* (New York:

Over and beyond such specific effects, feminist studies, and I believe, Foucaultian practice, share with cultural studies a view of theoretical work as "a critical political intervention," to cite Stuart Hall (*CS* 294). More than Foucault, however, British cultural studies since the late 1950s has drawn on a tradition of Western Marxism that includes Althusser and Bourdieu, and the work of Richard Hoggart (*The Uses of Literacy*, 1957), Raymond Williams (*Culture and Society*, 1958), and E. P. Thompson (*The Making of the English Working Class*, 1963) to interrogate the forms and processes of cultural productions and the politics of meaning, especially those that create and sustain exclusions ("Introduction," *CS* 3ff). Opposed to fixed subject matter and resolutely open to new methodologies (Lacanianism, deconstruction, the new ethnography), cultural studies can serve as a useful model for the new studies of sexuality. Thus the often expressed fear that the academic success of cultural studies will erode its founding antidisciplinary, oppositional impulse needs to be heeded by the new studies of sexuality. The self-conscious auto-critique that cultural studies promotes when it wrestles with blindness to differences is, of course, essential to all work in the politics of power-knowledge. Even more important, the crisis which catalyzed the new studies of sexuality, and with which I began, like the crisis in the humanities that motivated cultural studies, according to Bratlinger (1–33) can—and should—continue to produce local resistances, as Foucault emphasizes. And resistance, for my part, still represents one important way of mediating the critic's ironic position in a sexually permeated culture.[38]

---

Routledge, 1992) 18–20, hereafter *CS*. See Hall, "Cultural Studies and Its Theoretical Legacies," *CS* 282. One study of sexuality in this volume is Laura Kipnis, "(Male) Desire and (Female) Disgust: Reading *Hustler*," 373–404.

[38]For a history of British cultural studies, its key influences and texts, see Carolyn Steedman, "Culture, Cultural Studies and the Historians," *CS* 613ff; Nelson, *JMMLA* 32, and Bratlinger 23ff. Although identified with an opposition to "high" culture and a focus on the popular culture of working-class lives, cultural studies aims to examine cultural formations in all periods; see *CS* 11ff; Nelson, *JMMLA* 31–33, 41; and Paul Smith, "A Course in 'Cultural Studies'," *JMMLA* 24 (Spring 1991): 40–41. On the opposition to fixed method and disciplinarity, as well as the fear of recuperation, see in *CS*, "Introduction" 2; Paul Gilroy, "Cultural Studies and Ethnic Abso-

## IV

The fields and subfields that have converged and cross-fertilized to produce the new studies of sexuality define the contours of *Discourses of Sexuality: From Aristotle to AIDS*. The essays in this volume, selected from a year-long series of lectures, seminars, and conferences at the University of Michigan's Institute for the Humanities, feature work in women's, gay and lesbian, African-American, new historicist and new historical, visual, psychoanalytic, and cultural studies. The span that the fourteen essays represent, from the AIDS crisis back through the early-modern period to classical Greek medical and hetero/homoerotic discourses, illustrates the historical grounding that these new studies of sexuality have embraced.

As my own (partial) archaeology of the field has emphasized, this volume of essays is not only imprinted by feminist studies; it is informed by Foucault's reconceptualization of the study of sexuality, beginning with the titular *discourses*, that immense compendium of concepts and themes, cultural representations and manifestations, institutions and value systems about sex, which "our civilization has required and organized" and in which "power and knowledge are joined together" (1:33, 100). Recognizing the importance of Foucault does not mean sacralizing him, however, as the first part of this volume, "'The History of Sexuality': Reopening the Question," makes clear. In keeping with the ideal of continuous critique that I posited for the new studies of sexuality, and with the Foucaultian practice of self-critique, in the introduction to *The Archaeology of Knowledge*, for instance, the essays in Part I enlist various (inter)disciplinary and methodological perspectives to examine deficiencies and blindspots in his work—regarding women and persons of color, his understanding of classical culture and eighteenth-century history, but even more important, his conception of the sexual subject.

In "The Politics of Pleasure: Female Sexual Appetite in the Hippocratic Corpus," Leslie Dean-Jones upholds Foucault's con-

lutism" 187ff; and David Glover and Cora Kaplan, "Guns in the House of Culture" 223; see also Nelson, *JMMLA* 25–32. Despite "self-critique" in cultural studies, the problem of racism continues; see Stuart Hall 282ff and Glover and Kaplan 222.

structionist theory of sexuality but argues that he mistakenly assumed that female sexuality in classical Greece was assimilated to the male's desire for the pleasure of intercourse and his capacity to control this impulse.   According to the dominant medical model of the period, insists Dean-Jones, women have physical exigencies that need to be fulfilled by intercourse but no knowledge and thus no control of this impulse—a phallocentric view that might nonetheless allow women to signal, but not admit to, a desire for sexual pleasure that would put their virtue into question.   From a different historical perspective, Lynn Hunt's "Is There a Subject in *The History of Sexuality?*" stresses yet again the maleness of the Foucaultian subject.   Indeed, Foucault ignored most of the gender and feminist implications of his work, writes Hunt, even though his theory of power is nonpatriarchal, and his view of the body as the site for the deployment of discourses helped feminist historians underscore the genderedness of subjectivity.   More broadly, however, Hunt casts doubt on the historicity of the Foucaultian subject, in examining his view of the eighteenth century in *The History of Sexuality, Volume 1*.   Hunt concludes that it was not the deployment of sexuality that produced a new subject in that era, as Foucault argued, but that a new concept of subjectivity induced the deployment of sexuality.[39]

Subjectivity in Foucault and his exclusive reliance on discourses to study sexuality are the objects of Abdul JanMohamed's critical essay.   Applicable to white, Euro-American bourgeois society, Foucaultian "discourse" cannot analyze "Sexuality on/of the Racial Border," insists JanMohamed.   At that site, sexual transgression is accompanied by silence, not discursive amplification, and slaves, like their descendants, are controlled by violence and by juridical prohibitions that are systematically broken by white men but are not subject to appropriation by confessional technologies.[40] Through his reading of Richard

---

[39]In *The History of Sexuality, Volume 1*, Foucault observed what Hunt and other historians have often criticized: "People are going to say that I am dealing in a historicism which is more careless than radical" (150).

[40]It should be noted that Foucault specifies that "the history of sexuality . . . must *first be written* from the viewpoint of a history of discourses"(1:69; my emphasis), not "only be written." It is possible that Foucault was driven by his polemical, counter-historical claims to pass over the repressive role of the law and the state, which he had emphasized in *Mad-*

Wright's *Native Son*, JanMohamed dramatizes the internal mechanisms of racialized sexuality: specularity and projection; the relation between castration and rape; and the exchange and use value of racialized women in a phallic economy.

JanMohamed's conclusion that racialized sexuality requires different methods from those of Foucault leads to a far more global critique by Catharine A. MacKinnon of all current approaches to the history of sexuality, but notably Foucault's, as "orgasmic" histories that silence the specificity of sexual practices. Asking "Does Sexuality Have a History?" MacKinnon argues that unequal status, sexual abuse, and the eroticization of aggression against women are factors so constant that they seem beyond the grasp of any history, much less of "sexuality," which she terms the set of practices that inscribes gender as unequal in social life. Beyond her exploration of such silences and gaps, MacKinnon suggests how their inclusion, exemplified by the work of Diane Russell and Eva Keuls, would help to reconstruct histories of sexuality.

Part II, *Regimes of Knowledge and Desire*, pursues Foucault's preoccupation with powerful discourses that "know" or claim to promote discovery of "the truth"—what he called "the games of truth"(2:7)—and that both confine and extend sexuality, desire, pleasure.[41] The essays in this section feature narratives in the age of discovery, Malthusian concepts, Freudian psychoanalysis, as well as latter-day theories of repression and studies of demographics. The contradictions and ambiguities that the essays expose undermine the perceived rigidity and authority of these discourses. So doing, the three essays question traditional views of sexuality in the Renaissance, the industrial revolution, and in Freudian psychoanalysis.

In "The Work of Gender and Sexuality in the Elizabethan Discourse of Discovery," Louis Montrose investigates a proto-colonialist economy, using the new historicist methods he has helped to define. The gendering of the New World as female and the sexualizing of its exploration and conquest, which was accomplished by the destruction of the indigenous world, was prevalent in sixteenth-century Europe, and in the writings of

---

*ness and Civilization: A History of Insanity in the Age of Reason* (New York: Random House, 1965).

[41]On the interplay of power and pleasure, see also Foucault 1:44–49; of power and desire, 1:81–90.

Walter Ralegh that Montrose examines. The discourse of discovery also inscribes contradictions in the construction of male subjectivity (Englishmen vs. Spaniards) and in the gendered and sexual articulation of the anomalous monarch, at once a woman and the ruler who authorizes the conquests of her male subjects. Thomas Laqueur's "Sex and Desire in the Industrial Revolution" explores the interrelation of two other discourses: the history of the industrial revolution on the one hand, of sexuality on the other. Weighing the evidence of demographic studies on fertility and natality during this revolution, Laqueur, like Foucault before him, challenges the repressive thesis. Analyzing the close connections between discourses of the marketplace and of sexuality, Laqueur reveals ideological tensions about "free exchange" of goods and sex as a threat to the social order—contradictions that still operate today.

Where Laqueur primarily cites discourses of "normal" sexuality, Teresa de Lauretis' close reading of *Three Essays on Sexuality* aims to grasp Freud's ambivalent view of "Sexuality and Perversion," the lesbian in particular. Agreeing that Freud only conceptualizes a heterosexual male subject, that he forecloses the difference of gay sexuality and excludes lesbian sexuality altogether, de Lauretis nonetheless shows that his notion of "normal" psychosexual development and thus of "normal" sexuality is inseparable from the perverse manifestations of "sexual instinct." Indeed, Freud suggests both that instinctual life involves a set of transformations, some of which are defined as normal, and more conservatively, that a "normal" instinct pre-exists its possible deviations, according to de Lauretis. The first and more radically culturalist notion, she concludes, can help to build a counter-theory of sexuality from the Freudian inscription of "the perversions."

The first seven essays of *Discourses of Sexuality*, especially those of Dean-Jones, JanMohamed, Montrose, and Laqueur prefigure *The Constructed Body* examined in Part III. A metonymy for sexuality itself, the body has generated so much work in recent years that it constitutes a field in its own right (I have elsewhere dubbed it "bodyology"). Extending the postmodern assault on subjectivity, this "denaturalized" body is no longer the basis for an autonomous, essential self. As Foucault wrote in *Discipline and Punish*, "the body is the inscribed surface of events, traced by language and dissolved by ideas, the locus of a dissociated self, adopting the illusion of a substantial unity—a volume in disintegration." This body is not the subject of the subject but the historical site of subjugated knowledge, a biopolitical object constructed within "the mechanics of power," says Foucault, which "seeps into the very grain of individuals, reaches right into their bodies, permeates their gestures, their posture . . . ."[42] In the essay most visibly influenced by Foucault in this section, specifically by *The History of Sexuality, Volume 3 (The Care of the Self)*, David Halperin illustrates the cultural constructedness of the sexual body and the historicity of sexual categories and subjects. His close reading of a second-century dialogue ascribed to Lucian, which features two men debating whether women or boys are better vehicles for male sexual pleasure, confronts the modern, Western distinction between hetero- and homo-sexuality. The denaturalized body thus reveals the contingency of modern practices, for Halperin, and destabilizes the binary opposition between heterosexuality and homosexuality that structures contemporary discourses of homophobia.

Where Halperin, like Foucault, examines men's inscription of their sexual bodies, Patricia Yaeger, Joanne Leonard, and Mae Henderson foreground the specificity of women's representations. For the body, the antithesis of mind or spirit in Western thought, the incarnation of what drags humanity down to animality and prevents its immortality, has been identified with "the inferior"—the female, the brute lower classes, the non-white races. Women's bodily experiences have thus been silenced, especially the act of birthing, according to these essays. In "The Poetics of Birth," Yaeger urges feminists to articulate the repressed stories of gestation and parturition in literary discourse. Underscoring, like Halperin, the links between theoretical and

---

[42]Quoted in Biddy Martin, "Feminism, Criticism and Foucault," *New German Critique* 27 (Fall 1982): 6. This is not the body rediscovered two decades ago, resurrected as the repressed term of occidental binarity, that laughing, Bakhtinian body whose lower stratum could subvert whatever state culture erected as sacred; nor the Kristevan, preoedipal, semiotic body whose revolutionary force could subvert the Father's law, the Cixousian hysterical, excessive body, or the liquid, unbounded, unwalled, but always connected, Irigarian body whose lips speak together. In retrospect, these theorists constructed an uncolonized space that escaped the grasp of culture's police and could counteract the imperialism of mind—a blissful vision that seems decidedly dated at this postmodern twilight of the century.

political work, Yaeger's proposed investigation of the tropes and principles governing the presentation or concealment of the story of reproduction in literary and cultural texts would offer new directions for a reproductive politics. She sketches such a poetics in her analysis of stories by Katherine Anne Porter and Eudora Welty, which manifest the culture's terror of female reproductive labor. The violence and pain of that labor, its bodily connection to sexuality, loss, and desire dominate Joanne Leonard's "Miscarriage/Ms Carnage and Other Stories," a visual essay that brings together selections from three bodies of her work—*Of Things Masculine* (c. 1965), *Dreams and Nightmares* (1971-72), and *Journal of a Miscarriage* (1973). This unpublished journal, which the artist has kept from public view, was begun during a pregnancy, continued during a miscarriage, and concluded with a period of intense longing for a child.

An intense maternal love that murders is the powerful theme of Toni Morrison's *Beloved*, the presiding work in Mae Henderson's essay on "The Body as Historical Text." The child that Sethe killed, with a knife across her throat, to save her from bondage—from the scarred back that figures the enslaved body's history—is a symbol of the repressed that haunts the living, writes Henderson. Conjured up by Sethe, Beloved's mysterious reappearance restores a personal past charged with political significance. This birthing of memory casts motherhood as a primary metaphor of history, Henderson observes, and delivery spells the possibility of a speakable past free from patriarchal white discourse. The belief that the female body can construct a history by—and for—African-Americans, like Yaeger's faith in the political significance of "a poetics of birth," affirms the efficacy of individual and collective agency in ways that seem to go beyond Foucaultian resistance. And yet, in what may well have been a utopian leap of faith, Foucault declared: "[we can] aim . . . to counter the grips of power with the claims of bodies, pleasures and knowledges, in their multiplicity and their possibility of resistance. The rallying point for the counterattack against the deployment of sexuality ought . . . to be . . . bodies and pleasures" (1:157).[43]

---

[43]In this gesture, Foucault seems to hark back to the blissful, unconstrained body I identified above. See also Nancy Fraser's "Foucault's Body-Language: A Post-Humanist Political Rhetoric?" in *Salmagundi* 61 (Fall

*The Constructed Body* is necessarily represented in *AIDS and the Crisis of Modernity*, although this final section of *Discourses of Sexuality* echoes and extends the earlier parts, as well as passages in this introduction.  Judith Butler's "Sexual Inversions" grapples with the challenge that the AIDS epidemic poses to a historical paradigm in *The History of Sexuality, Volume 1*.  In the shift from premodern to modern power, argued Foucault, when the law ceased to defend the polis against the threat of death, epidemics, and famine and became preoccupied with the maintenance of life, the fictive category of "sex" was deployed for the production and regulation of bodies and sexuality.  This inversion of sex and sexuality, proper to modern power, presupposes the end of epidemics, Butler observes, and calls Foucault's 1976, pre-AIDS analysis into question.  Rethinking this Foucaultian inversion, Butler transforms the diagnostic category, "invert," into a strategic "inversion" of sex and sexuality that contests the notion of identity and offers a political challenge to  regimes that produce the death-bearing subject of AIDS.  In a complementary challenge to visual discourses, Douglas Crimp exposes the implications of "Portraits of People with AIDS" on network and public television and in fine arts photography.  To be sure, the demands of activists for "positive images"'of PWA self-empowerment can make a negative representation positive, Crimp acknowledges, but it leaves the stereotype of the AIDS subject in place.  By contrast, Crimp shows that Stashu Kybartas' *Danny*, an independent video, may not repudiate the stereotype, but it sexualizes the person with AIDS and thereby reveals the political unconscious of other representations—the fear of—and the desire to eliminate—gay male sexuality altogether.

The need for "Invented Moralities: Values in an Age of Uncertainty" is demonstrated in Jeffrey Weeks' culminating essay.  Where Foucault meditated at the end of his life on the classical ethical problem of *The Use of Pleasure* and *The Care of the Self*, Weeks confronts the absence of firm guarantees and determinate social goals at the twilight of the twentieth century—an uncertainty emblematized by the AIDS epidemic.  Is it possible, Weeks asks, to find values today without surrendering to absolutism or fundamentalism?  His answer—a fitting optimistic close to this volume—is to affirm that "we" have an opportunity to reinvent

---

1983): 55–70, for the possibility that the body constitutes a transcendental signifier in Foucaultian theory.

or rediscover values that allow "us" to live with the only irreducible truth of the contemporary world: human, social, and especially, sexual diversity.  In so doing, Weeks proclaims radical pluralism to be the real challenge of living with uncertainty and sexual diversity to be crucial to the definition of a humanistic society.

Just as *Discourses of Sexuality* critiques, extends, and recasts Foucault's practice, it exposes its own lacunae and blindspots, and thus the work needed, in my view, the new directions to be taken in studies of sexuality in the years ahead.  As the essays of Weeks and Crimp, Henderson and Yaeger most clearly illustrate, the concern with agency and resistance, beyond the recognition that the self is interpellated and constructed, should lead to more intensive analyses of the ways in which specific subjects operate within—and against—sexual discourses in specific situations.  Such work will help to elaborate more dynamic and nuanced models of the relations among discourses and subjects and their effects on each other.  Moreover, this work may generate new questions about the unconscious and its formations, which have been displaced by the dominant paradigm of the constructed subject, even though it was the Freudian unconscious that radically subverted the unitary, autonomous, essential subject.[44] The relation of the unconscious to the socially constructed self poses a future challenge.

To date, work on the subject of sexuality, although substantial and consequential, has principally involved female, gay and lesbian white middle-class subjects.  The powerful, unmarked term—the heterosexual male—and the construction of his sexuality receive far less attention in this volume, as in the new studies of sexuality. Still, the essays of JanMohamed, Montrose, Laqueur, and Halperin point to needed work in men's sexual studies.  Along with JanMohamed and Montrose, Henderson signals the lacunae in this and other new studies of sexuality regarding the practices of persons of color and of the working classes under all conditions, including proto- and post-colonialism

---

[44]Symptomatically, de Lauretis' is the only essay in this volume to analyze the Freudian subject. See also her essay in *Theatre Journal* 177. Judith Butler's *Gender Trouble: Feminism and the Subversion of Identity* (New York: Routledge, 1990) seems to be at the forefront of this effort to remember the unconscious.

and imperialism.[45] Until societies, communities, and periods other than "our own" are examined, the new studies of sexuality will tend to impose "our" sexual categories and institutions on "theirs," as Halperin observes, and will fail to achieve meaningful comparative and crosscultural perspectives.

Beyond anthropology and other social sciences, the new studies of sexuality must extend its crossdisciplinary dialogues to the biological sciences. Following feminist critiques of science in the 1980s, which exposed the ideologically laden—misogynist, racist, capitalist—foundations and implications of scientific discourses and findings, confirmed their social embeddedness, and thus undermined their claims to (and "our" fetishizing of) objectivity and truth, the new studies of sexuality must join with historians and researchers to probe the cultural meanings of biological data on sex and sexuality. Is all of "nature" made by humanity and history? To what extent is it possible to determine whether every scientific datum is within the grasp of cultural ideologies? Such questions are not only crucial to studies of sexuality; they are key to developing an alternative set of practices and another scientific method.[46]

---

[45]The inattention to the heterosexual male is analogous to the failure to deconstruct whiteness in ethnic studies. Of course, I do not intend to re-rigidify the hetero/homosexual opposition, but the binary makes the unmarked term visible. On the inflection of sexuality by class, the best anthology to date is Kathy Peiss and Christian Simmons, eds., *Passion and Power: Sexuality in History* (1989).

[46]For a good review of feminist critiques of science, see Helen Longino and Evelynn Hammonds, "Conflicts and Tensions in the Feminist Study of Gender and Science," *Conflicts in Feminism* 164–83. Sandra Harding has proposed that the natural sciences be viewed as social sciences so that their social embeddedness can be more readily investigated; see her *Whose Science? Whose Knowledge* (Ithaca; Cornell University Press, 1991) 14–15, 300ff. See also Haraway's effort to speak of "the social relations of science and technology," in her influential "A Cyborg Manifesto: Science, Technology, and Socialist-Feminism in the Late Twentieth Century," *Simians, Cyborgs and Women* 165. As Haraway explains, "science is part of the process . . . of constituting the category of nature in the first place. . . . We are far from understanding precisely what our biology might be . . ." ("The Biological Enterprise: Sex, Mind and Profit from Human Engineering to Sociobiology," in *Simians* 45).

Finally, the new studies of sexuality must not only look to other disciplines; they must self-consciously question the field's configuration and its investment in privileged categories. Why, for example, has there been an extraordinary amount of work on "the body" in recent years? In one sense, it is logical that the body, once thought to be the metonym of nature, would follow upon the deconstruction of gender and sexuality, thereby removing another foundational concept. In another sense, however, "bodyology" parallels the complex obsession with the body in late capitalist consumerist societies, the anorexic/bulimic object that engages, at one and the same time, in a feeding frenzy and a relentless thinning, fasting, tightening, and sculpting. And from still another perspective, this fascination with the body coincides with the moment of its disappearance—the dying AIDS body most dramatically, but also the death of a "natural body," replaced by cosmetic and sex-change surgery, genetic engineering, scientifically produced wombs, and other "organs without bodies."[47]

Although it is difficult, perhaps impossible, to understand the meanings of discourses at the moment "we" inhabit them, it seems clear, even now, that bodyology does not mean liberty and does not say "no to power." Such understanding may or may not occur in a field that is, like sexuality and subjectivity, in an ongoing process of construction, change, flux. The new studies of sexuality, like this volume, embody Foucault's characterization of his *History of Sexuality* as an essay, that is, "the assay or test by which . . . one undergoes changes." His and these studies are "the record of a long and tentative exercise that [needs] to be revised and corrected again and again" (2:9), an exercise in which no single discourse of sexuality has the last word.

---

[47]See in addition to Haraway's "Cyborg Manifesto," Arthur and Marilouise Kroker, eds., *Body Invaders: Panic Sex in America* (New York: Saint Martin's Press, 1987); Rosi Braidotti, "Des Organes sans corps," *Les Cahiers du Grif* (Paris: Editions Tierce, 1987): 7–21.

# PART ONE. "THE HISTORY OF SEXUALITY": REOPENING THE QUESTION

# THE POLITICS OF PLEASURE:
## Female Sexual Appetite in the Hippocratic Corpus

### Lesley Dean-Jones

Although Michel Foucault admits that the ancient Greek code of sexual ethics he investigates in *The Use of Pleasure: The History of Sexuality, Volume 2* was "an elaboration of masculine conduct carried out from the viewpoint of men in order to give form to their behavior," he believes that with some modifications the model of masculine behavior was transferable to feminine behavior and that in classical Greece a woman was expected "to establish a relationship of superiority and domination over herself that was virile by definition."[1] Foucault reached his conclusions about the forms of masculine sexual behavior to a large extent by considering of the general medical works of the Hippocratics; had he paid more attention to the description of female sexual experience in the gynecological works of the Corpus, he would not so readily have assimilated the medical conception of a woman's relationship with herself in sexual matters to the virile model so readily. In Foucault's model, the intense pleasure associated with sexual intercourse has the important function of stimulating a man's appetite for copulation; but the Greeks believed the intensity of this pleasure could tempt a man to copulate too often for his own good. Foucault argues that the Greeks perceived sexual pleasure as necessary to human well-being but

An earlier version of this paper was presented at the Columbia University Seminar on Women and Society in April 1987 and, in a revised form, at the Conference on Women and Ancient Medicine at Brown University in October 1988. I would like to thank Helene Foley and David Konstan for giving me the opportunity to present the paper, all members of those meetings who made suggestions on my presentation, and the commentators on the two occasions—Judith Hallett and Sally Humphreys. I have received helpful suggestions from many scholars during the revision of this paper, too many to note individually though I am grateful to them all, but I would like to thank David Halperin especially for his support, encouragement, and insightful criticisms. The advice and suggestions from my colleagues have strengthened the paper in many respects; any shortcomings that remain are my own responsibility:

[1]Trans. Robert Hurley (New York: Pantheon, 1985) 22–3 and 83.

beneficial only if mastered so that it could be used in the right way. To be able to use his body's promptings toward sexual intercourse, an agent had to be able to recognize and control them. There is no room for this concept of "the use of pleasure" in the Hippocratic gynecology.

In the first volume of *The History of Sexuality*[2] Michel Foucault rejects the assumption that human sexuality is an enduring constant, to be more or less taken for granted, repressed or revealed in divers cultures. He analyzes it instead as a product of social forces, a construct modeled around those aspects of sexual behavior that are considered problematic by the powers within a society, which accept certain options in these contested areas of sexual behavior as normal. This influences the scientific knowledge of the day (itself a locus of power) to sanction those options as natural and condemn the alternatives as unhealthy. In relation to these focal points of sexual conduct individuals within any given society identify and differentiate themselves and others as subjects of desire and hence define their sexuality.

Foucault begins his "history of desiring man" by examining the prescriptions and interdictions on sexual behavior among the classical and early Hellenistic Greeks (c. 450–300 B.C.). Since he believes sexuality is largely the product of the interplay between power and knowledge, Foucault restricts his examination to "texts whose main object, whatever their form (speech, dialogue, treatise, collection of precepts, etc.), is to suggest rules of conduct."[3] These texts are essentially the medical and philosophical writings of the period. As a result, his explication of what concerned the Greeks in matters of male sexual behavior focuses on the physiological effects of desire and the steps a rational man should take in reaction to these effects (what I shall term the "functional" aspect of sexual activity). Foucault does not discuss at any length the profound psychological aspect of *erôs* that informs so much tragedy nor the jokes in comedy against certain sexual practices not problematized in the "prescriptive" texts. Nor does he exploit the plastic arts, especially vase painting, which illuminate areas ignored in the literary evidence. Consequently, his analysis of the ideal of sexual

---

[2]*The History of Sexuality, Volume 1: An Introduction*, trans. Robert Hurley (New York: Pantheon, 1978).
[3]Foucault 1:12.

behavior for a Greek male is somewhat one-dimensional.[4] But it is one dimension, and an important one. The two ruling principles of Greek life upon which this ideal is based, *gnôthi seauton* ("know yourself") and *mêden agân* ("nothing to excess"), are fundamental enough to all Greek thought that other literary genres can be seen to accept the basic tenets that "prescribed" normative sexual behavior (though they may be less sanguine about the possibility of adhering to these tenets or more explicit about what they preclude).

Most literary genres in classical Greece depict women as suffering the same sort of erotic desires (licit and illicit) as men and, like men, as striving to fulfill or repress these desires. However, the Hippocratic gynecological treatises—among the medical works that Foucault considered one of the chief repositories of normative sexual behavior—are anomalous in this regard. The women of the Hippocratic gynecology differ from the heroines of tragedy and comedy not in their lack of desire for anyone other than their husbands nor in the success or failure of their attempts to control such desire but in the physiological imperative of their bodies to intercourse without any desire and in their complete inability to control their bodily appetite for sex even if they wanted to.

Because this study is conceived primarily to contest Foucault's assimilation of the female to the male model of sexual appetite in the medical texts, I will be concerned almost exclusively with the functional aspect of female sexual experience in classical Greece. There are obviously many other facets to this complex subject, and I do not mean to claim that the medical model[5]

---

[4]For more detailed reviews of Foucault see (among others) Martha C. Nussbaum, *New York Times Book Review* 10 November 1985: 13–14; Mary Lefkowitz, *Partisan Review* 52 (1985): 460–66; Eva Keuls, *The Philadelphia Inquirer* 26 January 1986: 7; G. E. R. Lloyd, *New York Review of Books* 13 March 1986: 24ff.; David Halperin, *American Journal of Philology* 107 (1986): 274–86.

[5]Although I refer to "the Hippocratic model" throughout this paper, it should be clearly understood that the gynecological texts of the Corpus are the products of several authors who disagree with one another on some issues. Hermann Grensemann (*Knidische Medizin Teil I* [Berlin: de Gruyter, 1975], *Hippokratische Gynäkologie* [Wiesbaden: Steiner, 1982], *Knidische Medizin Teil II* [Stuttgart: Steiner, 1987]) has shown that the three-volume treatise on the diseases of women (*De Mulieribus [Diseases of women]* I, II and *De*

dictated or even approximated the sexual experience of most women in classical Greece. As with men, the medical texts provided biological reasons for individuals to conform to their society's code of sexual behavior. While this functional model might not obtrude on an individual's actual sexual activity, most would prefer to articulate their activity in forms ordained as "natural" by those with expert knowledge; they could have recourse to the medical model to justify their own or criticize another's sexual behavior from an apparently objective standpoint. Unlike the functional accounts of male sexual appetite in the Hippocratic Corpus or of male and female sexual appetite in Aristotle's biology (which while giving short shrift to psychological affects do not eliminate the role of erotic stimuli or willpower in withstanding the body's desires), the female sexual appetite described in the Hippocratic gynecology *precludes* directed desire and the exercise of self-control over the body's imperative to intercourse. Whereas in the case of men the medical texts of classical Greece present an aspect of sexual experience different from but compatible with that presented in other genres, in the case of women the medical texts present a different sexual experience altogether. I will refer only briefly to examples of female sexual desire and behavior in other genres to illustrate this divergence, though obviously a great deal more could be said on this score.

It is immediately clear that the Greek notion of male "sexuality" differed from that prevalent today: what many

---

*Sterilibus [On sterile women])* is a compilation of at least three hands, which he labels A, B, and C. However, the fact that the chapters could be integrated to work as a unity shows that the authors were operating with basically the same concept of the female body. Moreover, the independent treatise *De natura muliebri (On the nature of women)* consists largely of chapters attributed to author A in Grensemann's schema, while author C has been identified with the author of *De semine (On generation)* and *De natura pueri (On the nature of the child)*, and possibly also of *De virginibus (On the diseases of young girls)* (I. M. Lonie, *The Hippocratic Treatises On Generation, On the Nature of the Child, Diseases IV* [Berlin: de Gruyter, 1981]). The three remaining treatises of the gynecology, *De superfetatione (On superfetation)*, *De foeti exectione (On the excision of the fetus)*, and *De septimestri/octimestri partu (On the seventh/eighth month of the fetus)*, contain in a condensed form some of the material found in the other treatises. The gynecology is therefore a cohesive group of treatises, and while I will have occasion to refer to deviations within the gynecology from "the Hippocratic model," the term is legitimate.

would consider the principal term in their own sexual identity (hetero-, homo-, or bisexual) was meaningless to the Greeks. They never "problematized" the sex of the object of desire *per se*, though age and class were important considerations. This is not to say that a man might not display a preference for one sex or the other, but this did not differentiate his sexual identity from the next man's. Nor is there any evidence in the medical texts that the Greeks were overly concerned about the mode by which sexual desire reached its culmination; there are no recommendations or condemnations of particular positions in copulation, for example.[6] These and related issues are what Foucault would term the "morphology" of sexual behavior, and they were not, he claims, of primary interest to the Greeks in delimiting the norms of this conduct. What did engage their interest was what he terms the "dynamics" of the activity.[7] By this Foucault means the internal affects that caused a man to indulge in sexual intercourse. The form of the object of desire (other than that it should be of an appropriate age and status) and of the means of pleasuring (other than that it should derive from penetrating rather than being penetrated and should be performed in private) were irrelevant in determining a man's sexual identity; the important elements were the ease with which the desire was stimulated and the frequency with which it was satisfied. A man who too often felt the attractions of either sex lacked *sôphrosynê* ("continence"), and he who indulged his lust too frequently lacked *enkrateia* ("self-mastery"). The aspect of sexual conduct considered important for a man's identity was his success or failure in displaying these two qualities.

The Greek ideal was not, as in the later Christian ethic, a total renunciation of sexual pleasure as a sin; pleasure had its uses. The association of intense pleasure with sexual intercourse ensured that men would have an appetite for the act and there-

---

[6]Though K. J. Dover shows by the use of vase painting throughout his study *Greek Homosexuality* (London: Duckworth, 1978) that some practices were more appropriate in certain circumstances than others, for example, intercrural copulation is shown between older men and their younger *erômenoi* ("ones who are loved") but anal copulation is usually shown only between men of the same age (98–99). Moreover, it was considered despicable for any man to derive pleasure from being penetrated (100–9). To this extent "morphology" was a concern of the Greeks.

[7]Foucault 1:42.

fore secured the continuation of the species, though it must be noted that the natural impulse extended only as far as the ejaculation of semen. The receptacle into which it was emitted and whether or not conception resulted were immaterial to the quality of a man's desire and his pleasure.[8] Although the impulse to intercourse and the emission of semen at the sight of beauty was a natural and strong desire, to give way to it too frequently would cause physical debility because semen was a vital and precious bodily fluid. On the other hand, emitting the correct amount of semen could prevent an excess of fluid from building up in the body and maintain a man's health. To refrain from intercourse altogether, therefore, led not only to a lack of descendants but also to the risk of disease for the man involved. *Sôphrosynê* restricted the occasions on which an object stimulated a man's desire for intercourse, and by consciously exercising *enkrateia* a man limited the frequency with which he indulged that desire so that he was not led by pleasure to emit more semen than was good for him.

This model identified the active and proper pleasure of intercourse with penetration and ejaculation. The Greeks of the classical period considered it a disgrace for a free adult Greek male to be the passive object satisfying another's desire and an even greater disgrace if he enjoyed this role.[9] This contumely of passivity also attached to those who failed to control their own desires and indulged in intercourse whenever they felt the urge, even if they were always the penetrating agent. It was a man's moral responsibility and to his own ultimate advantage to avoid being dominated by another's or his own sexual pleasures.

For the Greeks both forms of passivity (being penetrated and being ruled by sexual desire) symbolized the female. In the case of penetration the symbolism resulted from the definition of the male role as active. As regards being at the mercy of one's passions, it was an axiom of the society that women had a

---

[8]If this were not the case, homosexuality would be stigmatized as unnatural more often than it is. Dover (60–68) demonstrates that this stigma is rare in the classical period outside certain strands of Plato's, and perhaps Aristotle's, philosophies.

[9]Foucault 1:187–255 gives an excellent analysis of the problems this caused the Greeks in validating their model of homosexual lovers, which required that one member of the pair be permanently cast as an *erômenos*.

greater appetite for sex and less self-control than men.[10] However, insofar as she was female, penetration was not disgraceful for a woman, and subjection to another's desires (which had more to do with determining the frequency with which she had intercourse than did her own wishes) was her proper role. In and of itself this denies a woman any power to use her pleasure. Foucault recognizes that *sôphrosynê* and *enkrateia* played a different role for women than for men, ensuring that they observed the rules laid down for them by others rather than determining for themselves when to indulge in intercourse;[11] but even with this modification, his model casts women, like men, as subjects of desire in the strength and frequency with which the sight of beauty incited them to want intercourse and the success with which they consciously subjugated their impulses. Moreover, by examining one passage in the medical writers (discussed below pp. 68–70) Foucault concludes that the model for all sexual activity was the virile "ejaculatory schema." He states that "the female act was not exactly the complement of the male act; it was more in the nature of a duplicate."[12] This presumes that the pleasure of ejaculation was thought to have the same uses for the female as for the male: to incite her to procreate and to evacuate an excess of seed building up in her body.

From the medical and philosophical texts, therefore, Foucault constructs a functional model of female sexual appetite by which women, like men, were thought a) to be impelled toward intercourse by the pleasure they would derive from union with a specific object, b) to possess the capability of controlling this impulse, and c) to benefit from resisting it on occasion.

Although these three criteria may fit the image of desiring women in other genres, none of them is applicable to the dominant model of the female in the Hippocratic Corpus. The medical authors concurred in the cultural belief that women had a voracious sexual appetite, but they did not believe that it was initi-

---

[10]See K. J. Dover, "Classical Greek Attitudes to Sexual Behavior," *Arethusa* 6 (1973): 64–65. Even in the *Lysistrata*, where the women's sex strike eventually forces the men to capitulate, abstention from sex is shown to be just as frustrating, if not more so, for the women as for the men. The strike is only maintained by Lysistrata's vigilance in preventing most of the women from slipping off home.

[11]Foucault 1:146.

[12]Foucault 1:129.

ated by specific objects that caused a woman to desire the pleasure of ejaculation in intercourse.  A woman's appetite for sex was a purely physiological phenomenon not necessarily associated with any psychological affects.

And whereas a man was expected for his own good to check the physiological phenomena that naturally followed upon his desire, it was impossible for a woman to control her appetites, nor was it beneficial to her health that she should do so.

Most other genres are concerned with the affective rather than the functional aspect of sexual appetite, and in these, including the Platonic dialogues,[13] the female experience approaches much closer to that of the male.  At one point, however, Plato describes a physiological compulsion to sexual intercourse in which the same types of differences between men and women appear as in the Hippocratic model, though Plato comments that the experiences of both are "owing to the same causes." As Plato's account is a concise comparison of a type that does not occur in the Hippocratic Corpus, it will be convenient to use it as a preface:

> And the marrow, inasmuch as it is animate and has been granted an outlet, has endowed the part where its outlet lies with a love for generating by implanting therein a lively desire for emission.  Wherefore in men the nature of the genital organs is disobedient and self-willed, like a creature that is deaf to reason, and it attempts to dominate all because of its frenzied lusts.  And in women again, owing to the same causes, whenever the matrix or womb, as it is called, which is an indwelling creature desirous of child-bearing, remains without fruit long beyond the due season, it is vexed and takes it ill; and by straying all ways through the body and blocking up the passages of the breath and preventing respiration it casts the body into the uttermost distress, and causes, more-

---

[13]For a discussion of Plato's theory of *erôs* see David Halperin, "Platonic *Erôs* and What Men Call Love," *Ancient Philosophy* 5 (1985): 161–204 (which includes an excellent bibliography on the subject) and "Plato and Erotic Reciprocity," *Classical Antiquity* 5 (1986): 60–80. Although the passage in the *Timaeus* does contain affective language, the subjects of the affections are the reproductive organs rather than their human owners, so there is still very little of the psychological involved in this account.

over, all kinds of maladies; until the desire and love of
the two sexes (*hekaterôn*) unite them.

*(Timaeus* 9 1b-d)[14]

This passage attributes sexual appetite in both men and women
to the independent desires of the reproductive organs. Although
nothing is said about either men or women gaining ascendancy
over their reproductive organs, *Timaeus* 86c-d describes sexual
intemperance caused by an excess of seed in the marrow of the
spinal column as one form of unrighteousness (*ponêria*) in men,[15]
and in 90e women are said to be born from men who lived un-
righteously (*adikôs*) in their previous incarnation; that is to say,
an inability to control the body's physiological processes fits a
man to become a woman.[16] What triggers desire for intercourse
in the man is not explained, but the penis' desire to "dominate
all" (*pantôn kratein*) implies that objects are involved, even if in-
discriminately chosen. Moreover, although the penis is said to
have a "love for generating" this is a by-product of what it really
desires: emission and possession. On the other hand, the womb
needs no object at all to trigger its lusts,[17] just an extended period of abstinence from procreation. And intercourse without a
successful conception will not satisfy a woman's reproductive organ.

No classical Greek text assumes that the male physiological
predisposition to emit semen will be triggered in the complete absence of any object. The beauty of a wife, a young boy, a prostitute, or a mental image stimulated involuntary emotional and
physical reactions that sought consummation in the emission of

---

[14]Trans. R. G. Bury, *Plato VII*, Loeb Classical Library (Cambridge,
Mass.: Harvard University Press, 1929) 249–51.

[15]*Timaeus* defines all forms of evil as the involuntary result of disease.

[16]Elsewhere in Plato, however, women are treated as full moral agents,
and in the *Republic* he acknowledges that some women will have the moral
capacity to become Guardians.

[17]In other dialogues, discrimination among possible love objects is an
important element in Plato's theory of desire for both men and women. In
the *Symposium* 206c-e Diotima tells Socrates that only the beautiful can call
forth the desire to procreate. Elsewhere desire is always contingent upon an
agent perceiving something as good and beautiful that he realizes he lacks,
for example, *Phaedrus* 253e; *Lysis* 204b.

seed, not the engendering of a child.[18] The physical reaction was natural, and difficult to master, but a respectable Greek citizen was expected to possess *sôphrosynê*, which would protect him from the charms of any and every beauty; when he was affected, his *enkrateia* would enable him to subdue all but the most essential and appropriate compulsions to fulfill his desires. It was recognized that some, because of their *akrateia* ("lack of self-control"), were prone to finding almost every body of a certain type stimulating and were unable to restrain their impulses whenever they saw a body that appealed to them,[19] while others because of their *akolasia* ("self-indulgence") went looking for beautiful bodies to arouse their lust, far from subduing their desires when they appeared.[20] Thus, in the male the satisfaction even of immoderate sexual appetites still depended upon some object of desire. Rape was attributed to the assailant's arousal at the sight of the victim rather than to his initially undirected physiological need.[21]

The medical works are silent about the occasions or objects that stimulate the desire for intercourse in men; their phrase for male sexual activity is usually "to use intercourse" or "sexual pleasures" (*chrêsthai lagneiêsi* or *aphrodisioisi*) without any suggestion of what object this should take. But their emphasis on curtailing rather than promoting intercourse makes it plain that they believe men tend to overindulge in the activity because something other than their bodies' requirements stimulates them to it.[22] The Hippocratics prohibit capitulating to the desire to

---

[18]For example, Aristophanes, *Nubes* 1075–82; Xenophon, *Hieron* I 31–33; *Cyropaedia* V 1.19 and VI 1.31; *Lysias* I 8. Most of these occasions would be instances of *epithymia* rather than *erôs*. The latter was a more exclusive passion involving emotional and psychological commitment beyond the consummation of any desire.

[19]For example, Xenophon, *Symposium* IV 38.

[20]A trait particularly common in tyrants, see Aristotle *Politica* V 10.

[21]Euripides fragment 840; Xen., *Cyr.* 6.1.31–3; Menander *Epitrepontes* 1123.

[22]The evidence for the functional model of male sexual appetite is taken from the general works of the Hippocratic Corpus (cited by volume, page, and line number from *Oeuvres complètes d' Hippocrate*, ed. E. Littré (Paris 1839–61; reprint Amsterdam: A. M. Hakkert, 1962); it may therefore be objected that the injunctions refer to women as much as to men. However, advice on the amount of exercise a man should take in such forms as

emit semen stimulated by external objects when this goes beyond the body's internal compulsion. It is true that they advise more intercourse during the winter than the summer, but the recommended amount of intercourse for the summer is "as little as possible" (*hôs hêkista*). The winter increase is recommended because that season is much wetter than the summer and the body could become too moist if fluids were not evacuated.[23] For the same reason older men are advised to have more intercourse than younger and men with moister constitutions than men with drier.[24] Generally, however, the danger was not that men would deprive their bodies of the sexual exercise they needed but that their desires would lead them beyond their physical needs and result in pathological conditions. Consumption of the back, for example, was thought to be particularly common in newlyweds and those who loved intercourse (*philolagnous*) because they dried their marrow out too much.[25] Intercourse is very rarely part of therapy for male patients;[26] the Hippocratics much more frequently prescribe abstention in the recovery phase of an illness.[27] However, at least one Hippocratic recognized that a man's desire for intercourse could be so strong as to lead him to indulge in it although he had been told specifically that his body really needed him to conserve semen.[28] Even when the emission

---

gymnastics and wrestling with no suggestions of parallel pursuits in which women could take part (for example, *De Victu [On regimen]* 2.64 [6.580.14–18]; *De internis affectionibus [On internal affections]* 30 [7.246.14–17]), and descriptions of symptoms affecting testicles or scrotum, with no references to the equivalent female genitalia (for example, *Int.* 44 [7.276.2]) show that the body the Hippocratics had in mind in the general works was the male, not the human, body. Cf. Lesley Dean-Jones, "Women's Bodies," *Classical Greek Science* (Oxford: Oxford University Press, 1992) forthcoming.

[23]*Vict.* 3.68 (6.596.9–10).

[24]*Vict.* 1.35 and 2.58 (6.516.6–9 and 6.572.1–4).

[25]*De morbis (On diseases)* 2.51 (7.78.14–15). For the dangers associated with too much intercourse see Foucault 1:118–20.

[26]But cf. *Vict.* 3.80 and 85 (6.628.1 and 6.636.12–13).

[27]For example, *Vict.* 3.73 (6.614.8–9); *Morb.* 3.16 (7.148.19–21); *Int.* 31 and 32 (7.250.9–10).

[28]*Morb.* 2.73 (7.112.7–8). In such a situation, the author says, the patient should at least fast and take vapor baths before indulging in intercourse.

of semen was totally involuntary and resulted simply from an excess of bodily fluid that found release during sleep, the emission was accompanied by images of sexual intercourse.[29] Thus, although the Hippocratics do not discuss at any length the psychological aspect of sexual desire, they considered it integral to the sexual appetites of the male body.[30]

While the Hippocratic Corpus is more concerned with the functional aspect of sexual activity than with the object of a man's sexual desire or the frequency with which it is stimulated, the medical model of male sexual appetite is compatible with other works concerning male sexual behavior in encouraging the exercise of *sôphrosynê*. Men can feel the urge for sexual inter-

---

[29]*Sem.* 1 (7.470.21–472.4). This could be caused by the reckless habit of sleeping on the back, see Diokles of Karystos, *Regimen* in Oribasius, *Collections des médecins*, eds. U. Bussemaker and C. Daremberg (Paris: Imprimerie Nationale, 1858) 177. Most medical texts do not discuss the content of the dreams, but the terms for the phenomenon of emission during sleep usually contain the root *oneir*, for example, *Morb.* 2.51 (7.78.19) and are better translated as "wet dream" rather than as "nocturnal emission," which suggests no affective aspect.

[30]*De aire, aquis, locis (Airs, waters, places)* 22 (2.82.1–4) seems to expect that autoeroticism will sometimes be initiated in the absence of sexual desire (somewhat absentmindedly), but its effect is to remind the practitioner of sexual intercourse and so keep him potent. That at least seems to be the sense of the passage citing lack of masturbation as one of the reasons for Scythian impotence:

> They always wear trousers and go upon horseback most of the time, so that they do not handle their genitals, and from the cold and tiredness forget about desire and intercourse and feel no sexual impulse before they become impotent.

Diogenes the Cynic supposedly masturbated openly in the agora, explaining that ejaculation was a physical need just like hunger and should be no more shameful an activity than eating (Diogenes Laertius 6.2.46). This view is not necessarily any more exclusively functional than the Hippocratics in separating the male desire to emit semen from an object or from a sexually pleasurable sensation. It is not known what provoked this need in Diogenes, nor what mental images he conjured up while he masturbated. But, even if his need to ejaculate was totally physiological, even if he was stimulated by the sight of no particular person, conjured up no erotic images nor even felt any pleasure beyond the removal of pain, at the very least he was conscious of what his body wanted.

course beyond what their bodies need; the urge, therefore, is not entirely physiological, and those who frequently desire to ejaculate semen are too easily affected by external objects, which may or may not be appropriate. As long as they do not consummate their desire and drain the body of its vital fluid, however, the lack of *sôphrosynê* will not affect them physically; thus the Hippocratics do not concern themselves with that aspect of sexual experience, though they recognize it implicitly. Like other genres of literature, however, the Hippocratic Corpus does expect men to be able to know and control their sexual appetites, threatening those who fail to display *enkrateia* in matters of sexual activity with a variety of sanctions, albeit pathological rather than moral.

In contrast, women have a physiological appetite for intercourse before they even know what it is. In *De Virginibus* the Hippocratic author attributes the suicidal tendencies of young virgins to the fact that their menarchal blood is trapped inside their bodies and, as it has no egress, moves from their wombs to their hearts and lungs, causing the insanity that prompts them to hang themselves or jump down wells. The author thinks the best cure is to marry the young woman off as quickly as possible so that her womb might be opened up and the blood drained out. Young women have a physiological need for intercourse but no conscious desire for it or knowledge of what it is they need. The satisfaction of their appetite is not even tied to any pleasure beyond simple relief of the pressure of blood on their heart, which may not happen immediately anyway.

Throughout her reproductive years, when she is not pregnant, intercourse fulfills this same function for an adult woman; it keeps her womb open and heats the blood so that it flows more easily.[31] Failure to have intercourse does not result in the retention of semen, causing erotic dreams or easily aroused desires[32] but in the retention of menstrual blood, causing consumption, hemorrhoids, or gout.[33] Intercourse not only prevents the womb from closing over; it also anchors it in place within the body with

---

[31]*Mul.* I 2 (8.14.5–16.2); *Sem.* 4 (7.476.12–15).

[32]Though *Mul.* I 5 (8.28.16) may imply that a surfeit of material in a woman who has eaten a lot when she is not really hungry might cause sexual desire.

[33]*Mul.* I 2 (8.18.18); *Epidemicae historiae (epidemics)* IV 24 (5.164.9–10); *Aphorismi (Aphorisms)* VI 29 (4.570.6).

the weight of semen or ideally with a fetus. If the womb becomes too dry, and therefore too light, it can become displaced
into any part of the body cavity or the head, causing headaches,
menstrual difficulties, loss of voice, foaming at the mouth, and
general torpor.[34] Less frequent intercourse makes these physiological reactions more likely, but the womb does not close over or
become displaced at the sight of an individual the woman finds
attractive, nor is the phenomenon attended with images of—or
desires for—sexual gratification. Because the body's need for intercourse is not attached to a desire for pleasure, which could
lead individuals to want more intercourse than was good for
them, the physiological insistence of a woman's body on intercourse does not signify a lack of *sôphrosynê*.[35]

Even if the womb did close over and move in response to
erotic stimuli when the body had no need of intercourse—as a
man's penis might become engorged with semen at the sight of a
woman or boy though his body had no need to evacuate excess
fluid—a woman had no chance of mastering this response unaided, as a man might nullify an erection by *enkrateia*. Paola

[34]*Mul.* II 123–26 (8.266.11–272.8); *Mul. Nat:* 2, 3 and 8 (7.312.14–316.8,
322.11–324.9).

[35]There are some references to female desire in the Corpus, but few of
them refer unambiguously to a simple desire for intercourse. For example,
*Mul.* I 5 (8.28.16) refers to desire in conjunction with a pathological
condition (see n. 32). *Mul.* I 6 (8.30.21-2) describes those women who
menstruate less than normal as not being *mnêsitokos* ("philoprogenitive")
implying that other women are. This seems to refer more to a desire for
having a child than for the intercourse necessary to produce one. Cf. *Mul.* I
24 (8.62.20), where the woman's desire is a desire for conception rather than
intercourse. At *Mul.* I 12 (8.48.15–17), a treatment to promote conception, a
woman is said to *orgci* at the end of her menstrual period, but this could be
translated either as "feel desire" or as "be ready to bear." The passage
continues to say that a woman must desire her husband on the other days if
her womb is in the best condition (*en têsin allêsin hêmerêsin himerousthai chrê
tou andros, ên arista echôsin hai hysterai*). This statement is the closest the
Hippocratics get to saying that desire for sexual pleasure *per se* is good for a
woman. Even here, though, her sexual activity is restricted to her husband,
and no limit is placed on the amount or frequency of the desire she should
feel since it could not lead her to harm her body by overindulgence without
him (see below, 64–65). *Himerousthai* may be more accurately rendered here
as "welcome her husband's advances."

Manuli has demonstrated[36] that the preferred destinations of the womb (brain, heart, liver) were all possible seats of the *psychê* ("life-force") and that the Hippocratic image of the womb, like Plato's, was of an independent entity within the woman's body that could master the woman's *psychê* with its own desires. One popular method for ensuring the womb's return to its correct position was to sit the woman on some sweet-smelling perfumes and to burn mule-dung under her nose. The womb would flee from the bad smell and be attracted toward the good, as a god is invoked by incense. Helen King has argued that the Hippocratics develop an entirely mechanical model to explain the movements of the womb;[37] when it becomes dry and hot through lack of intercourse it is attracted to the moister, cooler organs in the body. She believes it is only by reading back from Plato that modern interpreters have attributed to the womb its own desires. It is true that the Hippocratics rationalize the womb's movements by the attraction of the dry to the moist (they believe it can also be attracted to the bladder), but this is not sufficient to explain why it should ever end up in the head. Nor does it explain why it should respond to the application of foul and sweet smells.[38] Without endowing the womb with the status of an independent animal as Plato had, the Hippocratics made it the seat of a woman's sexual appetite and divorced it from her conscious control by allowing it to stifle those organs in which the consciousness was thought to lie. A woman therefore had no chance to exercise *enkrateia* over her appetite for sex.

In the Hippocratic model there is no need for the average woman to exhibit *enkrateia*. The Hippocratics never suggest that

---

[36]"Fisiologia e patologia de femminile negli scritti ippocratici dell'antica ginecologia greca," *Hippocratica: Actes du colloque hippocratique de Paris 4–9 Septembre 1978*, ed. M. Grmek (Paris: Editions du Centre national de la recherche scientifique, 1980) 393–408.

[37]"From Parthenos to Gyne: The Dynamics of Category," diss., University of London, 1985, 113–15.

[38]This treatment was retained in the second century A.D., after dissection had proved that a woman's womb was held in place by tendons so that its tendency to rise upwards when it became too light was held in check to some extent. Soranus, a second century A.D. physician, castigates those who used odor therapy, objecting that "the uterus does not issue forth like a wild animal from the lair" (*Gynaecologia* 3.29, trans. Owsei Temkin, *Soranus' Gynecology* [Baltimore: Johns Hopkins, 1956] 153).

intercourse should be restricted for women as part of a normal regimen,[39] and no pathological states result from too frequent intercourse. In contrast to men, women are much more at risk from too little sexual activity, and their therapy often includes recommendations for intercourse, though usually in forms similar to "let her go to her husband" (*para ton andra itô*)[40] rather than to "use sexual pleasure." Until she becomes pregnant a woman's menses are always in danger of being retained and her womb of becoming displaced; the more influxions of semen there are, the less likely this is to occur, and a woman is safest when conception has finally taken place.

This model has obvious advantages for the male position in the social structure of classical Greece. Men had an opportunity to choose their wives and also to have their desire stimulated and satisfied outside the home.[41] The medical model of male sexual appetite and behavior validates not only the need for but also the desire for intercourse as normal and, insofar as the desire is simply for emission, says nothing about how or with whom the act should be performed. While the medical model worked against the man's fulfilling any and every desire, it did not lay down a quantitative minimum or maximum, so an individual could claim to feel excessively "moist" if he believed he was having more than the "average" amount of intercourse. Women had little control over the choice of their husbands and often wed considerably older men who remained their only sex partners for the duration of the marriage. Hence the form "let her go to her husband" in the injunctions to women to have intercourse. If their natural appetite for sex were a desire for pleasure that was

---

[39]The occasions on which women are advised to abstain from sex (for example, *Mul.* I 12 [8.48.19]; *Mul.* II 143, 144 and 149 [8.316.12 and 326.17–18]; *Steril.* 230 [8.444.17–18]) are in a preliminary stage of treatment of hitherto barren women preparatory to intercourse with a view to becoming pregnant or in the recovery from childbirth, see G. E. R. Lloyd, *Science, Folklore, and Ideology* (Cambridge: Cambridge University Press, 1983) 84, n. 103 and King 121. The recommendations for abstention apply only to particular occasions, not to the overall frequency with which women should indulge in intercourse.

[40]For example, *Mul.* I 60 (8.122.4); *Mul.* II 128 (8.276.8), see n. 35.

[41]Though courtesans cost money, and while it may have been accepted practice to frequent them, the regular sexual partners of most poorer men would surely have been their wives; see Dover 63–64.

awakened only by objects of desire without which they had no need of intercourse, then the subjugation of their bodies to their husbands was demonstrably unjust; and if an object of desire did function as the provocation of a natural need, even the limited contact they had with members of their own households (male and female) posed a possible danger. The Hippocratic model allowed a husband to have intercourse with his wife whenever he wished without taking her desires into consideration, literally "for her own good." If a man failed to have intercourse with his wife as often as she needed it, the woman would be driven not by her unfulfilled longing for pleasure to another lover but by her pathologically dry womb to a Hippocratic doctor.

In denying women the possibility of mastering their own sexual appetites, the Hippocratic model further justified their subordinate position to men. Women could not refuse to grant their husbands sexual favors because this would backfire on the women themselves, who would eventually be the more incapable of suppressing their need for their spouses, even if they felt no desire for them; still the Hippocratics did acknowledge occasions when a woman, for pathological reasons, did not welcome her husband's sexual advances.[42] Her need to have fluid put into the womb rather than to emit anything herself also ensured that a woman could not turn to her female companions to free her from sexual dependence on her husband.[43] For the same reason she could not dispense with the need of her husband through masturbation. *De aëre, aquis, locis* 9 (2.42.2–3) says that women do not get stones in the bladder as much as men because they do not masturbate.[44] Even if a wife resorted to a dildo on occasion,

---

[42]For example, *Mul.* I 24 and 57 (8.64.5–6 and 114.12–13), *Mul.* II 177 (8.358.21–360.1), *Steril.* 227 (8.436.12).

[43]Female homosexuality was recognized among the Greeks, but after the archaic period it was very rarely mentioned; when it was, it was generally described in derogatory terms as unnatural; see Dover, 171–84. Of course, this need not mean that women did not have fulfilling homosexual relations in reality.

[44]Again, this does not mean that women did not in fact masturbate and enjoy it, simply that the functional model claimed it could not fulfill their natural sexual appetite. Sarah Pomeroy, in *Goddesses, Whores, Wives and Slaves* (New York: Schocken, 1975) 87–88, suggests that masturbation was viewed as an acceptable sexual outlet for citizen wives, citing such evidence as representations of dildos on vase paintings and references to the use of

in the Hippocratic model it could not benefit her because it failed to inject semen into her womb.[45] The women who are portrayed as using dildos in literature are described as wearing them down, which may imply that they were thought to cause as much frustration as gratification. A woman needed a man to control her passions, and that man and the occasions on which he had intercourse with her need not be of her own choosing to be successful.

There is notoriously little, if any, evidence about how women in classical Greece viewed their position in society. It may seem that if they accepted the functional model of male and female sexual appetites on any level, they would be reduced to chattels and renounce any chance to have their own sexual desires taken into consideration; but the model could also be used to ensure that women got the sexual attention they wanted from their husbands, including any whose husbands might try to avoid intercourse with their wives as a form of contraception without their wives' agreement.[46] The fact that her health depended on

---

them in the *Lysistrata*. However, as Catherine Johns points out *in Sex or Symbol: Erotic Images of Greece and Rome* (Austin: University of Texas Press, 1982) 102–3, a woman has no need of such equipment to excite herself, though many men would like to think that she has. The descriptions of women lusting after dildos in *Lysistrata* and (later) Herodas' *Mime* 6 reflect how men would like to think women masturbated rather than actual women's practices, and the vase paintings probably represent entertainments that were staged for men by courtesans rather than wives.

[45]Therapy involving a cucumber which is explicitly likened to a penis *(Steril.* 222 [8.430.20–1]) prepares a woman to receive her husband, rather than substituting for conjugal relations. It may be significant that the few methods of contraception recommended in the Hippocratic Corpus do not advocate any type of barrier method. They describe a potion that when drunk protects against pregnancy for a year *(Mul.* I 76 [8.170.7–8]) or allows the semen to enter the womb before expelling it *(Sem.* 5 [7.476.17–19]). Aristotle mentions that some women anoint the labia with oil so that the semen will slip out before reaching the womb *(HA* VII 3 583a23–25). The Hippocratics do not recommend this nor any barrier method (which some women must have used) because it would deprive the womb of the moisture it needs to remain healthy.

[46]Pomeroy (49 and 68) suggests that this may have been a common form of birth control. However, a married couple did hope for some children from a marriage, and as Pomeroy shows (69) the mortality rate of children made it advisable to bear more than the minimum one son for "insurance"

her husband's sexual attentions meant that a certain amount of intercourse with one's wife was seen as a duty among Greek men.  In the sixth century Solon passed a law that any man married to an *epiklêros* ("heiress") should have sex with her at least three times a month; but since it was imperative for the continuation of the *epiklêros'* father's line and fortune that she have a son as soon as possible, Solon may have considered this to be more frequent than was normal among married couples. This is not to argue that women for whom this would be an unsatisfying sex life actually displayed hysterical symptoms in order to have their repressed sexual desires met by treatments such as bandaging beneath the breasts or foul-smelling fumigations applied to the nose.[47]  The threat of developing such symptoms would allow women to remind their husbands of their conjugal duties without appearing to challenge the male's sexual mastery or to threaten the integrity of the *oikos* with desires that would seek an outlet elsewhere.  A woman could also use the functional model of male sexual appetite to suggest to her husband that he restrict his extramarital sexual activity for his own health without challenging his socially sanctioned right to such activity.

Once again, the functional model of sexual appetite was not the only or the most important aspect of classical Greek concerns about sexual behavior.  But the different models for men and women gave both a forum in which to make their sexual needs known without challenging the relationship between the sexes upon which their society depended.[48]  It justified the societal

---

purposes. Given the number of treatments for promoting conception in the Corpus and the fact that even today couples do not always succeed in engendering a child as soon as they start trying, it cannot be assumed that women gave birth to their allotted "quota" early in their child-bearing years. Furthermore, among those who did, a belief in the efficacy of other forms of birth control, however unfounded, would postpone resignation to celibacy.

[47]See Bennet Simon, *Mind and Madness in Ancient Greece* (Ithaca: Cornell University Press, 1978) 242–44.

[48]I am defining "society" as *polis* + *oikos*. Women were of course excluded from direct participation in the affairs of the *polis*, but they did not necessarily share the male perception that this was the more important of the two aspects of society. If, as seems probable, most women valued their

ideal of secluding of women from men outside the *oikos* (unscrupulous males might attempt to take advantage of female sexual helplessness), thus allowing a married couple to develop a socially sanctioned relationship without either feeling that the woman was inherently distrusted.

The severing of the body's sexual appetite from conscious sexual desire is obviously not the model of female sexuality prevalent in Greek myth, tragedy, or comedy. Helen's passions are directed exclusively toward Paris, Medea's to Jason, and Myrrhine's to Kinesias.[49]    Athene takes the precaution of endowing Odysseus with special beauty when he leaves his bath to go to Penelope for the first time in twenty years. Nausikaa knows perfectly well what she wants from Odysseus even though only a young girl, and Aeschylus' *Suppliants* shows that young women could be well aware of what they did not want in a husband. Nor are females shown as incapable of controlling their passion. Kalypso, Kirke, and Nausikaa are all quite capable of relinquishing Odysseus when they are told to, though not without some regret. Nor has Penelope behaved in any unseemly fashion in the twenty years in which her womb has been unirrigated. To some extent Clytemnestra can be seen as mastering her passion for Aegisthus (if that is indeed what she feels for him) until she has achieved her designs, and Euripides' Electra is in complete control not only of her own sexual behavior but also of her peasant husband's. Phaedra is, of course, unable to control herself, but she too challenges the Hippocratic model since her husband Theseus would be unable to satisfy her. Even a good dose of burning mule dung would have little effect on her condition. She needs Hippolytus.

The majority of these women are masculinized in some way, and their stories normally end in disaster for them and all concerned with them. A Greek man would not wish to think he was leaving his *oikos* in the hands of such a creature, and a Greek woman would not like to think she was suspected of harboring the same propensity as these heroines. The functional model of

position in maintaining the *oikos*, they were not likely to undermine the social forms they thought protected their position.

[49]Any reference to compulsion from Aphrodite should not be taken to mean that the woman does not comply in the passion. A man's sexual attraction was often referred to Aphrodite without any intention of denying that the passion was real.

female sexual appetite rationalized and integrated the cultural belief that women constantly desired intercourse with the societal need for obedient and chaste wives who yet were always ready to produce heirs and citizens.

I do not mean to imply that the classical Greeks considered it impossible for a chaste wife to take pleasure in intercourse, but if the functional model of female sexual experience was to support the social relationship between the sexes, it could not allow pleasure to be either a stimulant for or a necessary concomitant to the satisfaction of female sexual appetite. The description of a woman's orgasm in *De semine* 4 (7.474.14.476.8) is indeed modeled upon a man's, as Foucault says, but unlike male orgasm it does not serve as incitement to intercourse, and if she fails to reach it, a woman is not left frustrated. In general, the Hippocratics believed that both the father and the mother had to contribute seed to the formation of the embryo. The father's seed was identified with the semen ejaculated at orgasm, and the author of *De semine* based his theory of the production of female seed on this model. Aline Rousselle has argued that this is evidence of the female oral tradition in the Hippocratics; women insisted that their husbands show consideration for their pleasure and bring them to orgasm if they wanted to beget children.[50] However, the passage does not suggest much female input.

> In the case of women, it is my contention that when during intercourse the vagina is rubbed and the womb is disturbed, an irritation is set up in the womb which produces pleasure and heat in the rest of the body. A woman also releases something from her body, sometimes into the womb which then becomes moist, and sometimes externally as well, if the womb is open wider than normal. Once intercourse has begun, she experiences pleasure throughout the whole time, until the man ejaculates. If her desire for intercourse is excited, she emits before the man, and for the remainder of the time she does not feel pleasure to the same extent; but if she is not in a state of excitement, then her pleasure terminates along with that of the man. What happens is like this: if into boiling water you pour another quantity of

---

[50]*Porneia: On Desire and the Body in Antiquity*, trans. Felicia Pheasant (Oxford: Blackwell, 1988) 27–28.

water which is cold, the water stops boiling.  In the same way, the man's sperm arriving in the womb extinguishes both the heat and the pleasure of the woman.  Both the pleasure and the heat reach their peak simultaneously with the arrival of the sperm in the womb, and then they cease.  If, for example, you pour wine on a flame, first of all the flame flares up and increases for a short period when you pour the wine on.  In the same way the woman's heat flares up in response to the man's sperm, and then dies away.  The pleasure experienced by the woman during intercourse is considerably less than the man's, although it lasts longer.  The reason that the man feels more pleasure is that the secretion from the bodily fluid in his case occurs suddenly, and as the result of a more violent disturbance than in the woman's case.

*(De semine* 4)[51]

In this model, the desire for sexual gratification does not prompt the woman to intercourse.  She begins to feel pleasure only after the man has penetrated her, and then she feels pleasure continually, sometimes—but only sometimes—rising to the peak of "excitement."  The friction of the penis in the vagina is sufficient to produce the pleasure; there is no mention of the clitoris although the Hippocratics' contemporaries knew about it and its effects.[52]  Furthermore, a woman's release of seed is not even tied to the secretion of the vaginal lubricant.  It is released directly into the womb and only appears outside it if the womb is open more than usual.  A woman's pleasure during intercourse is not tied to any physiological display on her part.

---

[51]Trans. Lonie 319–20.

[52]In "Diseases of Women in the Epidemics," *Die Hippokratischen Epidemien: Actes du colloque hippocratique 1984,* ed. Gerhard Baader (Stuttgart: Steiner, 1987) 31, Ann Hanson notes Xanthus of Lydia's remarks that the Lydian king had clitoridectomies performed on women in his harem to keep them young and beautiful; Hipponax and Aristophanes both refer to it under the name of *myrton* (myrtleberry), and it seems likely that Sappho used the word *nymphê* (bride) as a pun referring to both a bride and the clitoris. See Jack Winkler, "Gardens of Nymphs: Public and Private in Sappho's Lyrics," *Reflections of Women in Antiquity,* ed. Helene Foley (New York: Gordon and Breach Science Publishers, 1981) 78–81.

The Hippocratics avowed a belief in female seed principally to explain how a child came to resemble its mother, not to ensure that husbands be concerned with their wives' sexual enjoyment. Since male seed for procreation was provided by sudden ejaculation from the body and it was believed that the mother had to provide the same sort of fluid in order to contribute equally to the fetus, the Hippocratics connected female seed too with orgasm. The fact that women could display pleasure during intercourse supported this model, but it did not *require* any visible evidence of a woman's enjoyment. In the numerous Hippocratic therapies on how to make a barren woman conceive, there is no advice on how to excite a woman's passion to make her emit seed. Ann Hanson believes this is because of a sense of propriety,[53] but the Hippocratics do not shrink from naming any other part of the female genitals (vagina, cervix, labia) if it will serve a use in therapy. Thus, it seems unlikely that when dispensing advice on how to make a woman pregnant they would avoid mentioning how to arouse a woman to conscious pleasure if they thought it really made any difference to whether or not she ejaculated. In promoting conception, they focus on the menses, recognizing that the time of month most favorable to conception comes right after menstruation, when the womb is empty and the seeds can mingle unimpeded by menstrual fluid. This is true of the treatment to promote conception at *De mulieribus* I 12 (8.48.15–17, cf. n. 36), which while implying that a woman's desire is necessary for conception, states that, if a woman's womb is in the best condition, she must (*chrê*) desire her husband. Therefore, a man need not concern himself with rousing his wife's desires as long as she is healthy. If she fails to conceive because her desires were not aroused, her own physiology is at fault, not her husband's behavior. Similarly, *De mulieribus* I 17 (8.56.19–22) directs a man whose wife does not become pregnant immediately after menstruation simply to continue having sex with her as the activity itself will excite her desire; that is, she will eventually become pregnant. For the Hippocratics, a woman's enjoyment of sex is not proof that she will become pregnant; rather, becoming pregnant is evidence that she enjoyed intercourse.[54]

---

[53]Winkler 78–81.

[54]Soranus, a physician practicing in Rome in the second century A.D., is a sympathetic gynecologist, but because he accepts the theory that a woman has to have an appetite for sex to conceive, he is forced to assert that

Even the description of female orgasm in *De Semine* 4, therefore, does not return the Hippocratic functional female model of sexual appetite to the province of *sôphrosynê* or *enkrateia*. The woman feels a desire for sex only after her husband has initiated intercourse, and it is not possible that she should be left with unfulfilled desires as long as he injects some fluid into her womb. The functional model of the Hippocratics does not allow a woman to be a moral agent in her own sex life.

This is not the case in Aristotle's functional theory of intercourse and conception. Aristotle championed the strand of Greek thought that claimed only men contributed seed to the embryo while the mother merely provided the place and the material. This is frequently interpreted as extremely misogynistic, as a denial of maternity.[55] It has been argued that it would be more understandable to deny paternity, as is the case in other more primitive cultures.[56] But the Greeks can hardly be faulted for observing that human reproduction was sexual. Since they re-

---

if a woman becomes pregnant from a rape she must have unconsciously enjoyed it (*Gyn.* I 37).

[55]Maryanne C. Horowitz, "Aristotle and Woman," *Journal of the History of Biology* 9 (1976): 183–213; Stephen Clark, "Aristotle's Woman," *Journal of the History of Political Thought* 3 (1982): 177–91; Suzanne Saïd, "Féminin, Femme et Femmelle dans les Grands Traités Biologiques d'Aristote," *La Femme dans les Sociétés Antiques*, ed. E. Lévy (Strasbourg: AECR, 1983) 93–123; Silvia Campese, Paola Manuli, Giulia Sissa, *Madre Materia* (Torino: Boringhier, 1983). For an opposing view see Johannes Morsink, "Was Aristotle's Biology Sexist?" *Journal of the History of Biology* 12 (1979): 83–112, and *Aristotle on the Generation of Animals: A Philosophical Study* (Washington: University Press of America, 1982) 43–59.

[56]Horowitz cites Malinowski's work among the Trobriand islanders in 1903, but Malinowski himself later wrote, "The so-called ignorance of paternity is nothing else but a very imperfect knowledge that intercourse is a necessary though not sufficient condition of the woman being 'opened up' as my Trobriand friends put it," M. F. Ashley-Montagu, *Coming into Being among the Australian Aborigines* (London: Routledge, 1937) 3. Edmund Leach addressed the problem in "Virgin Birth," *Proceedings of the Royal Anthropological Institute* (1966): 39–49, and Melford E. Spiro responded in "Virgin Birth, Parthenogenesis and Physiological Paternity: An Essay in Cultural Interpretation," *Man* 3 (1968): 242–51. The articles generated a prolific correspondence. Most scholarly opinion now agrees with that of Malinowski's 1937 reappraisal.

alized that the father was necessary for reproduction, it is understandable that some Greeks developed theories explaining what a man provided that a woman could not furnish herself. She had a place to lodge the embryo and he did not (a womb); she had material to nourish it and he did not (menses). If she also provided seed, why did she not produce homunculi unaided? In fact, they did believe that some animals (for example, locusts and fish)[57] reproduced by parthenogenesis. Aristotle defines the male as that which generates in another and the female as that which generates within itself.[58] Far from negating maternity, Aristotle's system claims that if only one sex were to exist, it would have to be the female.[59] In contrast, the Egyptians (who also believed that the father was the only true parent of the child and the mother merely a receptacle for his seed) called those trees that produced fruit male; they were unaware of the process of pollination, and as they believed the father was the true parent, they assumed that a tree that produced fruit unaided must be male.[60] The same passage reveals that the Greeks followed the convention of calling fruit-bearing trees female. The denial that women and other female animals produced seed, therefore, was not motivated simply by a desire to downplay the importance of maternity. Aristotle's theory of unique roles for each of the sexes in reproduction was an attempt to answer a conundrum that the theory of female seed in animals did not fully address.[61]

Aristotle also denies that women produce seed for the very good reason that women said they could become pregnant without feeling any pleasure or emitting any fluid. Furthermore, many women who did experience pleasure and secrete moisture during intercourse did not conceive.[62] True, Aristotle accepted this female testimony because it supported his theories—he did not square his theory to fit a female report—but at least it meant

[57]*De generatione animalium (Generation of animals)* 741a 33–38.

[58]*Historia animalium (History of animals)* 489a 9–12; *GA* 716a 14–15.

[59]Of course, Aristotle has no doubt that the male is the superior sex but does not deny the facts of maternity as he knew them to support this view.

[60]Diodorus Siculus I 80.4.

[61]However, Aristotle could have claimed—and it would ultimately have been easier for him to do so—that men provided matter and women form.

[62]*GA* 727b 7–12.

that he would not assume that a woman who became pregnant after a rape had secretly enjoyed it.

Aristotle also used his own observations to argue that the vaginal lubricant could not be identified with seed. Unlike male seed, the liquid produced by a woman who felt pleasure during intercourse was emitted at a different place from that where the pleasure originated:

> An indication that the female emits no semen is actually afforded by the fact that in intercourse the pleasure is produced in the same place as in the male by contact, yet this is not the place from which the liquid is emitted.[63]

The liquid was emitted at the *os uteri*,[64] but what does Aristotle mean by the part of the female anatomy that is "the same place as in the male by contact"? Does it mean the place where the male penis comes into contact with the woman's body, i.e., the vagina? But this is too close to the *os uteri* to be so categorically differentiated from it, and it also makes "the same place" refer to a particular set of coordinates in space rather than, as the Greek suggests, a particular point on the female body that is analogous to a part of male anatomy and is pleasurably aroused when touched. The position on a woman's body corresponding most closely to the penis on a man's lies just below the pubes—the clitoris, which is indeed a place that can be aroused by touch but that does not emit moisture. As further indication that he was referring to the clitoris here, Aristotle insists at *GA* 739b 15 that it is the uterus itself rather than "the parts instrumental in copulation" (as some [*tines*] assert) that draws the semen into the womb. Now, the author of the pseudo-Aristotelian Book X of the *HA*[65] argues that the semen emitted at the *os uteri* was drawn into the womb *not* through the action

---

[63]GA 728a 31–34. Trans. A. L. Peck, *Aristotle XIII*, Loeb Classical Library (Cambridge, Mass.: Harvard University Press, 1942) 105.

[64]*GA* 739b 2. A further indication that the fluid is not semen as it would then have to be drawn into the womb. As Nature does nothing unnecessary, she would have arranged for the fluid to have been released directly into the womb if that were its ultimate destination.

[65]For a discussion of the authorship of *GA* X see Pierre Louis, *Aristotle: Histoire des animaux* (Paris: Société d'Édition "Les Belles Lettres," 1969) 147–55.

of the womb itself but through the action of a small passage the opening of which lay above the passage for urine and ran from there up to the front of the uterus.  When a woman is sexually aroused, this passage does not remain in the same state as normal but draws in air and effects the suction of semen into the womb.[66]  This seems to be a description, albeit misguided, of clitoral stimulation.  Thus if this author was one of the *tines* with whom Aristotle was disagreeing in *GA* 739b 15, he means to refer to the clitoris, not the vagina, by "the parts instrumental in copulation" and the part where a woman felt pleasure during intercourse.

Unlike the Hippocratics, then, Aristotle explicitly recognizes how and when women do take pleasure in sex.  However, because he does not think female pleasure is necessary for conception, Rousselle and others argue that he finds even less reason for husbands to be concerned with their wives' enjoyment.[67] This is disproved by the fact that he labels the clitoris an *organikon morion* ("instrumental part") as every such part in the body has to serve a purpose.[68]  He must therefore have thought that a woman's clitoris and orgasm perform some useful function.    Aristotle himself does not explain exactly what this function is, but the author of *HA* X, who equates the vaginal lubricant with female seed and thus has no need to elaborate any further use, says at 635b 26–28 that the vaginal lubricant acts as a saliva to make copulation easier.  The author of *HA* X was very much influenced by Aristotle[69] and may have tried to incorporate the latter's explanation of the vaginal lubricant while at the same time retaining his own belief in female seed.  Whatever Aristotle's theory, the author's teleological principles would lead him to assert that because a woman possessed a clitoris and could be stimulated during intercourse, it was to the advantage of both the male and female that she experience pleasure during intercourse.

Aristotle also thought that the desire for intercourse in both the male and the female could proceed from the need to emit fluid after remaining celibate:

---

[66]*HA* 637a 23–28.

[67]Rousselle (29) maintains that Aristotle "destroyed the traditional basis of reciprocal pleasure in heterosexual love-making."

[68]*De partibus animalium (Parts of animals)* 645a 15.

[69]See Louis 153.

In all the Vivipara those females which are barren are prone to sexual intercourse, because they are in a similar condition to males when their semen is ready, collected together, but is not being emitted, the evacuation of the menstrual fluid in females being the emission of semen, since, as has been stated earlier, the menstrual fluid is semen that is unconcocted. Hence, too, those women who are incontinent in the matter of sexual intercourse, cease from their passionate excitement when they have borne several children, because once the seminal residue has been expelled from the body it no longer produces the desire for this intercourse.[70]

He did not think that a woman's need for sex was caused by the womb's tendency to displacement within the body. He argued that as the testes and seminal ducts were known to be anchored in place in men, so must the womb be anchored in women.[71] Moreover, just as too much sex was injurious to a man's health, so were too much intercourse or too many pregnancies in the case of a woman.[72] The "using up" of a woman's seminal fluid depended on the menstrual blood which remained in her womb being constituted into a fetus by the male semen. Although a woman could still not be fully satisfied with another woman as a lover, nor with masturbation in Aristotle's model, at least she knows what she would be satisfied with.

Aristotle was aware that both sexes could be propelled beyond their need for sexual intercourse by the memory of past pleasures that caused desire for present gratification even when there was no build up of seminal material. To ensure that both sexes learned and practiced sexual temperance, Aristotle encouraged that they should be prevented from indulging in intercourse too young.[73]

---

[70]*GA* 773b 32–774a 6.

[71]*GA* 720a 11–12. At *HA* 582b 22–25 he makes the observation that a prolapsed womb has issued looking for sex, but this belief is not reflected in his general physiology and was probably discarded early in his career. It is significant that it reflects Plato's description in the *Timaeus* rather than any Hippocratic text, where a prolapsed womb is one of the conditions for which sexual abstinence is advised; see n. 39.

[72]*GA* 727a 22–25.

[73]*HA* 581b 11–21.

If the Greeks identified themselves and others as sexual beings in the success or failure of *sôphrosynê* and *enkrateia* in their sexual conduct, then in the Hippocratic model women had the chance neither to succeed nor fail in this arena and were denied the possibility of acting as moral agents. This supported rather than threatened the social order in classical Greece because it justified taking little account of a woman's preferences in the choice of a husband without conceding that many wives might be unsatisfied in their marriage. It also validated the separation of women from men without necessarily impugning their loyalty to their husbands' *oikoi*.

In Aristotle, the structure of male and female bodies is much more analogous than in the Hippocratics. As a result, his concept of male and female sexual appetite is also much more analogous. Nature has seen to it that both should be provoked to intercourse by strong pleasures but has also provided both with *sôphrosynê* and *enkrateia* to ensure that they use and do not abuse these pleasures. A woman is by nature a weaker moral agent than a man and a wife is therefore still subject to her husband's authority,[74] but as long as her husband is satisfying her needs for sexual pleasure, a woman can be expected to suppress inappropriate compulsions to intercourse.

Aristotle's model of female sexual functioning quickly became the dominant model in antiquity. Among the many reasons for this is that the form of social relationships between men and women began to change. The idea of romantic love as a basis for marriage began to take hold,[75] and it became acceptable, indeed necessary, that a wife feel and recognize erotic desires for her husband; thus her cognitive organs had to be unencumbered by her reproductive system. At the same time, in the Hellenistic and Roman periods women came into contact with men beyond the *oikos* much more frequently. Since their desire could be stimulated by someone other than a husband, or by a suitor who was not yet a husband, women had to have the capacity of subduing it themselves. Furthermore, once women were endowed in the functional model with the desire for intercourse and the ca-

---

[74]*Pol.* I 12–13 .

[75]For women's increasing participation in choosing their husbands see Pomeroy 129. For the growing association of romantic love with marriage see Robert Flacelière, *Love in Ancient Greece*, trans. James Cleugh (London: F. Muller, 1962) 187–213.

pacity to control this desire, as with men pathological sanctions were introduced to encourage women to exercise their *enkrateia* for their own good.  Later medical writers, therefore, take their cue from Aristotle and, in contrast to the Hippocratics, threaten women with the consequences of too much as well as too little intercourse.[76]

These functional constructs did not describe the actual sexual experiences of individuals within classical Greek society.  Their claim to scientific objectivity validated those sexual experiences of men and women that best supported the social organization of the period.  In the functional model of female sexual experience the amount of pleasure a woman was allowed to take in intercourse proceeded neither from cultural traditions nor from biological research but from political expediency.

Although this analysis of female sexual response in the Hippocratic Corpus contradicts Foucault's too-ready assimilation of male and female sexuality in classical Greece, it does, in fact, illustrate his more general thesis that human sexuality is a cultural variable, the construct and content of which are determined by what the loci of power and knowledge in a society consider desirable.  Had Foucault recognized that women are not simply modified men in their relations to these loci, he could have illustrated his theory synchronically within societies as well as diachronically through time.  As it is, Foucault's *The History of Sexuality* would be more aptly titled *A History of Male Sexuality*.

---

[76]For example, Soranus, *Gyn.* I 32; Aretaeus, *De causis et signis diutinorum morborum (On the causes and symptoms of chronic diseaseas)* II 5.

# FOUCAULT'S SUBJECT IN THE HISTORY OF SEXUALITY

## Lynn Hunt

*The History of Sexuality, Volume 1,* changed Foucault's status among historians. But not all at once. As late as 1987, Allan Megill was able to argue that Foucault could not be assimilated by historians: he was too solitary, too anti-disciplinary, too unwilling to adhere to the usual standards of historical scholarship to be accepted within the ranks. Like the books on prisons and madness, *The History of Sexuality* attracted social historians because of its subject matter, but it did not force a reconsideration of Foucault's work as a whole. According to Megill, social historians simply took from Foucault's work whatever suited their own purposes. Foucault was nevertheless important to history as a discipline because, in Megill's words, he "called attention to hitherto neglected fields of research" and because he fostered "a self-reflection that is needed to counteract the sclerosis, the self-satisfaction, the smugness that constantly threaten."[1]

Historians of sexuality have never been all that smug, since until very recently they have labored in their own private vineyards far from the centers of mainstream professional power. Foucault's introductory volume appeared at a time in the mid-1970s when the history of sexuality was just taking shape as a subject of research (French edition, 1976; English translation, 1978). In 1972, for example, Vern Bullough had proclaimed that "sex in history" was a "virgin field."[2] By the 1980s, however, a whole series of books began to appear that showed the imprint of Foucault's criticism of the so-called repressive hypothesis—that the truth of sex had been repressed by the powers that be and is only now being freed. They also shared his basic view that subjectivity, gender, and sexuality are fundamentally

---

[1]Allan Megill, "The Reception of Foucault by Historians," *Journal of the History of Ideas* 48 (1987): 117–41.

[2]Vern Bullough, "Sex in History: A Virgin Field," *The Journal of Sex Research* 8 (1972): 101–16.

shaped by discourse and representation.[3]   As Gayle Rubin concluded, *"The History of Sexuality* has been the most influential and emblematic text of the new scholarship on sex."[4]

The impact of Foucault's work is still resisted by mainstream historians, but it has increasingly moved to the center of the preoccupations of historians of sexuality and of feminist historians.[5]   Historians of sexuality have been more receptive to Foucault's work than historians of prisons or mental asylums before them.   There are at least two reasons for this receptivity: Foucault's work appeared before the field was well-established, and Foucault tied the history of sexuality to a larger philosophical project of reconsidering the meaning of the self in history. Thus, Foucault gave the history of sexuality a kind of philosophical legitimacy that it had previously lacked.   What Foucault himself described as his work on technologies of production, technologies of sign systems, and technologies of power had less resonance among historians, especially among those historians outside social history proper, than his last work on technologies of the self. [6]

Foucault's relatively warm reception among feminist historians is in fact more surprising, for when he actually comes to analyzing technologies of the self, the "individuals" he has in

---

[3]For a brief review, see Carol A. Pollis, "The Apparatus of Sexuality: Reflections on Foucault's Contributions to the Study of Sex in History," *The Journal of Sex Research* 23 (1987): 401–14.

[4]Gayle Rubin, "Thinking Sex: Notes for a Radical Theory of the Politics of Sexuality," *Pleasure and Danger: Exploring Female Sexuality*, ed. Carole S. Vance (Boston: Routledge, 1984) 267–319, quote 276.   For a recent critique by an   historian of Foucault's work on sexuality, see Roy Porter, "Is Foucault Useful for Understanding Eighteenth and Nineteenth Century Sexuality," *Contention* 1 (1991): 61–81.

[5]Some might question the very notion of a history of sexuality because it assumes that sexuality has a fixed meaning over time. Foucault himself pioneered the dismantling of all fixed categories—madness, medicine, and sexuality too—so it is worth remembering that sexuality can have no transcendental meaning outside of its historical development. For a Foucault-style critique of the concept of sexuality itself, see Arnold I. Davidson, "Sex and the Emergence of Sexuality," *Critical Inquiry* 14 (1987): 16–48.

[6]For a discussion of these various technologies, see David Latane, "At Play in the Field of Foucault: A Review of Some Recent Texts," *Critical Texts* 6 (1989): 39–58, esp. 50.

mind are always male. He defined technologies of the self as technologies "which permit individuals to effect by their own means or with the help of others a certain number of operations on their own bodies and souls, thoughts, conduct, and way of being, so as to transform themselves in order to attain a certain state of happiness, purity, wisdom, perfection, or immortality."[7] There are many problems with this formulation, not least the unreflective use of the term "individuals," but for the moment I will limit myself to the gender problems with the definition of technologies of the self.

In the introduction to volume 2 of *The History of Sexuality*, Foucault described how he came to this work:

> After first studying the games of truth (*jeux de verité*) in their interplay with one another, as exemplified by certain empirical sciences in the seventeenth and eighteenth centuries, and then studying their interaction with power relations, as exemplified by punitive practices—I felt obliged to study the games of truth in the relationship of self with self and the forming of oneself as a subject, taking as my domain of reference and field of investigation what might be called "the history of desiring man."[8]

The history of desiring man in volumes 2 and 3 of *The History of Sexuality* is told from the male viewpoint. This is a story about "an ethics for men: an ethics thought, written, and taught by men, and addressed to men. . . . A male ethics, consequently, in which women figured only as objects" (*The Use of Pleasure* 22).

Even when Foucault analyzes the new ethic of reciprocity in marriage (in volume 3, *The Care of the Self*), with its intensified valorization of "the other" and its aesthetics of shared pleasure (149), he does so from the male point of view. He concludes the section on the wife, for instance, with the remark that "The conjugalization of sexual activities that tends to localize legiti-

---

[7]Quote from Foucault's lecture, "Technologies of the Self," Latane 50.

[8]*The Use of Pleasure, The History of Sexuality, Volume 2*, trans. Robert Hurley (New York: Pantheon, 1985) 6. All subsequent references to specific volumes in *The History of Sexuality* will be given by volume and page number in the text. They include *The History of Sexuality, Volume 1, An Introduction*, trans. Robert Hurley (New York: Pantheon, 1980) and *The History of Sexuality, Volume 3*, trans. Robert Hurley (New York: Pantheon, 1988).

macy within marriage alone obviously results in their manifest limitation (at least for the husband, since this limitation has long been required of the married woman)" (185). What changes in the history of sexuality, then, is what changes for men. This self that "forms oneself as a subject" is a male subject intent on self-mastery. It is also an adult self. As Gad Horowitz has remarked, "Foucault's male antiessentialism represses knowledge of the child." Although Horowitz's own alternative theory based on a notion of transhistorical infancy is subject to its own criticisms, his analysis nevertheless draws attention to Foucault's presupposition of an adult subject in his definition of the self.[9]

Despite his emphasis on adult males, feminist historians find a certain comfort in Foucault, and it is not hard to see why this would be so.[10] If subjectivity, gender, and sexuality are shaped by discourse and representation (that is, by man-made convention) rather than by nature, then they are susceptible to change. Even though Foucault himself ignored most of the feminist and gender implications of his work, his focus on the body as the site for the deployment of discourses (whether discourses of madness, medicine, punishment, or sexuality) opened the way for a consideration of the gendering of subjectivity, if only because bodies in the West have long been associated with the low, the other, the repressed, the earthy, the disgusting, the sexual, and the female.[11] Foucault claimed that he was not interested in

[9]For some suggestive but incomplete remarks on this problem, see Gad Horowitz, "The Foucaultian Impasse: No Sex, No Self, No Revolution," *Political Theory* 15 (1987): 61–80, quote 71.

[10]I am purposely discussing Foucault's influence on feminist historians here, rather than feminists in general, since my interest focuses on Foucault as historian of sexuality. For a broader view, see, among others, Edith Kurzweil, "Michel Foucault's History of Sexuality as Interpreted by Feminists and Marxists," *Social Research* 53 (1986): 647–63, and Frances Bartkowski, "Speculations on the Flesh: Foucault and the French Feminists," *Power, Gender, Values*, ed. Judith Genova (Edmonton, Alberta, Canada: Academic Printing and Publishing, 1986) 69–79.

[11]See, for example, the essays in Lynn Hunt, ed., *Eroticism and the Body Politic* (Baltimore: Johns Hopkins, 1991); Klaus Theweleit, *Male Fantasies*, trans. Stephen Conway, Erica Carter, and Chris Turner, 2 vols. (Minneapolis: University of Minnesota Press, 1987–89); and Michel Feher, ed., *Fragments for a History of the Human Body*, 3 vols. (New York: Zone, 1989).

writing a history of mentalities that would discuss only how bodies were perceived; rather he wanted to write a "history of bodies" that got at how "what is most material and most vital in them has been invested" (1:152). Included in what is most material and most vital is the gendering of bodies, that is, how gender is itself produced in bodies.

By focusing on bodies, Foucault offered perspectives that help disengage us from a dreary, repetitive, totalizing history of patriarchy and misogyny. Sexuality for Foucault is "an especially dense transfer point for relations of power" (1:103), but these relations of power are not permanent or transcendent. Sexuality has a history, and it is very broadly defined. Included among the relations of power in sexuality are those between men and women, young and old, parents and children, teachers and students, priests and laity, government and the population. In Foucault's view, "There is no single, all-encompassing strategy, valid for all of society" (1:103), much less for all of Western history.

Foucault's sketch in volume 1 of the "four great strategic unities" taking shape from the eighteenth century onward seems to promise a consideration of gender along with the history of the deployment of sexuality: these strategic unities were 1) a hysterization of women's bodies, 2) a pedagogization of children's sex, 3) a socialization of procreative behavior (population control), and 4) a psychiatrization of perverse pleasure. Central to all of them was the family, "the crystal in the deployment of sexuality" (1:111), a prime agency of sexualization, and, we might add, the chief site for the establishment of gender differentiations.

It could be said that Foucault promises to displace the history of patriarchy with the history of sexuality. He sought to develop a nonpatriarchal theorization of power, though he did not use those words precisely. He complained, for example, that "the representation of power has remained under the spell of monarchy," and that "in political thought and analysis, we still have not cut off the head of the king" (1:88–89). I take this to mean that power has too often been conceived of as sovereign (centered on a particular point), juridical, prohibitive, and uniform, that is, easily located because defined by the law and essentially negative (it prohibits, it censors). In other words, and these are mine not Foucault's, power was modeled on the authority of the stern father. Instead of locating power in institutions, in the law, or in systems by which one group dominates over another, Foucault proposes to look at power as "multiplicity," "process," "chain," "disjunctions," "moving substrate," and "strategies" (1:92–93). In this view, there is no one location of power: "Power is everywhere; not because it embraces everything, but because it comes from everywhere" (1:93).

Foucault's view of power and of possible resistances to it have been much commented upon, and it is not necessary to take up those familiar arguments again here.[12] Two salient characteristics of his view should be emphasized in this context, however: 1) for Foucault, power and sexuality are closely entwined with each other, since power produces sexuality and gives it meaning, and yet 2) his view of power itself is surprisingly genderless. Replacing the law of the father, localized and clearly identified, is an amorphous or polymorphous, essentially neutered vision. Power seems most like a virus:

> my main concern will be to locate the forms of power, the channels it takes, and the discourses it permeates in order to reach the most tenuous and individual modes of behavior, the paths' that give it access to the rare or scarcely perceivable forms of desire, how it penetrates and controls everyday pleasure . . . in short, the "polymorphous techniques of power." (1:11)

This view of power might seem paradoxical given Foucault's emphasis on the male subject in his actual historical account of the development of sexuality. Indeed, it is paradoxical, and I will argue that it constitutes the central tension—if not contradiction—in Foucault's consideration of the self. The metaphors for the functional operation of power in volume 1 of *The History of Sexuality* are all genderless, while the individual presupposed in "the history of desiring man" in volumes 2 and 3 is gendered male.

I use the term *view of power* rather than *theory of power* because Foucault does not have a theory of power; he proposes a

---

[12]See, for example, the essays by David Couzens Hoy and Michael Walzer in *Foucault: A Critical Reader*, ed. David Couzens Hoy (London: Blackwell, 1986) 1–25 and 51–68. Hoy discusses, among other issues, the Habermas-Foucault debate.

view structured by a set of interlocking metaphors—"process," "chain," "moving substrate"—rather than a story of origins in the manner of contract theory, for example, or a causal analysis based on assumptions about human nature, as in Aristotle or even modern rational choice theory. The genderlessness of his view of power results, at least in part, from Foucault's insistence on the necessity of going beyond psychoanalytic theory. In volume 1 of *The History of Sexuality*, psychoanalysis is presented as a medical practice—hence part of the medicalization of sexuality in the nineteenth century—and as a theoretical discourse (1:5). As a theoretical discourse, however, it is limited by its emphasis on the "interrelatedness of the law and desire" (1:129), that is, by its attachment to the old "monarchical" model of power. The success—and for Foucault, the failure—of psychoanalysis was made possible by the fact that it "always unfolded within the deployment of sexuality, and not outside or against it" (1:131). It cannot therefore serve as a means for getting purchase on the operation of the system. Unfortunately, Foucault throws out the gendering of power, which is central to psychoanalytic theory, along with the psychoanalytical framework for analyzing the workings of the law of the father.[13]

This degendering of power has important consequences for Foucault's sense of "the individual." Although he promises a kind of history of the deployment of sexuality and along with it a history of the deployment of the self and subjectivity, his use of the term *individual* is often surprisingly ahistorical. The genderless functional operation of power is juxtaposed, uncomfortably and even inexplicably, with a profoundly gendered concept of the individual as adult male subject. The practices and techniques in the deployment of the self presumably vary over time, but subjectivity itself does not, at least not in volumes 2 and 3 of *The History of Sexuality*.

Foucault defined technologies of the self as technologies "which permit individuals to effect by their own means or with the help of others a certain number of operations on their own bodies and souls, thoughts, conduct, and way of being, so as to transform themselves." This is a distinctly modern or post-eighteenth century formulation, in which individuals are figured as separate beings with separate selves who are able to act upon

---

[13]On Freud's psychoanalytic theory of power, see Carole Pateman, *The Sexual Contract* (Stanford: Stanford University Press, 1988) 1–115.

themselves and even transform themselves. Indeed, such self-transformation is inconceivable without a notion of self-possession, of a self that owns itself and its own body. Thus, though the forms of self-transformation vary over time in Foucault's analysis, the grounds of its psychic possibility do not. Foucault extends this notion of the self-possessing, self-transforming individual right back to the Greeks, but he never devotes much attention to the exclusions implied in this notion of subjectivity. Upper-class adult men are the only ones who possess selves, but no history is offered of how this came to be.[14]

Foucault certainly intended to provide a history of subjectivity. Although he does not discuss the self or the subject very explicitly in volume 1 of *The History of Sexuality*, in the introduction to volume 2 he outlines the three axes that constitute sexuality: 1) the formation of sciences (*savoirs*) that refer to it, 2) the systems of power that regulate its practice, and 3) the forms within which individuals are able, are obliged, to recognize themselves as subjects of this sexuality (2:4). Foucault goes on to recognize that the third of these was much harder for him to investigate. He had the tools for the analysis of the first two—the formation of sciences and the systems of power—from his previous work, but "the problems were much greater" when it came to studying "the modes according to which individuals are given to recognize themselves as sexual subjects" (2:5). What follows in volumes 2 and 3 is in this respect disappointing precisely because Foucault's methods of approach were much better suited to the analysis of sciences and systems of power than they were to the analysis of the development of forms of subjectivity.

It is significant that Foucault's history of sexuality—like his previous histories of the clinic and the prison—turned on a period of time—the last half of the eighteenth century—that was at once the pivot of his analysis and the great hole in it. The "four great strategic unities" of volume 1—hysterization of women's bodies, pedagogization of children's sex, socialization of procreative behavior, and psychiatrization of perverse pleasure—all began to take shape, according to Foucault, in the eighteenth century. As he puts it, in a telling moment, "It was during the same period—the end of the eighteenth century—*and for reasons*

---

[14]See, for example, the history of how the male body came to be isolated from and set off against the female body in Theweleit, vol. 1.

*that will have to be determined,* that there emerged a completely
new technology of sex" (1:116; my emphasis).

Foucault identifies many of the elements in the transformation of the "technology of sex" (the term he uses in volume 1
rather than technologies of the self) in the eighteenth century.
The technology of sex expanded along three axes—pedagogy,
medicine, and demography—that made sex a secular and state
concern requiring the social body as a whole and "virtually all of
its individuals, to place themselves under surveillance" (1:116).
He then goes on to recognize that each of these three "privileged
areas" or axes had origins in the history of Christianity, yet he
nevertheless insists that a critical mutation took place at the
turn of the nineteenth century: "from that time on, the technology of sex was ordered in relation to the medical institution . . .
and . . . the problem of life and illness" (1:117). But Foucault
never offers an explanation for the reordering of the new technologies of sex at that time. He eschews such explanation in
part because he steadfastly resisted any request to offer a causal
analysis of an historical phenomenon. He remained focused on
how things changed, not why, though it is possible to question
how clearly these two—the how and the why—can be separated.

It is not possible in the space of one essay to offer either a
causal explanation for the emergence of the new technologies of
sex—were that desirable—or a complete narrative of the gendering of subjectivity, even in the presumably crucial eighteenth
century. As part of a preliminary effort to lay the groundwork
for such a history, I want to suggest that the terms of Foucault's
argument might be reversed. It is not the deployment of sexuality that solicits a new subject but rather a new version of subjectivity that solicits the deployment of sexuality. Foucault essentially equates technologies of sex (as he calls them in volume 1)
and technologies of the self; the deployment of new technologies
of sex, according to Foucault, produces a new kind of individual,
one defined by his capacity for self-surveillance ("sex became a
matter that required . . . individuals to place themselves under
surveillance" (1:116) and by his sexual identity. "It is through
sex . . . that each individual has to pass in order to have access
to his own intelligibility" (1:155). Although Foucault recognizes
the imaginary, constructed, and artificial meaning of this
definition of identity based on the truth of sex, he remains
trapped within it, in part because he only partially historicizes
subjectivity. He is in some sense a noteworthy victim of the

deployment of sexuality because he exaggerates its all-pervasiveness and cannot imagine a self other than the one newly deployed in the eighteenth century.

The best way to get at these issues in a preliminary way is through a brief examination of eighteenth-century pornography, especially the pornography of Sade, which was in many ways emblematic for Foucault.  Georges Van Den Abbeele has argued, for instance, that Sade is "as lucid and as important" for Foucault as Rousseau is for Derrida or de Man.  Sade represents both the birth and the death of literature to Foucault, yet as Van Den Abbeele concludes, "the woman's body graphically revealed in Sade becomes unmarked and occulted in Foucault's persistent refusal to consider the pertinence of sexual difference to the historical deployment and implementation of discursive practices."[15] Sade has a peculiar place in Foucault's writing; he serves as a kind of patron saint and precursor but only after his writing has been purged of its obsession with the dynamics of gender difference and gender obliteration.

Along with medicine, psychiatry, and prostitution, pornography is cited by Foucault as one of the major means by which pleasure and power overlap and reinforce each other in the modern deployment of sex (1:48).  Yet Foucault says surprisingly little about pornography in *The History of Sexuality*; the word does not even appear in the indexes to the three volumes of the English edition.  Once again, the eighteenth century might be imagined as crucial to the story since pornography began to take shape as a distinctive modern practice in the eighteenth century. Only a few isolated works of pornography were published before the first great explosion of publication in the 1740s in France and England, and by the 1790s, most of the modern themes of pornography had been summarized and catalogued in the works of Sade.[16]  In the eighteenth century, moreover, pornography was published explicitly as what Foucault has called a *scientia sexualis*; it was a procedure for telling the truth of sex that had been supposedly repressed by church and state until then.  Just

---

[15]"Sade, Foucault, and the Scene of Enlightenment Lucidity," *Stanford French Review* 11 (1987): 7–16, esp. 15.

[16]There is surprisingly little written on the early history of Western pornography. I base my remarks on the papers given at a conference on "The Invention of Pornography" at the University of Pennsylvania, October 4–5, 1991.

as Foucault would have predicted, the more attention church and state paid to repressing pornography, the more it was in fact written, published, and read.

In *The History of Sexuality*, Foucault assimilates pornography, especially Sade, to the confessional; "one could plot a line going straight from the seventeenth-century pastoral to what became its projection in literature, 'scandalous' literature at that." He imagines Sade taking up the injunction to discourse in the treatises of spiritual direction: "Not only will you confess to acts contravening the law, but you will seek to transform your desire, your every desire, into discourse" (1:21). Sade took up with a vengeance this injunction or incitement to discourse, as his many and often long novels show. Up to this point, Foucault's analysis simply repeats the main lines of Barthes' comparison of Sade and Loyola. Barthes had already noticed "the same writing: the same sensual pleasure in classification, the same mania for cutting up . . . the same enumerative obsession."[17]

Foucault goes beyond Barthes, however, when he criticizes Sade for never freeing himself from "the mechanisms of the old power of sovereignty" or the "prestige of blood" (1:148). Although Sade carried out an "exhaustive analysis of sex," he still linked this to old notions of sovereignty:

> In Sade, sex is without any norm or intrinsic rule that might be formulated from its own nature; but it is subject to the unrestricted law of a power which itself knows no other law but its own; if by chance it is at times forced to accept the order of progressions carefully disciplined into successive days, this exercise carries it to a point where it is no longer anything but a unique and naked sovereignty: an unlimited right of all-powerful monstrosity. (1:149)

This analysis of Sade is remarkably acute, but it makes Sade into a precursor of Foucault in a way that Foucault himself fails to recognize.

To make this clear, it is essential to look at each one of the claims in this passage in turn. 1) For Sade, sex is without any norm that might be formulated from its own nature; Foucault

[17]Roland Barthes, *Sade, Fourier, Loyola*, trans. Richard Miller (New York: Hill and Wang, 1976; French edition 1971) 3.

himself argues that there is no hidden essential truth in sex. Sade's position in this respect represented the culmination of the eighteenth century pornographic tradition, which was largely dedicated to uncovering the conventional and arbitrary nature of sexual relations in European society.  2) In Sade, according to Foucault, sex is subject to the unrestricted law of a power which itself knows no other law than its own; is this not the Foucaultian power that is "omnipresent," "the moving substrate of force relations which, by virtue of their inequality, constantly engender states of power" (1:93)?  3) If by chance power in Sade is at times forced to accept the order of progressions carefully disciplined into successive days, this exercise carries power to a point where it is no longer anything but a unique and naked sovereignty; does this not remind us of that disciplinary power described by Foucault that slips so easily between the prison, the factory, the school, and the family with its constant demand for self-surveillance?  Consequently, if Foucault denounces this vision of power as "an unlimited right of all-powerful monstrosity," is he not in effect criticizing his own notion of power?  Although Foucault explicitly rejected the old model of power based on the "Sovereign-Father" and criticized both Freud and Sade for remaining subject to this "historical 'retro-version'" (1:150), his own, supposedly ungendered, version only increases "the unlimited rights of all-powerful monstrosity."

Foucault's aim to transcend historical retroversions founders on his own inability to offer an alternative account of the historical gendering of subjectivity.  Foucault neglects altogether this critical dimension of Sade's work and of all eighteenth-century pornography.  A brief consideration of Sade's novel *Philosophy in the Bedroom* will suggest some possible lines for such an alternative account.  *Philosophy in the Bedroom* was published in 1795 just after the end of the Terror in the French Revolution.  It offers a *reductio ad absurdum* of Enlightenment rationality and also of eighteenth-century notions of the individual.  The characters live in an "age of preoccupation with the rights of man and general concern for liberties."[18]  In the novel, Sade tells the story of the corruption of a fifteen-year-old girl, Eugénie Mistival, by

---

[18]English translations from *The Marquis de Sade: The Complete Justine, Philosophy in the Bedroom and Other Writings*, trans. Richard Seaver and Austryn Wainhouse (New York: Grove, 1965) 218. Further page references to this translation will appear in parentheses in the text.

three libertines, Madame de Saint-Ange, Madame's brother, and Dolmancé. It is true, as Foucault remarks, that Sade tries to retain some kind of sovereign model of power, largely through his portrayal of Dolmancé, who is the director of the sexual tableaux and the ultimate authority in the *boudoir*. In that sense, Sade tries to maintain a located, even centralized sense of power. Yet at the same time, the sexual action in the novel itself threatens to undo this fixity.

The novel explores the world that will follow from unfettered individualism. It begins from the premise that "all men are born free, all have equal rights" (318) and proceeds to instantiate a world in which all social ties are progressively dissolved by the force of individual desire. As Eugénie has learned, "Nature caused man to be born alone, all independent of other men" (284). In a reversal of Rousseau, who began from the same premise, Sade does not argue for the moralizing of the individual through the social. Sade's logical unraveling of the social world shows the problems posed by the new world of separate individuals, by the egotism of desiring "man," by the self-possession of the self-transforming man. In this world, the individual can become anything; Eugénie, the example of what can be learned about the self, is transformed into a libertine in the space of a few hours. She learns that incest should be the basis of republican government, that rape is less problematic than theft, and that theft is only a form of property redistribution. She learns too that "we owe nothing to our parents . . . because the rights of birth establish nothing" (284), and she cooperates in the plan to kill her own mother. In this world, love is at base only desire, and desire is at base egoistic. The social is threatened with constant dissolution, and the only certain systems of power are those carefully controlled by one or a few men within a small, claustrophobic space. As Barthes remarked, the Sadian space is a highly formal "solitary," which forms the basis of a social autarchy, the only form of social life that is possible for the Sadian imagination.[19]

This is not the place to review the enormous literature about Sade or to go into a detailed analysis of even this one novel.[20]

---

[19]*Sade, Fourier, Loyola*, 16–17.

[20]I discuss the novel in terms of family issues raised by the French Revolution in Lynn Hunt, *The Family Romance of the French Revolution* (Berkeley: University of California Press, 1992).

My main point is that such a novel, with its profound analysis of the relationship between the individual and the social, could only be written after the Enlightenment of the eighteenth century had put forward several new, interrelated propositions about the individual and the social world. Eighteenth-century materialism posited an individual encapsulated in a self-contained body and inhabiting a social world of like bodies in motion. Desire rooted in the body was imagined as the motor of social development, and from this model followed a concept of power as the management of such bodies in motion. Materialism was in some sense inherently democratic too, since it emphasized the likeness of individual bodies; it individualized and socialized desire at the same time (desire was located in the individual but generalized by the very mass of individuals). It also opened the way to a radically new vision of social change, in which individuals acting together (or governments) could self-consciously transform the social world. Sade's novel can be read as an exploration of the meaning of materialism for social and political as well as individual affective life.

The materialist view of the individual was responsible for that central characteristic of the new technology of sex, which Foucault defined as the demand that the social body as a whole and "virtually all of its individuals" place themselves under surveillance. Surveillance was necessary because the new desiring individual, imagined as fundamentally egotistical, threatened constantly to undermine the requirements of the social. Sade captured this same need for surveillance in his endless obsession with establishing rules. The famous pamphlet inserted in the novel—"Frenchmen, Yet Another Effort If You Would Be Republicans"—advocates the establishment of large, hygienic temples of Venus in every town, where "the most absolute subordination will be the rule of the individuals participating" (316–17).

It is no accident that the novel, including the pornographic novel, took decisive new forms in the eighteenth century; both are about the desiring subject and the new fragility of the social world inhabited by such individuals.[21] It is no accident, as Robert Darnton has shown, that pornography was classified with

---

[21]Jean Marie Goulemot, *Ces Livres qu'on ne lit que d'une main: Lecture et lecteurs de livres pornoqraphiques au XVIIIe siècle* (Aix-en-Provence: Alinea, 1991).

"philosophical books" (i.e., materialist tracts) by both the police and booksellers in eighteenth-century France.[22]  It is no accident that Sade published *Philosophy in the Bedroom* right after the Terror had shown the problems of reconstructing the social world on the basis of this new materialist vision.  In all of these do-mains — the novel, pornography, philosophy, and politics — people were working through their hopes and anxieties about the shape of the social world once deference, birthright, and monarchy were gone; was desiring "man" an adequate basis for social rela-tionships?  Perhaps not without constant surveillance and self-discipline.

Sade has one last lesson to offer about the consequences of eighteenth-century materialism for the desiring subject.  His work is obsessed not only with rules but also with gender, in par-ticular with the threat that gender boundaries will disappear in the similarities of desire.  Dolmancé defends sodomy with the claim that "it is so sweet to change sex, so delicious to counter-feit the whore, to give oneself to a man paramour, to avow one-self his mistress!" (247).  It is also possible, he argues, for women to transform themselves into men, though he is charac-teristically brief on this subject.  If all individuals are equally de-siring subjects, then what will found the difference between men and women?  Will these not just be two positions among many that the self-transforming individual can take up or lay down?  As if to answer this question, Dolmancé insists finally on female inferiority and uses for the first time a distinctly political image: a man in the moment of sexual pleasure feels a desire for despo-tism, Dolmancé claims; "'tis then he dominates, is a *tyrant*" (345).  This can be dismissed in Foucault's terms as Sade's un-willingness to discard a monarchical model of power, but it is noteworthy that this power has now retreated from the social and political world onto the grounds of sex and nature.  Sade recognized that gender differentiation in his new world was in fact very difficult to reinscribe, and power was very difficult to locate.

The questions raised by Sade's novel in 1795 are with us still, so it would be ungenerous in the extreme to fault Foucault for failing to answer all of them.  Yet for all his fascination with Sade as both beginning and end of modern life, perhaps Foucault

---

[22]Robert Darnton, *Edition et sédition: L'Univers de la littérature clandes-tine au XVIIIe siècle* (Paris: Gallimard, 1991).

did not exploit Sade to the fullest. What is so compelling still about Sade's vision is his interweaving of notions of the self, sexual desire rooted in the body, gender differentiation, and the polity. Foucault systematically underrated the importance of gender differentiation in these interrelationships and so missed the chance to develop a history of the gendering of subjectivity (using gendering here to refer not only to male and female but also to alternative subject positions within male and female, such as Sade's own fascination with the passive sodomite). Without that history, there can be no real history of the self, no history of the forms within which individuals are able, are obliged, to recognize themselves.

# SEXUALITY ON/OF THE RACIAL BORDER: FOUCAULT, WRIGHT, AND THE ARTICULATION OF "RACIALIZED SEXUALITY"

## Abdul R. JanMohamed

Foucault's *History of Sexuality* has liberated us from a reliance on "repression" as the monological explanation of the political economy of "sex," power relations, cultural and ideological structures and dynamics, and the forms that individual and collective subjectivity have taken. In doing so, Foucault offers new methods and approaches that are powerfully enabling and new fields that need to be investigated. One such field, which lies at the edge of Foucault's description of sexuality but which he does not examine in any detail, can be defined at the point where the deployment of sexuality intersects with the deployment of race, a field that I would call "Racialized Sexuality."[1]   But precisely when one begins to apply Foucault's positive "analytics" of sexuality to this field, one discerns some of the theoretical limitations of his method.  At the most general level, these limitations stem from his definition of "power."  At the more specific level of his history of sexuality, these limitations are products of a Eurocentric focus.   Yet in spite of these limitations, the fecundity of Foucault's theory suggests precisely the manner in which the field of "racialized sexuality" can be mapped.

Given the problems and the suggestiveness of Foucault's work on sexuality, this essay attempts to read against the grain of his work in order to go beyond its horizons.  In doing so, I will take up only those aspects of the problematics of power that af-

I would like to thank Domna Stanton for inviting me to present an earlier draft of this paper at the Institute for the Humanities at the University of Michigan and for her cogent criticisms of that draft. The paper has benefited a great deal from both. I would also like to thank Norma Alarcon, Judith Butler, Kimberle Crenshaw, Smadar Lavie, and Michael Sprinker, whose comments and suggestions have been very helpful.

[1]While I do not put "race" in quotation marks in order to indicate its problematic nature, I use it throughout this essay to stand for a complex social construction by a racist society. Even though this term does not represent any sort of essence, the cultural and ideological experience and value it designates are historically very real.

fect the mapping of racialized sexuality. I will argue that Foucault's insights into sexuality cannot be applied *tout court* to this field because he failed—his few remarks about Nazism notwithstanding—to examine the intersection of the discourses of sexuality and race. However, this essay is not designed to offer an alternate "history of racialized sexuality," a field that remains to be defined and described; the brief remarks toward the end of the essay on Richard Wright's *Native Son* are included only to indicate the *kinds* of complications that need to be considered in defining racialized sexuality.[2] This essay, then, is a polemical reading of Foucault's notion of the history of sexuality; it offers only hypothetical "conclusions." Its main function is to clear a theoretical space within which the economy and function of racialized sexuality can be articulated more systematically.

Although Foucault's method for analyzing sexuality is enabling, his definitions of power and descriptions of its mode of operation are of limited use for mapping the field of racialized sexuality. Power, according to Foucault, is a polyvalent, polymorphous, and ubiquitous cultural force that permeates all social space and mediates, in one form or another, all human interaction; indeed, power is immanent to all forms of human exchange. This concept of power thus functions as the general equivalent of exchange. As Foucault puts it, "power must be understood in the first instance as the multiplicity of force relations immanent in the sphere in which they operate and which constitutes their own organization"; moreover, "the moving substrate of force relations, . . . by virtue of their inequality, constantly engender states of power."[3] To the extent that unequal force relations produce it, power thus functions like a form of equivalence through which modes of unequal exchange in force relations are

---

[2]Indeed, a considerable body of work on the literary, as well as the critical, register has already been done in this area by women of color. In the black literary tradition, the articulation of racialized sexuality by men such as Wright must be modified by interventions of writers such as Alice Walker, Toni Morrison, and Gail Jones. The present essay does not engage this work because it is concerned with scrutinizing Foucault's ultimately ethnocentric description of sexuality.

[3]Michel Foucault, *The History of Sexuality, Volume 1: An Introduction* (New York: Pantheon, 1978) 92 and 93. All further references to this volume will be incorporated in the text of the essay.

negotiated and can be analyzed. As a result, Foucault's theory is most useful for describing how power *circulates* but less so for defining how it can be syphoned off, like surplus value, and how it comes to be *accumulated in institutional forms*, like capital. To be sure, Foucault does admit that the "institutional crystallization [of power] is embodied in the state apparatus, in the formulation of the law, [and] in various social hegemonies," but, in rightly cautioning that these structures must not be assumed "as given at the outset," he adds that these institutions "are *only* the *terminal* forms power takes" (1:93, 92; my emphasis). By characterizing the institutional crystallizations of power as "terminal" forms, Foucault refuses to trace the significant modifications to which power is subject in the process of crystallization and the effect of "accumulated" power when it reenters the circuits of exchange. Foucault's termination of the circuits of power at their supposedly "terminal" end leads, it seems to me, to an inadequate appreciation of the "prohibitive" or "negative" nature of accumulated, institutionalized power, which, I will argue, is precisely the form of power crucial to the mapping of racialized sexuality.

Foucault's bracketing of power at the macro, institutional end is balanced by a similar bracketing at the micro end of the circuit. The difficulty at this end is caused by an inadequate articulation of the intersection of temporality and subjective agency through which all power has to pass. "Power," he claims, "is not something that is acquired, seized, or shared, something that one holds on to or allows to slip away; power is exercised from innumerable points, in the interplay of nonegalitarian and mobile relations" (1:94). This definition is consonant with his radical emphasis on the discursive determination of subjectivity. Yet one needs to probe further the tension between the different temporalities inherent in "exercise" and "mobility." Are the relations of power so mobile that they cannot be "arrested," even momentarily, so that the subject can "exercise" some form of decision-making relevant to the force relations at hand? How can one "exercise" power that is not "acquired, seized, or shared" in some way *at the moment* that one is in fact "exercising" it? A subject who "exercises" power controls it, even if momentarily and even if s/he is only "exercising" the options among various discursive formations that have constituted her or his subjectivity. To maintain otherwise is to posit a universe that is totally deterministic, one in which subjects have no agency whatsoever.

Foucault indeed seems to be articulating such a universe: "Power relations are both intentional and *nonsubjective*"; lest he be misunderstood, he adds that while power is always exercised with "a series of aims and objectives" such goals do not "[result] from the choice or decisions of an individual subject" (1:94–95; my emphasis).

While Foucault's radical bracketing of the circuits of power at the macro and micro ends may constitute the blindness that enables his brilliant articulation of the circulation of power, the field of racialized sexuality can be adequately articulated precisely at the points that Foucault brackets, points that intersect in the very formation of slavery. Within the confines of United States slave and Jim Crow societies, racialized sexuality exists at the point where the virtual powerlessness of certain subjects intersects with the massive prohibitive power of various state and civil apparatuses, power that, it must be emphasized, is always underwritten by the actual or potential use of massive coercive violence.

## I

All social relations, including sexuality, that are grounded in this intersection are primarily defined and controlled, it seems to me, by what Foucault calls "juridico-discursive" prohibitions rather than by the will to knowledge/power that lies behind the discourses involved in the production of fields such as sexuality. Juridical prohibitions are extremely powerful in this space because all socio-political-cultural relations on the racial border are predicated on the definition of the "other," in this case the black American, as nonhuman, as a being who does not belong to the human realm of the master's society and who consequently has no "rights" within that society. As Orlando Patterson has demonstrated, all slave societies incorporated slaves as "socially dead" beings, that is, as beings who had no *de facto* and, more important in this context, no *de jure* access to the civil and political apparatuses of the given society. Because these humans were defined as property, the social, political, and legal rights of slaves barely exceeded those of farm animals: juridically, they lived in a state of almost total powerlessness, under massive institutional prohibitions that mediated all their social relations.[4] In Foucaultian terms one would say that juridical prohibitions are "immanent" to the very organization of "the multiplicity of force relations" that constitute slave and Jim Crow societies.

In the United States, emancipation ended the legal definition of the slave as property and recognized the African-American as a legal subject; however, various Jim Crow laws soon ensured that the descendants of slaves had no more access to civil and political society than did their ancestors. In spite of the various "equal but separate" emendations, the Jim Crow juridical prohibitions continued in effect until the civil rights legislation of the 1950s and 1960s, which was the first moment, I would argue, when black Americans had anything like equal access to civil and political society.

Since it is not possible to begin exploring in any detail the historical effects of juridical prohibitions on the field of racialized sexuality in the space available here, I want to cite just one contemporary legal case, which illustrates the historical range of the effects of juridical prohibitions. In 1982–83, Susie Guillory Phipps unsuccessfully sued the Louisiana Bureau of Vital Records to change her racial classification from black to white.[5] The descendant of an eighteenth-century white planter and a black slave, Phipps was designated "black" on her birth certificate in accordance with a 1970 state law requiring that anyone with at least one-thirty-second (3.125 percent) part "Negro blood" be classified as black. (This 1970 law, it should be noted, was enacted to supersede an even more arbitrary Jim

---

[4]Orlando Patterson, *Slavery and Social Death* (Cambridge: Harvard University Press, 1982). According to Patterson, "the most distinctive feature of the slave's powerlessness was that it always originated . . . as a substitute for death, usually violent death." However, in all slave societies, the condition of slavery did not dissolve the slave's prospect of death; rather death was conditionally commuted and could be revoked at the master's whim. The implication is that in order to live the slave had to acquiesce in his own powerlessness; by asserting himself in any significant way against the master, he courted death. Thus in "his powerlessness the slave became an extension of his master's power. He was a human surrogate, re-created by his master with god-like power in his behalf" (4–5).

[5]This case is derived from its discussion in Michael Omi and Howard Winant, *Racial Formation in the United States: 1960–1980* (New York: Routledge, 1986) 57.

Crow statute that relied on "common report" to determine an infant's race.) In the course of the case, Phipps' attorney called on a retired Tulane University professor who cited research indicating that most people classified as "white" in the South have one-twentieth (5.0 percent) black ancestry. This case, like many others, demonstrates one of the most blatant contradictions on the racial-sexual border. Although juridical prohibitions were historically used to demarcate strictly the civil and political boundary between "black" and "white," and to confine civil and political rights to one side of that border, the very existence of "racially mixed" individuals like Phipps, as well as the "whites" with 5 percent black ancestry, proves that the *sexual* boundary between the two races was systematically violated. The "racial mixture" resulting from this violation of the racial-sexual border in turn necessitated further juridical classifications, prohibitions, repressions, and the comedy of ratios such as that involved in the Phipps case.

Of the many questions raised by the highly selective permeability of the racial border, the most important methodological considerations are the following: Why does the sexual violation of the socio-political borders not call into question the validity and the enforcement of the entire racial border, including its civil and political demarcations? Why does the regular crossing of the racial border through racialized sexuality not enter the daylight of discursivity along with other supposedly "hidden" aspects of sexuality? And, finally, why does white racist society not produce racialized sexuality through the kind of "dense discursivity" utilized in the production of white bourgeois sexuality?[6]

---

[6]I do not wish these questions to imply that the construction of racialized sexuality is altogether different from that of bourgeois sexuality. The two overlap and differ in complicated ways. For instance, white society's decision to silence the construction of racialized sexuality contrasts with a tense desire within black American culture—as evinced, for example, by the works of Alice Walker, Gail Jones, Toni Morrison, James Baldwin, and Richard Wright—to investigate and articulate its effects on the construction of the racialized subject.

## *II*

Foucault does not answer these questions, of course. Indeed, since his interest lies in developing an "analytics" rather than a "theory" of power and hence in describing the discursive deployment of white bourgeois sexuality,[7] Foucault appropriately avoids the assumption that "juridico-discursive" prohibitions are originary and sufficient forms of control. However, in my view, the draconian nature of the slave code and Jim Crow laws and their systematic enforcement through violence justify the use of "juridico-discursive" prohibitions as the ground for the construction of racialized sexuality. One can, of course, analyze the mobility of force relations that preceded the crystallization of slavery as an institution and racism as an ideological formation, but relations of power within this crystallized institution and this formation, including sexual relations, are subject to some of the five principal features of the juridico-discursive model that Foucault eschews.

Foucault correctly criticizes the "homogeneity of power" assumed under the principle of *the uniformity of the apparatus* (1:84–85).[8] However, the proposition central to this regulation, that it "schematizes power in a juridical form, and defines its effects as obedience," is perfectly applicable to slave societies to

---

[7]Foucault is quite clear about the class origins of "sexuality" as a formation: "it was in the 'bourgeois' or 'aristocratic' families that the sexuality of children and adolescents was first problematized, and feminine sexuality medicalized." The working classes, he argues, "managed for a long time to escape the deployment of 'sexuality'." Or again, "we must say that there is a bourgeois sexuality, and that there are class sexualities. Or rather, that sexuality is originally, historically bourgeois, and that, in its successive shifts and transportations, it induces specific class effects" (1:120, 121, and 127, respectively). Foucault does hint, without systematic elaboration, that the bourgeoisie subjected the resisting working classes to specific aspects of the "deployment of 'alliances'" (1:121). The articulation of such a deployment might offer intriguing parallels with a similar deployment in the construction of racialized sexuality that I explore below.

[8]This portion of his critique seems particularly motivated by a desire to avoid a vulgar Marxist notion, wherein power operates in a uniform manner "from the agencies of social domination to the structures that constitute the subject himself" (1:85)

the extent that the *intended*, as opposed to actual, effect of juridical control is obedience. The apparatus, though, does not intend to deploy its subjects in a uniform manner: rape, the forceful possession of female slaves by their white masters, is permissible, while any version of the opposite relation, one between a black male slave and a white woman, is strictly prohibited. According to another of Foucault's principles of juridico-discursive formation, *the insistence of the rule*, "power is essentially what dictates its law to sex. Which means first of all that sex is placed by power in a binary system: licit and illicit, permitted and forbidden" (1:83). This precisely describes the habitual appropriation of the female slave and the symbolic and often literal castration of the male slave, which functions ·as the drastic mark of the prohibition. Another rule, *the logic of censorship*, is, according to Foucault, quite contradictory: "The logic of power exerted on sex is the paradoxical logic of a law that might be expressed as an injunction of nonexistence, nonmanifestation, and silence" (1:84). Under the principle of *the cycle of prohibition* Foucault repeats the same notion in the personified voice of prohibition: "Renounce yourself or suffer the penalty of being suppressed; do not appear if you do not want to disappear. Your existence will be maintained only at the cost of your nullification" (1:84). While not intended for this purpose, Foucault's characterization of the double bind constructed by the cycle of prohibition is one of the most eloquent descriptions of the central dilemma that slave and Jim Crow societies create for their victims. The cogency of this personified injunction is aptly demonstrated by its range of applicability. It succinctly represents the injunction against the offspring of the master and the female slave, which is depicted, for instance, by Harriet Jacobs. And it summarizes the effects of this same injunction that Ralph Ellison systematically explores in *Invisible Man*: according to the fundamental logic of racism and racialized sexuality, its victims can exist only if they accept their invisibility.

Finally, according to the rule of *negative relation*, the effects of power, says Foucault, "take the general form of limit and lack." Power "introduces discontinuities, separates what is joined, and marks off boundaries" (1:82). This is the central principle around which slavery and racism consolidate themselves, in my view. Power is used in this context to institute a radical demarcation and denial of kinship between two groups while one of them intimately and brutally exploits the other.

Foucault's characterization of prohibitive juridico-discursive power, which relies on "a taboo that plays on the alternative between two nonexistences" (1:84), captures the essence of the "existence" of slaves: they can either choose the "social death" of slavery, which strips them of existence within the master's society, or they can opt for "actual death," which frees them from slavery but at the cost of their actual and their social existence. My insistence on the overwhelming determining role of juridical prohibitions does not contradict Foucault's deep suspicion of the centrality of "the law" since his critique is rightly directed against the assumption that this "law" has ontological validity. What I am asserting, on the contrary, is that the juridical prohibitions that determine life on the racial and sexual borders are not ontological but socio-political constructs, which demarcate major divisions in a potential continuum of kinship.

While racialized sexuality shares some of the features of juridico-discursive formations that Foucault wishes to avoid, it overlaps with his four positive methodological rules or "cautionary prescriptions." According to the *rule of immanence*, "between techniques of knowledge and strategies of power, there is no exteriority, even if they have specific roles and are linked together on the basis of their difference" (1:98). Racialized sexuality, unlike its bourgeois counterpart, links power and knowledge in a negative, inverse relation: the perpetuation of white patriarchy and the preservation of its self-image require that it deny a "scientific-discursive" knowledge of its sexual violation of the racial border. The *rule of continual variations* implies that "relations of power-knowledge are not static forms of distribution," where one group has accumulated all power and the other none but that these relations "are matrices of transformation" (1:99). Because racialized sexuality is characterized by a relative paucity of discursive articulation and a relatively uneven distribution of power, it tends to become an even more powerful "matrix of transformation" than bourgeois sexuality. The *rule of double conditioning*, that is, the mutual and symbiotic dependence of overall strategy and local tactics or "local centers" of discursive formation, is central to the allegorical structure of the peculiar "silence" that characterizes racialized sexuality. Similarly, the *rule of the tactical polyvalence of discourses*, which posits that discourses of sexuality must be mapped "as a series of discontinuous segments whose tactical function is neither uniform nor stable" (1:100), must take into account the tactical silences and articulations, the varied authorization and positioning of speaking subjects, and, most important, the manner in which "identical formulas" can serve apparently contradictory objectives. Finally, this rule necessitates the recognition that discourses "are tactical elements or blocks operating in the field of force relations; there can exist different and even contradictory discourses within the same strategy; they can, on the contrary, circulate without changing their form from one strategy to another, opposing strategy" (1:100–2). (This apparently contradictory circulation, I will argue, is precisely the process through which Wright's attempted inversion, in *Native Son*, of the repeated white patriarchal crossing of the racial-sexual border and its construction of the racialized subject needs to be read.)

### III

While racialized sexuality shares various features with the formulations on either side of Foucault's grand divide between juridico-discursive constructs and "sexuality" as a modern discursive formation, the most important characteristic that distinguishes racialized from white bourgeois sexuality is its strategic, rather than merely tactical, deployment of a peculiar "silence." Racialized sexuality has never been subjected to dense discursive articulation, which was the basis of bourgeois sexuality. Sexuality, says Foucault, was articulated "at the point of intersection of a technique of confession and a scientific discursivity" (1:68). The will to knowledge regarding sexuality, which he claims as a particular trait of "the modern Occident," made the rituals of confession function within the norms of scientific discourse and transformed desire itself into a discourse that produced "sexuality." This apparatus for producing an ever greater quantity of discourse about "sex" operated through various tactics—the codification of the inducement to speak; the medicalization of confession; the ascription of certain characteristics to "sex," such as inexhaustible causality and infinite latency; the specific methods of interpretations such as psychoanalysis, and so on—and consolidated itself around various centers: pedagogy, medicine, psychiatry, criminal justice, and modes of "social control . . . which screened the sexuality of couples, parents and children, [and] dangerous and endangered adolescents." As a discourse produced by these methods and sites, sexuality "in turn created further incentives to talk about it" (1:29–31). This kind of dense discursivity never existed on the racial border, where sexuality developed as a separate center.

Racialized sexuality refused or failed to develop a dense discursivity primarily because white patriarchy's sexual violation of the racial border—the master's rape of the female slave—was an "open secret." But this "common knowledge" could not be admitted to the realm of even a pseudo-scientific discursivity lest it undermine the socio-political impermeability of that border, which was of course essential to the very structure of racism and slavery. This contradiction leads to the "one drop of black blood" criterion, which simultaneously provides a means of denying miscegenation and augmenting the supply of slave labor. The need to deny the "open secret" leads, moreover, to the formation of an internally contradictory juridical discourse around racialized sexuality, aptly symbolized by the Phipps case. On the po-litical-libidinal register the necessity for this "open secret" can be traced to the white master's sexual desire for a slave. Since this desire implicitly admits the slave's humanity, it undermines the foundation of the border—the supposed inhumanity of the black other, her putative ontological alterity. Unable or unwilling to repress desire, the master silences the violation of the border and refuses to recognize, through any form of analytic discursivity, the results of the infraction. This peculiar silence prevents the development of the kind of confessional and "scientific" discursivity central to the deployment of sexuality as Foucault defines it. There are, of course, pseudo-medical texts written by white doctors who claim to have fathomed "Negro sexuality,"[9] but these are pale and infrequent imitations of the dense analytic discourses of white bourgeois sexuality. Even when the discourse of racialized sexuality approximates some of the central tropes of bourgeois sexuality, it is never subject to the same kind of appropriation. Thus, the "hysterization of women's bodies" is paralleled on the racial-sexual border by the hysterization of the black body, which is also represented as saturated with sexuality. However, unlike the woman's body, the black body is never "integrated into the sphere of medical practices" nor "placed in

---

[9]See, for instance, I. A. Newby's discussion of these pseudo-medical texts in *Jim Crow's Defense: Anti-Negro Thought in America, 1900–1930* (Baton Rouge: Louisiana State University Press, 1965).

organic communion with the social body" (1:104).  To the contrary, it is the hystericized, oversexualized body of the black male that is used by the discourse of racialized sexuality to reinforce the hysterical boundaries between the two racialized communities.  Sexuality on the border was not a construct that could be administered through *analytic* discourse.

On the other side of the racial divide, black Americans were condemned to silence through a twofold strategy.  Because they were considered inhuman, their speech was judged insignificant.  This view is codified in the statutes that prevented blacks from bearing witness against whites: since blacks were not legal subjects, their testimony had no legal standing.  This was coupled with the legal interdiction of black education and later the segregation and the systematic impoverishment of that education, which was also designed to induce silence.  However, as the abundance of black literature now available demonstrates, these injunctions could not overcome the will to knowledge; but this will was manifested in a literary register, not in the medical, psychiatric, and confessional textuality that Foucault describes.

This deployment of silence, wherein those who could speak did not want to and those who did want to speak were prevented from doing so, produced racialized sexuality as a discursive formation.  In this dynamic structure, where silence and repression play a strategic rather than a tactical or local role, sexuality becomes an even more dense transfer point for relations of power.  Like the sexuality that Foucault describes, racialized sexuality is a "network in which the stimulation of bodies, the intensification of pleasures, . . . the formation of special knowledges, [and] the strengthening of controls . . . are linked to one another" (1:105–6).  But the "furtive reality" of this sexuality and its resistance to being turned into a surface network by analytic discourse are part of its immanent specificity.

Though it saturates every social relation, sexuality in this formation produces a discourse that is in many ways an inversion of that which produces bourgeois sexuality.  In contrast to the *analytic* imperative that underlies bourgeois sexuality, racialized sexuality is structured by a set of *allegorical* discourses: silence and repression  weave a limited configuration of symbols and desires that are deeply resonant but never available to pseudo-scientific methods.  Whereas bourgeois sexuality is a product of an empiricist, analytic, and proliferating discursivity, racialized sexuality is a product of stereotypic, symbolizing, and condensing discursivity: the former is driven by a will to knowledge, the latter by both a will to conceal its mechanisms and its own will to power.

Like colonialist literature, as I have argued elsewhere, racialized sexuality is structured by and functions according to the economy of a manichean allegory. The cognitive framework of the machinery of this allegory is "a field of diverse yet interchangeable oppositions between white and black, good and evil, superiority and inferiority, civilization and savagery, intelligence and emotion, rationality and sensuality, self and other, subject and object." Such a system functions by first reducing the colonized or racialized subject to a generic being that can be exchanged for any other "native" or racialized subject.

Once reduced to his exchange-value in the colonialist signifying system, s/he is fed into the manichean allegory, which functions as the currency, the medium of exchange, for the entire colonialist discursive system. The exchange function of the allegory remains constant, while the generic attributes themselves can be substituted infinitely (and even contradictorily) for one another.

The aim of this allegorical discursive structure is to maintain the *positional* superiority of the European in relation with the other, "to reproduce the native in a potentially infinite variety of images, the apparent diversity of which is determined by the simple machinery of the manichean allegory," and to transform social, historical, and cultural dissimilarities into universal, metaphysical differences.[10] It is an economy under the sway not of an "*analytic knowledge*" or a "*logic*" of sexuality and power but of an "*allegorical coding*" or a "*mytho-logic*" of sexuality, race, and power.

---

[10]"The Economy of Manichean Allegory: The Function of Racial Difference in Colonialist Literature," *Critical Inquiry* 12 (Autumn 1985): 59–87. The citations are from pages 63, 64, and 66. That article does not theorize how gender functions within the allegorical structure, as the present essay begins to do.

## IV

If bourgeois sexuality is produced by scientific and pseudo-scientific discourses, the allegorical structures that characterize racialized sexuality seem to reveal themselves better in fictive discourses, which manifest the process through which the economies of these structures are negotiated. In the brief space available here I want to sketch an important feature of the economy of racialized sexuality through Richard Wright's *Native Son*, for that novel, by forcing its protagonist, Bigger Thomas, to cross the racial-sexual border in the reverse direction, provides a glimpse of its underlying economy.

Wright's overall fictive project consisted of an archaeological excavation of the racialized subject, of the various discursive strata that gradually sediment to construct that subject. As I have argued in detail elsewhere, Wright thoroughly internalized the psycho-political-sexual structures of racist discourses and the process whereby they construct the subject but then began to deconstruct these formative structures in his autobiographies and fiction.[11] His primary goal was to expose the operation of these structures and to indicate possible modes of resistance. Although mainly preoccupied with the dialectic of death as the central mechanism of these structures, he also reveals the dynamics of racialized sexuality as a secondary, but by no means unimportant, feature of his work.

Wright focuses on one crucial mode by which racialized sexuality operates: the "feminization" or "infantilization" of the black man within a phallocentric system. Relying sometimes on a literal and more often on a symbolic form of castration, the economy of racialized sexuality is dedicated not only to obstructing the subjugated man's access to the phallus but also to a ritual cleansing, through the mechanism of projection, of the guilt involved in white patriarchy's selective violation of its own general prohibitions against crossing the racial border. Wright brilliantly investigates the economy of castration in his last novel, *The Long Dream*, but in *Native Son*, where he is just beginning to

---

[11]"Negating the Negation as a Form of Affirmation in Minority Discourse: The Construction of Richard Wright as a Subject" *The Nature and Context of Minority Discourse*, ed. Abdul R. JanMohamed and David Lloyd (New York: Oxford University Press, 1990) 102–23.

explore the problematic of racialized sexuality, he casts it in terms of rape. Wright proceeds from the perspective of a protagonist so profoundly castrated that he experiences himself as an already "feminized" black male who needs to (re)assert his "manhood" through rape and murder. The fundamental premise of *Native Son*, which Wright entirely fails to examine critically, is that the protagonist can become a "man" through rape and murder and overcome the racialization of his subjectivity. While the novel intends to depict how Bigger can surmount the debilitating effects of racism, it demonstrates in fact that the phallocratic order can foreclose effective forms of resistance and can position some black males in such a way that they are incapable of asserting their "manhood" against racism except by replicating phallocratic violence against women. In addition to probing the dialectic of death, the novel then provides insights into the way in which racialized sexuality channels political and libidinal energies.

In exploring the libidinal economy of this novel, "rape" needs to be treated as a "positivity," in Foucault's terms an "*historical a priori*" that "defines a field in which formal identities, thematic continuities, translations of concepts, and polemical interchange may be deployed."[12] An analysis of the "tactical efficacy" of rape must begin, however, by explaining how and why the politics of kinship, which in Foucault's view are more important in the deployment of alliance than of sexuality, are subverted by the racist prohibition. If kinship and thus society are established through the "exchange" of women between men, according the dubious logic of a phallocratic society, then racism, which is predicated precisely on a denial of "kinship" between whites and blacks, prevents the development of familial bonds by prohibiting the "legal" "exchange" of women across the color line. Here a distinction must be maintained between "*exchange*," which assumes a certain degree of consent between men, and "*appropriation*," which does not. On the racial-sexual border white women were never "exchanged" between white and black men, and black women were forcefully appropriated, raped (rather than "exchanged") by white men. In addition to the effects of rape on black women, the belief of the racist society that black men's consent to the possession of black women is irrele-

---

[12]Michel Foucault, *The Archaeology of Knowledge* (New York: Random House, 1972) 127.

vant represents yet another form of castration, for it eliminates or severely undermines the paternal and fraternal functions.

Within this highly charged matrix, Wright characterizes sexuality in general and rape in particular as the paradigm of all modes of crossing the racial boundary. As he says in the preface to *Native Son*, "So volatile and tense are [racial] relations [on the border] that if a Negro rebels against rule and taboo, he is lynched and the reason for the lynching is usually [given as] 'rape'."[13]   Wright's narrative restatement of the effectivity of rape is more specific:

> Every time [Bigger] felt as he had felt that night, he raped. But rape was not what one did to women. Rape was what one felt when one's back was against a wall and one had to strike out, whether one wanted to or not, to keep the pack from killing one. He committed rape every time he looked into a white face. He was a long, taut piece of rubber which a thousand hands had stretched to the snapping point, and when he snapped it was rape. But it was rape when he cried out in hate deep in his heart as he felt the strain of living day by day. That, too, was rape. (213–14)

Thus the deep, wrenching penetration of the racialized subject by racist discourses, which are responsible for the very formation of that subject, is represented by Wright as "rape." In fact he characterizes the entire region of the racial border as defined by rape. Rape is simultaneously the metonymy of the process of oppressive racist control (as in the first quotation) *and* a metaphor for the construction of the racialized subject (as in the second quotation): regardless of gender, the racialized subject is always already constructed as a "raped" subject in Wright's view. Rape thus subsumes the totality of force relations on the racial border, which is in fact always a sexual border.

This definition of the racial border as the zone of rape must underlie any analysis of the three (rather than simply the two self-evident) rapes in *Native Son*, rapes which change from the symbolic to the literal during the course of the novel. In the first case, in which Bigger assaults his male friend Gus to distract

---

[13]Richard Wright, *Native Son* (New York: Harper and Row, 1940) xii. All further references to this novel will be incorporated in the text.

them from their fear of robbing a white store, Wright ends the fight with several apparently gratuitous gestures: Bigger mounts Gus and then forces him to lick his knife. These gestures, I would argue, simultaneously represent fellatio, castration, and rape. Given the insistent specularity of the scene (the narrative insists six times that Bigger is projecting his fear onto Gus), Bigger is in effect castrating and raping himself. He is ritualistically and perhaps obsessively rehearsing the racist construction of his own subjectivity: he is symbolically raping himself so that he will not have to cross the racial border with aggressive intentions against white men and their property.

In the second case, which is characterized by an equally strong specularity, Bigger stifles Mary just as he feels society has been suffocating him. He has penetrated white society by destroying one of its cherished symbols (Mary), just as the racial system penetrates him. That he substitutes his own severed head for hers in a dream suggests that he is destroying himself as well as her. However, unlike the rape of Gus-and-himself, which is designed to keep him within the confines of the ghetto, the putative rape and actual murder of Mary-and-himself allow Bigger to break out beyond the limits of the racial border. They give him a kind of security and power that transform his subjectivity: "The knowledge that he had killed a white girl they loved and regarded as their symbol of beauty made him feel the equal of them, like a man who had been somehow cheated, but had now evened the score" (155). This feeling becomes a substitute for the security his knife and gun had provided him. Thus the violent "appropriation" of Mary's sexuality not only allows Bigger to enter into a system of "exchange" with white men and become their "equal"; it also permits him to enter the symbolic realm and possess the phallus: the aggressive phallic symbols are replaced by knowledge-as-power. Yet in his "liberation" Bigger still remains subject to the logic of the phallocratic system.

In the third case, Bigger's gruesome rape and murder of his black companion Bessie is utilized by both the narrative and white society in the novel as a substitute for the supposed rape of Mary. The court argues that if he raped Bessie, he must have raped Mary too and succeeds in convicting him though it lacks evidence that he committed the act. Because Wright is loath to portray Bigger as a victim, unjustly prosecuted for the putative rape of Mary and her accidental death, the narrative urgently "requires" Bessie's rape and murder to "prove" Bigger's "guilt." Thus Bessie's rape and murder are inserted by the court and the narrative into the exchange system that Bigger entered by killing Mary; Bessie's primary function is to be a medium of exchange for the value of Mary. The novel thus suggests that in the economy of racialized sexuality, white women represent exchange value between white and black men, whereas black women represent only use value for both. If Mary constitutes a metaphor of desire on the racial border, then Bessie functions as a metonymy of that metaphor.

These rapes and murders, in which race, sexuality, power, and knowledge intersect, are matrices for the transformation of Bigger, very much in keeping with Foucault's "rules of continual variations" (1:99). Through the possession and murder of a white woman Bigger enters the phallocentric circuit of exchange and equivalence, but in the process he also discovers a form of use value that is instrumental in the reconstruction of his subjectivity. Wright was perfectly aware that slave and Jim Crow societies had created economies that syphoned off almost the entire production of the black man as well as the "reproduction" by black women as surplus value. However, in killing Mary and thereby facing his own death, Bigger discovers the use value of his own actual (as opposed to social) death. In the narrator's words, Bigger "had murdered and created a new life for himself. It was something that was all his own, and it was the first time in his life that he had had anything that others could not take from him" (101). The new life that he discovers at the point of death constitutes a value that can be of "use" only for him; it has no exchange value, and it is impossible for his masters to appropriate it as a surplus.

By navigating his character through the explosive field of racialized sexuality, Wright discovers an approach to "liberation" from the confines of social death. Ironically, however, this emancipation exacts a terrible price: Bigger is only able to find "liberation" by inscribing himself in a subject position analogous to that of the white master. His symbolic and literal rapes and murders all involve victims who, in different ways, occupy subject positions of "social death." It seems he can be free only by imposing on others a choice between social and actual death. *Native Son* turns out to be a profoundly specular novel; it holds up a mirror to the structure and economy of phallocratic society, but it is unable to escape or undermine them.

## V

*Native Son* illustrates that within the discursive formation of racialized sexuality the process of racialization is always already a process of sexualization, and the process of sexualization is also always already—or at least functions as if it were—a process of racialization. Thus while racialized sexuality condenses within itself a complex socio-political-libidinal relation of race and gender, this formation also constitutes an important border in relation to bourgeois sexuality. This becomes clear in contrasting the two formations of sexuality with respect to the differences that Foucault describes between the deployments of alliance and of sexuality.

According to Foucault, the deployment of alliance is "a system of marriage, of fixation and development of kinship ties, of transmission of names and possessions." The deployment of sexuality was constructed "around and on the basis" of the deployment of alliance, over which it was superimposed without completely supplanting it (1:106–107). To consider U.S. slave society and its Jim Crow extension in light of this description of alliance is to see that racialized sexuality contains some of the elements of alliance: fixation—the strict, yet sexually permeable, demarcation of rigid racial boundaries; kinship ties—the bonding of a timocratic society through its degradation of slaves, the negative inscription of kinship on the racial border, and the systematic destruction of kinship among slaves; and, most important, the transmission of possessions—the transformation of slave subjects and their sexuality into property that is to be kept in the master's possession at all costs, a transformation marked by the displacing of African names with those of the masters.

Further examination of Foucault's detailed comparison of deployments of alliance and sexuality confirms the divergence between bourgeois and racialized sexuality. Foucault writes:

> The deployment of alliance is built around a system of rules defining the permitted and the forbidden, the licit and the illicit, whereas the deployment of sexuality operates according to mobile, polymorphous, and contingent techniques of power. The deployment of alliance has as one of its chief objectives to reproduce the interplay of relations and maintaining the law that governs them; the

deployment of sexuality, on the other hand, engenders a continual extension of areas and forms of control. For the first, what is pertinent is the link between partners and definite statutes; the second is concerned with the sensations of the body, the quality of pleasures, and the nature of impressions. . . . Lastly, if the deployment of alliance is firmly tied to the economy due to the role it can play in the transmission or circulation of wealth, the deployment of sexuality is linked to the economy through numerous and subtle relays, the main one of which, however, is the body—the body that produces and consumes. (1:106–7)

Even a cursory examination of these oppositions shows that racialized sexuality replicates more features of the deployment of alliance than of bourgeois sexuality. Thus racialized sexuality is characterized by juridico-discursive prohibitions, by the need to maintain a law, and by the subtle operations of a manichean allegory which constantly distinguishes the licit from the illicit. Similarly, the structures of slave society, and those of racialized sexuality that emerge from that society, are tied not only to the transmission and circulation of material wealth but to its very production. Foucault's summation of the structure of the deployment of alliance applies almost entirely to racialized sexuality: "In a word, the deployment of alliance is attuned to a *homeostasis of the social body*, which it has the function of maintaining; whence its privileged link with the law; whence too the fact that the important phase for it is 'reproduction'" (1:107; my emphasis). One of the primary functions of racism, which underpins U.S. slavery and racialized sexuality, is to maintain the homeostasis of the social body—the firm division between whites and racialized "others"—through a complex allegorical discursivity. A slave society also aims to reproduce the bodies of slaves, a primary source of its wealth; but at a more general level it is also driven by an anxiety, which is central to its allegorical machinery, to reproduce itself as a system of division. As these instances confirm, racialized sexuality originates from the politics of alliance, just as white bourgeois sexuality does; yet each form of sexuality is neither identical to its common source (alliance) nor to the other form. In fact, they are opposed to each other in some fundamental ways: one is characterized by a will to knowledge and hence by an analytic discursivity, the other by a will to conceal and hence by an allegorical discursivity.

The two forms of sexual discourse can be further distinguished by their different intentionalities toward the family. Foucault argues that the family lies at the intersection of "sexuality and alliance: it conveys the law and the juridical dimension in the deployment of sexuality; and it conveys the economy of pleasure and the intensity of sensation in the regime of alliance" (1:108). If the cohesion of the family has a crucial mediating function between alliance and bourgeois sexuality, then the economy of racialized sexuality utilizes the racialized, "othered" family in precisely the opposite way: racialized sexuality is predicated on the fracturing, rather than the unity, of the "black" family. This process, which can only be briefly sketched here, involves the destruction of the paternal and maternal functions within the enslaved family;[14] the continued "feminization" of the black male, which is simultaneously symbolic and material; and then, as in the Moynihan report,  a convoluted "masculinization" of the black woman.[15]

Foucault's provocative and emancipatory theory of "sexuality" thus has a limited applicability despite or perhaps because of his implicit assumption that its development was a universal rather than a specifically white, bourgeois, Euro-American phenomenon. These limitations become clearer within the larger social context of Euro-American bourgeois history. For instance, Foucault claims that the deployment of sexuality was accompanied by a transformation in the deployment of "death": the oppressive monopoly of the state in utilizing "death" to coerce "life" gave way to a nurturing enhancement of "life" in the modern period; along with the increasing technological control of disasters such as famines and epidemics, this transformation liberated "life" from the external specter of "death" (see Foucault 1:135ff.). But in making such an assertion, Foucault fails to acknowledge that throughout much of the modern period "death" was continually deployed as a "means of

---

[14]The most eloquent and penetrating expression of the horror involved in the destruction of the maternal function is, of course, Toni Morrison's *Beloved*, while the destruction of the paternal function is depicted with equal strength and subtlety in Alice Walker's *Third Life of Grange Copeland*.

[15]See *The Negro Family: The Case for National Action Report* (Washington, DC: U.S. Govt. Print. Office, 1965).

production" by the European nations throughout the colonies, particularly in the form of slavery.[16]  Because this "older" deployment of death takes place at the "margins" of European society, in the Americas for instance, Foucault never inquires whether this "enhancement of life" at the center (so crucial for the development of its "sexuality") may depend on the "deployment of death" on the borders of the various Euro-American empires.  He never examines how the symbolic and material economies of these empires mediated between the deployment of death at the margins and the enhancement of life at the center, how, indeed, the center has thrived on the margins.  The gaze that Foucault casts on the deployment of sexuality and "life/death" is clearly not panoptic: it is profoundly limited by a Eurocentric horizon.

In order to conceptualize a more comprehensive "sexuality," the three Foucaultian criteria for mapping the discourses that constitute "sexuality" must be taken seriously: a *"dispersion of* centers from which discourses emanated, a *diversification* of their forms, and the complex deployment of the *network connecting them"* (1:34; my emphasis).  This would permit a definition of white bourgeois sexuality as a center and racialized sexuality as a separate center,[17] and the relation between them as negative and specular.  It is negative because racialized sexuality seems to define the very border of white bourgeois sexuality.  Racialized sexuality delineates the point at which the will to knowledge, which in bourgeois sexuality compels discourse to permeate all facets of socio-sexual relations, begins to abate.  And while the will to power is profoundly intertwined with the will to knowledge in the deployment of bourgeois sexuality, at its border or its margins, where racialized sexuality deploys itself, the will to knowledge detaches itself from the will to power; or, to put it differently, the intentionalities of the will to power and the will to knowledge do not coincide in the transition from bourgeois sexu-

---

[16]For the political economy of death, see Patterson; Michael T. Taussig, *Shamanism, Colonialism, and the Wild Man: A Study in Terror and Health* (Chicago: University of Chicago Press, 1987); and Joseph C. Miller, *The Way of Death: Merchant Capital and the Angolan Slave Trade: 1830–1930* (Madison: University of Wisconsin Press, 1988).

[17]Of course, in order to be really comprehensive, one would also have to map other regimes of sexuality that existed and still exist in other cultures.

ality to racialized sexuality. The two are characterized by very different ratios of power and knowledge.

Like the deployment of "sexuality" as a putatively "universal" phenomenon, Foucault's "*history*" of that "sexuality" is also characterized by a tendency to confine itself to a more or less homogeneous, ethnocentric field. The history of "bourgeois" and "racialized" sexualities is deployed in a relation of negative specularity: the first can write itself as "universal" only if it averts its gaze from the second, its dark other, which stares from across the racial border and demands an equal historical articulation. But even in so radical a critic as Foucault, the Eurocentric gaze is consistently blind to the various forms of sexualities that it implicitly constructs as its alterities. As a result, fields such as "racialized sexuality" will have to be investigated by different methods, by procedures that will have to be emancipated from an ethnic and cultural narcissism—a narcissism that may well be an integral part of "sexuality" itself.

# DOES SEXUALITY HAVE A HISTORY?

## Catharine A. MacKinnon

It definitely does, if history is what historians do. This history—as defined by Freud and his successors, who see sexuality as a fundamental motive force in history; as pursued by Foucault and his followers, who see sexuality as socially created out of disciplinary power and discourses of knowledge—this history has been the history of pleasure and seeking it, of repression and derepressing it. The history these historians of sexuality write is the history of desire: of the impelled, compelled, wanting, grasping, taking, mounting, penetrating, thrusting, consummating. It is a history of ecstasy and its prohibition or permission. It is a history of the active, the striving. It is what Nietzsche called a "monumental" history[1] (envision here the Washington Monument), an orgasming, ejaculating history of getting some.

On my reading, this version of sexuality's past includes most but not all of what goes under the rubric "history of sexuality." Taken to a particular pinnacle in the collections *Pleasure and Danger*[2] and *The Powers of Desire*,[3] it also animates sexology-inspired retrofit versions of gay and lesbian history and

---

©Catherine A. MacKinnon 1990, 1991, 1992. Originally presented September 12, 1990, as a lecture sponsored by the University of Michigan Institute for the Humanities and the Law School, as part of the Institute's year-long study of the "Histories of Sexuality."

[1]Friedrich Nietzsche, *The Advantages and Disadvantages of History for Life*, trans. Peter Preuss (Indianapolis: Hackett Publishing Co., 1980) 14–15.

[2]Carole S. Vance, ed., *Pleasure and Danger: Exploring Female Sexuality* (Boston: Routledge & Kegan Paul, 1984). There are exceptions to this characterization in the collection, notably the essay by Kate Millett on sex between adults and children. When she asks "Adults can turn around and hit you at any moment. They can send you off to bed. Who wants a relationship with a lover who has this sort of authority?" it is clear she is in the wrong book.

[3]Ann Snitow, Christine Stansell, and Sharon Thompson, eds., *Powers of Desire: The Politics of Sexuality* (New York: Monthly Review Press, 1983). Again, not all of the contributions fit this characterization.

the history of prostitution.[4] It is the history of what makes historians feel sexy. In it, prostitutes are agents. In law, agent means someone whose strings are being pulled by someone else. Historians of sexuality mean someone who is actively choosing, pulling their own strings. Prostitutes are the freest of those who choose; you can tell because they make such a stigmatized choice. Why those who become prostitutes are always those with the fewest choices is not part of this history—maybe because facing this is not sexy. Even some gay male historians seem to need to know that a woman is being bought and sold for sex, somewhere, or being a man loses its meaning. This same spirit lives in the historical analysis of rape law as surplus repression and incest and sexual abuse of children as intergenerational sex. It motivates the argument that pornography is an institution of sexual equality and the only historical problem is that women are comparatively deprived of access to using women the way men use women. Particularly in the defenses of sadomasochism, historical and current,[5] we are told that hierarchy is equality and slavery is freedom, maxims that everywhere but sex are recognized as an Orwellian mind-fuck but pass in this area as profundity and daring.

This history of sexuality has certain imperatives, of which I want to mention just a few. First, sex is good and more sex is better. You need to know this to understand that when Foucault says that to say yes to sex is to not say no to power,[6] he is not criticizing sex. In this history, to sexualize something, like

---

[4]See, for example, Jeffrey Weeks, *Sex, Politics and Society: The Regulation of Sexuality since 1800* (New York: Longman, 1981); John D'Emilio, *Sexual Politics, Sexual Communities: The Making of the Homosexual Minority in the United States, 1940–1970* (Chicago: University of Chicago Press, 1983); Judith R. Walkowitz, *Prostitution and Victorian Society* (Cambridge: Cambridge University Press, 1980) and "Male Vice and Female Virtue: Feminism and the Politics of Prostitution in Nineteenth-Century Britain," in *Powers of Desire* 419–38.

[5]See, for example, George Bataille, *Death and Sensuality* (New York: Walker, 1962); Samois, *Coming to Power* (Boston: Alyson, 1982); Pat Califia, "Feminism and Sadomasochism," *Coevolution Quarterly*, 33 (Spring 1982): 33-40.

[6]"We must not think that by saying yes to sex, one says no to power." Michel Foucault, *The History of Sexuality, Volume 1: An Introduction*, trans. Robert Hurley (New York: Vintage Books, 1980) 157.

power, is to exonerate it, to urge its free expression.  The norm is teleological and goal-oriented, such that as more sex occurs, history progresses.  Second, sex is pleasure.  It follows from the history of sexuality as the history of pleasure that it cannot be the history of oppression—except insofar as it is a history of re-sistance to the oppression of pleasure and getting it, a history of overcoming denials of pleasure's expression.  Third, this sexual-ity, to have a history, must change.  It must come in periods: how desire is defined, how pleasure is got, who does what to whom, how pleasure is restrained, how these restraints are dan-gerously and heroically broken.  Sexuality must behave in this way or history is not had, at least not in the genealogical sense.  One example is Foucault's analysis that sexuality was invented in the nineteenth century.  Then it turns out it also existed in classical Greece, but never mind.  The sexuality he serves us is the rise and deployment of the desiring subject, sexuality as the life and times of desiring man in bondage and being disciplined and loving every minute of it, and loving his struggle to get out of it even more.[7]  The upshot is that when desiring man gets more or sees more or feels better or worse about what he gets or sees (and seeing sex is a form of getting it), history is made.  A new day dawns.  A new period is ushered in.  The earth moves.

Now it actually helps the project of historicizing this sexual-ity that so much of sexuality is relational, happens between peo-ple and hence dies with them, and all these people are dead.  There is no one around to tell the historians of sexuality to their face that this account of how it was is not what happened to them.  This makes it all so much more indeterminate, so beauti-fully subject to endlessly varied interpretation, so Rorschach-like.  Hence, in the title of this series, "Histories of Sexuality," one wonders how sexuality escaped the plural.  Here we have the perfect academic subject.  Now we can all have an erotic experi-ence of the text and get tenure too.

Against this backdrop, my question is, what does any of this have to do with reality, or even realities?  What, in particular,

---

[7]There seems to me a deep underlying continuity of sadomasochism in Foucault's work between his analysis both of torture and its replacement with disciplinary power.  See Michel Foucault, *Discipline and Punish*, trans. Alan Sheridan (New York: Vintage Books, 1979), and his version of what sexuality, *per se*, is about.

does this history of this sexuality have to do with what people practice, or practiced, as sex?

This is a difficult question because, first of all, what really happens in sex is hidden. Consider heterosexual intercourse, the dominant form of sexual practice. Mostly, people don't do it in public. And whatever intimacy goes along with it, and sometimes does, tends to be ephemeral. Pornography might be a nonephemeral presentation of what actually happens in sex. This is true of the most abusive pornography and of written pornography, but to make visual pornography out of conventional heterosexual intercourse, you have to have sex in a way that nobody who has sex has sex. You have to have it so everything shows, so that the camera can see what's going on. Generally when people have sex, they have it in such a way that if you look at them you don't see much. And much of the essence of what goes on is not subject to external observation.

Reproduction might be regarded as hard evidence. But it has only an occasional relation to what people actually practice as sex. All this like boys masturbating in circles seeing who can ejaculate the farthest and men putting money in slots to salivate over women in glass boxes with nothing on—I am not convincible that all of this is even about practicing up for reproduction. Technically, one would only have to have intercourse two or three times in a lifetime, a few more for good measure, to produce most of the current world's population. Additionally, the practices of sexual abuse, while they leave some material tracks on soft tissue and bones (with which one would think physical anthropologists could do *something*) as well as on the spirit—this is not spoken of, so also leaves no trace. So if you consider what people actually do as sex, it becomes clear that a great deal of its reality is going to be intrinsically inaccessible to history. This is especially true, I would argue, for sexual abuse because its victims have not been permitted to speak, far less to write their own history. How can you write a history of what is practiced as sex when those who have been abused through sex have no way of telling you what happened to them? They can hardly tell you now, and they are all around you.

How do we face these problems and still give sexuality a history? History's answer—at least mostly, and I will speak about some of the exceptions—has been, so much the worse for facing these problems. We write about what we can get at, based on what we do have, which is painted on vases, forget about what we don't have, who and what are excluded, who is not permitted to paint on vases. We act as if what we have is all there is. We forget about the meaning of what is not there, not known, maybe even not knowable. In other words, the silence of the silenced is filled by the speech of those who have it and the fact of the silence is forgotten in this noisy discourse about sexuality which then becomes its history.

This raises the question, what _do_ we know about what is practiced as sex? Can we get at it with live people? We are beginning to have some real answers to this question, largely as a result of the contemporary movement for the liberation of women. Most of it is new information. It has not been known before. One thing we have learned is that sex, as practiced, includes abuse, of women and children principally. They are abused in the name of sex, in the course of the practice of sex, in order for men to get the pleasure that defines sex. There is a lot of this abuse, but its numbers are less the point than its impact on one's possible experience of sex and its meaning for the relationship of sexual practice to how social life is lived.

We have this information because the women's movement has, it seems for the first time in history, created conditions under which the speech of those who have been abused and fetishized, those who have not painted on vases—centrally women—has been validated and legitimized. As a result, it has been heard. The best study is by Diana Russell[8] giving us the first real information that we have ever had on the incidence of sexual abuse. Her interviewers went to 930 San Francisco households selected at random, women who spoke the languages of those they were interviewing, and asked women about their experiences of sexual assault. In a revolutionary methodological procedure, they believed what the women said, wrote it down, and treated it as though it were data. Among the things she found were that 44 percent of all women had been victims of rape or attempted rape at least once in their lives, and a great many more than once. She found that abuse of women of color was far more frequent than the average for all women. She found that 38 percent of young girls had been sexually molested

---

[8]Works from the study include Diana E. H. Russell, _Sexual Exploitation: Rape, Child Sexual Abuse, and Sexual Harassment_ (Beverly Hills: Russell Sage, 1984), _Rape in Marriage_ (New York: Macmillan, 1982), and _The Secret Trauma: Incestuous Abuse of Women and Girls_ (New York: Basic Books, 1986).

or violated or abused in some way by some person in authority
or a family member, usually someone older, someone close and
trusted, before they reached the age of majority. These figures
completely dwarf any reported rates of these crimes. About a
tenth, it would appear, of rapes are reported. She confirmed
that women are most often sexually abused by men they know
or with whom they are close. If you add up all the forms of sexual harassment, violation, abuse, intrusion, being yelled at on
the street, being subjected to flashers, obscene phone calls, she
found that only 7.5 percent of women reported none of them,
ever.[9]

Have our histories of sexuality seriously considered that
something like this might have been going on before? How would
it change sexuality's histories if it were? What creative methodologies might we devise to expose this in the past, since its victims likely took it to their graves? How would we read the
record we have differently, in light of it? How do you analyze
the absence of a trace of something? Wouldn't you think that
these possible facts might be at least as significant as Foucault's
"hysterization of women's bodies"[10] (which, by the way, he
never really analyzes) in how sexuality, is, note the militaristic
term, deployed? That is, if sexuality is practiced against women
in the process of men's pursuit of pleasure, isn't that significant?
When you know that you have been kept from knowing this information by stigmatizing of assaulted women so that the violation was a shameful fact about her that never went away instead of a shameful fact about what was done to her such that
no one rested until it was made right; when you know that now
you have this information for the first time, wouldn't your analysis of the past have to change?

I take the primary historical impulse to be not forgetting
what happened. It leads me to an historical hypothesis about
women's experience of sexuality historically, once sexual abuse
is included within it. Probably, whatever there was of pleasure
in the past has been amply documented in all this elegiac writing. I would hypothesize that while ideologies about sex and
sexuality may ebb and flow, and the ways they attach themselves to gender and to women's status may alter, that the actual practices of sex may look relatively flat. In particular, the

---

[9]Diana Russell did this calculation at my request on her data base.
[10]Foucault, *History of Sexuality* 1:104.

sexualization of aggression or the eroticization of power and the fusion of that with gender such that the one who is the target or object of sexuality is the subordinate, is a female, effeminized if a man, is relatively constant. And that hierarchy is always done through gender in some way, even if it is playing with gender or reversing gender or same-gendering, it is still all about gender. Gender hierarchy is either being played with or played out. The hypothesis would be that the practice of misogyny as sex may have been present all along. Even if it is being practiced in a more virulent form here and now, maybe we could find it in history, lying there like a snake coiled on a cold day. The implicit argument here is this: if you measure the history of sexuality against a standard of sexual equality, defined here as the absence of sexual force as normative, variation may not be the most prominent feature of the historical landscape. The timelessness of this picture, among its effects, highlights the implicit assumption of inequality in the variation models.

For such suggestions, feminists have been called ahistorical. Oh, dear. We have disrespected the profundity and fascination of all the different ways in which men fuck us in order to emphasize that however they do it, they do it. And they do it to us. If that hasn't changed all that much, enough to fit their definition of what a history has to look like, I submit to you that that is not our fault.

So what *has* changed? If it has got to change to make a history, what is different? If the landscape has to have edges like a field has to have walls for us to get our minds around it—I am alluding here to what I think is one of the most important things the study of women has to offer, which is its relative edgelessness, its non-neatly divided, unpartitioned quality—one needs to ask, what would a change be? I am not here disputing all the changes historians have found in the landscape of sexuality. I am saying that underneath all of these hills and valleys, these ebbs and flows, there is this bedrock, this tide that has not changed much, namely male supremacy and the subordination of women. By this standard—under which equality would be a change—what *has* changed?.

In the modern period, there have been some changes for the worse, away from equality. Women are expected to like sexual force better and better, partially as a product of the movement for sexual liberation and partially as a result of what produced that movement. Freedom for women's sexuality becomes freedom for male sexual aggression. During this period, it appears that the actual level of sexual abuse to which women are subjected has escalated. Age cohorts show a dramatically greater likelihood of rape if a woman matures during the sixties than if she matures during the thirties.[11] The FBI statistics—and the FBI is always the last to know—show increases as well.[12] One also finds some indications of a drop in the age of the average rapist, which would dramatically increase the pool of men that women might legitimately take as a security risk. One used to be able to feel safe with thirteen- or fourteen-year-old boys, but this cannot be assumed anymore, when five- or six-year-old boys are raping babies.[13]

I also think that more and more children are being sexually assaulted, including boys. The studies show a figure of 2-14 percent of boys are sexually abused as children.[14] I think it is much higher. There are lots of reasons boys don't report. They include the shame and stigma of being treated like a girl—not a problem for girls, who are treated as who they are. For boys, there is a drop in status; raped men also experience this. There is also the tendency of girls, as they grow up, to face as abuse their experiences of sexual abuse as children. Whatever they

[11]Russell, *Sexual Exploitation* 55–57. ("The tragic finding of this survey is an alarming increase in the true rape rate over the years.") It is true that women feel more able to report now, but this compares women reporting under the same conditions about being assaulted during different times. It is also possible that younger women are more likely to report rape than older women.

[12]In 1987, the forcible rape total rose 15 percent over 1982 and 42 percent over 1977, according to the Justice Department. In 1989, it rose 7 percent over 1985 and 14 percent over 1980. From 1983 to 1987, the female forcible rape rate rose 11 percent. *Uniform Crime Reports* (1987, 1988, 1989, 1990). Note these are *reported* rapes, those that are not "unfounded" by the police.

[13]Elizabeth Holtzman, "Rape—The Silence is Criminal," *New York Times* 5 May 1989: sec. 1, 35. Ms. Holtzman reports "startling increases in rape by teenagers" such that New York City, in the two years before her article, saw a 27 percent increase in rape arrests of boys under eighteen and a 200 percent increase of boys under thirteen. No such trend has yet registered in federal crime statistics.

[14]David Finkelhor, *Child Sexual Abuse: Theory and Research* (New York: Free Press, 1984).

experienced as children, by the time of their late 20s, 30s, or 40s, they remember it, and they clearly feel that it was not all right with them: not then, not now. Even if it felt like sex, even if that is all they have ever known as sex, it was abuse. With boys, some of them make the abuse into sex. However they experienced it at the time, as adult men, it becomes a liberating, a loving education, what they wanted. The abuse is sexualized, hence it is not abuse, which means it is not reported as such.[15]

Another change is the explosion in the pornography industry. Social life is increasingly saturated with it and its sexualized misogyny. We also have more information on the internal dynamic of pornography: the more pornography one consumes, the more violent and aggressive it needs to be to produce a sexual response.[16] Pornography increasingly desensitizes its consumers to abuse, as it sexualizes increasingly intense violation. This makes more and more force necessary for sexual arousal. Looking for what makes things move, if we know there is more sexual abuse, perhaps an explanation for it might be the one thing that is documented to make people experience abuse as sex.[17] That is, there is a connection between these changes.

Now let's go back to our histories of sexuality. These histories, on the whole, do not theorize gender. For example, Foucault in his second volume, *The Use of Pleasure*, brackets male dominance, the subjugation of women, and the prohibition of incest at the outset as essentially outside history. This is because "the extent and constancy of these phenomena in their various forms are well known."[18] Having gotten the flat and unbounded out of the way, we can proceed with sexuality and its history. Gone with them is a *discussion* of the role of misogyny in sexuality and the place of rape, sexual harassment, forced prostitution, and pornography—sexual practices from objectification to murder. I know no grounds for believing these practices to be unique

[15]This is an impression, a sense influenced by discussions of the subject with Andrea Dworkin, not an interpretation for which evidence is yet available.

[16]See citations at n. 6, p. 304 in my *Toward a Feminist Theory of the State* (Cambridge: Harvard University Press, 1989).

[17]Diana E. H. Russell, "Pornography and Rape: A Causal Model," *Political Psychology* 9 (1988): 41–74.

[18]Michel Foucault, *The Uses of Pleasure*, trans. Robert Hurley (New York: Pantheon Press, 1985) 14.

to our time. Suggestions are otherwise. What do they mean for the historians' precious sexuality?

At this point, I would reverse the usual assumption that sexual abuse is exceptional and cabined off and means nothing for what people generally practice as sex. I would argue that sexuality is the set of practices that inscribes gender as unequal in social life. On this level, sexual abuse and its frequency reveal and participate in a common structural reality with everyday sexual practice.[19] The erotic sexualizes power differentials; the experience of hierarchy is the experience of sex under unequal conditions. The historical task would be to explore and map this location and to capture it as a dynamic, one that happens always through gender. Then we would see how much racism, genocide, homophobia, and class exploitation we could explain. This would not be a history of who gets pleasure and how, but a history of who uses who for pleasure and how they get away with it.

Sources that help me in this project include a book by Eva Keuls, *The Reign of the Phallus*, which gives a rather different interpretation of classical Greece and those vases.[20] German scholar Klaus Theweleit has written a brilliant study, *Männerphantasien*, meaning men's fantasies, translated under the less threatening title, *Male Fantasies*, about the deployment of male sexuality in and as fascism culminating in Nazism.[21] One almost forgives him his Freudianism because the analysis and the materials are so rich, perceptive, and evocative. An English historian, Sheila Jeffreys, has written two excellent books. *The Spinster and Her Enemies* treats the suppression of the early feminist critiques of the use of sex for the subjection of women in England before and after the First World War.[22] *Anticlimax* traces the development of sexology as the science of the suppression of women's attempts to resist exploitation through inter-

---

[19]I argue this in more depth in chapter 7, "Sexuality," in *Toward a Feminist Theory of the State*.

[20]Eva C. Keuls, *The Reign of the Phallus: Sexual Politics in Ancient Athens* (New York: Harper and Row, 1985).

[21]Klaus Theweleit, *Male Fantasies, Volume 1: Women, Floods, Bodies, History*, trans. Stephen Conway, with Erica Carter and Chris Turner (Minneapolis: University of Minnesota Press, 1987).

[22]Sheila Jeffreys, *The Spinster and Her Enemies: Feminism and Sexuality, 1880–1930* (Boston: Pandora Press, 1985).

course from the Second World War to toda:
also English, has written an exceptional w(
about the rise of the drivenness of male sexu
an imperative.  He traces the thrust to gettin
particularly stunning analysis of Charcot's
spectacle and of the spectralization process, :
looked-at thing.  He understands gender.[24]  T.
*Making Sex*, historically traces how models o     ____ difference
have been predicated on views of the body and the place of nature in sexuality and reproduction.  While the treatment could
use a tighter grasp on the politics of male dominance, gender
ideology is effectively disconnected from known biology.[25]  Indeed, in his history, destiny is closer to making anatomy than
the other way around.  You may have heard of the book by Jeffrey Masson, *The Assault on Truth*, which gives an historical account of Freud's rejection of his original belief that his patients
were sexually assaulted when they said they were—giving rise
to his theories of fantasy, the unconscious, and repression.  It
seems Freud could not hold onto the belief that all those men
could actually have hurt all those children. [26]

Rather than a monumental history, the project building here
is a critical history: in Nietzsche's terms, the history of those
who suffer and are in need of liberation.[27]  Especially for women,
but not for women alone, such a history would rely on not forgetting what you know and refusing to forget what you cannot
know.  It would reject the posture of dominance in making the
history that feels good.  It would be an insubordinate history.  Its
task would be to give sexuality a history so that women may
have a future.

---

[23]Sheila Jeffreys, *Anticlimax: A Feminist Perspective on the Sexual Revolution* (London: The Women's Press, 1990).

[24]Stephen Heath, *The Sexual Fix* (New York: Shocken Books, 1982).

[25]Thomas Laqueur, *Making Sex: Body and Gender from the Greeks to
Freud* (Cambridge, Mass: Harvard University Press, 1990).

[26]Jeffrey Moussaieff Masson, *The Assault on Truth: Freud's Suppression
of the Seduction Theory* (New York: Farrar, Straus and Giroux, 1984).

[27]Critical history "belongs to the living man . . . so far as he suffers
and is in need of liberation" (Nietzsche 14).

## Discussion[28]

**Question:** It seems to me that Foucault's approach to sex and power and his argument that sexuality is socially constructed could produce an opening for a more gendered analysis of sexuality. Why, then, do you regard him as a theorist who simply works along in the same old Freudian way?

**Answer:** In regard to the connection between knowledge and power, my theory of sexuality was first conceived in the very early 1970s in the context of the women's movement. As a result, when Foucault's work on sexuality came out in translation, to the extent some of his analysis developed similar connections, I did not read him with the same sense of discovery that many people seemed to, since I had my analysis before. It still amazes me that when he writes some of the same formal arguments feminists have made, but leaves gender out, it is taken as pathbreaking. I would have liked to see him take feminism seriously. I will never forgive him for dying before I could confront him with it.

It does seem to me that for a man who understands so much about epistemology, power, knowledge, and law, it takes the tenacity of genius to avoid gender as nearly completely as he does. I think his denial of gender is fundamental, and necessary to his perspective. He says, to say yes to sex is not necessarily to say no to power. Closer to reality is: to say yes to sex is to say yes to power. The point is, his statement was not a critique. He was not saying, "now here's what's wrong with sex: on my analysis, it's about power." He lacks that critical edge. Unless you see gender, the consequences of sex being about power for men and powerlessness for women, hence revealing a sytematic problem, are invisible.

Power in Foucault is everywhere in general, hence nowhere in particular. Some of his most wonderful insights involve minute social actions and interactions. But diffusion of power to him looks like fragmentation of power to us. Feminists see a structure to the diffusion, making it totalized and pervasive. We see power everywhere at once but not no place in particular or

---

[28]The following discussion accompanied Catharine A. MacKinnon's lecture at the Institute for the Humanities.

everywhere equally. It solidifies into fixed molds, takes rigid forms, and constitutes certain social divisions. For Foucault, power is constantly in flux and being rearranged and reinvented, even as it is being enforced. For us, it is always being reproduced and enforced. We analyze powerlessness a lot more than he does, too, hence our focus on sexual abuse and his bracketing of it. For him, power reposes nowhere and with no one in particular, so it doesn't necessarily mean hierarchy, certainly not gender hierarchy. It means that I can pick up a piece of it, play with it, use it or resist it, and get off.

When he misses gender, he misses how power is organized sexually, hence socially. He sees sexuality structured so that repression keeps some people from getting access to pleasure, while at the same time keeping them obsessively focused on it. The tension between that structuring and that attempt to get it is his sexual crucible. What he misses is that desire itself, including his, is constituted here, that gender is this crucible, and that society—with sexuality itself, not just its control—is structured along these lines, which are lines of power. I am attempting to suggest what I find useful in Foucault; at the same time, what he misses—namely, women and women's subordinate status as—is, I think, fairly fatal.

**Question:** In what way can we express sexuality's history so that women can have a future without recreating a genre of historical pornography?

**Answer:** We could start by putting pornography in the Smithsonian, where we keep other extinct species and atavisms and avatars of the past. It is difficult to talk real about sexuality without at times participating in some of its abuses through words. But this is not because it is difficult to avoid speaking pornography.

Let me give you an example. In connection with the pornography ordinance forwarded by Andrea Dworkin, the brilliant feminist writer, and me, the Minneapolis City Council conducted hearings. A lot of people came to talk about the ways they had been violated through pornography. A gay man spoke movingly about how as a boy he had learned from heterosexual pornography that to love a man meant to accept his violence; as a result he had accepted the abuse of his first lover, because he wanted to be loved by men. (I hope this disabuses anyone who was about to conclude that any of this is biological.) Women and girls told of the role of pornography in a shattering array of sexual abuse. The record of the hearings is a record of abuse in which people speak in graphic and sometimes explicit terms about sex. Which is not to say it is sexually explicit in the legal sense. It is not pornography. It documents sexual abuse in a way that presents the abuse as abuse.

One way to give sexuality its history is to create a written record of the reality of this abuse in a way that does not sexualize it. I know people take the view that sexuality is in the mind of the observer, but as it turns out, what is sexual is a great deal more socially determined than people think. I have not heard that our hearings have been used as masturbation materials.

There was one disturbing incident that substantiates your concern about how to create a history of sexuality without making it pornography. *Penthouse* took some of the Minneapolis accounts—not from the hearings but from a press conference in support of the ordinance—and put them in pornography, in *Penthouse Forum*. A native American woman found in her mailbox her story ripped out of *Forum* with "We're going to get you, squaw" scrawled on it. They took her resistance to violation and turned it into a way she could be further violated, intimidated, threatened, harassed, and reduced. They can do this. But *they* made her pornography; she didn't; she just provided the material. In one way or another, we are all always that kind of material; only some of it is also part of fighting back and some of it is not.

What I end up thinking is that we have got to leave a trace. They have endless vehicles for sexualizing our abuse. They use us any way they can, including every form of resistance we invent. The question is, what are *we* going to do. They make pornography out of us, out of Andrea Dworkin, for example. Every time we go into rooms like this, we have to wonder how many of you have read about us first in pornography, as pornography. This is done to us because we oppose it, but it is also done to all women simply because we are women.

We are trying to make sexuality have a history by drawing a line across it called equality. Our goal is to give it a past called inequality, so it isn't this flat continuous tide with little ebbs and flows marking all the variations we have ever been permitted to know. This work *will* be used to make us into more pornography. Until we win, both our silence and our speech can be and will be made into pornography at any time. If we had the power to stop that, we would have the power to stop them from abusing us, from making sexual abuse into sex and accounts of sexual abuse into pornography in the first place.

I do know that we have produced a lot that does not seem to be useable as pornography. For example, contrast *Deep Throat*, the film that Linda Marchiano was forced to make as "Linda Lovelace," with *Ordeal*, her account of being forced to make it. See the difference between her version and theirs. As one measure of it, *Deep Throat* is the largest grossing film in pornography's history, by some reports. *Ordeal* is hardly even an underground success. If people responded to *Ordeal* the way they respond to *Deep Throat*, we could track it financially. The woman speaking in her own voice, saying "This is how I was forced," is not the same, sexually, as the woman through the pornographer's eye view, even when she is being forced in exactly the same way she describes being forced in the book. The difference is between abuse as sex and abuse as abuse—it is a vexed difference when abuse of women is sex, but it is a difference we nonetheless have been able to make.

**Question:** Do you have a view on whether or not the stories and names of rape victims should be printed or not?

**Answer:** Yes, I do. I think that if a woman doesn't want her name printed, she should not be made into pornography, so to speak, by the media. One of the reasons women don't report rape is they don't want to be this kind of pornography; that is, they don't want their abuse made into a spectacle for other people's sexual pleasure. It is bad enough having to go to court where you have to make pornography of yourself in order to explain what happened to you, to recount the abuse, while some observers get sexual pleasure out of your pain. The public presentation and representation of her rape is something a woman should have control over. This does not mean that the press should be prohibited from publishing information about rapes.

If a woman wishes the account of her own rape to appear in the media, that's fine. It is a courageous choice. Of course, it is easier to come forward if you are white and your assailant is a Black stranger, because you are more likely to be believed, rather than further assaulted, by the media. It is marginally more likely to be believed that this was not something you wanted, that you were forced.    The hierarchy of credibility women encounter on reporting is racist.    (In reality, most rapes are within racial groups;    overwhelmingly white women are raped by white men and Black women by Black men.)    In spite of this, Black women have brought some of the earliest and most innovative cases of sexual abuse to court; they brought legal claims before there were recognized legal claims to bring.

I do not agree that the way to bring rape into the light of day, to reduce its social shame and stigma, is through making an involuntary display of victims.  This disclosure is not the media's decision to force.  Once a woman is raped, she ought at least to be entitled to decide whether she wishes to become a vehicle of social change.

**Question:** You emphasized the importance of taking women's reports of their sexual experiences as being accurate and truthful.  You also claim that it is impossible to have equality in heterosexual sex.  What do you say, then, to women who sincerely report that they have experienced mutuality and equality in heterosexual sex?  Are they just victims of false consciousness?

**Answer:** "False consciousness" is not a term I use; I sometimes say that I think people are wrong.  I regard those who say they have sex under conditions of equality somewhat the way I regard those who tell me they have never been discriminated against.  My first reaction is, I am really happy for you; my next reaction is, maybe you are missing something; my final reaction is, just wait.

The truth is that women and men experience sexuality under conditions of inequality between the sexes.  Gender is a division of power; sexuality, in my argument, is a dynamic in that.  A similar analysis can be made of work as an exploitive process through which value is created; and through that process, people are constructed as members of classes.  This does not mean that no worker ever has a good day or nobody has fulfilling work.  It does not mean that there is no such thing as "my work," or that opposition to the class structure in which people struggle out forms of fulfillment is impossible.  It just means that it is *never not there.*

What I have found lately, particularly with younger men, is that something is going on out there with these men for whom the women's movement and feminism are part of the taken-for-granted obviousness of their lives. They are struggling deeply with this issue of having sex as equals. Deeply, in their bodies, they do not want to oppress women. It is not that they like to think they are not oppressing women while getting all the benefits of doing so. They do not want to live in a world that is like that. They do not say that I am wrong about this. They are the first to say that this problem *does* exist. The women who are with them don't say: I don't have this problem; all the sex we have is equal; reality may be gendered everywhere else but not in my bedroom; when we go in there we are level equals. In other words, the people who could most credibly say, "I'm not doing that," are the last to say it, because they are facing the difficulty of not doing it. I suspect there is an inverse relation between actually confronting this problem in your own life and saying you have solved it.

It seems to be easier at the beginning of a relationship to think you have solved this problem. Having observed cycle after cycle of many of my friends, it seems we have, on average, about two weeks of equality.

There is a lot of hope on this subject, hope that is hard to justify on the basis of experience and easier to explain on the basis of myth. I think many people, particularly women, want what I want. They want equality. Some seem to want it so hard that they want themselves into thinking they already have it, even though society remains unequal. I want us to face inequality so that we can actually have equality—as a rule not an exception, a reality not a dream.

**Question:** Following up on the last question, would you comment on those who say that you're right about inequality being everywhere but that women genuinely take pleasure in sex, at least a lot of the time, and that it's not all abusive. Anthologies such as *Powers of Desire* essentially say that. The historical record of women taking pleasure and getting some is an important piece of the story, but it doesn't seem to be part of your story at all. You're saying that sex as it is now does not necessarily amount to equality, but it is an important imperative for women.

**Answer:** Any woman who wants to talk about how much pleasure she gets out of unequal sex has a forum and a publisher. The pornographers will sign her up if no one else will. Getting pleasure is not my particular agenda; getting equality is. If sexual pleasure is in the way, we need to think about it. A small number of women with loud voices, magnified through every available means of publication, have argued that they love it the way it is. There is no lack of this story being told out there but a glut of it.

It seems to me that this fact documents the way male supremacy uniquely works: it creates its subordinate group that eroticizes its subordination, enjoys it, feels fulfilled by it, believes this is what a woman really is. The imperative is to make the perfect fuck available to us all as the limit of our quest. Some women say that is what they want. Giving us that was what the sexual revolution said it was about. Some of us apparently have what we wanted, at least so they say, so I guess their problems are solved. Some of the rest of us still have a problem, though: women are being savaged through the way that imperative freed and legitimated male sexual aggression.

It would help if those who make your point made it the way you did: equality is important but pleasure is too. I have not heard the *Powers of Desire* crowd say that meaningful equality was important in this area. This is because it is essential to their position that inequality is not a problem for sex so long as it produces pleasure, that inequality in the pursuit of orgasm is bliss. Their basic query is not what about equality but what about our orgasms. If we have equality, what would become of the power difference that gives sex its charge, they wonder. How can we have sex if we have equality, they want to know. History will (finally) end, the population problem will be solved, people will have sex two or three times at carefully plotted moments in order to have children, a few more for good measure. . .

Unlike you, I see no concession from them that equality matters on any level approximate to pleasure. The two are regarded as antithetical. I myself do not disagree that people eroticize dominance and subordination. I theorize this very thing. It would be very surprising if men eroticized dominance, practiced it, and enforced it over women, and there were no women who eroticized subordination. The surprise is that so many of us don't, that so many women do not enjoy force, don't like to be raped, and that everybody knows what "being fucked" means.

**Question:** In a lesbian relationship, is the power relationship different? And could you comment on lesbian erotica?

**Answer:** In one way, the power relationship is different in a same-sex context, both for women and for men, and in another way it is not. It is altered because the people are not unequal on the basis of sex. But it is not altered because power is not absent. (I think Foucault would be the first to agree with me on that, except he didn't mind, and I do.) Power is there both in the construction of sexuality and in social life as a gendered individual. Women and men are still women and men in the world, even when they are gay or lesbian. That makes lesbian women distinctively subordinated within a subordinate group, women, and gay men distinctively subordinated within a dominant group, men.

The paradigm of sex that is eroticized in society for us all, I think, is top-down sex, in the hierarchical sense. When you alter the gender piece, you make the power divisions less automatic and can open a space for greater equality, but the top-down structure of sexuality as such does not necessarily go away. Heterosexuality is constructed around gender, as the dominant paradigm of sex; homosexuality is constructed around gender, as the subordinated paradigm of sex. Both are deeply invested in gender, if in different ways. It is important to a gay man, for example, that it is a *man* he is with. In that sense, gender, therefore power—however rearranged—is there.

A great deal of so-called lesbian erotica is pornography. Men buy it and men use it. "Lesbian" is a theme in male pornography: two for the price of one. Men get to watch women doing what men think women do when men are not around. Lesbianism here is a male sexual taste. Your question is, is lesbian pornography any different, or what could make it different? Andrea Dworkin and I define pornography as graphically sexually explicit materials that subordinate women. Power is obviously involved because subordination is involved. Erotica seems to mean anything that is not pornography that people feel is sexual. Now the question is, if no one is being subordinated, is it sex to anyone? Is erotica a null set?

In sexual materials "by women, for women," the hierarchy between the consumer and the women in the materials is still there. The women are things, the consumers are persons. This is a political argument, not a legal argument, that a hierarchy is there. This raises the question: why do we need a person made into a thing before we can experience ourselves sexually? What is this "I—it" relation in sex? How is that "ours"? What is lesbian about that? If lesbian sexuality, as many argue, criticizes the deep structure of male dominant sexuality, affirms women and explores what equal sex and life could be like, what are we doing making women into things? How does it improve using women that women are using them? Should we dignify it as a special case of the use of women because it is for women? The critique of heterosexuality central to lesbian feminism is totally sold out here, as is even a simple-minded critique of sexism.

There is also the political question of why is sex pictures and why are pictures sex. Does the camera *do* anything, is the question. How come, with sex, it has to be in pictures or it can't happen? How come people don't have a sexuality or know about sex unless they see it in a picture? How come when you see a picture of sex you are supposed to have sex? Why is it that is the way sex is? Say you see a picture of Mount Everest, a good picture, with the wind and snow blowing. You will say, I got a real chill. But if somebody puts a thermometer in your mouth, your temperature will not go down, and nobody will think it is a less good picture. When you look at pornography, the penis is supposed to go up, you are actually supposed to experience sex. Why, and what does this tell us about sex itself ?

# PART TWO.  REGIMES OF KNOWLEDGE AND DESIRE

# THE WORK OF GENDER AND SEXUALITY IN THE ELIZABETHAN DISCOURSE OF DISCOVERY

## Louis Montrose

"Guiana is a countrey that hath yet her maydenhead"
—Sir Walter Ralegh, *The Discoverie . . . of Guiana*

*I*

In a recent essay on gender as a category of historical analysis, Joan Wallach Scott advances two integrally connected propositions: "Gender is a constitutive element of social relationships based upon perceived differences between the sexes, and gender is a primary way of signifying relationships of power."[1] The first proposition "involves four interrelated elements: first, culturally available symbols that evoke multiple (and often contradictory) representations"; "second, normative concepts that set forth interpretations of the meanings of the symbols, that attempt to limit and contain their metaphoric possibilities" (43); third, the realizations of those various alternative or contestatory possibilities that are marginalized or suppressed by the normative or dominant, and which must be recovered by subsequent critical-historical analysis; and fourth, the employment of such historically specific (though not necessarily stable or consistent) cultural representations in the making of gendered subjective identities. Scott's second proposition refers to gender as one of the fundamental modes in which ideological and material realities are organized:

---

An earlier version of this essay has been published as "The Work of Gender in the Discourse of Discovery," *Representations* 33 (Winter 1991). For the present version, I have made some revisions, cuts, and additions to the text, and have considerably shortened the notes.

[1]Joan Wallach Scott, *Gender and the Politics of History* (New York: Columbia University Press, 1988) 42.

Established as an objective set of references, concepts of gender structure perception and the concrete and symbolic organization of all social life. To the extent that these references establish distributions of power (differential control over or access to material and symbolic resources), gender becomes implicated in the conception and construction of power itself. (45)

From this perspective, as "a persistent and recurrent way of enabling the signification of power in the West," the discourse of gender is not always or necessarily "literally about gender itself" (45). Among the flexible strengths of this analytical model are that it conceptualizes gender in terms of the reciprocally constituted and historically variable categories of Man and Woman; and that it also comprehends such gender systems as themselves reciprocally related, in multiple and shifting ways, to other modes of cultural, political, and economic organization and experience. Furthermore, to view gender representations historically—in terms of a multivalent ideological process that perpetually generates, constrains, and contests cultural meanings and values—is to reveal, beneath the apparent stability and consistency of collective structures, myriad local and individual sites of social reproduction, variation, and change.

This analytical model provides a theoretical groundplot for the particular historical and critical, local and individual, concerns of the present essay. At the center of these concerns is the gendering of the proto-colonialist discourse of discovery prevalent in Western Europe in the sixteenth century; the projection into the New World of European representations of gender—and of sexual conduct, a distinct but equally *cultural* phenomenon—and the articulation of those representations with new projects of economic exploitation and geo-political domination. I discuss some instances of the gendering of the New World as female and the sexualizing of its exploration, conquest, and settlement. The frame of reference for this discussion is not a closed or autonomous discourse of gender or sexuality but rather an open field of historically specific ideological conjunctures and exchanges, within which issues of gender and sexual conduct participate.

Early modern Europe's construction of its collective Other in "the New World"—its construction of the "savage" or the "Indian"—was accomplished by the symbolic and material de-

struction of the indigenous peoples of the western hemisphere, in
systematic attempts to destroy their bodies and their wills, to
suppress their cultures, and to efface their histories. This process
of proto-colonialist "othering" also engages, interacts with, and
mediates between two distinctive Elizabethan discourses: one, articulating the relationship between Englishmen and Spaniards;
the other, articulating the relationship between the female
monarch and her male subjects. The latter discourse is inflected
by the anomalous status of Queen Elizabeth—who is at once a
*ruler*, in whose name the discoveries of her male subjects are authorized and performed; and also a *woman*, whose political relationship to those subjects is itself frequently articulated in the
discourses of gender and sexuality.[2] The paradoxes and contradictions implicit in each of these discourses are foregrounded
when they are brought together in a conjuncture with the discourse of discovery. Within the intertwined and unstable terms
of collective national and gender identity, I focus upon an individual   Englishman   and   Elizabethan   subject—Sir   Walter
Ralegh—whose production of these discourses in his writings and
performances is marked by the idiosyncracies of his personal history and situation.

The writings of critics, too, are necessarily subject to historical and idiosyncratic marking. I remain uncomfortably aware
that the trajectory of this essay courts the danger of reproducing
what it purports to analyze: namely, the appropriation and effacement of the experience of both native Americans and women
by the dominant discourse of early modern European colonialism
and patriarchy. It is necessary, I believe, not only to resist such
a dominant discourse but also to resist too rigid an understanding of its dominance. In other words, it is not only necessary to
recover instances of overt resistance and transgression but also
to anatomize those elements of heterogeneity and instability,
permeability and contradiction, within the dominant discourse

---

[2] I have discussed other aspects of this discourse in detail in earlier
studies.   Of particular relevance are "'Shaping Fantasies': Figurations of
Gender and Power in Elizabethan Culture," *Representations* 2 (Spring 1983):
61–94; and "The Elizabethan Subject and the Spenserian Text," *Literary
Theory/Renaissance Texts*, ed. Patricia Parker and David Quint (Baltimore:
Johns Hopkins University Press, 1986) 303–40. A few passages from those
earlier studies reappear in the present essay in revised form.

that perpetually forestall ideological closure.[3]  My concern is to locate and discover a few of the textual sites where this dominant discourse is under stress.  That said, I should add that I resist the illusion of having wholly resisted my own complicity in its operations.

## II

By the 1570s, allegorical personifications of America as a nude female with feathered headdress had begun to appear in engravings and paintings, on maps and title pages, throughout Western Europe.[4]  Perhaps the most resonant of such images is Jan van der Straet's drawing of Vespucci's discovery of America, widely disseminated in print in the late sixteenth century by means of Theodore Galle's engraving (fig. 1).[5]  Here a naked female figure, crowned with feathers, upraises herself from her hammock to meet the gaze of the armored and robed male figure who has just come ashore; she extends her right arm toward

---

[3]I discuss some of these larger issues of theory and method more fully in "New Historicisms," *Redrawing the Boundaries of Literary Study*, ed. Giles Gunn and Stephen Greenblatt (New York: Modern Language Association, in press).

[4]See Hugh Honour, *The New Golden Land: European Images of America from the Discoveries to the Present Time* (New York: Pantheon, 1975) ch. 4, esp. plates 76–84.

[5]See the reproduction of van der Straet's drawing in Claire le Corbeiller, "Miss America and Her Sisters: Personifications of the Four Parts of the World," *Metropolitan Museum of Art Bulletin*, 2nd ser. 19 (1961): 209–23; fig. 1, 211 ("The Discovery of America, by Jan van der Straet [Stradanus]. Flemish, about 1575. Pen and bistre heightened with white").  Galle's engraving was originally issued in the early 1580s as the first in a set of twenty based on drawings of Stradanus, with the general title *Nova Reperta*; all the other engravings in this series illustrate inventions and technologies. The twenty engravings of *Nova Reperta* and the additional four engravings of *Americae Retectio* (celebrating Columbus, Vespucci, and Magellan) are reproduced in *"New Discoveries": The Sciences, Inventions and Discoveries of the Middle Ages and the Renaissance as represented in 24 engravings issued in the early 1580s by Stradanus* (Norwalk, Connecticut: Burndy Library, 1953).

Figure 1. *America*, c. 1580.
Engraving by Theodor Galle after a
drawing by Jan van der Straet (c.
1575). Photo: The Burndy Library,
Norwalk, Conn.

him, apparently in a gesture of wonder—or, perhaps, of appre-
hension. Standing with his feet firmly planted upon the ground,
Vespucci observes the personified and feminized space that will
bear his name. This recumbent figure, now discovered and
roused from her torpor, is about to be hailed, claimed, and possessed as *America*. As the motto included in Galle's engraving
puts it, "Americen Americus retexit, & Semel vocavit inde sem-
per excitam"—"Americus rediscovers America; he called her
once and thenceforth she was always awake." This theme is
discreetly amplified by the presence of a sloth, which regards the
scene of awakening from its own shaded spot upon the tree behind America. Vespucci carries with him the variously empow-
ering ideological and technological instruments of civilization, exploration, and conquest: a cruciform staff with a banner bearing
the Southern cross, a navigational astrolabe, and a sword—the
mutually reinforcing emblems of belief, empirical knowledge, and
violence. At the left, behind Vespucci, the prows of the ships

that facilitate the expansion of European hegemony enter the pictorial space of the New World; on the right, behind America, representatives of the indigenous fauna are displayed as if emerging from an American interior at once natural and strange.

Close to the picture's vanishing point—in the distance, yet at the center—a group of naked savages, potential subjects of the civilizing process, are preparing a cannibal feast. A severed human haunch is being cooked over the fire; another, already spitted, awaits its turn. America's body pose is partially mirrored by both the apparently female figure who turns the spit and the clearly female figure who cradles an infant as she awaits the feast. Most strikingly, the form of the severed human leg and haunch turning upon the spit precisely inverts and miniaturizes America's own body form. In terms of the pictorial space, this scene of cannibalism is perspectivally distanced, pushed into the background; in terms of the pictorial surface, however, it is placed at the center of the visual field, between the mutual gazes of Americus and America, and directly above the latter's outstretched arm.

I think it possible that the represented scene alludes to an incident reported to have taken place during the third of Vespucci's alleged four voyages and recounted in his famous Letter of 1504. I quote from the mid-sixteenth-century English translation by Richard Eden:

> At the length they broughte certayne women, which shewed them selves familier towarde the Spaniardes: Whereupon they sent forth a young man, beyng very strong and quicke, at whom as the women wondered, and stode gasinge on him and feling his apparell: there came sodeynly a woman downe from a mountayne, bringing with her secretly a great stake, with which she gave him such a stroke behynde, that he fell dead on the earth. The other wommene foorthwith toke him by the legges, and drewe him to the mountayne, whyle in the mean tyme the men of the countreye came foorth with bowes and arrowes, and shot at oure men. . . . The women also which had slayne the yong man, cut him in pieces even

in the sight of the Spaniardes, shewinge them the pieces, and rosting them at a greate fyre.[6]

The elements of savagery, deceit, and cannibalism central to the emergent European discourse on the inhabitants of the New World are already in place in this very early example.  Of particular significance here is the blending of these basic ingredients of proto-colonialist ideology with a crude and anxious misogynistic fantasy, a powerful conjunction of the savage and the female.

This conjunction is reinforced in another, equally striking Vespuccian anecdote.  Vespucci presents a different account of his third voyage in his other extant Letter, this one dated 1503 and addressed to Lorenzo Piero Francesco de Medici.  Like the other letter, this one was in wide European circulation in printed translations within a few years of its date.  Here Vespucci's marvelous ethnography includes the following observation:

> Another custom among them is sufficiently shameful, and beyond all human credibility.  Their women, being very libidinous, make the penis of their husbands swell to such a size as to appear deformed; and this is accomplished by a certain artifice, being the bite of some poisonous animal, and by reason of this many lose their virile organ and remain eunuchs.[7]

The oral fantasy of female insatiability and male dismemberment realized in the other letter as a cannibalistic confrontation of alien cultures is here translated into a precise genital and domestic form.  Because the husband's sexual organ is under the

---

[6]*A treatyse of the newe India . . . after the description of Sebastian Munster in his boke of universall Cosmographie*, trans. Rycharde Eden (London, 1553) rpt. in *The first Three English books on America*, ed. Edward Arber (1885; rpt., New York: Kraus Reprint, 1971) 39.  Latin, Italian, and French editions seem to have been in print within three or four years of the original date of Vespucci's letter.  It was on the basis of this work that, in 1507, the cosmographer Martin Waldseemuller first used the name "America" on a map to mark the southern region of the New World.

Throughout this study, I have silently modernized obsolete typographical conventions in quotations from Elizabethan texts.

[7]*The Letters of Amerigo Vespucci*, ed. Clements R. Markham, The Hakluyt Society, 1st series, n. 90 (1894; rpt., New York: Burt Franklin, n. d.) 46.

control of his wife and is wholly subject to her ambiguous desires, the very enhancement of his virility becomes the means of his emasculation.

In the light of Vespucci's anecdotes, the compositional centrality of van der Straet's apparently incidental background scene takes on new significance: It is at the center of the composition in more ways than one, for it may be construed as generating or necessitating the compensatory foreground scene which symbolically contains or displaces it. In van der Straet's visualization of discovery as the advance of civilization, what is closer to the horizon is also closer to the point of origin: It is where "we" have come from—a prior episode in the history of contacts between Europeans and native Americans and an earlier episode in the history of human society; and it is now what must be controlled—a cultural moment that is to be put firmly, decisively behind us. In the formal relationship of proportion and inversion existing between America's leg and what I suppose to be that of the dismembered Spanish youth, I find a figure for the dynamic of gender and power in which the collective imagination of early modern Europe articulates its confrontation with alien cultures. The supposed feminine guile and deceit that enable the native women to murder, dismember, and eat a European male are in a relationship of opposition and inversion to the vaunted masculine knowledge and power with which the erect and armored Vespucci will master the prone and naked America. Thus, the interplay between the foreground and background scenes of the van der Straet-Galle composition gives iconic form to the oscillation characterizing Europe's ideological encounter with the New World: an oscillation between fascination and repulsion, sympathy and estrangement, desires to destroy and to assimilate the Other; an oscillation between the confirmation and the subversion of familiar values, beliefs, and perceptual norms.

Michel de Certeau reproduces the engraving of Vespucci's discovery of America as the frontispiece of his book, *The Writing of History*. As he explains in his Preface, to him this image is emblematic of the inception of a distinctively modern discursive practice of historical and cultural knowledge: This historiography subjects its ostensible subject to its own purportedly objective discipline; it ruptures the continuum "between a subject and an object of the operation, between a *will to write* and a *written body* (or a body to be written)." For de Certeau, the history of this modern writing of history begins in the sixteenth century with "the 'ethnographical' organization of writing in its relation with 'primitive', 'savage', 'traditional', or 'popular' orality that it establishes as its other." Thus, for him, the tableau of Vespucci and America is

> . . . an inaugural scene . . . the conqueror will write the body of the other and trace there his own history. From her he will make a historied body—a blazon—of his labors and phantasms. . . .
> What is really initiated here is a colonization of the body by the discourse of power. This is *writing that conquers*. It will use the New World as if it were a blank, "savage" page on which Western desire will be written.[8]

"America" awakens to find herself written into a story that is not of her own making, to know herself only as a figure in another's dream. When called by Vespucci, she is interpellated within a European history that identifies itself simply as History, single and inexorable; this history can only misrecognize America's history as sleep and mere oblivion. In 1974, when a speaker at the first Indian Congress of South America declared, "today, at the hour of our awakening, we must be our own historians," he spoke as if in a long suppressed response to the ironic awakening of van der Straet's America, her awakening to the effacement of her own past and future.[9]

Although here applied to a graphic representation that is iconic rather than verbal, de Certeau's reflections suggestively raise and conjoin issues that I wish to pursue in relation to Sir Walter Ralegh's *Discoverie of the large, rich, and beautifull Empire of Guiana* (1596) and some other Elizabethan examples of "writing that conquers."[10] These issues include consideration of

[8]Michel de Certeau, *The Writing of History*, trans. Tom Conley (New York: Columbia University Press, 1988) xxv–xxvi.

[9]Address by Justino Quispe Balboa (Aymará, Bolivia) before the first Indian Congress of South America, October 13, 1974; quoted in Michel de Certeau, *Heterologies: Discourse on the Other*, trans. Brian Massumi (Minneapolis: University of Minnesota Press, 1986) 227.

[10]Ralegh's *Discoverie* was first published separately in London in 1596 and went through three editions in that year; it was soon reprinted in the second edition of Richard Hakluyt's monumental collection, *The principal navigations, voyages traffiques & discoveries of the English nation*, 3 vols.

the writing subject's textualization of the body of the Other, neither as mere description nor as genuine encounter but rather as
an act of symbolic violence, mastery, and self-empowerment; and
the tendency of such discursive representation to assume a narrative form, to manifest itself as "a historied body"—in particular, as a mode of symbolic action whose agent is gendered
masculine and whose object is gendered feminine. Rather than
reduce such issues to the abstract, closed, and static terms of a
binary opposition—whether between European and Indian, Culture and Nature, Self and Other, or, indeed, Masculine and
Feminine—I shall endeavor to discriminate among various
sources, manifestations, and consequences of what de Certeau
generalizes as the "Western desire" that is written upon the putatively "blank page" of the New World; and to do so by speci-
fying the ideological configurations of gender and social estate, as
well as national, religious, and/or ethnic identities, that are
brought into play during any particular process of textualization.

## III

The Elizabethan discovery of America is textualized in a report written by Arthur Barlowe and addressed to Sir Walter
Ralegh. Fortuitously, it was on the fourth of July in 1584 that
"the first voyage made to . . . America" at the "charge, and direction" of Sir Walter Ralegh "arrived upon the coast, which we
supposed to be a continent, and firme lande."[11]  This abundant

---

(London, 1598–1600). Illustrated translations were printed in the Latin and
German editions of Théodore de Bry's *Americae*, part 8 (Frankfurt, 1599). I
quote the *Discoverie* from the modern edition of Hakluyt, *Principal Navigations*, 12 vols. (Glasgow, 1904; rpt. New York: Augustus M. Kelley, 1969) 10:
338–431. All parenthetical page references will be to vol. 10 of this edition.

[11]Arthur Barlowe, "The first voyage made to the coastes of America,
with two barkes, wherein were Captaines Master Philip Amadas, and Master Arthur Barlowe, who discovered part of the Countrey, now called Virginia, Anno 1584: Written by one of the said Captaines, and sent to sir Walter Raleigh, knight, at whose charge, and direction, the said voyage was set
foorth," *The Roanoke Voyages 1584–1590: Documents to illustrate the English
voyages to North America under the patent granted to Walter Raleigh in 1584*, ed.

country is called, by the "very handsome, and goodly people" who already inhabit it, "Wingandacoa, (and nowe by her Majestie, Virginia)" (98–99). The Elizabethan antiquary William Camden soon records that Virginia is "so named in honour of Queen Elizabeth, a virgin."[12]    Significantly, the naming of "Virginia" was "the first such imperious act sanctioned by an English monarch."[13]  Having authorized her subjects' acts of discovery and symbolic possession, the English monarch assumes the privilege of naming the land anew and of naming it for herself and for the gender-specific virtue she has so long and so successfully employed as a means of self-empowerment.   Queen Elizabeth participates in an emergent colonialist discourse that works to justify and, symbolically, to effect the expropriation of what it discovers.   Typically, this discourse denies the natural right of possession to indigenous peoples by confirming them to be heathens, savages, and/or foragers who neither cultivate the land nor conceptualize it as real property; or it may symbolically efface the very existence of those indigenous peoples from the places its speakers intend to exploit.  What was Wingandacoa is now rendered a blank page upon which to write Virginia.  Thus, the Virgin Queen verbally reconstitutes the land as a feminine place unknown to man; and by doing so, she also symbolically effaces the indigenous society which already physically and culturally inhabits and possesses that land.  In this royal renaming of Wingandacoa as Virginia, considerations of gender difference interact with considerations of ethnic difference; the discursive power of the inviolate female body serves an emergent imperialist project of exploration, conquest, and settlement.

Although England's first American colony was claimed in her name and named in her honor, Queen Elizabeth herself demonstrated little enthusiasm or material support for the various colonizing ventures that ignited the energy, imagination, and desire of many of her restive male subjects.  Preeminent among

David Beers Quinn, The Hakluyt Society, 2nd ser., nos. 104, 105 (London: Hakluyt Society, 1955) 2 vols. (continuously paginated) 91–92.

[12]William Camden, *Annals* (1585 ed.) extract rpt. in *The Original Writings and Correspondence of the Two Richard Hakluyts*, ed. E. G. R. Taylor, 2 vols., The Hakluyt Society, 2nd ser., nos. 76–77 (1935; rpt. in one vol., Nendeln, Liechtenstein: Kraus Reprint, 1967) 2:348.

[13]John T. Juricek, "English Territorial Claims in North America under Elizabeth and the Early Stuarts," *Terrae Incognitae* 7 (1976) 11.

those subjects was Walter Ralegh. Ralegh's tireless promotion of exploration and colonization was driven by intellectual curiosity and by a patriotic devotion to the creation of an overseas empire that would strengthen England against Spain both economically and strategically; and it was also driven by his extraordinary personal ambition. In his social origins, Ralegh was the youngest son of a modest though well-connected west country gentry family. Thus, he was wholly dependent upon the queen's personal favor not only for the rapid and spectacular rise of his fortunes but also for their perpetuation; in the most tangible and precarious way, Ralegh was Elizabeth's creature. The strategy by which he gained and attempted to maintain the royal favor was systematically to exploit the affective ambiguity of the royal cult; to fuse in his conduct and in his discourse the courtship of the queen's patronage and the courtship of her person.[14]

Observing Elizabeth's open display of intimacy with Ralegh during the Christmas festivities at court in 1584, a German traveler recorded that "it was said that she loved this gentleman now in preference to all others; and that may be well believed, for two years ago he was scarcely able to keep a single servant, and now she has bestowed so much upon him, that he is able to keep five hundred servants."[15]   In surveying the leading courtiers attending upon the queen at this event, Von Wedel had already noted the Earl of Leicester, "with whom, as they say, the queen for a long time has had illicit intercourse," and Sir Christopher Hatton, "the captain of the guard, whom the queen is said to have loved after Lester" (263). Such opinions—which seem to have been offered readily to Von Wedel by his native English informants and which he duly noted in his diary—suggest that many at court did not regard the queen's perpetual virginity as a literal truth. This is not to suggest that they therefore necessarily regarded it as a mere fraud—although

---

[14]On Ralegh's self-fashioning in writing, speech, and conduct, see Stephen J. Greenblatt, *Sir Walter Ralegh: The Renaissance Man and His Roles* (New Haven: Yale University Press, 1973). The standard documentary biography and edition of Ralegh's extant letters is still that of Edward Edwards, *The Life of Sir Walter Ralegh . . . Together with His Letters*, 2 vols. (London: Macmillan, 1868).

[15]"Journey through England and Scotland made by Lupold von Wedel in the years 1584 and 1585," trans. Gottfried von Bülow, *Transactions of the Royal Historical Society*, ns 9 (1895): 265.

there is surviving testimony that at least a few of the queen's subjects thought precisely that. Many at court may have regarded the royal cult as a necessary and effective, collectively sustained political fiction, as a mystery of state quite distinct from the question of whether or not Elizabeth Tudor was a woman who had yet her maidenhead. Whatever the precise nature and degree of Ralegh's intimacy with Queen Elizabeth, in 1587 he succeeded Hatton as Captain of the Guard; in both physical and symbolic terms, he now officially protected, and controlled access to, the queen's body. However, whatever honors, offices, patents, and leases the queen might grant to her favorite, without clear title to great manorial lands he had no secure source of income and status and no hope of founding and sustaining his own lineage. What the royal patent for Virginia and the subsequent commission for Guiana gave to Ralegh was the prospect of possessing vast riches and vast lands, a prospect that would never be available to him at home in England.[16]

Although, in the later 1580s, Ralegh was displaced as the queen's preeminent favorite by the Earl of Essex, he nevertheless continued to enjoy considerable royal confidence and favor. In 1592, however, Queen Elizabeth learned of Ralegh's secret marriage to her namesake, Elizabeth Throgmorton, one of the young ladies attendant at court, and of the birth of their first child. Both offenders were imprisoned in the Tower for several months, and Ralegh continued in disgrace and away from the court for some time longer. In the extravagant and fragmentary

[16]Joyce Youings, "Did Ralegh's England Need Colonies?" *Raleigh in Essex 1985: Privateering and Colonisation in the Reign of Elizabeth I,* ed. Joyce Youings, Exeter Studies in History, n. 10 (Exeter: University of Exeter, 1985) 54, points out both the rapid elevation and the precariousness of Ralegh's social standing:

> Raleigh was knighted in January 1585, being then already member of parliament for Devon, both of these unusual achievements for a virtually landless gentleman. Later that year he was to succeed . . . as Lord Warden of the Stanneries, High Steward of the Duchy of Cornwall and Lord Lieutenant of Cornwall. As such he would enjoy power and patronage, but no landed inheritance, without which there was no future for his line. . . . Even if he invested what cash he had in English land rather than in colonial ventures, land suitable for gentlemen, that is manors and other revenue-producing property, was no longer readily available, even for purchase.

complaint, *The Ocean to Cynthia*, Ralegh wrote of the queen as his royally cruel mistress: "No other poure [power] effectinge wo, or bliss, / Shee gave, shee tooke, shee wounded, shee apeased."[17] Perhaps it cannot be decided, finally, whether to attribute the queen's anger toward Ralegh (and toward other noblemen and courtiers in his circumstances) to the sexual jealousy of a mistress, betrayed by her lover; to the moral outrage of a virgin and the guardian of virgins, victimized by male lasciviousness; or to the political perturbation of a militarily and fiscally weak ruler, whose attempts to maintain an absolute command over her courtiers' alliances and their attentions had been flagrantly flouted. Indeed, the various and conflicting recorded perceptions and attitudes of Elizabethan subjects strongly suggest that such undecidability is itself the historically relevant point; that it is, in fact, a salient feature of the Elizabethan political system. A strategic ambiguity which might be manifested as paradox, equivocation, or contradiction, it was of potential if limited utility both to the monarch and to her (male) subjects. For the latter, however—as Ralegh's case demonstrates—it also carried considerable potential liabilities.

We may regard with a certain skepticism the claim that Queen Elizabeth's virtues inspired virtuous conduct in her subjects; however, there is no doubting that the courtly politics of chastity bore acutely upon the commander of the Guiana voyage. An anonymous letter concerning the circumstances of Ralegh's disgrace in 1592 provides a thematic link between that episode and the discourse of his *Discoverie* in 1596:

> S. W. R., as it seemeth, have been too inward with one of Her Majesty's maids. . . . S. W. R. will lose, it is thought, all his places and preferments at Court, with the Queen's favour; such will be the end of his speedy rising. . . . All is alarm and confusion at this discovery of the discoverer,

---

[17]*The 11th: and last booke of the Ocean to Scinthia*, printed from the undated holograph in *The Poems of Sir Walter Ralegh*, ed. Agnes M. C. Latham (1951; rpt. Cambridge, Mass.: Harvard University Press, 1962) 27, lines 55–56. Conjectures as to the date of *The Ocean to Cynthia* range from 1589 to 1603, with the period immediately following the 1592 disgrace perhaps most often endorsed.

and not indeed of a new continent, but of a new incontinent.[18]

Although of uncertain provenance and authenticity, this wittily scurrilous text does help to foreground and contextualize the *Discoverie*'s recurrent references to Ralegh's restraint of himself and his subordinates, his repudiation of concupiscence, and his strategic tempering/temporizing of his announced quest for wealth and power.

In his dedicatory epistle to Lord Howard and Sir Robert Cecil, Ralegh represents both the conduct of his discovery and the account in which he discovers it as intended to mollify the queen's displeasure and to regain her favor:

> As my errors were great, so they have yeelded very grievous effects. . . . I did therefore even in the winter of my life, undertake these travels . . . that thereby, if it were possible, I might recover but the moderation of excesse, & the least tast of the greatest plenty formerly possessed. . . . To appease so powreful displeasure, I would not doubt but for one yeere more to hold fast my soule in my teeth, till it were performed. (339)

Indeed, Ralegh goes so far as to suggest that the narrative of his exploit should be read as a penitential journey, an act of fleshly purgation undertaken to expiate the incontinent lapse in his devotion to the queen:

> I have bene accompanyed with many sorrowes, with labour, hunger, heat, sickenes, & perill. . . . [They] were much mistaken, who would have perswaded, that I was too easefull and sensuall to undertake a journey of so great travell. But, if what I have done, receive the gracious construction of a painefull pilgrimage, and purchase the least remission, I shall thinke all too litle. (339–40)

---

[18]Quoted in Edward Thompson, *Sir Walter Ralegh: The Last of the Elizabethans* (London: Macmillan, 1935) 83. The letter was first printed in J. Collier, "Continuation of New Materials for a Life of Sir Walter Raleigh," *Archaeologia* 34 (1852): 161.

Read in the context of Ralegh's fall from grace, the *Discoverie* operates on the model of Book II of Spenser's *Faerie Queene* (1590), as a compensatory "Legend of Sir Walter, or of Temperance." The hero of this exemplary autobiographical narrative of restrained desire and deferred gratification eschews both Avarice and Lust, both Mammon and Acrasia:

> If it had not bin in respect of her highnes future honor & riches, [I] could have laid hands on & ransomed many of the kings & Casiqui of the country, & have had a reasonable proportion of gold for their redemption: but I have chosen rather to beare the burden of poverty, then reproch, & rather to endure a second travel and the chances therof, then to have defaced an enterprise of so great assurance, untill I knew whether it pleased God to put a disposition in her princely and royal heart either to folow or foreslow the same. (342–43)

> I neither know nor beleeve, that any of our company one or other, by violence or otherwise, ever knew any of their women. . . . I suffered not any man . . . so much as to offer to touch any of their wives or daughters: which course so contrary to the Spaniards . . . drewe them to admire her Majestie, whose commaundement I tolde them it was. (391)

In short, Ralegh's discovery of a new continent discovers him to be newly continent. As if to redress his conduct with Elizabeth Throgmorton, in these and a number of other passages Ralegh pointedly defers the desired consummation with Guiana until a royal blessing has been secured. Nevertheless, it is the prospect of that consummation that drives the narrative.

Himself a man from a society in which women—with one extraordinary exception—are politically invisible, Ralegh is predisposed to characterize the indigenous societies of the New World as if they are exclusively masculine. The Tivitivas, for example, "are a very goodly people and very valiant, and have the most manly speech and most deliberate that ever I heard, of what nation soever" (382–83). Ralegh admires these alien nations for their collective virility. Nevertheless, at a higher level of abstraction and under stronger rhetorical pressure, these apparently masculine societies—societies from which women have already been verbally effaced—are themselves rendered invisible by a metonymic substitution of place for persons, a substitution of the land for its inhabitants. However, this land which is substituted for its manly inhabitants is itself gendered feminine and sexed as a virgin female body:

> To conclude, Guiana is a countrey that hath yet her maydenhead, never sackt, turned, nor wrought, the face of the earth hath not bene torne, nor the vertue and salt of the soyle spent by manurance, the graves have not bene opened for golde, the mines not broken with sledges, nor their Images puld downe out of their temples. It hath never bene entred by any armie of strength, and never conquered or possessed by any christian Prince.
>
> (428)

In this concluding exhortation of his masculine readership, Ralegh's description of Guiana by means of negatives conveys a proleptically elegiac sympathy for this unspoiled world, at the same time that it arouses excitement at the prospect of despoiling it. His metaphor of Guiana's maidenhead activates the bawdy Elizabethan pun on "countrey," thus inflaming the similitude of the land and a woman's body, of colonization and sexual mastery.[19] By subsuming and effacing the admired societies of Amerindian men in the metaphorical female Other of the land, he "naturalizes" the English intent to subjugate the indigenous peoples of Guiana as the male's mastery of the female. The ideology of gender hierarchy sanctions the Englishmen's collective longing to prove and aggrandize themselves upon the feminine body of the New World; and, at the same time, the emergent hierarchical discourse of colonial exploitation and domination reciprocally confirms the hegemonic force of the dominant sex/gender system.[20]

---

[19]See, for example, Eric Partridge, *Shakespeare's Bawdy* (1948; rpt. New York: E. Dutton, 1960) s. v. "country" and "country matters."

[20]Joan Wallach Scott (48) observes that "hierarchical structures rely on generalized understandings of the so-called natural relationships between male and female. . . . Power relationships among nations and the status of colonial subjects have been made comprehensible (and thus legitimate) in terms of relations between male and female."

As Michel de Certeau suggests in his discussion of van der Straet's icon, the "historied" and gendered body of America calls attention to the affinity between the *discovery* and the *blazon*, two Renaissance rhetorical forms that organize and control their subjects—respectively, the body of the land and the body of the lady—by means of display, inventory, and anatomy. As Nancy Vickers has remarked, "the blazon's inventory of fragmented and reified parts [is] a strategy in some senses inherent to any descriptive project."[21] Typically, in both the blazon and the discovery, the dynamics of this descriptive situation are gendered in a triangulated relationship: A masculine writer shares with his readers the verbal construction/observation of a woman or a feminized object or matter; and in doing so, he constructs a masculine subject position for his readers to occupy and share. Puttenham's *Arte of English Poesie*, a compendium of Elizabethan courtly rhetoric and rhetorical strategies for the negotiation of social interactions at court, identifies the rhetorical operator of the blazon as "your figure of *Icon*, or resemblance by imagerie and portrait."[22] Puttenham exemplifies the *Icon*, first by citing "Sir Philip Sidney in the description of his mistresse excellently well handled," and then by piecemeal quotation from one of his own panegyric poems to Queen Elizabeth, a blazon

> written of our sovereign Lady, wherein we resemble every part of her body to some naturall thing of excellent perfection in his kind, as of her forehead, browes and haire. . . . And of her lips. . . . And of her eyes. . . . And of her breasts. . . . And all the rest that followeth. (244)

[21]Nancy Vickers, "'The blazon of sweet beauty's best': Shakespeare's *Lucrece*," *Shakespeare and the Question of Theory*, ed. Patricia Parker and Geoffrey Hartman (New York: Methuen, 1985) 95–115, quotation from 95. For an introduction to the literary history of the woman:land trope, see Annette Kolodny, *The Lay of the Land: Metaphor as Experience and History in American Life and Letters* (Chapel Hill: University of North Carolina Press, 1975) esp. 10–25. Drawing upon the work of Kolodny, Vickers, and others, Patricia Parker discusses rhetorical and ideological aspects of the woman:land trope—the interplay of gender, commerce, and property—in *Literary Fat Ladies: Rhetoric, Gender, Property* (New York: Methuen, 1987) 126–54.

[22]George Puttenham, *The Arte of English Poesie* (1589) ed. Gladys Doidge Willcock and Alice Walker (Cambridge: Cambridge University Press, 1936) 244.

Puttenham's *Partheniades* were conceived and presented as a New Year's gift, as a rhetorical instrument for ingratiating himself with the queen and eliciting some reciprocal benefit. The symbolic control of a feminized object of description by means of division and analogy has an institutional basis in the privileged masculine access to the discourses of law and rhetoric. When an Elizabethan lawyer and rhetorician like Puttenham can display in print an example of how he has, by figure, "excellently well handled" his royal mistress, he is giving an explicitly political charge to a poetic figure already marked by the politics of gender.

Queen Elizabeth might not only be figured in an erotic blazon but might also be troped in the similitude of land and body. In the special case of a queen regnant, the representational strategies of this trope of gender might well serve to aggrandize the sovereign rather than to subordinate the woman. Her own naming of Virginia for herself is a variation on such a rhetorical strategy; another, from one of her speeches, will be discussed below. Here I want to consider the "Ditchley" portrait of Queen Elizabeth (c. 1592), by Marcus Gheeraerts the Younger (fig. 2). The Ditchley icon realizes the tropological equivalence of land and woman in the conjunction of a cartographic image with a royal portrait. This striking painting, the largest known portrait of the queen, represents her standing, like some great goddess or glorified Virgin Mary, with her feet upon the globe and her head amidst the heavens. The cosmic background divides into sunlight and storm; according to the now fragmentary sonnet inscribed on the canvas, these signify, respectively, the heavenly glory and divine power of which the queen is the earthly mirror. She stands upon a cartographic image of Britain, deriving from Christopher Saxton's collection of printed maps. Like Saxton's 1583 map, the painting divides England into counties, each separately colored, and marks principal towns and rivers. Much of the monarch's island nation is enclosed by the hem of her gown, a compositional feature perhaps recalling the iconography of the *Madonna della misericordia*. This representation of Queen Elizabeth as standing upon her land and sheltering it under her skirts suggests a mystical identification of the inviolate female body of the monarch *with* the unbreached body of her land, at the same time that it affirms her distinctive role as the motherly protectress of her people. But the painting also asserts, in spectacular fashion, the other aspect of Elizabeth's androgynous personal symbolism: her kingly rule; it affirms her power *over* her land and *over* its inhabitants. The cartographic image transforms the *land* into a *state*; and by the division of the land into administrative units, its inhabitants are marked as the monarch's political and juridical subjects.[23] Ralegh's writings and performances display a striking split between hyperbolic elaborations of such royal fictions and oblique counter-gestures of resistance that are both rank- and gender-specific. Ralegh's figuration of his own and his fellows' relationship to Guiana constitutes one such belligerent though displaced gesture of resistance to official figurations of the relationship between the woman ruler and her masculine subjects.

Queen Elizabeth names the eastern seaboard of North America, in her own honor, *Virginia*. When her "trusty and welbeloved servant Walter Raleighe" describes the northeast interior of South America as a virgin, the rhetorical motive is not an homage to the queen but rather a provocation to her masculine subjects: "Guiana is a countrey that hath *yet* her maydenhead" (*Discoverie* 428; my italics). There exists an intimate relationship between the figurations of these two places, as there does between Elizabeth and Ralegh themselves: It is as if the queen's naming of Virginia elicits Ralegh's metaphor of Guiana's fragile maidenhead. Addressing Ralegh in a dedicatory epistle to his edition of Peter Martyr's *De orbe novo* (1587), Richard Hakluyt imagines "your Elizabeth's Virginia" as Ralegh's bride, her depths as yet unprobed for their hidden riches (*Writings and Correspondence of the Two Richard Hakluyts* 2:360–61 [Latin], 367–68 [trans.]). Hakluyt takes imaginative liberties in Latin;

---

[23]On Saxton's maps and the ideological implications of Elizabethan and Jacobean cartography, see Victor Morgan, "The Cartographic Image of 'The Country' in Early Modern England," *Transactions of the Royal Historical Society*, 5th ser. 29 (1979): 129–54; and Richard Helgerson, "The Land Speaks: Cartography, Chorography, and Subversion in Renaissance England," *Representing the English Renaissance*, ed. Stephen Greenblatt (Berkeley and Los Angeles: University of California Press, 1988) 326–61. Helgerson's thesis is that "the cartographic representation of England . . . strengthened the sense of both local and national identity at the expense of an identity based on dynastic loyalty. . . . Maps thus opened a conceptual gap between the land and its ruler" (332). His judgment that the Ditchley portrait, however, "enforces the royal cult" (331) accords with my own reading.

Figure 2. Marcus Gheeraerts the
Younger, the "Ditchley" portrait of
Queen Elizabeth, c. 1592. Photo:
National Portrait Gallery, London.

however, it is difficult to imagine that Ralegh himself, in a
printed address to the queen's subjects, would be so impolitic as
to represent the plantation of Virginia in the same terms that he
uses to represent the conquest of Guiana. If he cannot write explicitly of Virginia's rape, as he can of Guiana's, this is because
the queen and her courtier share a common discourse of discovery, grounded in a territorial conception of the female body. It is
telling that, when the seemingly inevitable image of Virginia's
defloration actually enters print, it does so after the death of
Queen Elizabeth and as a rape perpetrated by the indigenous inhabitants of what was once Wingandacoa:

When Virginia was violently ravished by her owne ruder Natives, yea her Virgin cheekes dyed with the bloud of three Colonies . . . disloyall treason . . . confiscated whatsoever remainders of right the unnaturall Naturalls had, and made both them and their Countrey wholly English.[24]

In Purchas's tract, the English colonists have now become identified with the land that they have expropriated; and the natives, having proven themselves to be unregenerately savage, have provided the final and definitive justification for their dispossession.

## IV

Ralegh can claim no more than to be the first *Englishman* to explore parts of the Orinoco basin and to discover those parts to *English* readers. His text cannot and makes no attempt to erase the footprints of the Spaniards who have preceded him everywhere he goes and who have either knowingly or unknowingly provided almost all of the practical information as well as the fantasies that have generated the motives and underwritten the execution of his project. Spanish tales are the sources repeatedly invoked by Ralegh in his strained and circumstantial attempts to substantiate his own claims for the existence of "the great and golden citie of Manoa," which was said to have been founded somewhere in Guiana by the Incas after the fall of Peru. His descriptions of the wondrous riches of El Dorado are merely extrapolated from the Spanish narratives of Peru, which he cites (see esp. 355–58). What is perhaps his most artfully circumspect and obfuscating position occurs near the end of the *Discoverie*:

Because I have not my selfe seene the cities of Inga, I cannot avow on my credit what I have heard, although it

---

[24]"Virginias Verger" (1625) Samuel Purchas, *Hakluytus Posthumus or Purchas His Pilgrimes*, 20 vols. (Glascow: James MacLehose, 1906) 19:229. I owe this reference to Peter Hulme, *Colonial Encounters: Europe and the Native Caribbean, 1492–1797* (London: Methuen, 1986).

> be very likely, that the Emperour Inga hath built and
> erected as magnificent palaces in Guiana, as his ances-
> tors did in Peru, which were for their riches and
> rarenesse most marvellous and exceeding all in Europe,
> and I thinke of the world, China excepted, which also the
> Spaniards (which I had) assured me to be true. (424–25)

Ralegh's final position concerning the existence of Manoa ultimately relies upon assurances from the rivals and enemies who
are temporarily within his power; furthermore, whatever their
credibility, the precise subject of these Spanish assurances is
rendered conspicuously obscure and ambiguous by Ralegh's syn-
tax. In effect, the very Spaniards whom Ralegh's text repeatedly represents as the cruel and deceitful foes of Englishmen and
Indians alike are also the authorities upon whose knowledge and
experience Ralegh has pursued his own discovery.

The *Discoverie* is haunted by a self-subverting irony, one
that it nowhere explicitly confronts but does frequently if
obliquely register, such as when the writer anxiously strives to
authenticate his narrative. This epistemological and ideological
destabilization arises from Ralegh's repeated need to ground his
own credibility upon the credibility of the very people whom he
wishes to discredit. One of the central ways in which Ralegh attempts to obfuscate this predicament of dependency upon and
identification with the enemy is through an absolute distinction
of the Englishmen's sexual conduct in the New World from that
of the Spaniards. The rhetorical operations of gender performed
in the *Discoverie* are considerably more complicated than the familiar trope of the female land might at first suggest. This com-
plication is in part related to the pervasive Spanish presence in
Ralegh's text and in the country it purports to discover.

Ralegh's ironic discovery of the Spaniards' prior discoveries
drives home to his English readers the embarrassment of England's cultural and imperial *belatedness*. Many Elizabethan writers voice a nagging concern that—in military, commercial, and/or
artistic terms—the English are a backward and peripheral nation. This concern is usually manifested as an anxious and impatient patriotism. For example, in *A Relation of the Second
Voyage to Guiana*, Laurence Keymis writes that

> it were a dull conceite of strange weaknes in our selves,
> to distrust our own power so much, or at least, our owne
> hearts and courages; as valewing the Spanish nation to

be omnipotent; or yeelding that the poore Portugal hath that mastering spirit and conquering industrie, above us.[25]

Keymis was Ralegh's lieutenant and performed this "second Discoverie" (441) in 1596, under Ralegh's instructions; his written account was printed in the same year.   As this passage from Keymis clearly suggests, a belligerent and chauvinistic national consciousness is almost invariably expressed in the terms and values of a collective national character that is culturally encoded as masculine.   Such encodement leads all too predictably to imagery such as Ralegh's, which figures England and Spain as manly rivals in a contest to deflower the new-found lands: At the beginning of his *Discoverie*, Ralegh invites his readers to "consider of the actions of . . . Charles the 5. who had the maidenhead of Peru, and . . . the affaires of the Spanish king now living" (346); at the end, he invites them to consider that "Guiana is a countrey that hath yet her maydenhead" (428).   In order to represent Ralegh's discovery of Guiana iconically, the scenario of van der Straet's drawing might be triangulated: Upon coming ashore, the Englishman discovers America in the arms of a Spaniard.

The ubiquitous figure of the Spaniard is an unstable signifier in the text of Ralegh's *Discoverie*: He is at once an authority to be followed, a villain to be punished, and a rival to be bested. For the Englishmen in the New World, the Spaniards are proximate figures of Otherness: In being Catholic, Latin, and Mediterranean, they are spiritually, linguistically, ethnically, and ecologically alien.   At the same time, however, England and Spain are linked together in an encompassing European system of economic, social, and political structures and forces; and they share an ambient Christian and classical cultural, moral, and intellectual tradition.   The sign of the Spaniard in English discovery texts simultaneously mediates and complicates any simple antinomy of European Self and American Other.

---

[25]Laurence Keymis, *A Relation of the Second Voyage to Guiana. Performed and written in the yeere 1596* (London, 1596); rpt. in Hakluyt, *Principal Navigations* (1598–1600). I quote Keymis' *Relation* from the 1904 ed. of Hakluyt, *Principal Navigations* 10:487.   Parenthetical page references will be to vol. 10 of this edition.

We can begin to observe how gender and sexual conduct are figured into this complex textual play of Otherness by juxtaposing two passages from Keymis' *Relation of the second Voyage to Guiana*. Near the end of his narrative, Keymis asks his English readers, rhetorically:

> Is it not meere wretchednesse in us, to spend our time, breake our sleepe, and waste our braines, in contriving a cavilling false title to defraude a neighbour of halfe an acre of lande: whereas here whole shires of fruitfull rich grounds, lying now waste for want of people, do prostitute themselves unto us, like a faire and beautifull woman, in the pride and floure of desired yeeres. (487)

Here the already familiar similitude of the earth and the female body—"fruitfull rich grounds" and "a faire and beautifull woman"—is activated through a peculiarly dissonant and degraded fantasy of *self-prostitution*. It is as if the writer's imagination of the New World has taken corruption from his already disconcerting representation of the old one: We are exhorted to repudiate our homegrown and familiar greed and fraudulence not because they are immoral but because they are paltry; they must be reconceived on a grander scale, in the large, rich, and beautiful empire of Guiana.

In an earlier passage, Keymis writes of the Indians' present predicament that:

> For the plentie of golde that is in this countrey, beeing nowe knowen and discovered, there is no possibilitie for them to keepe it: on the one side they coulde feele not greater miserie, nor feare more extremitie, then they were sure to finde, if the Spaniardes prevayled, who perforce doe take all things from them, using them as their slaves, to runne, to rowe, to bee their guides, to cary their burthens, and that which is worst of all, to bee content, for safetie of their lives, to leave their women, if a Spaniard chance but to set his eye on any of them to fancie her: on the otherside they could hope for, nor desire no better state and usage, then her Majesties gracious government, and Princely vertues doe promise, and assure unto them. (472)

The Indians who are the collective subject of this passage are exclusively the Indian *men*; "their women" are the (male) Indians' most valued and most intimate possessions, serving to define and to make manifest their own freedom and masculinity. One of the most conspicuous ways in which the Spaniards assert their enslavement of native American men is precisely by their casual use of the bodies of native American women. In Keymis' representation of the Spaniards, the rape of the Indians' lands and the rape of "their women" go hand in hand. In the case of Englishmen, however, male sexual aggression against the bodies of native women has been wholly displaced into the exploitation of the feminized new-found land. Indeed, the Englishmen's vaunted sexual self-restraint serves to legitimate their exploitation of the land. Furthermore, such male desires for possession have been subjected to a form of reversal, in that Keymis' discourse renders Englishmen not as territorial aggressors but rather as passive beneficiaries of the animated land's own desire to be possessed: "Fruitfull rich grounds, lying now waste for want of people, do prostitute themselves unto us, like a faire and beautifull woman." The sexual conduct of European men in the New World is sometimes explained away as the unbridled expression of an essential male lustfulness. It might be more useful to understand it as an ideologically meaningful (and overdetermined) act of violence. This violence is impelled by, enacts, and thus reciprocally confirms the imperatives of appropriation, possession, and domination that characterize the colonialist project in general, imperatives that are themselves discursively figured in gendered violence.

The topic of sexual conduct can become a point of convergence for a multiplicity of discourses—among them, gender, ethnicity, nationality, and social estate. I write of ethnicity and social estate rather than race and class because, in the Elizabethan context, some of the contemporary assumptions implicit in the terms race and class do not seem to be either adequate or appropriate.[26] For example, concerning class: Not only different cate-

---

[26]Compare Eve Kosofsky Sedgwick, *Between Men: English Literature and Male Homosocial Desire* (New York: Columbia University Press, 1985) 11: "The subject of sex [is] an especially charged leverage-point or point for the exchange of meanings, *between* gender and class (and in many societies, race)." As Sedgwick herself notes, the constitution and interrelation of

gories of social rank but also different systems of social categorization and stratification sometimes overlapped, contradicted, or
excluded one another.   And concerning race: Prejudicial early
English perceptions of native Americans—unlike contemporaneous perceptions of Africans—were not given a physical basis in
their appearance and skin color but were based exclusively upon
their supposed savagery.  Furthermore, issues of class and race
might be conflated.  The statuses of "Indians" and "the meaner
sort" of English people were sometimes analogized: Indians were
said to be like English rogues and vagabonds; and unruly English
forest dwellers, like Indians.[27]
   A particularly instructive example of Elizabethan discourses
of sex, gender, ethnicity, nationality, and social rank in convergence is provided in the following extended passage from
Ralegh's *Discoverie*, a small part of which I have already quoted:

> [The Arwacas] feared that wee would have eaten
> them, or otherwise have put them to some cruel death
> (for the Spaniards, to the end that none of the people in
> the passage towards Guiana or Guiana it selfe might
> come to speach with us, perswaded all the nations, that
> we were man-eaters, and Canibals) but when the poore
> men and women had seen us, and that wee gave them
> meate, and to every one something or other, which was
> rare and strange to them, they beganne to conceive the
> deceit and purpose of the Spaniards, who indeed (as they
> confessed) tooke from them both their wives and daugh-
> ters dayly, and used them for the satisfying of their owne
> lusts, especially such as they tooke in this maner by
> strength.  But I protest before the Majestie of the living
> God, that I neither know nor beleeve, that any of our

these categories—including "the subject of sex"—are societally and historically variable.
   [27]For varying interpretations of attitudes toward North American Indians in sixteenth- and seventeenth-century English writings, see Karen Or-
dahl Kupperman, *Settling with the Indians: The Meeting of English and Indian
Cultures in America, 1580–1640* (Totowa, New Jersey: Rowman and Lit-
tlefield, 1980); and Bernard Sheehan, *Savagism and Civility: Indians and Englishmen in Colonial Virginia* (Cambridge: Cambridge University Press, 1980).
Kupperman emphasizes social rank as the fundamental category of difference and hierarchy, while Sheehan emphasizes savagery.

company one or other, by violence or otherwise, ever
knew any of their women, and yet we saw many hundreds, and had many in our power, and of those very
yong, and excellently favoured, which came among us
without deceite, starke naked.

Nothing got us more love amongst them then this
usage: for I suffered not any man to take from any of the
nations so much as a Pina, or a Potato roote, without
giving them contentment, nor any man so much as to offer to touch any of their wives or daughters: which
course so contrary to the Spaniards (who tyrannize over
them in all things) drewe them to admire her Majestie,
whose commaundement I tolde them it was, and also
wonderfully to honour our nation.

But I confesse it was a very impatient worke to
keepe the meaner sort from spoyle and stealing, when we
came to their houses: which because in all I coulde not
prevent, I caused my Indian interpreter at every place
when wee departed, to knowe of the losse or wrong done,
and if ought were stolen or taken by violence, either the
same was restored, and the partie punished in their
sight, or else was payed for to their uttermost demand.

(390–91)

By a fine irony that Ralegh fails to appreciate, the spectral
New World cannibals who so horrified and fascinated sixteenth-
century European writers and readers appear to the equally
horrified Arwacas to be Englishmen. The English unmask the
Spanish deception by reversal: They offer to feed meat to the Indians rather than to eat them. (This is also a reversal in another sense, since perhaps the most commonly recorded initial
gesture of friendship made toward Europeans by New World
peoples was to offer food.) Ralegh purports to have learned from
the Indians that the Spaniards have misrepresented the English
as anthropophagi: Through this heavily mediated pattern of assertion and denial, Ralegh's text voices the Englishmen's own
consuming desire to consume the Indians' land and goods; it registers a fleeting intimation that the "man-eaters, and Canibals"
of the New World are actually a projection—and, by this means,
a legitimation—of the Europeans' own predatory intentions toward their hosts.

Whereas the English bestow gifts upon the Indians, the Spaniards take from them, using Indian women "for the satisfying of their owne lusts." Although, for purposes of contrast to the Spaniards, it would have been necessary only to reaffirm the absence of sexual violence from English behavior, Ralegh insists that to the best of his knowledge none in his company, "by violence, *or otherwise*, ever knew any of their women" (my italics). And he goes out of his way to suggest that this chaste conduct has been heroically maintained against the great temptations posed to the male concupiscible appetite by the young, well-favored, and naked women whom the Englishmen have held in their power. Ralegh is at pains to inhibit any culturally inscribed predisposition in his (masculine) readers that would identify the naked maidens in his text as conventional allegorical personifications of Lasciviousness and Indolence—such as those that populate the exotic pleasure gardens of Spenser's Legend of Temperance (*Faerie Queene*, book 2, cantos 6 and 12). Although he credits reports that the Amazons are both violent and lustful, the women whom he claims to have actually encountered in Guiana Ralegh represents as neither deceitful nor predatory—such attributes tend to be reserved for the Spanish men. However, in this passage and elsewhere, his contrary emphasis upon feminine innocence and vulnerability, upon the potential victimage of women, simultaneously disempowers them and legitimates their condition of dependency. It also reduces them to functioning as the collective instrument for making comparisons and marking differences among *men*. It is crucial to Ralegh's text that what is at issue in this construction of masculinities is not male sexual prowess but, on the contrary, the ability of European men to govern their concupiscible appetites. In *The Book named The Governor*, Sir Thomas Elyot writes that

> continence . . . is specially in refraining or forbearing the act of carnal pleasure, whereunto a man is fervently moved, or is at liberty to have it. Which undoubtedly is a thing not only difficult, but also wonderful in a man noble or of great authority, but as in such one as it happeneth

to be, needs must be reputed much virtue and wisdom, and to be supposed that his mind is invincible.[28]

Ralegh's concern with sexual conduct is not inscribed within an autonomous discourse about human, masculine, or personal sexuality; rather, it is the somatic focus of concerns that are fundamentally ethical, social, and political.[29] "We saw many hundreds, and had many in our power": It is precisely their refusal to abuse their own position of mastery over the Indians that is the measure of the Englishmen's collective self-mastery, that provides proof of the ascendancy of (what Sidney would call) their erected wits over their infected wills. And this self-mastery might not only help them to distinguish themselves, as *Men*, from Women, to whom unruliness and lasciviousness were traditionally ascribed; it might also help them to distinguish themselves, as *Englishmen*, from the lustful and un-self-governable Spaniards. Here misogyny subserves anti-Spanish sentiments, and both serve the Englishmen's project to master the savages of America.[30]

However, having made this moral distinction among men exclusively upon the ground of national difference, Ralegh goes on to say that he had to exercise vigilant control over the inherent tendency toward lawlessness among "the meaner sort" within his own company. He now shifts categories so as to mark

[28]Sir Thomas Elyot, *The Book named The Governor* (1531) ed. S. Lehmberg, Everyman's Library edition (London: Dent, 1962) 203–4.

[29]On "sexuality" as a specifically modern, Western, and bourgeois mode of subjectification and subjectivity, see Michel Foucault, *The History of Sexuality, Volume 1: An Introduction*, trans. Robert Hurley (New York: Pantheon, 1978); Robert A. Padgug, "Sexual Matters: On Conceptualizing Sexuality in History," *Radical History Review* 20 (1979): 3–23; David M. Halperin, "Is There a History of Sexuality?," *History and Theory* 28 (1989): 257–74.

[30]On the ideology of female unruliness in early modern Europe, see, for example: "Women on Top," Natalie Zemon Davis, *Society and Culture in Early Modern France* (Stanford: Stanford University Press, 1975) 124–51; D. E. Underdown, "The Taming of the Scold: The Enforcement of Patriarchal Authority in Early Modern England," *Order and Disorder in Early Modern England*, ed. Anthony Fletcher and John Stevenson (Cambridge: Cambridge University Press, 1985) 116–36; and Linda Woodbridge, *Women and the English Renaissance: Literature and the Nature of Womankind, 1540–1620* (Urbana: University of Illinois Press, 1984) passim.

hierarchical social differences among the Englishmen themselves. Now, within the restricted domain of Englishness, "the meaner sort" have become structurally equivalent to Spaniards—just as, in other Elizabethan and Jacobean ideological contexts, they are negatively represented as analogous to Indians. If gentlemen have the capacity and the duty to govern themselves, they also have the prerogative and the obligation to govern their social inferiors, who are incapable of self-government. To quote Sir Thomas Elyot once more,

> To him that is a governor of a public weal belongeth a double governance, that is to say, an interior or inward governance, and an exterior or outward governance. The first is of his affects and passions, which do inhabit within his soul, and be subjects to reason. The second is of his children, his servants, and other subjects to his authority. (*The Book named The Governor* 183)

Although it is "worke to keepe the meaner sort from spoyling and stealing," the perceived necessity that the gentleman undertake this burdensome duty defines and legitimates the hierarchical ordering of society; and by performing it, he 'reciprocally confirms the congruence of his status with his virtue.

The rhetorical shifting and swerving of Ralegh's text invite some scrutiny. In the first paragraph of the long passage quoted above, Ralegh represents the Englishmen as antithetical to the Spaniards, on the basis of their disinterested generosity toward the Indians: "Wee gave them meate, and to every one something or other, which was rare and strange to them"; in the second paragraph, we are circumstantially informed that although Ralegh forbade his men "so much as to offer to touch any of their wives or daughters," he did permit them to take other forms of Indian property, as long as reparation was made; in the third paragraph, we learn that Indian property was in fact being "stolen or taken by violence" by some of these same gift-giving Englishmen, though not without punishment by their commander. If English virtue becomes a little soiled in the working, an occasion is nevertheless provided to demonstrate containment of the poorer sort's petty thievery by the moral rectitude and judicial vigilance of their betters. Yet it is precisely by an emphatic insistence upon both triviality and scrupulosity—"I suffered not any man to take from any of the nations so much as a Pina, or a

Potato roote"—that this discourse obfuscates the magnitude of the theft being contemplated and prepared by Ralegh himself, which encompasses nothing less than the entire land and everything in it.

The circuitous movement of Ralegh's discourse at once admires the Indians for their innocent trust and displaces onto the Spaniards the implicit betrayal of that trust which is at the heart of the English enterprise. What Ralegh seems to be evading—and what his text nevertheless intermittently discovers—is a recognition that the most massive deception of the Indians is being perpetrated by Ralegh himself. And although evaded, this self-compromising perception may be surfacing obliquely in Ralegh's emphatic characterization of the Indian maidens who were held in his power as being "without deceit, starke naked": Here the insidious erotic provocations of female nudity have been transformed into an emblematic, exemplary—and, perhaps, an obscurely self-admonitory—honesty. An appropriate gloss on Ralegh's naked maidens is provided by the emblem of the Graces in Spenser's Legend of Courtesy (1596):

> Therefore they alwaies smoothly seeme to smile,
> That we likewise should mylde and gentle be,
> And also naked are, that without guile
> Or false dissemblaunce all them plaine may see,
> Simple and true, from covert malice free.[31]

Ralegh exhorts his English readers to liberate the Indians from Spanish exploitation and oppression; and at the same time, he incites them to plunder Guiana for themselves. The ideological coherence of the *Discoverie* is destabilized by a fundamental contradiction in its hortatory aims, a moral contradiction between charity and avarice. In this intolerable situation, in which the Other is always threatening to collapse into the Same, feminine figures must be textually deployed in an attempt to keep Spaniards and Englishmen apart. Thus, distinctions between Man and Woman, and between European and Indian, may both qualify and be qualified by the pervasive textual operation of distinctions between Englishmen and Spaniards that are made on the basis of national identity, cultural and religious values, and

---

[31]Edmund Spenser, *The Faerie Queene*, ed. A. C. Hamilton (London: Longman, 1977) Book 6, canto 10, stanza 24.

social behavior. It is precisely by constructing and reiterating a moral opposition between Spanish lust and tyranny, on the one hand, and English continence and justice, on the other—an opposition epitomized in the contrasting conduct of Spanish and English men toward Indian women—that the discourses of Englishmen such as Ralegh and Keymis obscure the fundamental *identity* of English and Spanish interests in Guiana: "For the plentie of golde that is in this countrey, being nowe knowen and discovered, there is no possibilitie for [the Indians] to keepe it" (Keymis, *Relation* 472); "We came both for one errant . . . both sought but to sacke & spoile them" (Ralegh, *Discoverie* 414). Greed is here the common denominator of "Western desire."

## V

Ralegh frequently writes respectfully and admiringly of the native Americans whom he purports to have encountered during his discovery. They are worthy to be the prospective allies and tributary peoples of the Empress Elizabeth. I think it important to acknowledge such sympathetic representations of various indigenous individuals and groups, while at the same time remaining aware that the very condition of sympathy may be enabled by prior processes of projection and appropriation that efface the differences and assimilate the virtues of the Indians to European norms. Furthermore, such instances of apparently enlightened familiarization cannot be considered in isolation from Ralegh's projection of radical and hostile Otherness elsewhere. This projection operates in two general directions, toward the foreground and toward the margins of the known world; and it also operates in two discourses, which might be called the discourses of morality and of wonder. In the discourse of morality, as I have already suggested, this Otherness is constituted in the proximate, ubiquitous, and tangible Spaniards. In the discourse of wonder, Otherness is figured in the spectacular myth of El Dorado, the Inga of Manoa (356–61), who is frequently represented as an imperial oppressor of Ralegh's tribal allies; and also in those residual Herodotean and Mandevillean curiosities such as anthropophagi, acephali, and Amazons, who haunt the margins of Ralegh's text and of whom he writes only circumspectly and at second hand. Unsurprisingly, from this latter catalogue of marvels it is the Amazons who most arouse Ralegh's interest.

Ralegh discovers the Amazons to his readers more than once during the meandering discourse of his journey. Although these occurrences may appear to be incidental to the *Discoverie*'s narrative, they have an integral place in its textual ideo-logic of gender and power. The matriarchal, gynocratic Amazons are the radical Other figured but not fully contained by the collective imagination of European Patriarchy.[32] Sixteenth century-travel narratives often recreate the ancient Amazons of Scythia in South America or in Africa. Almost invariably, the Amazons are relocated just beyond the receding geographical boundary of *terra incognita*, in the enduring European mental space reserved for aliens. The notion of a separatist and intensely territorial nation of women warriors might be seen as a momentous transformation of the trope identifying the land with the female body. Implicit in the conceptual shift from *the land as woman* to *a land of women* is the possibility of representing women as collective social agents. Predictably, such a disturbing notion produces a complex and at best morally ambiguous male representation of female agency. In any event, such women as the Amazons are not merely assimilable to the landscape; nor are they assimilable to the goods and chattels possessed by the men of their group. Unlike the other indigenous societies described by Ralegh, in the case of the Amazons it is the women who are synonymous with the political nation; indeed, Amazon men are literally nonexistent. And as a particular (and particularly extreme) construction of the female gender, the Amazons enter into complex and multiple articulations, not only with the textual figurations of masculinity in the *Discoverie* but also with its other significant female representations: the women among the native American peoples

---

[32] I use the term "Patriarchy" to describe a system of social and domestic organization hegemonic in early modern England, in which authority resided in a male "head"—whether father, husband, elder, master, teacher, preacher, magistrate, or lord. On the political theory of patriarchy in early modern England, see Gordon J. Schochet, *Patriarchalism in Political Thought* (New York: Basic Books, 1975); on the interplay of theory and practice at the level of household and village, see Susan Dwyer Amussen, *An Ordered Society: Gender and Class in Early Modern England* (Oxford: Basil Blackwell, 1988).

encountered by Ralegh, who are victimized by the Spaniards; and the queen of England, to whom Ralegh himself is subject.

It is a discussion about the circulation of gold and other commodities among the peoples situated between the Orinoco and the Amazon that provides the immediate occasion for Ralegh's lengthy digression on the remarkable tribe for whom the latter river had been named:

> [I] was very desirous to understand the truth of those warlike women, because of some it is beleeved, of others not. And though I digresse from my purpose, yet I will set downe that which hath bene delivered me for trueth of those women. . . . The memories of the like women are very ancient as well in Africa as in Asia. . . . In many histories they are verified to have bene, and in divers ages and provinces: but they which are not far from Guiana doe accompany with men but once in a yere, and for the time of one moneth, which I gather by their relation to be in April: and at that time all kings of the borders assemble, and queenes of the Amazones; and after the queenes have chosen, the rest cast lots for their Valentines. . . . If they conceive, and be delivered of a sonne, they returne him to the father; if of a daughter they nourish it, and reteine it: and as many as have daughters send unto the begetters a present; all being desirous to increase their owne sex and kind: but that they cut off the right dug of the brest, I doe not finde to be true. It was farther tolde me, that if in these warres they tooke any prisoners that they used to accompany with those also at what time soever, but in the end for certeine they put them to death: for they are sayd to be very cruell and bloodthirsty, especially to such as offer to invade their territories. (366–67)

This Amazonian anti-culture precisely inverts European norms of political authority, sexual license, marriage and child-rearing practices, and inheritance rules. Such conceptual precision suggests that it was not merely the antiquity and wide diffusion of the idea of the Amazons that compelled Ralegh and his contemporaries to entertain seriously the possibility of their existence. Elizabethan perception and speculation were structured by the cognitive operations of hierarchy and inversion, analogy and antithesis. By the logic of these operations, a conceptual space for reversal and negation was constructed within the world picture of a patriarchal society. Among those figures that might occupy this space were the Amazons. Since they didn't exist, it proved necessary to invent them—or, in the case of the New World, to reinvent them.

Ralegh's ethnography of the Amazons divides into two antithetical parts, each largely defined by their collective conduct toward alien men: The first is focused upon the Amazons' orderly, periodic, and eminently civilized ritual cohabitation with men of neighboring tribes. Because it is performed for purposes of procreation—in order to insure the perpetuation of "their owne sex and kind"—this apparently remote Amazonian practice is not without relevance to the always sensitive Elizabethan succession question. It may be that Ralegh was obliquely criticizing the queen's earlier refusal to marry and her ongoing refusal to designate a successor. In any case, the relevant point is that the centrality that had been given to such matters of state from the very inception of Elizabeth's reign predisposed Englishmen to take a keen interest in the ways in which other actual or imagined societies might structure the processes of political succession and social reproduction. Taking place at the margins of the Amazons' territory, on the boundary between matriarchal and patriarchal societies, this sexual rite serves to mark the feminine and masculine genders as mutually exclusive and, simultaneously, to mediate their radical difference through sexual intercourse. The second, strongly contrasted part of the digression is a brief but sensational account of the impulsive and random mixing of violence and lust in the Amazons' conduct toward their masculine captives. This latter mode of Amazonian behavior—an irascible and concupiscible distemper provoked by attempts "to invade their territories," to violate their body politic—inverts and doubles the violent and lustful conduct frequently associated with the masculine Spanish invaders. In Ralegh's narrative of the Amazons' response to invasion, sexual conduct takes the form of reciprocal aggression between the genders rather than a practice of either procreative or abstinent virtue. Construed as a struggle between women and men for the control and disposition of their own and of each other's bodies, the sexual is here synonymous with the political. Gender and rule, sex and power: These are the concerns that preoccupy Ralegh in his desire "to understand the truth of those warlike women"; we might expect such concerns to be of more than incidental interest to a gentleman who is subject to a woman monarch.

Although Amazonian figures might at first seem suited to strategies for praising a woman ruler, they are not conspicuous among the many encomiastic mirrors of Queen Elizabeth produced by her own subjects.[33] The one notable exception, the heroic Amazon Queen Penthesilea, may have been acceptable and appropriate precisely because she sacrificed herself not for the Amazonian cause but for the cause of patriarchal Troy, the mythical place of origin of the Britons. Otherwise, the sexual and parental practices habitually associated with the Amazons must have rendered them, at best, an equivocal means for representing the Virgin Queen. She herself seems to have been too politic, and too ladylike, to have pursued the Amazonian image very far. However, she could transform it to suit her purposes. If report speaks true of her, she did so most notably when she visited Tilbury in 1588, in order to review and to rally the troops that had been mustered in expectation of a Spanish invasion. According to the subsequent recollection of Thomas Heywood, among others, on that momentous occasion the queen of England was "habited like an *Amazonian* Queene, Buskind and plumed, having a golden Truncheon, Gantlet, and Gorget, Arms sufficient to expresse her high and magnanimous spirit."[34] The theme of her speech was by then familiar to her audience:

---

[33]For a sense of the ubiquity of Amazonian representations in Elizabethan culture, see the valuable survey by Celeste Turner Wright, "The Amazons in Elizabethan Literature," *Studies in Philology* 37 (1940): 433–56; and, for Amazons and viragos in Elizabethan and Jacobean dramatic and nondramatic writings, see Simon Shepherd, *Amazons and Warrior Women: Varieties of Feminism in Seventeenth-Century Drama* (Brighton: Harvester Press, 1981). For analyses and speculations regarding Amazonian representations of Queen Elizabeth, see Winfried Schleiner, "*Divina virago*: Queen Elizabeth as an Amazon," *Studies in Philology* 75 (1978): 163–80; and Gabriele Bernhard Jackson, "Topical Ideology: Witches, Amazons, and Shakespeare's Joan of Arc," *English Literary Renaissance* 18 (1988): 40–65.

[34]Thomas Heywood, *The exemplary lives and memorable acts of nine the most worthy women of the world* (London, 1640) 211. Among Heywood's three "Heathen" female worthies is the Amazon "Penthisilaea" (96–109); the ninth and culminating female worthy is, of course, England's late queen (182–212).

Let Tyrants fear, I have always so behaved my self, that
under God I have placed my chiefest strength, and safeguard in the loyal hearts and good will of my subjects.
. . . I know I have the bodie, but of a weak and feeble
woman, but I have the heart and Stomach of a King, and
of a King of *England* too.[35]

Elizabeth's strategy of self-empowerment involves a delicate balance of contrary gestures. On the one hand, she dwells upon the
feminine frailty of her body natural and the masculine strength
of her body politic—a strength deriving from the love of her people, the virtue of her lineage, and the will of her God. In other
words, she moderates the anomalous martial spectacle of feminine sovereignty by representing herself as the handmaiden of a
greater, collective and patriarchal will. On the other hand, she
subsumes the gesture of womanly self-deprecation within an assertion of the unique power that inheres in her by virtue of her
office and nation. Her feminine honor, the chastity invested in a
body that is vulnerable to invasion and pollution, is made secure
by the kingly honor invested in her body politic.  She adds,
defiantly:

I . . . think foul scorn that *Parma* or *Spain*, or any Prince
of Europe should dare to invade the borders of my Realm,
to which rather then any dishonour shall grow by me, I
my self will take up arms, I my self will be your General,
Judge, and Rewarder of everie one of your virtues in the
field.

Queen Elizabeth's putative speech presents the threat of invasion in the most intimate and violent of metaphors, as the attempt by a foreign prince to rape her. Like the iconic effect of
the Ditchley portrait, the rhetorical force of this speech is partly
due to Elizabeth's identification of corporeal with geopolitical
boundaries, to her subtle application of the land:body trope to
herself: She identifies her virginal female body with the clearly
bounded body of her island realm, threatened with violation by

---

[35]The speech is recorded in an undated letter: "Dr. [Leonel] Sharp to
the Duke of Buckingham," undated letter printed in *Cabala, Mysteries of
State, in Letters of the great Ministers of K. James and K. Charles* (London,
1654) 259. Sharp had been present in the queen's retinue at Tilbury.

the masculine Spanish land and sea forces personified in King Philip and the Duke of Parma. Such an illegitimate sexual union would contaminate the blood of the lineage and dishonor not only the royal house but the whole commonwealth. The Roman matron Lucretia submitted to and was ritually polluted by sexual violation, and her suicide was required in order to cleanse the social body. In contrast, the royal English virgin will defend and preserve both herself and her state. If Queen Elizabeth at Tilbury resembles the Amazons in her martial stance, she differs from them in leading an army of men. By insisting, however impractically, that she herself will be the leader of her army, the queen implies that she will not be merely the passive object of male power—even if the intended use of that power is to protect her against the aggression of others. Thus, Elizabeth's own gendered, metaphorical discourse anticipates Ralegh's: England is a country that has yet her maidenhead—and Ralegh's virgin queen, not wholly unlike his Amazons, will prove herself a virago toward those who offer to invade her territories.

In the wake of the Armada's failure, Ralegh can tell all the tribes he encounters in the New World that the queen will protect them as she has protected herself, her own people, and the Protestant cause in Europe:

> I made them understand that I was the servant of a Queene, who was the great Casique of the North, and a virgine . . . that shee was an enemie to the Castellani in respect of their tyrannie and oppression, and that she delivered all such nations about her, as were by them oppressed, and having freed all the coast of the Northren world from their servitude, had sent mee to free them also, and withall to defend the countrey of Guiana from their invasion and conquest. (*Discoverie* 353–54)

However, at the very end of his narrative, in a characteristically shameless display of his duplicity, Ralegh invites Elizabeth to betray the Indians' trust; in effect, he exhorts her to emulate "the Castellani in respect of their tyrannie and oppression" by undertaking her own conquest of Guiana:

> For whatsoever Prince shall possesse it, shall be greatest, and if the king of Spaine enjoy it, he will become unresistable. Her Majestie hereby shall confirme and

strengthen the opinions of all nations, as touching her great and princely actions. And where the South border of Guiana reacheth to the Dominion and Empire of the Amazones, those women shall hereby heare the name of a virgin, which is not onely able to defend her owne territories and her neighbours, but also to invade and conquer so great Empires and so farre removed. (431)

Ralegh insinuates that Elizabethan imperial designs upon the Empire of Guiana might be extended to the Empire of the Amazons, that a woman who has the prerogative of a sovereign, who is authorized to be out of place, can best justify her authority by putting other women in their places. Ralegh's rhetorical tactic for convincing the queen to advance his colonial enterprise is apparently to associate her ambiguously with the Amazons and then to offer her a means by which to distinguish herself from them. He seeks to persuade the queen not merely to emulate the Amazons' vigilant territoriality but to overgo them by emulating the Spaniards' rampant invasiveness. In effect, by appropriating the royal tropes of female self-empowerment such as those employed in Elizabeth's Tilbury speech, Ralegh endorses a martial and heroic—a manly and kingly—image of female authority. But he does so precisely in order to bend the royal will to his own designs. Suffice to say that Her Majesty was unyielding.

## VI

Ralegh's exhortation of Queen Elizabeth to overgo the Amazons by offensive warfare and to out-maneuver King Philip of Spain by possessing Guiana is immediately preceded by an exhortation of his general male readership, who are potential volunteers and investment partners for the conquest and settlement of Guiana. Employing a gender-specific rhetorical strategy distinct from that addressed to the queen, Ralegh elaborates a geography of Elizabethan male desire, discovering that "there is a way found to answer every mans longing" (342). The object of this overdetermined desire encompasses identity and security, knowledge, wealth, and power. It seeks to know, master, and possess a feminine space—or, in the language of Ralegh's Virginia patent, "to discover search fynde out and view . . . to have

holde occupy and enjoye"; it is a desire that is most vividly realized as the prospect of deflowering a virgin.   In his prefatory address "To the Reader," he bids them to "consider of the actions
of both Charles the 5. who had the maidenhead of Peru, and the
abundant treasures of Atabalipa, together with the affaires of
the Spanish king now living" (346); and, at the end, he exhorts
them to emulate King Philip's father by taking Guiana's maidenhead just as he had taken Peru's.   In urging these English
gentlemen to emulate the rapacious and spectacularly successful
Spanish imperialism that now threatens England's very existence, Ralegh holds out to them the prospect of rewards graded
to their various statuses:

> The common souldier shall here fight for golde, and pay
> himselfe in steede of pence, with plates of halfe a foote
> broad, whereas he breaketh his bones in other warres for
> provant and penury.  Those commanders and chieftaines
> that shoot at honour and abundance shall finde there . . .
> rich and beautifull cities . . . temples adorned with golden
> images . . . sepulchres filled with treasure. (425)

As is common in the promotional literature for Elizabethan colonizing ventures, Ralegh envisions exploration, trade, and settlement   abroad   as   an   escape   valve   for   the   frustrations   of
disaffected or marginalized groups, and as a solution to endemic
socioeconomic problems at home: "Her Majestie may in this en-
terprize employ all those souldiers and gentlemen that are
younger brethren, and all captaines and chieftaines that want
employment" (430).   Thus, the potentially riotous malcontents
among Her Majesty's male subjects may displace their thwarted
ambitions into the conquest of virgin lands.   Himself a younger
brother, a soldier, and a gentleman in need of advancement,
Ralegh might well be considered a special case of the general social problem that he here seeks to redress to his own inestimable
advantage.

     Together with his company, and his readers, Ralegh encoun-
ters in the New World the presence of England's implacable
Spanish foe—the specular figure of desiring European Man.
Thus recontextualized in the body of Guiana and in the body of
Ralegh's book, the Englishmen's relationship to the Spaniard
manifests itself as a disturbing oscillation between identity and
difference, between the acknowledgment and the obfuscation of

their common longing.  Ralegh can reassure his English gentleman readers that, although "Charles the 5 . . . had the maidenhead of Peru," there remain in the New World other countries
that have yet their maidenheads.  It is not the English monarch
but rather her masculine subjects who are exhorted to emulate
the king of Spain.  Whether as the virgin protectress of the Indians or as their Amazonian conqueror, Queen Elizabeth cannot be
comfortably analogized to Charles V; she cannot take maidenheads.  As I have tried to show, the conjunctures, exchanges,
and contradictions between the categories of gender and nation
could be employed to produce moral distinctions between Englishmen and Spaniards.  But they could also dispose English
subjects to identify with Spaniards and with the king of Spain
himself on the basis of their manly rivalry for possession of the
female land.  In the face of a tangible Spanish threat to what
were perceived to be the mutual interests and shared identity of
English men and women of all estates, Queen Elizabeth's Tilbury
speech may have been relatively successful at producing an
identification of the collective social body with the feminine body
of the monarch.  However, for its masculine Elizabethan readers,
the violent rhetoric of Ralegh's *Discoverie* generates identifications with the agency of England's masculine enemies; and
in this very process of identification and emulation, these Englishmen will necessarily be alienated from their own sovereign,
who cannot occupy the position of the agent in such a gendered
and sexed discourse.

The final sentence of the *Discoverie*, following immediately
upon Ralegh's exhortation to the queen to overgo the Amazons,
balances against its initial deferential gestures an ultimate assertion of the subject's resolve: "I trust . . . that he which is King
of all Kings and Lord of Lords, will put it into her heart which is
Ladie of Ladies to possesse it, if not, I will judge those men worthy to be kings thereof, that by her grace and leave will undertake it of themselves" (431).  Ralegh has good reason to doubt
that the queen will be moved to action by his own imperial vision.  The requisite phrase, "by her grace and leave," does little
to qualify the assertion of a strong, collective, and defiant response by the queen's masculine subjects to her anticipated lack
of enthusiasm.  Invoking the aid of an emphatically masculine
God, Ralegh employs the epithet, "Lord of Lords" to figure superlative authority and potency; in contrast, his epithet for his
monarch, "Ladie of Ladies," figures superlative feminine gentil-

ity. The *Discoverie*'s final clause—"I will judge those men worthy to be kings thereof, that by her grace and leave will undertake it of themselves"—envisions the queen's most manly subjects, like so many Tamburlaines, seizing the opportunity to repudiate their unworthy subjection and to make themselves kings by their deeds. Nor does Ralegh's perfunctory gesture of deference to the queen neutralize his bold, final symbolic act, in which he arrogates to himself the authority to judge who is worthy to be a king. It seems to me that this closing period of Ralegh's *Discoverie* manifests a considerable strain between two Elizabethan subject positions and two different notions of the "subject": a strain between the subject's courtship of and deference to his queen, and his contrary impulse to assert his own masculine virtue and to put his sovereign in her place as a woman. Nevertheless—and the point cannot be made too strongly—however clever and rhetorically skillful the arguments and insinuations of Ralegh's text, they exerted no discernible power over the queen's policies. Whatever personal predispositions or pragmatic military, diplomatic, and fiscal considerations may have governed Elizabeth's refusal to endorse Ralegh's grandiose scheme, she was also, in effect, resisting his attempts to discursively construct and delimit her gender identity and her sovereignty, to shape her fantasy and to control her will.

Ralegh emphasizes that the Englishmen "had many" of the Indian women "in [their] power" (391); and he represents territorial conquest as the enforced defloration and possession of a female body. Such forms of discursive intimidation and violence may be identified as the compensatory tactics of a masculine Elizabethan subject who is engaged with his monarch in a gendered struggle for mastery and agency, authority and will. If we widen our perspective, however, Queen Elizabeth herself may be understood to be a feminine subject who had been engaged since the very beginning of her reign in compensatory tactics of her own. Elizabeth's political genius was to appropriate and maintain a space for feminine authority within the dominant masculine and patriarchal structures of Tudor society. However, to the extent that such tactics became a successful strategy of power, they also tapped the alternating current of misogyny in her ostensibly adoring and obedient masculine subjects.[36] Such atti-

---

[36]Here I am using *strategies* to connote practices by which a dominant ideology seeks to maintain or extend its hegemony and *tactics* to connote im-

tudes of hostility, distrust, and contempt were expressed toward women and toward the category of Woman; and they were also expressed toward the sovereign, often indirectly or equivocally but also occasionally with remarkable bluntness.  Thus, to formulate Ralegh's practices in terms of "compensatory tactics" may be merely to reobjectify Woman as the threatening Other of the masculine subject: His own objectification of and violence toward women have now been rendered understandable—perhaps even sympathetic.  Such a formulation becomes complicit in the very tactics that it seeks to describe.

Many who have not read Ralegh's *Discoverie* may, nevertheless, be familiar with the phrase, "Guiana is a countrey that hath yet her maydenhead."  It has been cited and quoted frequently in studies of English Renaissance culture and has been made the subject of discourses ranging from ideological analysis to prurient anecdote.  Our contemporary discourses about rape emphasize its character as an act of rage rather than an act of desire.  Some would therefore deny it the status of a specifically sexual crime; others argue compellingly that, to the contrary, rape is a socially sexed crime that must be contextualized within a larger system of gender politics.  Whether the rape is physical or metaphorical, whether its object is a woman, a man, or a "countrey," that object is positioned as feminine. [37]  These emphases have relevance to Ralegh's notorious metaphor—and, certainly, to the ways in which we critically re-present it.  My immediate concern has been with the historically and textually specific work performed by this metaphor in Ralegh's *Discoverie* and with its articulation among other rhetorical/ideological elements in the collective Elizabethan discourse of discovery.  The female body maps an important sector of the Elizabethan cultural unconscious; it constitutes a veritable matrix for the forms of Elizabethan desire and fear.  The feminized topographical and textual spaces of the new-found land; the heroic, fecund, and ra-

provised appropriations of dominant practices by marginalized subjects. This distinction is indebted to Michel de Certeau, *The Practice of Everyday Life*, trans. Steven Rendell (Berkeley: University of California Press, 1984).

[37] I am indebted to the discussion of this controversy in Teresa de Lauretis, "The Violence of Rhetoric: Considerations on Representation and Gender," *The Violence of Representation: Literature and the History of Violence*, ed. Nancy Armstrong and Leonard Tennenhouse (London: Routledge, 1989) 239–58, esp. 244–45.

pacious Amazons; the young, well favored, and naked maidens of
Guiana; the pure and dangerous, politic and natural bodies of the
queen of England: It is through the symbolic display and manip-
ulation of these gendered and historied bodies—in discursive acts
of violence or adoration, or of violent adoration—that what
Ralegh calls "every mans longing" is given a local habitation and
a name.

The subject of Ralegh's *Discoverie* is a masculine subject, a
masculine subject who is textually defined not in terms of his
subjective experience of sexuality but rather by means of a complex process of social positioning.  The narrative and descriptive
movements of Elizabethan texts construct multiple—and potentially contradictory—subject positions for writers and readers by
means of continually shifting and recombined sets of oppositional
or differential terms, terms that are culture-specific in their content and resonance.  The project of Ralegh's prose tract, as of
Spenser's heroic poem, is (in the words of Spenser's Letter to
Ralegh, appended to *The Faerie Queene* in 1590) "to fashion a
gentleman or noble person in vertuous and gentle discipline." In
both texts, this fashioning is produced in a conjunction of
identifications and distinctions that are made in terms of gender,
nation, religion, social estate, and condition of civility or savagery (which we might call ethos).  The system of Aristotelian
ethics that provides a foreconceit for Spenser's Legend of Temperance also provides the conceptual framework within which
Ralegh thinks his own daily actions and interactions.  But
whereas Spenser's polysemous allegorical fiction works explicitly
toward a general system of moral virtue, Ralegh's ostensibly fac-
tual narrative inscribes elements of such ideological schemata
into its intended representations of particular persons and
events.

I have suggested some of the ways in which, through the
observation/construction of his narrative and descriptive objects,
the writing subject obtains coordinates for the constant if often
subliminal process by which he locates his own shifting position
in moral and social space.  Ralegh's observations of the
Spaniards, of the warriors of Guiana and "their women," of the
Amazons, and of "the meaner sort" of Englishmen all work in-
terdependently so as to exemplify in Ralegh himself the ethical
and political congruence of the temperate man and the governor,
the national and social congruence of the Englishman and the
gentleman.  At the same time that the persona of the author is

dialectically fashioned in relation to the personae narrated and described in his text, he is also so fashioned in relation to the readers whom he constitutes by addressing them in his text. In the case of Ralegh's *Discoverie*, as I have already suggested, these gender- and status-specific objects of address include Queen Elizabeth herself, who is obliquely addressed and directly discussed throughout the text; Lord Howard and Sir Robert Cecil—two of the most powerful men in England, to whom the *Discoverie* is dedicated and directly addressed; and a general readership of Elizabethan masculine subjects—gentlemen, soldiers, potential investors and colonists—who are explicitly addressed in an initial epistle and at the close of the work.

However distinctive in detail, Ralegh's individual relationship to Queen Elizabeth was shaped by a cultural contradiction that he shared with all members of his gender and social estate: namely, the expectation that he manifest loyalty and obedience to his sovereign at the same time that he exercised mastery over women. His relationship to Howard and Cecil was also conditioned by a cultural contradiction, one specific to men of the social elite and the political nation: namely, that while mastery of oneself and one's social inferiors was central to the ideology of the gentleman, the extreme degree of stratification in Elizabethan society meant that most relationships between gentlemen were also hierarchical and required elaborate if often subtle forms of deference toward social superiors. In his strategies of address to his general readership, Ralegh must make his appeal in terms of the interests, desires, and national identity he has in common with them, but without compromising the position of distinction and superiority that is the basis of his claim to authority over them. A dissonance that is intermittently registered throughout the text of the *Discoverie* is powerfully foregrounded and heightened when, in the rhetorical violence that marks his final address to these readers, Ralegh abandons his previous claim and responsibility to govern their appetites. This dissonance between Ralegh's representation of his own conduct as temperate and judicious and his incitement of others to conduct that is passionate and rapacious has a multiple and contradictory ideological import that lies beyond the controlling intentions of the writing subject: It both affirms and subverts—and, thus, destabilizes—the identification of the masculine subject with the authority of his feminine sovereign; it destabilizes the moral distinction of the virtuous Englishman from the degenerate

Spaniard, and of the reasonable gentleman from the sensual commoner; and it destabilizes the legitimacy of civil European attempts to possess savage America. Of the prospective exploitation of Guiana, Ralegh declares triumphantly that "there is a way found to answer every mans longing." However, the textual operations of his *Discoverie* discover the way to be errant and the answer, equivocal.

# SEXUAL DESIRE AND THE MARKET ECONOMY DURING THE INDUSTRIAL REVOLUTION

## Thomas W. Laqueur

Neither "sex," "sexuality," nor "desire" appears in text-books of the industrial revolution, and yet contemporaries, as well as subsequent historians, talk about them endlessly. Thomas Malthus made the seemingly irrepressible power of sexual desire the central axiom of his work on population, one of the foundational texts of nineteenth-century political economy. The classical sources on the social history of the period—Engels, Gaskell, Kay-Shuttleworth, not to speak of parliamentary investigations, medical tracts, and novels—revel in observations on the subject: on prostitution (newly christened *the* social evil); on lasciviousness among the young and especially young working-class girls; on domestic practices, scarcely novel, like the sharing of beds and sleeping rooms by parents, children of both sexes, and lodgers, which now deeply shocked middle-class witnesses; on masturbation; and generally on a diffusely but powerfully felt loss of social control over sexuality. (By "sexuality" I mean one's sense of oneself as a desiring subject, a homosexual, a heterosexual, for example, each with a great variety of possible erotic, culturally determined shadings of whatever might be biologically given.)

Moreover, as nineteenth-century observers well understood and philosophers since Frederich Nietzsche have emphasized, sexual desire is not simply a measurable biological property but is itself a product of historical forces. It is both generated and deployed by social practices and by the vast array of often contradictory literature of which it is the focus. Factories, cities, shops, markets, novels, and medical tracts were all themselves engines of desire and not just sites for indulging or writing about it.

Focusing on eighteenth- and nineteenth-century England, this essay asks why two seemingly distinct histories—of the industrial revolution on the one hand and of sexuality on the other—should be so thoroughly imbricated. The general answer is that talk about sex in the Western tradition has always been talk about society and so, too, during the industrial revolution. Marriage, sexual intercourse, and reproduction form the most basic connections between individuals and generations, the mi-

crocosmic arena where the most intimate aspects of human existence intersect with the demands of the culture and society beyond. (Their meaning and consequence, of course, vary
significantly over time, between men and women, and among different social strata.). Little wonder that one of the great transformations of human history would be refracted in both how humans managed their sexuality and how they understood it.[1]

More specifically, I will offer an answer in two parts: the
first in terms of what "really happened," the second through an
examination of the relation between discourses of the marketplace on the one hand and discourses of sex and desire on the
other. There was, in fact, a demonstrable, dramatic increase in
access to heterosexual intercourse, a sort of sexual democratization, which made it easier to couple and which constituted for
contemporaries a frightening sign that the bonds of the old social
order had come asunder. But there was also a deep and pervasive understanding that economic rationality alone could not motivate capitalism and market behavior. There was more to in-
dustrialism than science in the service of progress. Passion and
desire were integral to the new order, and there was no clear
conceptual boundary between its sexual and economic manifestations. In principle nothing distinguished the acceptable from the
dangerous: the free market in labor from the morally far more
ambiguous openness of a marriage regime relatively unfettered
by constraints of land or fixed livelihood; the freedoms of the
marketplace in goods and services from the marketplace of sex;
the threats posed to the family by an explicitly amoral public
economic sphere from the threats posed by prostitution; the elab-

---

[1]This paper deals almost entirely with the debate about working-class
sexuality, although there would be a great deal to say about other classes.
The attack on the  alleged promiscuity of the aristocracy was central to the
radical political critique of the old regime; bourgeois sexuality was crucial to
the creation of middle-class subjectivity in all its luxuriant variety. Demographic data of course cover all classes, but the trends discussed here apply
to the working classes alone. Age of marriage went up, not down, among the
better off; celibacy rates probably rose. Since  aristocrats were traditionally
large consumers, the question of how economic desire could be managed was
discussed almost entirely with regard to the middling sorts or lower classes,
who before the eighteenth century were considered as consumers only of necessities. Excessive consumption of the traditional sort, like excess sexuality, was one of the charges radicals leveled against an aristocratic order.

orately theorized individualism of liberal society from its perversion in the socially corrosive power of autoerotic self-absorption;
the rapid circulation of money and commercial paper—so enticing
and yet so seemingly ephemeral and ungrounded—from the ef-
fervescent qualities of eros.

In an economic and social order where, as Marx noted, "all
that is solid melts into air," where "man is at last compelled to
face with sober senses his real conditions of life and his relations
with his kind," the discourses of sexual passion and desire reiterate, reinforce, and intertwine the imaginative connections between the worlds of the body and the worlds of the market.[2]
Even in the early eighteenth century, when social theorists
looked for metaphors through which to understand the exuberant
new marketplace, they turned to the realms of eros: the future is
sought passionately and inconstantly in love and speculation;
credit is a woman and inconstant like Fortuna.[3]

I hope that these quotes and this essay bring together two
domains of the history of the first industrial revolution that are
usually considered as altogether distinctive: the sexual desires of
the body and the economic desires of men and women as consumers in the marketplace. I first ask what can be learned
about their relation from contemporary accounts; then from demography, which at the very least registers the onset and consequences of heterosexual intercourse; and finally from various
texts of political economy and social observation, which conflate
the two worlds of desire in ways that demonstrate their intrinsic
and inextricable links.

## The Question of Repression Posed

Some contemporaries certainly thought that the industrial
revolution brought the welcome dawn of a new era of libidinal
repression. Francis Place, one of the leading working-class radicals of the period, for example, wrote his autobiography as an
instance of this development, an exemplary story of rising moral

---

[2]Karl Marx, *The Communist Manifesto*, *The Marx-Engels Reader*, ed.
Robert Tucker (New York: W. W. Norton, 1976) 476.

[3]J. G. A. Pocock, *Virtue, Commerce and History* (Cambridge: Cambridge
University Press, 1985) 99.

standards from his boyhood in the 1770s and 1780s to the post-Napoleonic era. "Smirched but not deeply stained," he tells how he was saved by his wife from a brutal low life and entered triumphantly into the new world of respectability, where the drunkenness, sexual license, and general dissipation of the decadent old world were but quaint bad memories.[4]    Numerous working-class autobiographies, not to speak of conversion narratives of the period, tell the same story. In his influential articles on eighteenth-century plebeian life, as well as his magisterial account of working-class formation, E. P. Thompson is more sympathetic than was Place to popular culture, but he nevertheless traces the same trajectory: from "picaresque hedonism" to class self-consciousness and political discipline[5].

This story, albeit in a new register, gains credibility from social theorists who raise it to a more abstract level and argue that it is precisely what they would have predicted. "Economic action" of the sort appropriate to a capitalist economy, Max Weber writes, requires "instrumental rationality," which supersedes both an "instinctual reactive search" for the immediate gratification of wants and "inherited techniques and customary social relations." The new mode of production, in this model, depends on the spread of a new personality type, one able to control animal urges and to delay the satisfaction of present wants for future gains, one governed by internal constraints and the capacity to abandon old practices for new, more rational ones.[6]

Freud translates this moral odyssey into a universal truth: the intensity of the pleasure to be had from psychical or intellectual labor—the sort of labor that makes human progress possible—is "mild as compared with that derived from the sating of crude and primary instinctual impulses." It is quite simply part of the order of things that civilization should be antagonistic to sexuality and that progress is bought at the price of "great sacrifices" of sexual gratification.[7]

---

[4]Graham Wallas, *The Life of Francis Place, 1771–1854* (London: George Allen and Unwin, 1918) 5–38.

[5]Edward Thompson, *The Making of the English Working Class* (New York: Vintage, 1966) 769ff.

[6]Max Weber, *Economy and Society*, ed. Guenther Roth and Claus Wittich (Berkeley: University of California Press, 1978) 1:63, 70.

[7]Sigmund Freud, *Civilization and its Discontents* (New York: W. W. Norton, 1961) 28.

Furthermore, a variety of cultural developments could be interpreted as both causing and reflecting a new era of sexual repression. Censorship played its part. Dr. Bowdler's *Family Shakespeare* appeared in 1804 without the intolerably lewd Doll Tearsheet in *Henry IV* or the word "body" anywhere; Jane Austen was criticized for allowing Lydia in *Pride and Prejudice* to happily survive her elopement. This was also the age of the masturbation phobia with its endless jeremiads on the mortal dangers of solitary pleasure; of the Society for the Suppression of Vice, founded in 1802; of woman supposedly unencumbered by lust—a putative angel in the house—and of the companionate marriage; of Methodism—Wesley himself preached celibacy and regarded marriage as distinctly second best, even if many of his followers did not agree;[8] and of Anglican Evangelicalism with its stern moralism—thousands of copies of Hannah More's tracts preached restraint, on all fronts, to the working classes. "Rational recreation" made headway, at least in the public sphere, against the old blood sports. The body, in short, was at a discount; "repression" and the new bourgeois world order seemed to fit very comfortably together.

Or did they? Certainly much qualitative evidence could be adduced for quite the opposite case. Parallel to the high and dry tradition of a Francis Place, chronicled most recently by Edward Thompson, there subsisted a low-life realm of London radicals who lived from pubs, pimping, and pornography.[9] If certain prescriptive texts suggest that the bourgeois family was at its core desexualized, others claim that its men folk at least profligately spent their newly gained money in a hugely increased libidinal economy. When Flora Tristan, the French socialist and feminist, visited England's "chief city," she reported that "there are in London from 80,000–100,000 women—the flower of the population—living off prostitution"; on the streets and in "temples raised by English materialism to their gods . . . male guests come to exchange their gold for debauchery." The number is exaggerated, probably wildly so, but the point is made nevertheless

---

[8]Henry Abelove, *The Evangelist of Desire: John Wesley and the Methodists* (Stanford: Stanford University Press, 1991).

[9]Iain McCalman, *Radical Underworld: Prophets, Revolutionaries, and Pornographers in London, 1795–1840* (New York: Cambridge University Press, 1988).

that where some saw repression, others saw an intimate link between sexual and economic life.[10]

The working classes, it is said by other bourgeois observers, were no more chaste than their betters. Frederick Engels in 1844 was repeating a longstanding commonplace when he noted with a hint of envy that "next to the enjoyment of intoxicating liquors, one of the principal faults of the English working-men is sexual license."[11] Just as novels were said by some to have corrupted the morals of impressionable young girls of the middling sort in the late eighteenth century, so it was supposed that "certain books [for example, the radical Richard Carlile's *Every Woman's Book* (1828), a guide to birth control for the working classes] have gone forth to inform depraved persons of a way by which they may indulge their corrupt passions and still avoid having illegitimate children."[12] The seemingly rootless denizens of the city suggested nothing so much as illicit, uncontrolled desire to bourgeois commentators of all ideological proclivities.

Statistics showing a remarkable rise in illegitimacy, particularly during the period 1750–1850, seem to lend credence to such views. Edward Shorter, for example, speaking from a very different moral perspective than nineteenth-century observers, categorically interprets these numbers to mean that the "liberation of the young" was finally nigh. He claims that the freeing of working-class youths from the sexual control of family and community led to a veritable "unleashing of sexuality," destroying "all competing passions (such as avarice or familial egoism) in the area of courtship." (Shorter seems to mean by this that they increasingly had intercourse as part of dating without concern for property or parental approval. It signals, for him, the first phase of the two-part libidinal revolution that would be completed in the 1960s.)

Shorter goes on to argue that masturbation, far from being suppressed during the industrial revolution, was largely unknown before that era and really only then came into its own as

[10]Flora Tristan, *London Journal, 1840*, trans. Denis Palmer and Giselle Pincetl (London: George Prior, 1980) 79.

[11]Frederick Engels, *The Condition of the Working Class in England, Karl Marx and Frederick Engels on Britain* (Moscow: Foreign Languages Publishing House, 1962) 161.

[12]Select Committee of the House of Commons on . . . 1831–32, *The Bill for Regulation of Factories* (706) xv, q. 3468.

part of the "premarital sexual revolution" that did so much to "modernize" affective relations generally. Shorter's evidence, like that of Jean-Louis Flandrin who makes a similar argument, is the silence of the sources. Almost nothing was said in medical literature about masturbation before the eighteenth century, and even in prescriptive religious texts it is lumped with other sexual sins: fornication, sodomy, adultery. (Even without assuming that discursive silences entail an absence in life, the question remains (see pp. 211–12 below) why "self-abuse" suddenly became such a pressing, much written about topic.) In any case, Shorter briefs a case that the industrial revolution, far from ushering in a new era of sexual repression, struck a blow for liberation. It first freed not the middle class but the working class, particularly working-class girls, who, through work outside the home, were supposedly emancipated from their preindustrial subjugation.[13]

Moreover, the old stereotype of a sexually repressed and repressive Victorian and even pre-Victorian middle class has recently been shown to be a gross simplification.[14] Peter Gay, in particular, has accumulated considerable evidence to the contrary. He argues that the antibourgeois diatribes of a Marx or a Flaubert, and of subsequent attacks on bourgeois sexuality as well, either stemmed from their more general criticism of the bourgeois as hypocritical—fine upstanding men seeing prostitutes and reading pornography in private—or were simply fanciful (the bourgeois wife silently suffering the attention of her husband). Gay paints a more nuanced picture of a generally healthy and varied sexual life in which married couples were likely to enjoy, and be advised by their doctors to enjoy, both foreplay and intercourse. After analyzing the extraordinarily explicit diary of a mid-nineteenth-century woman's sexual desires and satisfactions, Gay concludes that "the bourgeois record [diaries, medical accounts, marriage guides, novels] is full of such passions."[15]

---

[13]Edward Shorter, *The Making of the Modern Family* (New York: Basic, 1977) 119.

[14]F. Barry Smith, "Sexuality in Britain, 1800–1900: Some Suggested Revisions," *A Widening Sphere*, ed. Martha Vicinus (Bloomington: Indiana University Press, 1980) 182–98.

[15]Peter Gay, *Education of the Senses, The Bourgeois Experience* 1 (New York: Oxford University Press, 1984) 110.

## Demography and the Question of Repression

Faced with qualitative evidence that seems both to confirm and deny the "repressive hypothesis," I turn now to quantitative data in an effort to resolve the question. This will not be easy. Using modern survey techniques, it is notoriously difficult to secure reliable statistics even about contemporary sexual desire or behavior, and it is virtually impossible to do so for the nineteenth century. "Would more time have been spent on collecting the actual experiences of human beings," lamented the comparative anatomist and birth control advocate Richard Owen; but, in a field "so characterized by delicacy and silence," it was not.[16] Modern demographers, moreover, have been relatively uninterested in the proximate cultural determinants of fertility, those that might translate as affect or desire: "although [they] deal with sex and death," notes one of them, "they characteristically eliminate the pleasure from the former (hiding it under the category 'fecundability') and the terror of the latter (death tables being euphemistically called 'life tables'."[17] Still, there has been important demographic research relevant to the question, and I turn to it now.

There is no doubt that the population of England rose rapidly during the "long eighteenth century": 133 percent, from 4.9 million in 1680 to 11.5 million in 1820. Between 1791 and 1831 alone, the core years of the industrial revolution, it grew 72 percent from 7.7 million to 13.28 million, the fastest rate of increase anywhere in Western Europe, with the possible exception of Ireland.[18] Ever since Thomas Rickman collected vital statistics from a sample of parish registers in the early nineteenth century, demographers have been debating whether this unprecedented growth was due primarily to changes in mortality—in which case it would reflect various environmental factors but reveal nothing about sexual behavior—or to changes in fer-

---

[16]Thomas Laqueur, *Making Sex: Body and Gender from the Greeks to Freud* (Cambridge: Harvard University Press, 1990) 190.

[17]Daniel Scott Smith, "A Perspective on Demographic Methods and Effects in Social History," *William and Mary Quarterly* 39 (1982): 442–68, quote from 442.

[18]E. A. Wrigley, "The Growth of Population in England: A Conundrum Resolved," *Past and Present* 98 (February 1983): 121–150.

tility, which might reveal more. With the publication of Wrigley and Schofield's *Population History of England 1541-1871*—the fruits of over a decade's work by the Cambridge Group—the question seems finally laid to rest: mortality did fall; that is, life expectancy at birth increased by over six years, from about 32 in the 1670s and 1680s to almost 39 in the 1810s; but, more important, fertility rose and its contribution to population growth was on the order of two-and-a-half times greater than that of mortality.[19]

Specifically marital fertility, however, did not change much between the seventeenth and the nineteenth century; that is, women were not having more children for any given number of years at risk. But they did marry earlier, and fewer of them remained celibate than before, which meant that a larger proportion of women were likely to become pregnant in the first place. Between the middle of the seventeenth and the early eighteenth century, the celibacy rate seems to have been a more important variable as the percentage never married declined from about 25 percent in 1641 to around 10 percent between about 1690 and 1710. It remained around 10 percent, except for a low of about 5 percent in the cohort of 1741, for most of the eighteenth and early nineteenth centuries. After 1700 the drop in age of women's first marriage came to have the dominant effect: 26.6

---

[19](Cambridge: Harvard University Press, 1981). Wrigley and Schofield's conclusions on this point have been remarkably robust in the face of over a decade of scrutiny, despite debate about their *ad hoc* corrections for underregistration of births and deaths in the parish registers which are their primary source. For example, Peter Lindert, troubled by the differences between demographic patterns in Britain during the industrial revolution and in the Third World today, has argued that they increasingly overestimate crude birth rates for the period 1740-1815, resuming the correct level by 1840. This leaves their overall population estimates standing—crude death rates for infants were also underestimated—and also leaves intact the overall estimate for the relative importance of mortality and fertility over the whole period 1680-1840, but it would affect discussion of the 1740s to 1810s. See Peter Lindert, "English Living Standards, Population Growth, and Wrigley-Schofield," *Explorations in Economic History* 20 (1983): 134–149. No one, however, has proposed a compelling alternative to the Wrigley-Schofield model, and recent work on Germany—for example John E. Knodel's *Demographic Behavior in the Past* (Cambridge: Cambridge University Press, 1988)— has tended to support their emphasis on fertility.

for 1675–99; 25.7 for 1725–49; 25.3, 24.7, 23.7, respectively, for the next three quartiles to 1824. (These figures are based on family reconstitution of twelve parishes by the Cambridge Group; alternative numbers have been generated by Schofield and Weir in an effort to reconcile inconsistencies between age of marriage and celibacy data so that estimates for age of marriage for the 1741 cohort vary between 24.92 and 26.01, for 1791 between 23.63 and 22.64.) But the precise contribution of marriage age and percentage never marrying is also still being debated, and even if manipulations of necessarily incomplete data yield different absolute values there is little question that changes in nuptiality were critical to population growth.[20]

Sexual behavior was also changing outside of marriage, however. Despite a higher proportion of women marrying, and marrying younger, there was also what might seem, at first blush, a surprising increase in illegitimacy and prenuptial pregnancy. The illegitimacy ratio (illegitimate:all births) rose from 1.5 percent of births in the 1670s and 1680s to 3 percent by the middle of the eighteenth century, to 6 percent by 1810, and to almost 7 percent by 1850, after which it declined to around 4 percent by the end of the century. (In Western Europe generally during the late nineteenth century, both illegitimate and legitimate fertility again moved together, this time both downward.) Meanwhile the percentage of first births resulting from prenuptial conception rose from a little over 15 percent at the beginning of the period to between 30 and 40 percent by the end of the eighteenth and early nineteenth century.[21]

Wrigley and Schofield estimate that the fall in marriage age and in percentage never married, the rise of the illegitimacy ratio, and the fall in the mean age of maternity contributed 52 percent, 26 percent, 15 percent, and 7 percent, respectively, to the fertility component of the population growth rate.[22] But,

---

[20]E. A. Wrigley, "Marriage, Fertility and Population Growth in Eighteenth Century England," R. B. Outhwaite, *Marriage and Society: Studies in the Social History of Marriage* (New York: St. Martin's Press, 1982) 137–85; David Weir, "Rather Late than Never: Celibacy and Age at Marriage in English Cohort Fertility, 1541–1871," *Journal of Family History* 9 (1984): 341–355; Robert Schofield, "English Marriage Patterns Revisited," *Journal of Family History* 10 (1985): 2–20.

[21]Wrigley, "Marriage, Fertility,"

[22]Wrigley and Schofield 236–48.

whether these precise percentages are ultimately sustainable or not, the critical and seemingly inevitable conclusion is that a complex, interconnected set of social, economic, political, and cultural developments between the late seventeenth and early nineteenth century lowered the barriers to reproductive sexual intercourse, marital as well as extramarital.

Thus, for example, the age at first birth for married women was more or less the same as that of women who bore illegitimate children, which does not, however, mean that having children was generally divorced from marriage. The usual practice for parents of illegitimate children was to marry later: four-fifths of illegitimate children were also first children.[23] But it does mean, to put the case conversely, that whatever had limited entry into full reproductive life in the seventeenth century had lifted considerably by the early nineteenth. (Poor law records also suggest that the ability of individual women, communities, or parish authorities to enforce marriage after prenuptial pregnancy declined with the increased mobility of commercial and industrial society, which would account for some of the increase in bastardy.)

So much is clear. So, too, is the fact that population continued to increase without the preventive checks that had sustained a more or less homeostatic system before. But why and how nuptiality functioned, what caused the decline in age of marriage and rates of celibacy, is still very much debated.

Certainly Shorter's effort (see p. 191 above) to deduce the libidinal liberation of working-class women from rising rates of illegitimacy is seriously weakened by historical evidence.[24] Critics point out that except in a few sectors, more women did not, in fact, work outside the home than before; and when they did, it was out of a need to fulfil traditional family obligations in new settings—not the desire to be rid of them. Illegitimacy rates, moreover, were no higher in new industrial than in rural areas. And finally, as the evidence on p. 194 above shows, illegitimacy cannot be considered on its own but is part of a far broader, nuptiality-driven increase in fertility patterns.

---

[23]Wrigley, "Marriage, Fertility."

[24]Louise A. Tilly, Joan W. Scott, and Miriam Cohen, "Women's Work and European Fertility Patterns," *Journal of Interdisciplinary History* 6 (Winter 1976): 447–76.

Wrigley and Schofield's explanation is essentially Malthusian: rising wages make it easier for couples to accumulate enough resources to marry: people marry earlier, fewer remain unmarried, they have more children. Consequently, labor supply increases, real wages go down, and the opposite happens: later marriage, higher celibacy rates, a lower gross reproduction rate, that is, fewer children for each couple. There are several serious problems with this view, however. In the first place, the empirical connection between wage rates and population, although plausible, remains weak, in part because historical wage series themselves are flawed and in part because economic analysis has suggested that if population affected wages at all, it did so indirectly by influencing prices.[25] The Wrigley-Schofield model demands a forty-to-fifty year lag, which is unaccountably long and difficult to explain, between changes in wage rates and changes in marriage behavior. Furthermore, two nuptiality indicators, a lowered age of marriage and a smaller proportion of the population remaining celibate, do not consistently move together as the model would predict.[26] And finally, regional studies show that other factors are quite clearly at work. In the agricultural south, where wage rates were notoriously depressed, the female age of marriage probably dropped because of the sheer need to survive: there was a sharp decline in the demand for live-in female servants, who before had remained single until they had saved a nest egg; a depressed demand for labor due to enclosures lowered wages so far that single people, especially women, could not earn enough to survive alone; and poor law policy—subsidizing family's but not single people's income—may well have kept depressed wages from having their "natural" demographic effect just as Malthus had feared. One recent study, for example, of 214 parishes in southeast England found that family allowances positively affected birth rates and accounted, when other variables were controlled, for increased marriage fertility in a period of falling, or at best stable, real incomes.[27]

---

[25]Peter Lindert, "English Population, Wages and Prices," *Journal of Interdisciplinary History* 20 (Spring 1985): 609–634.

[26]J. A. Goldstone, "The Demographic Revolution in England: A Reexamination," *Population Studies* 40 (March 1986): 5–34.

[27]George Boyer, "Malthus was Right After All: Poor Relief and Birth Rates in South East England," *Journal of Political Economy* 97, n. 11

Protoindustrialization, and the resulting proletarianization of labor—that is, its dependence on wages—has also been adduced as the critical social and economic change affecting nuptiality and hence population growth.    In theory, since marriage age and the celibacy rate were supposedly kept relatively high by the difficulties of accumulating sufficient scarce resources—primarily land but also working capital—to set up an independent household, whatever would make such accumulation easier    would make access to marriage easier as well.    Thus, if young people were less dependent on family land, for instance, they would have easier access to marriage, which would be reflected in lower ages of marriage and a smaller proportion of the population who never married.    And indeed, a body of empirical work suggests that the age of marriage did drop precipitously in a community like Shepshead in Leicestershire—from a median for women of 26.8 in 1600–99 to 23.2 in 1700–49 and 20.6 in 1750–1824—seemingly in response to dramatic new opportunities in rural industry.[28]    A number of other studies for specific locales, in Britain and on the continent, present similar evidence.[29]

But there are also difficulties with proletarianization as a general explanation.    Marriage age dropped in parishes where there was no rural industry; and conversely in certain Belgian parishes studied by Gutman and Leboutte, for example, marriage age remained high despite new industry.    At the national level, proletarianization and protoindustrialization were associated in England both with declining fertility in the sixteenth and seventeenth century and with increasing fertility in the eighteenth.    This does not mean that there is no connection between industrial change and family strategies.    Certainly contemporary observers lamented the ease with which young couples could enter into a sexual relation under the new economic dispensation. But the mechanisms are far more complex than have been captured in any of the available models.

---

(February 1989): 93–114; K. D. M. Snell, *Annals of the Laboring Poor* (Cambridge: Cambridge University Press, 1985).

[28]David Levine, *Family Formation in an Age of Nascent Capitalism* (New York: Academic Press, 1977).

[29]Myron P. Gutman and René Leboutte, "Rethinking Protoindustrialization and the Family," *Journal of Interdisciplinary History* 14 (Winter 1984): 587–607.

In response to the absence of any clear relation between wage rates or other underlying economic factors on the one hand and nuptiality on the other, Henry Abelove has argued recently that demographers have simply misconceived the problem. It is not a question of nuptiality but of sexuality; not "what changed constraints on entry into marriage?" but what made "sexual intercourse so called more popular in late eighteenth century England?" The rise in production and the increased popularity of a sexual act, "which uniquely makes for reproduction," he speculates, are part of the same phenomenon which could "be called either capitalism or the discourse of capitalism or modern heterosexuality or the discourse of modern heterosexuality."[30] Factory discipline and the decline of foreplay go together. The attraction of this reformulation is that it posits—as I will argue in more detail below—that the economic and the sexual sphere are intimately connected.

The problem can be summarized thus: Compared to earlier periods, there was certainly open hostility to nonreproductive sexuality—to masturbation and homosexuality, if not openly to foreplay—and the incidence of "intercourse, so called" per capita was certainly higher because the barriers to marriage were lowered. Yet there is little evidence for the increased "popularity" of a specifically reproductive act in areas of new productivity or elsewhere.

Within marriage, where the vast proportion of reproductive intercourse took place, the sexual regime was largely unchanged. Based on the timing of first births nine or more months after marriage, demographers can calculate fecundability, the chance of becoming pregnant in the absence of birth control or postpartum nonsusceptibility during a menstrual cycle or month. Since women are, in fact, fertile only during a small number of days in the middle of the menstrual cycle, their chances of becoming pregnant are greatly increased with frequency of coition. Using a number of mathematical models that are much debated but

---

[30]Henry Abelove, "Some Speculations on the History of 'Sexual Intercourse' during the 'Long Eighteenth Century' in England," *Genders* 6 (November 1989): 127. Abelove uses the phrase "sexual intercourse so called" to suggest that one form of sexual intercourse—the heterosexual, penis in vagina with emission, act has been labeled as "intercourse" for cultural purposes, while all other sexual acts are designated by the names of sins or perversions.

fairly widely accepted within the range under discussion, demographers can work backwards from the actual data on fecundability to the coital rate that would make it possible.[31] In the case of England, the result is disappointingly dull: fecundability for every marriage cohort after 1600–49 is about .23 (23 out of 100), which corresponds to a coital rate of about .25 (1: 00= once a day), or once every four days.[32] (For certain European populations, Abelove's hypothesis *might* prove correct. Knodel finds a sizable increase in age-standardized fecundability from .21 in the cohort 1750–74 to .282 in 1875–99 in the fourteen German villages he studied, but he attributes the shrinking birth interval not to more frequent intercourse but to changes in breast-feeding practices, which in turn affect fertility because the hormone that induces milk production reduces the likelihood of ovulation.)[33]

Finally, not only age-specific marital fertility but also the general pattern of reproductive behavior failed to change dramatically during the long eighteenth century. Until the late nineteenth century England, and indeed Europe generally, remained a "natural fertility" regime, in which no discernible effort was made to stop childbearing completely after a given number of children had been born. Women would thus tend to have their last children near menopause, at around forty, no matter how many they had had before. This does not mean that the actual level of fertility did not vary among societies and that individual couples—or women—did not try to space births according to various cultural, economic, or idiosyncratic personal considerations. Indeed the method most within the control of women—the duration of lactation after each birth—seems to have been the most important of the means used.[34] During the

---

[31]R. G. Potter and S. R. Millman, "Fecundability and the Frequency of Marital Intercourse: A Critique of Nine Models," *Population Studies*, 39 (November 1985): 461–70.

[32]Chris Wilson, "The Proximate Determinants of Marital Fertility in England 1600–1799," *The World We Have Gained*, ed. Lloyd Benfield, Richard M. Smith, and Keith Wrightson (Oxford: Basil Blackwell, 1986) 203–30.

[33]Knodel, *Demographic Behavior*.

[34]Effective surgical abortion was extremely dangerous, and the widely sold abortifacients, when not also poisonous, were of doubtful efficacy; coitus interruptus and abstinence required the co-operation of men, which was usually not forthcoming and may even have been generally "unknown";

industrial revolution, in other words, sexual intercourse was still inextricably bound up with babies in the consciousness of the great majority of men and women.

The question of what happened to sex during the industrial revolution and its antecedents has now been partially answered. Within marriage, the evidence suggests, there was little change. But, as the barriers to nuptiality eased, access to sexual intercourse did become greater; the franchise, so to speak, for indulging in it was lowered. Beginning in the late seventeenth century and continuing well into the nineteenth—precisely how and why remains unclear—couples could marry with only a shadow of the claim on social and economic resources that had been required earlier. Sexual intercourse was thus literally "freer" because there was a freer market in matrimony, to which it was still inextricably linked.

But perhaps I should rephrase the question. Instead of asking whether there was more or less sexual intercourse, greater or fewer opportunities for the fulfillment of sexual desire or for its repression, more or less desire itself, one should ask instead why there was such a vast outpouring of talk on the subject during this period, how it articulated with other discourses, and how the various discourses of sexuality served to constitute, rather than merely reflect, their object.

---

birth control devices, especially those controllable by women, like the sponge, were next to useless.

One does not, of course, know whether a new family limitation regime would have come earlier if the technology had been available. But demographers tend to see it as a product of new mentalities, not of technologies, because it depended on widespread knowledge—and also adoption by men since women had long been willing to do so—of behavior or devices to stop reproduction entirely once a certain family size has been reached. In contrast simply to birth spacing, this step constitutes a radical and irrevocable shift in reproductive behavior—the so-called "fertility transition"—which falls outside the period under discussion. See Etienne van der Walle and John Knodel, "Europe's Fertility Transition: New Evidence for Today's Developing World," *Population Bulletin* 34, n. 6 (February 1980): n.p.; Susan C. Watkins, "Conclusion," Ansley Coale and Susan C. Watkins, *The Decline of Fertility in Europe* (Princeton: Princeton University Press, 1986) 420–49.

### *Discourses of Sex, Sexuality, and Desire*

"The central issue," the philosopher Michel Foucault argues, "is not to determine whether one says yes or no to sex . . . whether one asserts its importance or denies its effects . . . but to account for the fact that it is spoken about, to discover who does the speaking, the positions and viewpoints from which they speak." In this account desire is not a constant biological given that is more or less repressed; talk about sex produces desire and allows for a new sort of political control of the body. Specifically, Foucault argues that there was a vast expansion in the "discourse of sex": medical texts, tracts about masturbation, the initiation and elaboration of censuses, discussions about vital statistics, marriage manuals, moralistic pamphlets; that this varied and multivoiced literature—this discourse—imbricated the body in a new "technology of power"; and that while the old "absolutist" state displayed its authority by actually punishing the bodies of offenders, the new bourgeois order produced a vast "will to knowledge" about sex (among other things), which both incited the body's sexuality and allowed it to be controlled by various sorts of experts.[35]

The history of discourses about sex is thus very much part of the history of the industrial revolution and of the nineteenth century generally. It does not constitute a separate subject from that of this essay. In what follows, however, I aim to show, more specifically, how social, cultural, and economic concerns were thought about, imagined through, and given a special emotional urgency by an erotically charged body.

The Tory poet laureate Robert Southey hated Thomas Malthus' *Essay on the Principle of Population* in part because he detested political economy. But more particularly, Malthus profoundly threatened the traditional Christian view of a well-ordered, beneficent universe that reflected God's foresight and judgment. No matter how much the productivity of agriculture might be improved, no matter how much better humanity became, fertility would inevitably outstrip resources. To obey God's command to Noah that man be fruitful and multiply could

---

[35]Michel Foucault, *The History of Sexuality, Volume 1: An Introduction*, trans. Robert Hurley (New York: Pantheon, 1978) 11.

lead only to disaster. God, as the saying went, appeared to have invited too many mortals to nature's feast.

Of course, theologians and other evangelical thinkers worked to repair some of the damage that Malthus had wrought to their well-ordered world. In the first edition he admitted only the positive check of famine and the preventive check of ascetic abstinence as means of keeping the birth rate in check. But if, as he admitted in later editions, moral restraint—that is, postponing marriage until able to provide adequately for children—could work as well, then perhaps there was moral purpose in the universe after all. Either overpopulation was God's incentive to labor more, acquire more, conserve more so as to be able to have children later. Or it transformed the spiritual virtues of prudence and chastity into secular ones, which would be more easily practiced as economic progress brought moral and cultural improvement in its wake.[36]

But the worm was in the bud, and people like Southey knew it. He is appalled that Malthus would consider lust and hunger as equivalents. Both were equally independent "of the reason and the will." He is outraged that a book in which sexual reproduction looms large and vice figures prominently "for the preservation of good order" should be written in the vulgar tongue, available to everyone including women: "These were not subjects to be sent into circulating libraries and book-societies, and to be canvassed at tea-tables." How could it be "heard without indignation by one who had a wife, a sister, or a daughter"?[37]

Perhaps, too, Southey is indignant that Malthus insists on the absolute primacy of the sexual body in the political economy. Against Godwin, who held that in a perfectly rational society sexual passion would disappear, Malthus argues not only that sex is here to stay, and a good thing besides, but also that there is absolutely no reason whatsoever to believe that matters could be otherwise. The fact that "the passion between the sexes is necessary and will remain nearly in its present state" is as obvious, and requires as little apology, as that food is necessary for human existence. "No move towards the extinction of passion

[36]Boyd Hilton, *The Age of Atonement: The Influence of Evangelicalism on Social and Economic Thought* (Oxford: Clarendon Press, 1988).

[37]Robert Southey, "On the State of the Poor, the Principle of Mr. Malthus's Essay on Population, and the Manufacturing System," *Essays, Moral and Political*, 2 vols. (London: J. Murray, 1832) 1:150, 82.

has taken place in the five or six thousand years that the world has existed" (Malthus still accepts the estimate of the seventeenth-century bishop James Usher based on biblical genealogy); why should it take place now?  Sexual pleasure indeed is so satisfying that its deferral through late marriage—he thinks of it only in this context—is one of the "miseries" that might curb population growth: "Perhaps there is scarcely a man who has once experienced the genuine delight of virtuous love . . . that does not look back to the period as the sunny spot in his whole life, where his imagination loves to bask . . . and which he would most live over again."  No pleasures, he concludes, are "more real and essential" than the pleasures of the flesh.  And no one understood better than Malthus their relation to economy and society.[38]

The reproductive capacities of the body were, for Malthus, the sign of its individual well-being but also, paradoxically, of society's present or future sickness.[39]  Healthy bodies reproduce themselves geometrically; food supplies increase arithmetically, and as a result the bodies of future generations are less healthy—since they have less nutriment per capita available to them—than the ones that came before.  The old healthy body/healthy society homology had broken down, but the reproducing body had become the lens through which the conditions and tensions of political economy could be viewed with great clarity.

Nowhere was Malthus' vision darker than when discussing the poor law.  People are given money, which stands for value—in this case of food—while in fact they contribute no labor to produce it—or anything else for that matter.  Indeed, the poor are encouraged by child allowances, he fears (see p. 196 above),

---

[38]Thomas Malthus, *An Essay on the Principle of Population* (1798; Harmondsworth: Penguin, 1970) 146–47.  Since the context of this discussion is procreative function of marriage and the pain caused by its deferral, it is clear that Malthus' "virtuous love" refers to what others called "the pleasures of the marriage bed," "marital bliss," and the like.  No one at this time, except possibly radicals like Carlile, discussed sexual pleasure for its own sake outside of marriage.

[39]Catherine Gallagher, "The Body versus the Social Body in the Works of Thomas Malthus and Henry Mayhew," *The Making of the Modern Body* ed. Catherine Gallagher and Thomas Laqueur (Berkeley: University of California Press, 1987) 83–106.

to reproduce in direct violation of the law of the body, that is, they are being artificially allowed to escape the misery of sexual abstinence. (In a world without effective birth control each act of heterosexual intercourse represents a potential claim on sustenance.) More profoundly, however, for Malthus, human sexuality is the mark of the essential corporeality of the body, which, mixed through labor with external matter, is after all what produces value in a *labor* theory of value.

Malthus' theoretical commitment to such a corporeal standard is evident, too, in his critique of Adam Smith's view of money as a way of representing the comparative values of different products for purposes of exchange. According to Smith, a shilling's worth of wheat is by definition of the same value as, and exchangeable for, a shilling's worth of lace. But not so for Malthus. He argues that Smith is wrong in holding that increases in the production of labor are equivalent to increases in the productivity of land. All increases in revenue are not the same, and in fact a stock or a revenue will not be "real and effectual" in terms of maintaining labor, will not be "convertible into a proportional quantity of provisions" if it has "arisen merely from the produce of labor, and not from the produce of land." Buying, selling, trading—the activities of the marketplace—are, in short, less "real" in terms of the body than growing food. Malthus frames the distortions of the market in an extraordinary image of the beef cow fattened on food that should go to humans. The very high price of beef today, he argues, makes it profitable to raise such a beast not only on the best of grazing land but even on land that could, and formerly did, grow corn for human consumption. A fattened beef feeds far fewer laborers and their families than would the grain it consumes, that is, it is produced with a net caloric loss in the stock of food available for humans and consequently "may be considered, in the language of the French economists, as an unproductive laborer."[40]    In other words the chimerical, incorporeal qualities of circulation and exchange, of money and especially paper money, lead to a distortion of the regime of sex: men and women indulge in a pleasure that—based on tangible nutritional resources—they have no claim to. The changes in nuptiality discussed above are, therefore, like the fattened cow, evidence for the dangers of un-

---

[40]See Malthus 184, 187–188; Gallagher 96–97.

productive exchange, of bodies tricked into profoundly impermissible intercourse.

Desire, whether for sexual gratification or for consumer goods, lies still more deeply at the heart of theories of capitalism. A market economy, and especially an industrial economy, is predicated on social openness, on the notion that the satisfaction of desire—for goods, services, prestige—through labor is beneficial to both the individual and society. It stands in stark opposition to a society of ranks and orders in which convention and sumptuary legislation are meant to keep desire in check. But once the genie of desire is let out, how is it to be restrained when its attention turns to sex? A free labor and free exchange were to be sought after; one of free love was clearly not.

David Hume, the eighteenth-century Scottish philosopher and historian, lays out the theoretical grounds for the connection; nineteenth-century observers squirm when confronted with its implications. "Everything in the world," Hume points out, "is purchased by labor," the cause of which is "the passions"—pain and aversion in the old, precommercial world, pleasure and desire in the new. In the old world there was little to work for, little to buy, sumptuary restrictions on what one could own even if it were available and within financial reach, and a moral predisposition against the exercise of desire: a low wage economy with a backward-sloping supply curve of labor, to put it in modern terms. The state or a feudal lord, Hume argues, can always extract a certain amount of labor through taxes or dues and can try to prevent consumption through legislation, but theirs is an uphill battle against the resistance of men and women who have no attractive reasons to work. Employers or the state have to contend with the high marginal utility of leisure and use force, of arms or of hunger, to compel effort.

But "furnish him [the producer] with manufacturers and commodities, and he will do it himself." The carrot replaces the stick, not only externally but in the realms of the psyche: "govern men by other passions and animate them with the spirit of avarice." Both consumption and production thrive—and overall wealth grows—as a result of the unshackling of desire and the breakdown of restrictions on the passions and on social mobility. Desire stimulates supply by making laborers produce for the market rather than only for home consumption or the state, and the consequent growth of "industry, art, and luxury" in turn stimulates further desire by providing it with new objects for purchase: a high wage economy and a wage-elastic supply of labor, in modern terms.[41] (Hume here is siding with "high wages" in the eighteenth-century debate that raged between those who believed that the poor worked only to avoid starvation and if paid more would work less—the low-wage faction—and those who thought that they worked in order to consume and would work more if they had more money to spend—the high-wage faction.)[42]

At its most general level, this is a brief for the new social order in which a boundless drive toward self-improvement, embedded in every breast, was thought to benefit both the individual and society. It is also an argument about morality. Hume, like other early theorists of capitalism, wants to rescue avarice from its moral dungeon and show it to be a passion fit to govern other less benign ones like aggression. The exercise of economic self-interest becomes a beneficent and peaceful foil to dangerous, antisocial human propensities.[43]

But Hume's new positive valuation of desire does not stop with the less overtly carnal passion for clothes. There is psychologically only one sort of desire. He argues, for example, that "the natural appetite betwixt the sexes" is the "first and original principle of human society" because men in their wild uncultivated state would never be compelled by reason to join together. Love, of the sort that "arises betwixt the sexes" is more complex. Of all the "compound passions," none "better deserves our attention as well on account of its force and violence, as those curious principles of philosophy, for which it affords us an uncontestable argument." He goes on to propose that it is derived from the conjunction of three different passions: the "pleasing sensation arising from beauty; the bodily appetite for generation; and a generous kindness or goodwill."[44] The critical point here is not Hume's benign attitudes toward a passion more often condemned than so neatly dissected but the fact that his mode of analysis applies equally well to consumer goods. Thus, he ex-

---

[41]David Hume, "On Commerce," *Essays: Moral, Political, and Literary* ed. T. H. Green and T. H. Grose (New York: Longmans, 1898) 1:294.

[42]E. W. Gilboy, "Demand in the Industrial Revolution" R. M. Hartwell, *The Causes of the Industrial Revolution* (London: Methuen, 1967) 121–38.

[43]Albert Hirschmann, *The Passions and the Interests* (Princeton: Princeton University Press, 1977).

[44]David Hume, *A Treatise on Human Nature*, ed. L. A. Selby-Bigge (1739; Oxford: Oxford University Press, 1965) 394.

plains the relation of the direct to the indirect passions by the case of a "suit of fine cloths": "It produces pleasure from their beauty," which in turn produces the direct passions of volition and desire; but the clothes also raise the indirect passion of pride in their owners, which in turn gives new impetus to the original direct passion of desire and the will to satisfy it.[45]

The connection between desire for clothes, or indeed any other personal adornments, on the one hand and sexual desire on the other is not new.  It is standard fare among seventeenth century moralists: outward adorning of the hair leads to "whoredom," not to speak of "drinking, stealing, lying, murder, and HELL";[46] "vain apparel leads to whoring, drinking, gluttony, and envy";[47] "rolling in foreign silks and linens" is likened to "blind sodomites groping after their filthy pleasures," just as wearing French clothes is tantamount to getting a venereal disease.[48]   Ambition itself was regarded as the vanguard of all other vices, especially those of the flesh: "wherever you see pride in the front, sure lust marches in the rear."[49]   But by the late eighteenth century, moral valences had changed; desire itself was not intrinsically bad; it could not be condemned *tout court* but had to be judged by its objects on a case-by-case basis.

Under the guiding moral assumptions of commercial society "unnecessary expenses" and the desire to live always a little above one's station were far from vices.   They were virtues. Bernard de Mandeville in the 1720s had already argued that if pride and luxury were banished, goodly numbers of artisans would be starved within half a year.  But more pointedly, when observers in the 1780s and 1790s noted that the rural poor "pant to imitate" London fashions; that girls in the country had "the most longing desires" to ape their urban betters; that Wedgewood's customers for pottery or Foster's for carpets had "caught from example the contagion of desire," they were doing

---

[45]Hume, *Treatise* 438–439.

[46]T. H., *A Looking-Glasse for Women* (London: R. W., 1644) title page.

[47]George MacKenzie, *Moral Gallantry* (Edinburgh: Robert Broun, 1667) 125.

[48]William Petyt, *Brittania Languens, or a Discourse of Trade* (London: Thomas Dring, 1680) 302.

[49]Edward Ward, *Female Policy Detected: Or, the Arts of a Designing Woman Laid Open* (London: B. Harris, 1716) 21.

so with approval.[50]  The language of the marketplace speaks of a more open libidinal economy generally: "longing desires," "panting," the sense of being caught up in a maelstrom of want bridges the apparent chasm between material objects and the flesh.

But therein lies the mortal danger for many nineteenth-century bourgeois observers.  The old elision of the difference between consuming goods on the one hand and consuming sex on the other could not be raised to the level of a general principle.  And while these middle-class observers seem to have regarded their own class as sufficiently rooted in home, work, and family to resist the slide from one side to the other, the same did not hold for the working class.  They were perceived generally to be rootless and uncontrolled—a sort of social correlative of unrestrained id; working-class women in particular were seen as dangerously vulnerable to the freedoms, the allure, of the marketplace.  Girls' love of "dress and finery," the source of the effective demand that kept the cotton and silk mills, the ribbon and lace workshops going, also led them, it was said, into prostitution, "adding to their legitimate earnings in the mills, with which alone they could not indulge their passion to show."[51]  Prostitutes may be distinguished from factory girls by their clothes "though the costume and head-dress of the factory girls is not altogether different."[52]  As she contemplates illicit sexual intercourse with the wealthy landowner Donnithorne, Hetty Sorel in George Eliot's *Adam Bede* dreams vacantly about all the wonderful clothes she will have when she becomes lady of the manor.  Working-class women were thought to bear the dangers of uncontrolled desire that seemed to flow freely from one domain to another, from legitimate consumption to illegitimate sex.

More generally bourgeois observers of all stripes looked at the working class through the prism of illicit sex.  Like many of his contemporaries, Engels reproached their "unbridled search for pleasure"—one detects a certain wistfulness here—or their indecent sleeping arrangements (couples sharing their beds or

---

[50]Neil McKendrick, John Brewer, and J. H. Plumb, *The Birth of Consumer Society* (Bloomington: University of Indiana Press, 1985) 95, 28.

[51]*Appendix to the Second Report of the Commissioners, Trades and Manufactures*, 1843 (431) xiv, A6 para 42.

[52]Appendix E. 38.

their sleeping rooms with lodgers and children of both sexes).[53]
Here the offense is not simply wearing jewelry or dresses; nor
are comments like Engels' simply a response to measurable increases in vice. By their own admission social commentators
found these difficult to come by. James Kay-Shuttleworth, the
Manchester physician and reformer, notes that while crime can
be "statistically classed," "the moral leprosy of vice can not be
exhibited with mathematical precision." "Sensuality has no
record," he concludes.[54] The Manchester surgeon Peter Gaskell
provides a long footnote to explain why statistics on illegitimacy
are "worse than useless"—in fact, they show a higher rate in
agricultural than in manufacturing districts—and that one must
look beyond them to appreciate "the general licentiousness and
illicit intercourse which prevails" there.[55]

In passages like these, working-class sexuality represents
the exhilarating yet also terrifying lability, flux, and movement
of a capitalist economy and rapid industrialization. The social
discourses of sex during this period expose what is both omnipresent and indistinctly perceived. Examples abound.
Navvies, itinerant workers *par excellence* who built the railroads,
also had a reputation for exceptional potency, "a fine muscled
animal . . . grasping in one hand a pick by the shaft, and in the
other a woman by the waist."[56] In an industrial context, middle-
class observers like Peter Gaskell readily translate their fears
about individual and social mobility into accounts of the "almost
entire extinction of sexual decency" among mill artisans. The
problem is not the democratization of access to sex but of access
to respectable social position and authority. It is as if unbounded
upward mobility pollutes the social and specifically the sexual
body.

Parvenu master manufacturers—so Gaskell's analysis
goes—"sprung from the ranks of labourers . . . uneducated, of
coarse habits, sensual in their enjoyments," are presented with
"the facilities for lascivious indulgence afforded by the number of

[53]Engels 162.

[54]James Phillips Kay-Shuttleworth, *The Moral and Physical Condition of
the Working Classes employed in the Cotton Manufacture in Manchester* (1832,
rpt. Manchester: E. J. Morten, 1969) 62.

[55]Peter Gaskell, *Artisans and Machinery* (1836; London: Cass Reprint,
1968) 100.

[56]Terry Coleman, *The Railway Navvies* (London: Hutchinson, 1965) 162.

females brought under their immediate control." These rootless
master manufacturers, desperate for supervisors in their mills,
invest their young sons with authority and money: "Boys, at an
age when they should have been sedulously kept apart from opportunities of indulging their nascent sexual propensities, were
thrust into a very hotbed of lust." Accustomed to "unbridled indulgence," they do not marry their partners in crime although
these females, "known to have lived in a state of concubinage,"
have no problem in finding husbands. The licentious new economy has no bounds as it destroys what Gaskell imagines was the
old market in marriage.[57]

Many such discursive connections were made by nineteenth-
century observers between the sexual on the one hand and the
social or economic realms on the other: the sexual dangers of un-
supervised movement of the young and of adolescents with
money of their own, the heated atmosphere of mills (70 to 75°
F!) producing early puberty and desire in girls and bringing together numerous young people of both sexes in factories.
Gaskell's text emphasizes over and over again the nakedness,
the violations of the modesty, of female workers. Probably the
most famous and guilt-inducing picture in nineteenth-century social reform literature shows a girl, bare to the waist, pulling a
loaded cart. Everything in the new social order was heated up,
changeable, morally shaky, and sex was the prism through
which its dangers were imagined.

At a more general level, too, perverted sex was the sign of
perverted social relations; the bodies of the dangerous classes
were imagined as preternaturally fecund and productive of mon-
sters. Thus, Edwin Chadwick cites with approval the fantasies
of a negative utopia voiced by a stipendiary magistrate of the
Thames Police Office. From the "indigent and profligate generally," he moves to the case of a fish hawker—again fastening
upon an itinerant occupation—to the image of a race of "tub
men," "lower than any yet known," who would somehow spawn
if "empty casks were placed along the streets of Whitechapel."
In a few days each would have a tenant; they would breed; they
would prey upon the community; and in the end "there is no con-

---

[57]Gaskell 100.

ceivable degradation to which portions of the species might not be reduced . . . savages living in the midst of civilization."[58]

The leading Manchester sanitary reformer, Dr. James Kay-Shuttleworth, indulges a similarly Rabelaisian revery about a "licentiousness capable of corrupting the whole body of society, like an insidious disease." The notion that cities generally, industrial cities in particular, perhaps even industrial society as a whole is somehow dangerous, dark, and "unreadable"—so powerful in Engels' encounter with the walled off courts of Manchester—is evident here too. Moral contagion is an evil in its own right, but Kay gives it an economic twist. Ultimately, productivity suffers: "the population becomes physically less efficient . . . politically worthless as having few desires to satisfy, and noxious as dissipators of capital accumulated." Finally, a dissipated race multiplies, "licentiousness" continues to "indulge its capricious appetite," and a great, dense, morally impotent, stagnant blob of flesh is all that remains. Lesson: "Morality is worthy of the attention of the economist."[59]

Masturbation and prostitution are also, as their new names—the *solitary* vice, THE *social* evil—imply, primarily social pathologies that are understood through the perverted sexualized body. The political and sexual radical Richard Carlile makes a *reductio* argument for how the solitary vice must be construed as a threat to "the nature of human solidarity" and how little it appears to be a problem of excess or wicked sexual desire. Sociability and not repression is at stake. Carlile's *Every Woman's Book* (a reprint of a special issue of the *Red Republican*, which he published with his wife Jane) is a sustained attack on conventional sexual morality, a plea for freeing the passions, and a practical guide to birth control. Love is natural, and only its fruits can and should be controlled; marriage laws constrain excessively a passion that should not be forced or shackled; and so on. Carlile proposes that Temples of Venus be established, where young men and women could enjoy safe, nonreproductive, health-preserving, *extramarital* sexual intercourse. (Five-sixths of deaths from consumption among young girls resulted from want of sexual commerce and perhaps as much as nine-tenths of

---

[58]Edwin Chadwick, *Report from the Poor Law Commissioners on an Inquiry into the Sanitary Conditions of the Laboring Population of Great Britain,* 1842 (HL) xxvi p. 135.

[59]Kay-Shuttleworth 81–82.

all other illness, he suggested in his attempt to promulgate this utopian scheme.) But on the subject of masturbation Carlile, the sexual radical, is as shrill as the most evangelically inspired moralist or alarmist physician. Born of the cloister or its modern equivalents, where a diseased religion turns love into sin, "the appeasing of lascivious excitement in females by artificial means" or the "accomplishment of seminal excretion in the male" is not only wicked but physically destructive as well. Masturbation leads to disease of mind and body. Indeed, the "natural and healthy commerce between the sexes" for which he offers the technology is explicitly linked to the abolition of prostitution, masturbation, pederasty, and other "unnatural" practices.[60]

The contrast could not be clearer between a fundamentally asocial or socially degenerative practice—the pathogenic, solitary sex of the cloister—and the vital, socially constructive act of heterosexual intercourse. But the supposed physical and even moral evils of masturbation seem almost secondary to its status as a sign of underlying social pathology. The emphasis in "the solitary vice" should perhaps be less on "vice," understood as the fulfillment of illegitimate desire, than on "solitary," the channeling of perfectly healthy desire back into itself. The debate over masturbation that raged from the eighteenth century onward might therefore be understood as part of the more general debate about the unleashing of desire upon which a commercial economy depended and about the possibility of human community under these circumstances—a sexual version of the classic "Adam Smith Problem."

Prostitution is the other great arena in which the battle against the destructive power of unsocialized sex was fought. "Whoring," of course, had long been regarded as wicked and detrimental to the commonweal, but so had drunkenness, blasphemy, and other disturbances of the peace. Not until the nineteenth century did it rise to being "*the* social evil," a particularly disruptive, singularly threatening vice. Here I want to tell only a small part of the long story of this phenomenon. The critical point is that the social perversity of prostitution was thought to be visited on the individual bodies of prostitutes: they were gen-

---

[60]Richard and Jane Carlile, *Every Woman's Book or What is Love containing Most Important Instructions for the Prudent Regulation of the Principle of Love and the Number of a Family* (London, 1828) 18, 22, 26–27, 37–38.

erally regarded as an unproductive commodity.   Because they were *public* women; because so much traffic passed over their reproductive organs; because in them the semen of so many men was mixed, pell mell, together; because the ovaries of prostitutes, through overstimulation, were seldom without morbid lesions; because their Fallopian tubes were closed by too frequent intercourse; or, most tellingly, because they did not feel affection for the men with whom they had sex, they were thought to be barren or in any case very unlikely to have children.

Money, or more precisely a somehow illegitimate exchange of money, is the root of their strange biology.   Prostitution is sterile because the mode of exchange it represents is sterile. Nothing is produced because, like usury in medieval Christian theology, it is pure exchange.   A deep cultural uneasiness about money and the market economy is thus couched in the metaphors of reproductive biology.   More to the point here, fear of an asocial market takes on a new avatar in the claim that sex for money, coition with prostitutes, bears no fruit.   By the nineteenth century, the trope of the barren prostitute had a respectable pedigree reaching back to the early commercial cities of Renaissance Italy.   But the boundaries it guarded—between home and economy, between public and private, self and society—were both more sharply drawn and more fraught in the urban class society of the industrial and commercial revolutions than ever before.   Or at least contemporary observers thought so.   Society seemed to be in unprecedented danger from the marketplace.   And the sexual body bore the widespread anxieties about this danger.

While masturbation threatened to take sexual desire and pleasure inward away from family, prostitution took it outward. Perhaps even more than masturbation, it broke the barrier between home and market, which, in much social thought, was regarded as the safeguard for human solidarities against the disintegrative forces of the market.   The sterility of prostitutes and their other biological defects and dangers (as well as the illnesses resulting from self-abuse) are in this context not warnings against undue sexual pleasure or inadequate sublimation but rather representations of the dangers of withdrawal from family and other supposed shelters from money.[61]

---

[61]Laqueur 230–233.

Discourse is not the only lens through which to view the history of sexuality. Recently, the social history of class formation, and especially of middle-class formation, has been brought together with the history of gender relations and thus also of sex. Changes in the gendered division of labor in various industrial pursuits, mining, and agriculture have long been a staple of economic and social historians, although this history has not figured prominently in the ways in which labor and cultural historians have understood the making of the working class. Likewise, recent work has suggested the centrality of new, gendered, public and private spheres in the context of specific middle-class economic and social circumstances. The history of class formation, it is becoming clear, must also be a history of gender formation and hence also of sexuality.[62]

Thinking through what happened to sexuality and desire, I have argued, is part of a far more general effort to think through the human meanings of the industrial revolution in which the spheres of the market and of the flesh are not distinct. The paradoxes of commercial society, which had already plagued Adam Smith and his colleagues, the nagging doubts that a free market economy could in fact sustain the social body, haunt the sexual body: concerns about easing access to marriage, and therefore to sexual intercourse, bear the weight of these anxieties. Or, then, the sexual body haunts society and reminds it of its fragility. Modern laments that sex is used to sell are not about some accidental and transitory association of late capital-

---

[62]Leonore Davidoff and Catherine Hall, *Family Fortunes: Men and Women of the English Middle Classes, 1780–1850* (Chicago: University of Chicago Press, 1987) demonstrate however, with a massive amount of empirical data, "how middle-class men who sought to be 'someone,' to count as individuals because of their wealth, their power to command or their capacity to influence people, were in fact, embedded in networks of familial and female support which underpinned their rise to public prominence" (13). The middle classes, through the writings of moralists like Sarah Ellis and of a host of doctors and other professionals, sought to understand new gender relations not as the vagaries of social change, as mere cultural artifacts, but as the consequences of biology. Women were intrinsically suited to their roles in the home, their place as guardians of morality, their intimacy with children. Gender, in short, could be translated—if not always with complete conviction—back into sex.

ism.   They are rooted in an almost three-hundred-year-old history of desire, corporeal and commercial.

# FREUD, SEXUALITY, AND PERVERSION

## Teresa de Lauretis

"One must remember that normal sexuality too depends upon a restriction in the choice of object," wrote Freud in one of his lesser-known case histories, "Psychogenesis of a Case of Homosexuality in a Woman." "In general, to undertake to convert a fully developed homosexual into a heterosexual does not offer much more prospect of success than the reverse, except that for good practical reasons the latter is never attempted" (*SE* 18: 151).[1] The observation that the "practical reasons" of psychoanalysis as a clinical (social) practice were, as they still are, often at odds with its purer theoretical reason is hardly new or, consequently, very interesting. On the other hand, to read Freud's theories as "passionate fictions," as Leo Bersani and Ulysse Dutoit suggest, is a much newer and more interesting project, but one more risky and inevitably contested.[2] This is especially so if such a reading project is carried out in the context of feminist theory, and all the more so in the effort to articulate a theory of lesbian subjectivity.

Freudian psychoanalysis has been marked as the enemy of women more often than not throughout the history of Anglo-American feminism, and undoubtedly for very good practical reasons. But, as some feminists have persistently and impressively argued, there are also very good theoretical reasons for reading and rereading Freud. What has not yet been broached is how Freudian theories of sexuality relate to the passionate fictions of lesbian desire today, in the Eurowestern "first world," and it is this gigantic task that I have set for myself in the book of which this essay is the first chapter. The book, still in its early stages, is concerned with what I am tentatively calling *sexual structuring.* By that I mean the ways in which subjectivity, sexual identity, desire, and the sexual drives are oriented, shaped, formed, and reformed by representation, social images,

---

[1]References are to Sigmund Freud, *The Standard Edition of the Complete Psychological Works of Sigmund Freud*, trans. and ed. James Strachey, 24 vols. (London: Hogarth, 1953–74).

[2]Leo Bersani, and Ulysse Dutoit, *The Forms of Violence: Narrative in Assyrian Art and Modern Culture* (New York: Schocken, 1985).

discourses, and practices that make of each individual, historical being a singular psycho-socio-sexual subject.

The question of what is "normal" sexuality—the term inexorably and almost imperceptibly sliding into "normative"—has been a focal point of feminist criticism since Kate Millett's tendentiously vulgar portrait of "Freud" in *Sexual Politics*. It then quickly spread across the spectrum of feminist critical positions ranging from what may be called the anti-Freudian "right" (for example, Millett) to the neo-Freudian "left," for whom the value of psychoanalysis is its singular "insistence not upon the regularization or normalization of sexuality but upon the constant failure of sexual identity, its instability or even its impossibility," as Mary Ann Doane says *à propos* of the work of Jacqueline Rose (76).[3] More accessible than Lacan, Freud has had his supporters as well as his detractors among feminists, although apparently no one can resist an occasional joke on penis envy, or his maladroit association of weaving with pubic hair. According to a certain logic, by the very fact that I have used the phrase "rereading Freud," I must be counted among the supporters. Be that as it must.

My intention, however, is not to praise Freud or to bury him but literally to reread him. Yes, again. The incentive for this project came from writing an essay concerned with lesbian representation and (Rose and Doane notwithstanding) lesbian identity, in which I was trying to sort out one of the paradoxes that, to my mind, have both constrained and advanced the development of feminist thought in the past two decades. I called it the paradox of sexual (in)difference. Because that first attempt to articulate the discursive double bind in which my thinking was caught is relevant to what I will be proposing here, I take the liberty of reproducing the first four paragraphs of that essay, with slight modifications, below.

There is a sense in which lesbian identity could be assumed, spoken, and articulated conceptually as political through feminism—and, current debates to wit, *against* feminism; in particular through and against the feminist critique of the Western discourse on love and sexuality, and therefore, to begin with, the rereading of psychoanalysis as a theory of sexuality and sexual

---

[3]Mary Ann Doane, "Commentary: Post-Utopian Difference," *Coming to Terms: Feminism, Theory, Politics*, ed. Elizabeth Weed (New York: Routledge, 1989) 76.

difference. If the first feminist emphasis on sexual difference as woman's difference from man has rightly come under attack for obscuring the effects of other differences in women's psychosocial oppression, nevertheless that emphasis on sexual difference did open up a critical space—a conceptual, representational, and erotic space—in which women could address themselves to women. And in the very act of assuming and speaking from the position of subject, a woman could concurrently recognize women as subjects *and* as objects of female desire.

It is in such a space, hard-won and daily threatened by social disapprobation, censure, and denial, a space of contradiction requiring constant reaffirmation and painful renegotiation, that the very notion of sexual difference could then be put into question, and its limitations be assessed, both *vis-à-vis* the claims of other, not strictly sexual, differences, and with regard to sexuality itself. It thus appears that "sexual difference" is the term of a conceptual paradox corresponding to what is in effect a real contradiction in women's lives: the term, at once, of a sexual *difference* (women are, or want, something different from men) and of a sexual *indifference* (women are, or want, the same as men). And it seems to me that the racist and class-biased practices legitimated in the notion of "separate but equal" reveal a very similar paradox in the liberal ideology of pluralism, where social difference is also, at the same time, social indifference.

The psychoanalytic discourse on female sexuality, wrote Luce Irigaray in 1975, outlining the terms of what here I call *sexual (in)difference*, makes clear "that *the feminine occurs only within models and laws devised by male subjects. Which implies that there are not really two sexes, but only one. A single practice and representation of the sexual*" (Irigaray, *This Sex* 86).[4] Within the conceptual frame of that "sexual indifference," female desire for another female self cannot be recognized. Irigaray continues: "That a woman might desire a woman 'like' herself, someone of the 'same' sex, that she might also have auto- and homo-sexual appetites, is simply incomprehensible" in the phallic regime of an asserted sexual difference between man and woman which is predicated on the contrary, on a complete

---

[4]References are to Luce Irigaray, *This Sex Which is Not One*, trans. Catherine Porter (Ithaca, NY: Cornell University Press, 1985) and *Speculum of the Other Woman*, trans. Gillian C. Gill (Ithaca, NY: Cornell University Press, 1985).

indifference for the "other" sex, woman's. Consequently, Freud
was at a loss with his homosexual female patients, and his analyses of them were really about male homosexuality, she observes. "The object choice of the homosexual woman is
[understood to be] determined by a *masculine* desire and
tropism," Irigaray writes, and, I suggest, that is precisely the
turn of so-called sexual difference into "sexual indifference" (the
phrase first appeared in *Speculum* 28), a single practice and representation of the sexual.

> So there will be no female homosexuality, just a hommo-
> sexuality in which woman will be involved in the process
> of specularizing the phallus, begged to maintain the de-
> sire for the same that man has, and will ensure at the
> same time, elsewhere and in complementary and contra-
> dictory fashion, the perpetuation in the couple of the pole
> of "matter." (*Speculum* 101–3)

With the term *hommo-sexuality* [*hommo-sexualité*]—at times
also written *hom(m)osexuality* [*hom(m)osexualité*]—Irigaray puns
on the French word for man, *homme*, from the Latin *homo*
(meaning "man"), and the Greek *homo* (meaning "same"). In
taking up her distinction between the now common-usage
word *homosexuality* and Irigaray's *hommo-sexuality* or
*hom(m)osexuality*, I want to remark the conceptual distance between the former term, *homosexuality*, by which I mean lesbian
(or gay) sexuality, and the diacritically marked *hommo-sexuality*,
which is the term of sexual indifference, the term (in fact) of heterosexuality. I want to re-mark both the incommensurable distance between them and the conceptual ambiguity that is conveyed by the two almost identical acoustic images.[5]
    The point of the terminological distinction, as I saw it at the
time, based on my analysis of several kinds of lesbian texts, was
to suggest that there was no simple way of representing or even
thinking lesbianism cleanly outside of the discursive-conceptual
categories of heterosexuality, with its foundation in a structural
difference (masculine-feminine or male-female) that for all in-

---

[5]The preceding four paragraphs may be found in my article "Sexual
Indifference and Lesbian Representation," first published in *Theatre Journal*
and reprinted in *Performing Feminisms: Feminist Critical Theory and Theatre*,
ed. Sue-Ellen Case (Baltimore: Johns Hopkins University Press, 1990).

tents and purposes sustains a social indifference to women's subjectivities. I concluded that our current efforts at lesbian self-representation would continue to be unwittingly caught in the paradox of sexual (in)difference unless we somehow managed to separate out the two drifts of the paradox and then rethink homosexuality and hommo-sexuality at once separately *and* together. I was thus escalating the paradox into an actual logical contradiction.

It seems to me now that my effort to understand one form of sexual (in)difference (heterosexual-homosexual) from the perspective of the other (male-female), as articulated by Irigaray, was not altogether unproductive—all analogical thinking has its usefulness initially—but was inherently limited. By showing that a paradox, or a seeming contradiction, hides what is in effect an actual contradiction, I did not yet displace the terms of the contradiction, although I may have clarified them for myself. Moreover, in borrowing Irigaray's notion of hommo-sexuality, I was dependent on a perspective that did not include the possibility of a difference between heterosexual and gay male sexualities. This further limited the conceptual horizon in which a non-heterosexual, nonhom(m)osexual, but homosexual-lesbian female sexuality might be thought.

I became more sharply aware of these limitations in reading Naomi Schor's "Dreaming Dissymmetry," a critique of what she calls "the *discourse of in-difference* or of *pure difference*" in the work of Barthes and Foucault.[6] Schor forcefully argues that this French poststructuralist discourse on sexual difference "shades into sexual indifference" (49) in that, in discursivizing sex, it consistently desexualizes women even as it reclaims the feminine position for male sexuality or proposes a utopia of free-floating desire and sexual/gender indeterminacy.[7] Though not ostensively referred to Irigaray, Schor's term *in-difference* was very close to my *(in)difference*, I thought, except that she did not address directly the issue of a heterosexual-homosexual difference in her chosen authors. (But could it be a coincidence, I wondered, that she was speaking of Barthes and Foucault?) While I did share Schor's concern with the returning marginalization of

---

[6]Naomi Schor, "Dreaming Dissymmetry: Barthes, Foucault, and Sexual Difference," Weed 48.

[7]Rosi Braidotti, *Patterns of Dissonance: A Study of Women in Contemporary Philosophy* (London: Polity Press, 1991).

female sexuality in the philosophical, as well as the political, domain, I was struck by the ambiguity of the sexual *in-difference* she pointed to in Barthes and Foucault—an ambiguity that neither she nor they, for that matter, were willing to trace to a heterosexual-homosexual difference, which, it seemed to me, loomed large in the background.

Thus Schor's essay helped me to see the limitations of my own concept of *(in)difference*, particularly with regard to the equation I made between it and Irigaray's *hommo-sexuality*. For the latter concept not only underscores the exclusion, the inconceivability of lesbian sexuality (which is the point of her pun) but also forecloses the possibility of considering gay sexuality as another kind of male sexuality, one not homologous or easily assimilable to the "normal." Irigaray may or may not have intended this foreclosure, but I do not. Although I shall not concern myself with questions of male sexuality, I certainly could not preclude them, nor would I wish to, in my reading of what I call Freud's negative theory of the perversions, to which I now turn.

If, in works such as mine and many others, today one normally encounters the phrase *"normal" sexuality* with the word "normal" between quotation marks, it is because their authors, whether they have read Freud or not, partake of a cultural and intellectual climate that follows from his work in the first decades of the century and has retained some versions of his "passionate fictions." For it was Freud who first put the quotation marks around the "normal" in matters sexual. He did it at a time of general agreement on the natural (i.e., procreative) function of the sexual instinct, which was also interchangeably called "genital instinct" (Davidson 47).[8] And he did it by daring to pursue his exceptional insight—whether genius, vision, or fantasy—into what many see as a revolutionary theory of sexuality; or less romantically, if one attends to Foucault, he did it by making explicit and giving systemic (and highly dramatic) form to certain strategies of power-knowledge, certain strategies of social regulation that had long been in operation in dominant European cultures and that comprise the modern "technology of sex";

[8]References are to Arnold Davidson, "How to Do the History of Psychoanalysis: A Reading of Freud's *Three Essays on the Theory of Sexuality*," *The Trial(s) of Psychoanalysis*, ed. Françoise Meltzer (Chicago: University of Chicago Press, 1987–88) 39–64.

namely, "a hysterization of women's bodies . . . a pedagogization of children's sex . . . a socialization of procreative behavior . . . [and] a psychiatrization of perverse pleasure" (Foucault 1:104–5).[9]

These were indeed the four major themes of Freud's early work: the sexual instinct, revealed by the symptoms of hysteria and the neuroses at the join of the somatic and the mental; infantile sexuality, the Oedipus complex, with its attendant fantasies of parental seduction and the transformations of the sexual instinct at puberty; and the sexual aberrations—in short, the table of contents of the *Three Essays on the Theory of Sexuality* (1905). While the concern with the "normal" in sexuality is clearly of paramount importance to Freud at this time (for instance, he closes the third essay with advice for the "Prevention of Inversion"), nonetheless the very notions of a normal psychosexual development, a normal sexual act, and thus normal sexuality are inseparable in this work from the detailed consideration of the aberrant, deviant, or perverse manifestations and components of the sexual instinct or drive (*Trieb*).

In his 1975 introductory essay to the Harper Torchbooks paperback edition of the *Three Essays*, Steven Marcus remarks on the peculiar form of this text, which "in contrast to the grand expository sweep" of Freud's major writings, is made up of "small juxtaposed blocks of material . . . fragments that are both connected and easy to separate, manipulate, revise, or delete. They function as movable parts of a system" (xxi).[10] And a systematic, coherent theory is just what Freud is proposing, Marcus argues, against Freud's own insistence that it is "out of the question" that the essays "could ever be extended into a complete 'theory of sexuality'" (Preface to the third edition of 1915 *SE* 7:130). Freud's disclaimer notwithstanding, Marcus persists. Although the explosive material of the book is to be found in the second essay on infantile sexuality, he observes, it is at the end of the first essay on the sexual aberrations that Freud, having first disaggregated the perversions and the sexual instinct into component parts, then recomposes them into the neuroses. And

---

[9]Michel Foucault, *The History of Sexuality, Volume 1: An Introduction*, trans. Robert Hurley (New York: Random House, 1980).

[10] References are to Steven Marcus, "Introduction" to Sigmund Freud, *Three Essays on the Theory of Sexuality*, trans. James Strachey (New York: Basic Books, 1975) xix–xli.

*that is* his theory, for after all, Freud himself remarked that "the theory of the neuroses is psycho-analysis itself" (*SE* 16:379).

> In a bewilderingly brief few pages on the neuroses he has recapitulated the entire structure of the earlier part of the essay, which was, one recalls, about actually perverse sexual behavior.  But the recapitulation is now on the level of the neurotic symptom, of unconscious mental life, of fantasies, ideas, and mental representations.  It is, in other words, on the level of theory. . . . In the neuroses the language of sexuality begins to speak articulately, coherently, and theoretically. (xxxii)

If that is so, and if "neuroses are, so to say, the negative of perversions," as Freud himself put it (*SE* 7:165), then his theory of sexuality is based on both representations and practices of sex that are, to a greater or lesser degree, "perverse." A few paragraphs later he actually speaks of "positive and negative perversions" (*SE* 7:167), thus creating the impression that, as Jonathan Dollimore put it, "one does not become a pervert but remains one."[11]  Furthermore, the whole of Freud's theory of the human psyche, the sexual instincts and their vicissitudes, owes its material foundations and developments to psychoanalysis, his clinical study of the psychoneuroses; that is to say, those cases in which the mental apparatus and the instinctual drives reveal themselves in their processes and mechanisms, which are "normally" hidden or unremarkable otherwise.  In all these respects, the normal is only conceivable by approximation, more in the order of a projection than an actual state of being.  If "an unbroken chain bridges the gap between the neuroses in all their manifestations and normality" (*SE* 7:171), as Freud states, then the gap between pathology and nonpathology is bridged at both ends: between neuroses and normality, on one side, and between normality and perversions, on the other. That bridge is the sexual instinct in its various vicissitudes and transformations.

Freud's own ambivalence with regard to this issue—whether a normal instinct, phylogenetically inherited, preexists its possible deviations (in psychoneurotic individuals) or whether instinctual life is but a set of transformations, some of which are then

---

[11] Jonathan Dollimore, "The Cultural Politics of Perversion: Augustine, Shakespeare, Freud, Foucault," *Genders* 8 (1990).

defined as normal, i.e., nonpathogenic and socially desirable or admissible—is a source of continued but ultimately insoluble debate.[12] The concluding section of the first of the *Three Essays*, entitled "The Sexual Aberrations," which comes shortly after the well-known analysis of neuroses and perversions as the respective negative and positive of each other, offers one example among many in Freud's writings of the ambiguities, inconsistencies, uncertainties, and—in his own word—ambivalence *vis-à-vis* the topic at hand that have invited passionate interpretation and made his fictions eminently open texts.

> The conclusion now presents itself to us that there is indeed something innate lying behind the perversions but that it is something *innate in everyone*, though as a disposition it may vary in its intensity and may be increased by the influences of actual life. What is in question are the innate constitutional roots of the sexual instinct. In one class of cases (the perversions) these roots may grow into the actual vehicles of sexual activity; in others [the psychoneuroses] they may be submitted to an insufficient suppression (repression) and thus be able in a roundabout way to attract a considerable proportion of sexual energy to themselves as symptoms; while in the most favorable cases, which lie between these two extremes, they may *by means of effective restriction and other kinds of modification* bring about what is known as normal sexual life. (*SE* 7:171–72; my emphasis )

---

12 For example, here is one of the more liberal readings from Jean Laplanche and J.-B. Pontalis, *The Language of Psycho-Analysis*, trans. Donald Nicholson-Smith (New York: W. W. Norton, 1973) 420. "It is clear that when Freud attempts to ascertain the point at which the sexual instinct emerges, this instinct (*Trieb*) appears almost as a perversion of instinct in the traditional sense (*Instinkt*)—a perversion in which the specific object and the organic purpose both vanish." At this point, however, Laplanche and Pontalis are speaking specifically of infantile sexuality. In the preceding section on "Sexual Instinct," they write: "Psycho-analysis shows that the sexual instinct in man is closely bound up with the action of ideas or phantasies which serve to give it specific form. Only at the end of a complex and hazardous evolution is it successfully organized under the primacy of genitality, so taking on the apparently fixed and final aspect of instinct in the traditional sense" (417).

Shortly before this conclusion, Freud had been summarizing his first formulation of the sexual instinct ("The concept of instinct is thus one of those lying on the frontier between the mental and the physical" [*SE* 7:168]), a concept that would occupy much of his later work; and he had introduced the term *component instincts* thus: "perhaps the sexual instinct itself may be no simple thing, but put together from components which have come apart again in the perversions" (*SE* 7:162). The words "have come apart again" refer proleptically to a period in the individual's psychic life that will be the topic of the next two essays in the book, infantile sexuality and its transformations at puberty under the primacy of the genital organization of the sexual instincts; it is the period prior to the onset of mental forces, such as shame and disgust, which intervene to restrain the instinct "within the limits that are regarded as normal." The argument goes as follows.

In infantile sexual life the instinct was "predominantly autoerotic [and] derived from a number of separate instincts and erotogenic zones, which, independently of one another, have pursued a certain sort of pleasure as their sole sexual aim," whereas in puberty, with the appearance of "a new sexual aim," the sexual instinct becomes "subordinated to the reproductive function; it becomes, so to say, altruistic" (*SE* 7:207). Then the component instincts and erotogenic zones line up and combine to attain this new sexual aim which, Freud specifies, "in men consists in the discharge of the sexual products." But the earlier aim, the attainment of pleasure, is by no means displaced by this new aim, he adds, apparently speaking from experience: "on the contrary, the highest degree of pleasure is attached to this final act of the sexual process." For women, Freud admits, it may be otherwise; in fact, he has reason to suppose that "[the sexual development] of females actually enters upon a kind of involution" (*SE* 7:207). But no more is said of women at this time, except that "the intermediate steps" of the process leading from a sexuality of component instincts to one under the aegis of seminal discharge "are still in many ways obscure . . . an unsolved riddle" (*SE* 7:208). And not by coincidence, perhaps, this same word *riddle* will be the *leitmotiv* of the psychoanalytic inquiry into female sexuality from Dora onward (*SE* 7:120).

There is a certain discrepancy of tone, a marked change in emphasis between the two consecutive pages that close the first essay and open the second. Let me attempt to point them out

and suggest a possible explanation.   If normal sexual life (or
"what is known as normal sexual life," as Freud carefully notes
in the long passage cited above) could be said to be *brought
about*, to be achieved, even induced "by means of effective restriction and other kinds of modification" in the first essay on the
sexual aberrations (and this was an area of research hardly new
or controversial after several decades of work by sexologists like
Krafft-Ebing and Havelock Ellis, from which Freud admittedly
drew most of his material at the time), here, on the other hand,
in the second and third essays containing Freud's own, more
radical and enormously controversial hypothesis of infantile sexuality and its transformations at puberty, "normal" sexual life is
taken as the premise, rather than the end result, of sexual development and assumed to be coincident with adult, reproductive,
lawful heterosexual intercourse.

In the last two essays, in other words, it is no longer a matter of bringing about the normal by effective restrictions, by
channelling the component instincts and realigning the erogenous
zones in the service of the one socially admissible form of sexual
pleasure; there is instead the posing of an ideal norm, the normal, as the a-priori, the essential kernel, the original potential
and promise of sexual development, the seed that will come to
maturation after puberty in "normal sexuality."   It is as if heterosexuality were firmly in place from the beginning, in each
newborn, as the promise and fulfillment of each component instinct.   This is a far cry from the hypothesis of bisexuality offered to explain inversion and from other related statements in
the first essay such as the famous footnote addition, in 1915,
that "from the point of view of psycho-analysis the exclusive
sexual interest felt by men for women is also a problem that
needs elucidating and is not a self-evident fact based upon an attraction that is ultimately of a chemical nature" (*SE* 7:146).

To account for such discrepancy, it is not altogether unrea-
sonable to think that, in setting forth his original theory of infantile sexuality, with its component instincts and polymorphous
perversity, Freud saw that the sexual instinct must be theoreti-
cally restrained, rhetorically curbed, as it were, by the emphasis
on an ideal normal development which will save the theory from
itself partaking of the perversions which the first essay describes.   I do not mean to suggest that this latter emphasis
stems from expediency or is a hypocritical and merely rhetorical
strategy on Freud's part.   To impute this to Freud is not only a

banality on the level of Jeffrey Masson's, but a failure of reading, an inability to hear the difference between hypocrisy and ambivalence.  I think the two emphases more likely reflect a bona fide and structural ambivalence in his thinking, due to the logic of the argument and its heuristic premise driving it in one direction, and to the drift of his ideological, emotional, and affective convictions pulling in a contrary direction.  In support of this reading, which is not of much consequence in itself but will be of some consequence in the development of my argument, I will cite another and more extreme example of Freud's doctrinal inconsistency—the relation between instinct and object, painstakingly analyzed by Arnold Davidson in his reading of the *Three Essays*.

Freud's redefinition of the sexual instinct, Davidson argues, was a revolutionary in(ter)vention in the medical discourses of his time, an overturning of the "highly structured, rule-governed, conceptual space" in which "psychiatric theories of sexuality had operated since about 1870" (53).  Freud accomplished this in the first of the *Three Essays* "by fundamentally altering the rules of combination for concepts such as sexual instinct, sexual object, sexual aim" (62) and thus subverting the conceptual foundations of the notion of perversion and, in particular, its specific configuration in inversion.  In order to show that inversion was a real functional deviation of the sexual instinct rather than merely a difference in its direction or object, "one had to conceive of the 'normal' object of the instinct as part of the very content of the instinct itself" (52), Davidson writes.  And indeed he demonstrates that psychiatric theories of the time unanimously assumed that a specific object and a specific aim (i.e., members of the other sex and reproductive genital intercourse, respectively) were integral or constituent parts of the sexual instinct.  Freud, therefore, not only challenged the unanimously accepted view but "decisively replaced the concept of the sexual instinct with that of a sexual drive 'in the first instance independent of its object'" (54).

Here is the crucial passage from the *Three Essays*:

> It has been brought to our notice that we have been in the habit of regarding the connection between the sexual instinct and the sexual object as more intimate than it in fact is.  Experience of the cases that are considered abnormal has shown us that in them the sexual instinct and the sexual object are merely soldered together—a fact which we have been in danger of overlooking in con-

sequence of the uniformity of the normal picture, where the object appears to form part and parcel of the instinct. We are thus warned to loosen the bond that exists in our thought between instinct and object. It seems probable that the sexual instinct is in the first instance independent of its object; nor is its origin likely to be due to its object's attractions. (*SE* 7:147–48)[13]

Freud's originality, Davidson remarks, is not the introduction of a new word, *Trieb* in lieu of *Instinkt*, as other commentators have suggested, for the word *Trieb* was already used by his contemporaries, including Krafft-Ebing; the originality consists in the theoretical rearticulation that makes Freud's *Sexualtrieb* an altogether novel concept. And one whose ultimate implications Freud himself seemed unable to grasp.

Inevitably, at this point, Davidson too is led to speculate on the reasons for Freud's inconsistent reintroduction, later in the book, of notions such as perversion and genital primacy which, on the very strength of his argument in the first essay, have been deprived of their conceptual ground and hence must now appear vacuous or nonsensical. For example, in a brilliant piece of textual exegesis, Davidson shows how Freud simply cannot mean what he says when he appears to disagree with other medical writers only to reiterate their very argument.

[Freud's] claim that these writers are mistaken in asserting that an innate weakness of the sexual instinct is responsible for perversion, but that their assertions would make sense "if what is meant is a constitutional weakness of one particular factor in the sexual instinct, namely the genital zone," is astonishing, since this is, of course, exactly what they meant, and had to mean, given their conception of the sexual instinct. It is Freud who cannot mean to say that the absence of this particular factor, the primacy of the genital zone, is a condition of

---

[13] Freud upheld this view in the much later metapsychological paper on "Instincts and Their Vicissitudes": "The object [*Objekt*] of an instinct is the thing in regard to which or through which the instinct is able to achieve its aim. It is what is most variable about an instinct and *is not originally connected with it, but becomes assigned to it only in consequence of being peculiarly fitted to make satisfaction possible*" (SE 14: 122; my emphasis).

perversion. The last sentence of this paragraph reads, "For if the genital zone is weak, this combination, which is required to take place at puberty, is bound to fail, and the strongest of the other components of sexuality will continue its activity as a perversion." But the system of concepts Freud has been working with in the first essay requires a slightly different conclusion, one whose subtle modulation from Freud's actual conclusion must be emphasized. The appropriate formulation of the conclusion should read, "For if the genital zone is weak, this combination, which often takes place at puberty, will fail, and the strongest of the other components of sexuality will continue its activity." The differences between these two formulations represent what I have been calling Freud's attitude. (61)

Being perhaps of a cast of mind more philosophical than psychoanalytic, Davidson suggests that Freud's attitude or mental habits, formed in the conceptual-scientific mentality of his own time, "never quite caught up" with the new conceptual articulations he himself produced (63). This does not contradict, but rather complements, my own suggestion that one's most profound ideological and affective convictions may sometimes run counter to one's most brilliant critical or analytical insights. Nor, for that matter, does it contradict Freud's own view of the subject as divided between what it says and what it means, or what it knows and what it doesn't, even as, in the latter instance, it should know better.

I have stressed the obtrusive presence of ambivalence, inconsistency, and structural ambiguity in the *Three Essays* to suggest that, if they do amount to a systematic, coherent theory (as Marcus asserts) or to a restructuring of our conceptual space whereby the sexual drive can be thought quite independent of its object (as Davidson argues), then Freud's theory of sexuality is not exactly the normative and normalizing synthesis of late Victorian views that many take it to be; nor is it a dramatic rendering of Foucault's technology of sex; rather, it is a conception of sexuality whose structural, constitutive ambiguity has *not yet* been fully taken up in its furthest implications. Moreover, Freud's theory of sexuality, as set forth in the early writings and never fundamentally altered in the later ones, is much closer epistemologically to his acknowledged "discoveries" or original conceptual formulations, such as the agency of the unconscious in the mind and his topographical models of the psychic apparatus, than is usually recognized. In particular, I find a curious resemblance between his conception of sexuality in the *Three Essays* and the configuration of the psyche in his second model, with the triad of ego, id, and superego serving as a rough analogue for the exchanges among normality, perversion, and neurosis.

Before I go on to indulge in another bit of analogical thinking, fully aware that it may have limitations, I will offer one example of the kind of statement that has instigated my speculation. In *The Ego and the Id* Freud writes: "From the point of view of instinctual control, of morality, it may be said of the id that it is totally non-moral, of the ego that it strives to be moral, and of the super-ego that it can be super-moral and then become as cruel as only the id can be" (*SE* 19:54). The mind's threefold relation to morality, which evidently concerns Freud in this 1923 text as much as it did in the *Three Essays* of 1905, reproposes the three positions of the sexual instinct *vis-à-vis* morality in perversion, normal sexuality, and neurosis, respectively; it even redoubles the slippage of the last term into the first: the superego here rejoins the id as neurosis rejoined perversion in its negative form there. In this perspective, Freud's theory of sexuality could be seen as a system based on three interdependent agencies or modalities of the sexual, none of which is causally or temporally prior, and one of which, the normal, would be defined by reference to the other two (as the ego is by reference to id and superego), rather than vice versa.

In *The Ego and the Id*, where Freud lays out his tripartite model of the mind, the following passage occurs:

> There are two paths by which the contents of the id can penetrate into the ego. The one is direct, the other leads by way of the ego ideal; which of these two paths they take may, for some mental activities, be of decisive importance: The ego develops from perceiving instincts to controlling them, from obeying instincts to inhibiting them. In this achievement a large share is taken by the ego ideal, which indeed is partly a reaction-formation against the instinctual processes of the id. Psychoanalysis is an instrument to enable the ego to achieve a progressive conquest of the id.

From the other point of view, however, we see this same ego as a poor creature owing service to three masters and consequently menaced by three dangers: from the external world, from the libido of the id, and from the severity of the super-ego. Three kinds of anxiety correspond to these three dangers, since anxiety is the expression of a retreat from danger. As a frontier-creature, the ego tries to mediate between the world and the id, to make the id pliable to the world and, by means of its muscular activity, to make the world fall in with the wishes of the id. . . . But since the ego's work of sublimation results in a defusion of the instincts and a liberation of the aggressive instincts in the super-ego, its struggle against the libido exposes it to the danger of maltreatment and death. In suffering under the attacks of the super-ego or perhaps even succumbing to them, the ego is meeting with a fate like that of the protista which are destroyed by the products of decomposition that they themselves have created. From the economic point of view the morality that functions in the super-ego seems to be a similar product of decomposition.

(SE 19:55–56)

In contrast with the image of the ego as a poor creature in service to three masters, and with several other equally anthropomorphic similes that Freud uses to draw a picture of the ego (a man on horseback, a constitutional monarch, a politician, a submissive slave, a physician-analyst), the metaphor of the frontier-creature and the comparison to the protista convey the sense of an instinctual energy, a material but nonhuman living substance rather than a socialized or civilized person. Moreover, the figure of the ego as a frontier-creature is reminiscent of the formulation of the sexual instinct as one "lying on the frontier between the mental and the physical" (SE 7:168).

In reading this entire section on "The Ego's Dependent Relations," the frontier image seems by far the more precise in conveying Freud's concept of the ego as "a body-ego" (SE 19:27), a physical site of negotiations between the pressures coming from the external world, on one side, and those coming from the internal world, from the id's instinctual and narcissistic drives and from their representative, the superego, on the other. For the superego is derived from the child's Oedipal object-cathexes that have been de-eroticized and transformed into identifications: the superego derives from "the first object-cathexes of the id, from the Oedipus complex," Freud says, and thus "is always close to the id as its representative *vis-à-vis* the ego. It reaches deep down into the id and for that reason is farther from consciousness than the ego is" (*SE* 19:48–49). In other words, the ego is not located between the id and the superego, but is the frontier between them and the external word. The dangerous and exciting domain of the real, comprised of other people, social institutions, and so forth, on one side, and an equally treacherous domain, on the other—the internal world of instinctual drives, the libido with its vicissitudes, and the death drive—make that *frontier*-creature, the ego, a site of incessant material negotiations between them.

If my analogy with the triad of the *Three Essays* holds, then "normal" sexuality there would be in a position homologous to the position of the ego here. Normal sexuality would also be a frontier-creature, or a frontier-concept—not a particular sexual disposition or a mode of being of the sexual instinct itself but rather the result of particular negotiations in the process of mediation in which the subject must constantly engage—the mediation between external (social, parental, representational) pressures and the internal pressures of the sexual instinct (or the component instincts). And the latter's modalities would be perversion and neurosis, two sides of the same coin, each other's positive and negative faces, the twin modes of being of the sexual instinct. In this scenario, sexuality would not come in two varieties, "normal" and "perverse" (I omit "neurotic" since neurosis is but negative perversion, as Freud implies in the section subheaded "Reasons for the Apparent Preponderance of Perverse Sexuality in the Psychoneuroses" [*SE* 7:170–71]). Instead, one can imagine the sexual instinct as being made up of various component instincts—none of which would have a *necessary* priority since no originary relation binds the instinct(s) to a particular object—and having two modalities, positive and negative perversion, depending on the presence and degree of repression. Normal sexuality, then, would name a particular result of the process of negotiation with both the external and the internal worlds; it would designate the achievement, on the part of the subject, of the kind of sexual organization that a particular society and its institutions have decreed to be normal. And in this

sense, indeed, *normal* becomes totally coextensive and synonymous with *normative*.

I may put it another way by retracing my steps so far. The
theory of sexuality that emerged when I first read the *Three Essays* seemed to be comprised of two theories: one explicit and
affirmative, a positive theory of normal sexuality, and the other
implicit and negative, appearing as the underside or the clinical
underground of the first. I thought of the latter as Freud's negative theory of the perversions. However, a closer reading of the
text's conspicuous inconsistencies and self-contradictory assertions (most significant in Davidson's analysis of the relation of
the sexual instinct to its object[s]) has produced another picture.
It now seems to me that what I have called Freud's negative
theory of the perversions, the one neither he nor his followers
could propose or count as a theory of sexuality, actually constitutes Freud's theory of sexuality. The positive theory of normal
sexuality and normal sexual development that can be read, and
has indeed been read almost unanimously, in the *Three Essays*
now looks to me like the imposition of an historically determined
social norm on a field of instinctual drives which, as Freud's entire work and the increasing fortunes of psychoanalysis go to
prove, is not capable of much development but only of shifts,
readjustments, and more or less successful negotiations with a
real that is always waiting around the corner, at the frontier.

In using the terms "positive" and "negative" in reference to
the two theories of sexuality that coexisted in my former reading
of the *Three Essays*, I was playing with Freud's characterization
of neuroses as the negative of perversions; it always struck me
that, by phrasing it that way, Freud was in a sense qualifying
the perversions as positive. And surely, in his case histories, the
actual patients, those suffering or made dysfunctional from their
symptoms, are the neurotics and the hysterics, not the perverts,
most of whom would or did live as well as they could without the
help of psychoanalysis—think of the protagonists of "Psychogenesis of a Case of Homosexuality in a Woman," "A Case of
Paranoia Running Counter to the Psycho-Analytic Theory of the
Disease," "Leonardo," and better still, the fetishists who, Freud
writes, "are quite satisfied with [their fetish], or even praise the
way in which it eases their erotic life" (*SE* 21:152). With the
phrase "Freud's negative theory of the perversions" I meant
ironically to reverse his own definition of psychoanalysis as the
theory of the neuroses and to trope on the high-contrast quality

(as in a photographic negative) conferred to the perversions by the highlighting that is automatically set on the normal.

Since I made the analogy between the theories of the *Three Essays* and the economic model of the psyche in *The Ego and the Id*, however, I must remark on a further resonance between my terms and Freud's notion of a positive and a negative Oedipus complex in the latter work (*SE* 19:31–34). There, as well as in the *Three Essays*, the negative term, the "negative Oedipus complex," designates what is socially inadmissible (the girl's erotic attachment to the mother, the boy's to the father) and must therefore be transformed into identification, repressed, or sublimated, or all of the above. As for the positive term, the "positive Oedipus complex" (the girl's refocusing of her erotic cathexis from the mother onto the father, the boy's continued erotic, and now phallic, attachment to the mother) designates what Freud persists in calling the normal sexual development in the face of overwhelming evidence that such a development is rarer and less likely than it ought to be. In other words, in this case as well, at least for the girl, the positive or the "normal" is merely an approximation, a projection, and not a state of being. Once again the positivity of the normal is a function of social norm.

What if I were to take up my earlier intimation that Freud's views on sexuality in the *Three Essays* have not yet been sufficiently considered, especially with regard to the further implications of its structural, if not structured, ambiguity? What if, in other words, one were to follow the path of the component instincts left visible, if darkly, in the background of the picture? What if one set out to build a theory of sexuality along the negative trace of the perversion—let us say, fetishism? (After all, Jacques Lacan almost did.) Such theory might not, of course, account for the majority of people, but then the positive theory of sexuality does not either; and then again, the notion of "the majority of people" is as troubled as the notion of "the normal"—it, too, is at best an approximation and at worst a projection (of what I myself and you, reader, are not). At any rate, a theory of sexuality based on perversion, such as I have suggested, would be just as much of a fiction and no less passionate or even true, for those who live it, than the theory of an elusive and ever more troubled "normal" sexuality.

# PART THREE. THE CONSTRUCTED BODY

# HISTORICIZING THE SEXUAL BODY:
Sexual Preferences and Erotic Identities in the Pseudo-
Lucianic Erôtes

## David M. Halperin

First: the good news. Hard as it may be to believe, in these dark, Helms-ridden times, the United States Postal Service officially issued on January 19, 1990, a homosexual love stamp. The stamp displays in its uppermost register the heading "LOVE" in large, widely spaced black lettering. Underneath that rubric is a symmetrical design featuring two identical lovebirds, or doves, outlined in profile, facing each other, and blocked out in solid blue; centered between and below them is a solid red valentine-shaped heart, and beneath it is a symmetrically arranged vine tendril in solid green. The inspiration for this design—to judge from U.S. Postal Service Poster 669 (fig. 1), which advertises the stamp and which urges customers, moreover, to "Add a little Love to [their] collection"—apparently derives from traditional European-American quilting patterns. I say that the stamp promotes "homosexual" love because in conformity, no doubt, with age-old quilting conventions the two birds are not depicted in an anatomically explicit manner, and so it is difficult to determine whether they represent a lesbian or a gay male couple: their blue coloring, along with my own partisan sentiments, might incline me to favor the latter possibility, but the customary assignment of quilting work to collectives of women, the traditional association of lovebirds with women's domestic world, the poster's acknowledgment of one Dora B. Hamlin as the source of the quilt against which the stamp is photographed and its crediting of one Renée Comet as the photographer—all of these considerations combine to argue, perhaps, for the former interpretation. Whether the birds are gay or lesbian, however, they are clearly identical to each other in every respect, and they are in love: the heading "LOVE," the red, valentine-shaped heart, and (most important of all) the requirements of the symmetrical design, taken in conjunction, leave no room for escape from that queer conclusion.

Now: the bad news. My conclusion, inescapable though it may be, is one that almost nobody else seems to have drawn, so

Figure 1. By permission of the
Philatelic and Retail Services
Department, United States Postal
Service.

far as I am aware—neither the Postal Service, the public at large, nor lesbians and gay men in particular.[1] As if by magic, each person who views the stamp—no matter what her or his social location—instantly and unreflectively reconfigures the image, constructing the pair of lovebirds not only as male and female but as a heterosexual and, presumably, monogamous couple (the stamp is not taken to depict a one-night stand). The viewer may also perform a number of other, subsidiary operations on this visual text, such as installing the "male" bird on the right-hand side of the field and even magnifying "his" size in relation to that of "his" mate, so as to motivate as well as to justify a heterosexist reading. But nothing in the text itself—nothing, at least, that I have been able to detect—provides the slightest impetus for such collective hallucinations. Rather, the apparently universal and unconquerable urge to read off gendered, heterosexualized meanings from the innocent surface of this unoffending text springs—as the text's source in the figural repertory of European-American folk art implies—from the traditional codes or conventions for representing "love" in European-American culture. These codes, which also govern the culture's visual rhetoric, restrict the use of erotic symbols, such as the valentine-shaped heart, to heterosexual contexts and employ exemplary animals, such as lovebirds, to typify and thereby to naturalize

This paper was originally written to be delivered on Valentine's Day 1991 at a conference on "The Constructed Body" sponsored by the Institute for the Humanities at the University of Michigan in Ann Arbor. The version published here is very much the product of that occasion.

Other versions of this paper were presented at the University of Pennsylvania, the University of Chicago, Duke University, the University of Wisconsin, Pomona College, and the Universities of California at Berkeley, Santa Cruz, Los Angeles, and San Diego. The final version has benefited substantially from the discussion the paper received at all of those schools. I wish to thank in particular David Blank, Peter Burian, Arnold Davidson, Whitney Davis, David N. Dobrin, Page duBois, John Kleiner, Tom Laqueur, Paul Morrison, Ann Pellegrini, Ruth Perry, Heidi Rubin, Eve Kosofsky Sedgwick, Domna C. Stanton, and Tom Vogler for their helpful observations, which unfortunately I have not always known how best to exploit in recasting this paper.

[1]The sole exception known to me is Rebecca Kaplan, my student in the fall of 1990, who came independently to the same conclusion.

contemporary human social and sexual arrangements, such as monogamous, heterosexual marriage.   Common to all those rhetorical practices is a discursive strategy whose effect is to (re)produce "love" as an exclusively heterosexual institution and to convert, under the sign of "love," all pairs of ungendered, identically figured bodies into heterosexual couples: compare the image on the cover of *The New Yorker*'s 1991 Valentine's Day issue.   It takes nothing less than a combination of masculine names, explicitly gay identities, and matching fezzes to withstand the weight of heterosexual presumption, to judge by the example of Matt Groening's Akbar and Jeff (see fig. 2, the cover of the 1991 Valentine's Day issue of *The Advocate*, with accompanying story)[2]—though inasmuch as "Life is Hell," the cartoon in which they appear, is routinely syndicated in college newspapers without stirring the slightest breath of scandal, perhaps even that odd couple's resistance to heterosexual presumption is less successful than one might have supposed.

The point of this perverse little exercise has been to recall the currently trendy (if still undervalued) precept that the body is not only a thing but a sign: it functions as a site for the inscription of gendered and sexual meanings, among a great many other meanings.   Instead of treating the body as the "really real," after the fashion of various scientific positivists, or as that which lies outside of language, or meaning, or subjectivity, or discourse, or representation, or power, after the sentimental fashion of various poststructuralists, it might be more profitable to regard the body, after the constructionist fashion of Donna Haraway, as "a 'material-semiotic actor'" in "the apparatus of bodily production."[3]   Haraway's project is to denaturalize the body and to deconstruct the bourgeois concept of "self," which has so closely attached to it, through a radical critique of

---

[2]Doug Sadownick, "Groening against the Grain: Maverick Cartoonist Matt Groening Draws in Readers with Gay Characters Akbar and Jeff," *The Advocate* 571 (February, 1991): 30–35.

[3]Donna Haraway, "The Biopolitics of Postmodern Bodies: Determinations of Self in Immune System Discourse," *differences* 1, n. 1 (Winter 1989): 3–43, esp. 10–12, recast as "The Biopolitics of Postmodern Bodies: Constitutions of Self in Immune System Discourse," Donna J. Haraway, *Simians, Cyborgs, and Women: The Reinvention of Nature* (New York: Routledge, 1991) 203–30, 251–54, plates 2–11, esp. 208–9.

Figure 2. By permission of *The Advocate*.

scientific, and specifically of immunological, discourse. My own considerably more modest project in this essay is to denaturalize the sexual body by historicizing it, by illuminating its multiple historical determinations, and thereby to contest the body's use as a site for the production of heterosexual meanings and for their transformation into timeless and universal realities.[4] That, at least, is one way that scholarship can challenge the powerful cultural magic that continually (re)produces the sexual body as a heterosexual body and can interrupt the homophobic logic that ineluctably constructs "love" in exclusively heterosexual terms.

My chief exhibit is a late antique Greek text, entitled the *Erôtes*, the "Loves," the "Forms of Desire," or (as A. M. Harmon somewhat quaintly renders it) the "Affairs of the Heart," which has been preserved in medieval manuscripts among the writings of Lucian. Stylistic considerations, however, apparently prohibit ascribing the work to the authorship of that well-known Greek satirist; the text's most recent editor and translator, M. D. Macleod, attributes it to a late antique imitator of Lucian and assigns it to the early fourth century C.E., although his dating of the text has been disputed.[5] Detached at one stroke from any specific geographical, political, or cultural context by this scholarly sleight of hand and long relegated to the academic oblivion of Latin dissertations,[6] to the embarrassed silences of classical philologists, or to the recreational reading of bored graduate students in classics (which is how I first encountered it), this anonymous little work deserves nonetheless to acquire a prominent place in the emerging histories of sexuality, and in 1984 it in fact provided Michel Foucault with the vehicle for a characteristically subtle and brilliant analysis in a late chapter of *Le*

---

[4]For other efforts to historicize the body, see especially Barbara Duden, *Geschichte unter der Haut* (Stuttgart: Klett-Cotta, 1987), and Michel Feher, ed., *Fragments for a History of the Human Body*, 3 vols. (New York: Zone, 1989).

[5]M. D. Macleod, trans., *Lucian VIII*, Loeb Classical Library (Cambridge, Mass.: Harvard University Press, 1967) 147. Félix Buffière, *Eros adolescent: La Pédérastie dans la Grèce antique* (Paris: Belles-Lettres, 1980) 481, prefers a date in the second century C.E.

[6]Notably, Robert Bloch, *De pseudo-Luciani Amoribus* (Strasburg: Citruebner, 1907).

*Souci de soi.*[7]  Foucault's chief purpose was to contextualize the *Erôtes*, along with the opinions expressed in it, in the philosophical currents of late antiquity—the only possible historical and cultural context for it that can now be recovered.  I have a different, and admittedly cruder, purpose in view, as will appear presently.

The *Erôtes* is a notably sophisticated and elegant specimen of late antique luxury literature.  Taking the form of a philosophical dialogue, but designed to mock the moral pretensions and austere postures of traditional philosophers (especially the supposedly high-minded, Platonizing advocates of boy-love[8] who by late antiquity had become stock figures of fun in the erotic literature of Greece),[9] the work features a debate between two men, Charicles and Callicratidas, over the relative merits of women and boys as vehicles of male sexual pleasure.  As such, it belongs to a widely distributed genre of erotic writing which is represented in the surviving literature of the ancient world by Plutarch's *Eroticus* and by an extended passage in *Leucippe and Cleitophon*, a late Greek romance, or novel, by Achilles Tatius.[10] Similar debates can be found in medieval European and Arabic literatures,[11] in late imperial Chinese literature,[12] and in the lit-

---

[7]Michel Foucault, *Le Souci de soi*, Histoire de la sexualité 3 (Paris: Gallimard, 1984) 243–61.

[8]So Foucault, 3:261.  See, especially, *Erôtes* 23–24, 35, 48–49, 51, 53 (where Diotima's "steps" of love in Plato's *Symposium* [211c3] are impertinently transformed into a "ladder of pleasure"), and 54.

[9]See, for example, Plutarch, *Moralia* 751a, 752a; Lucian, *Dialogues of the Courtesans* 10; Alciphron 4.7; Athenaeus 13.572b.

[10]Plutarch, *Moralia* 748f-771e, and Achilles Tatius 2.33–38: commentary by Friedrich Wilhelm, "Zu Achilles Tatius," *Rheinisches Museum für Philologie* 57 (1902): 55–75.

[11]On the "Debate between Ganymede and Helen," and other such texts, see John Boswell, *Christianity, Social Tolerance, and Homosexuality: Gay People in Western Europe from the Beginning of the Christian Era to the Fourteenth Century* (Chicago: University of Chicago Press, 1980) 255–65.

Similarly, al-Samau'al ibn Yahyâ, a Jewish convert to Islam who died in 1180, composed a treatise entitled *Book of Conversations with Friends on the Intimate Relations between Lovers in the Domain of the Science of Sexuality*, which is largely given over to "a long and highly technical comparison between the anal sphincter and the muscles of the uterus"; the author, who includes in his discussion a striking account of sexual relations between

erature of "the floating world," the luxury literature of town life in seventeenth-century Japan.[13]

In the ancient Greek context, however, the existence of such a genre raises a number of provocative issues. For one thing, most Greeks seem routinely to have assumed that most adult Greek men—whatever their particular tastes—were at least capable of being sexually aroused both by beautiful women and by beautiful boys;[14] as I have argued elsewhere, "it would be a

women, invokes the authority of the Prophet to establish the superiority of women as sexual partners for men: see Danielle Jacquart and Claude Thomasset, *Sexuality and Medicine in the Middle Ages*, trans. Matthew Adamson (Princeton: Princeton University Press, 1988) 124–25. A more classical instance—"The Man's Dispute with the Learned Woman Concerning the Relative Excellence of Male and Female"—can be found in the 419th Night of *The Book of the Thousand Nights and a Night*, trans. Richard F. Burton (London: Burton Club, c. 1886) 5:154–63 (I wish to thank Joe Boone of the University of Southern California for helping me verify this reference); this corresponds to tales 390–93 in the J. C. Mardrus-Powys Mathers version of *The Book of the Thousand Nights and One Night* (New York: St. Martin's, 1972) 2:409–15: Boswell n. 257.

[12]See *Bian er chai* ("Wearing a Haircap but also Hairpins"), dated to the first half of the seventeenth century, with discussion by Keith McMahon, *Causality and Containment in Seventeenth-Century Chinese Fiction*, T'oung-pao Monograph 15 (Leiden: E. J. Brill, 1988); cf. Charlotte Furth, "Androgynous Males and Deficient Females: Biology and Gender Boundaries in Sixteenth- and Seventeenth-Century China," *Late Imperial China* 9, n. 2 (December 1988): 1–31. See, also, the first chapter of *Pinhua baojian* ("Precious Mirror for Judging Flowers"), published in 1849 by Chen Sen: commentary by Bret Hinsch, *Passions of the Cut Sleeve: The Male Homosexual Tradition in China* (Berkeley: University of California Press, 1990) 156–61. (I wish to thank Maram Epstein of the University of Michigan and Gregory M. Pflugfelder of Stanford University for kindly supplying me with these references.)

[13]On the *danjo yûretsu ron*—which is a modern Japanese designation for the largely seventeenth-century genre of erotic debate over the relative merits of women and boys as sexual partners for adult men—see the translator's introduction to Ihara Saikaku, *The Great Mirror of Male Love*, trans. Paul Gordon Schalow (Stanford: Stanford University Press, 1990) 7.

[14]I use *boy* here, when speaking about Greek sexual practices, in something of a technical sense: the term *boy* translates the Greek word *pais*, which refers by convention in Greek sexual discourse to the junior partner in a pederastic relationship, or to one who plays that role, regardless of his ac-

monumental task indeed to enumerate all the ancient documents in which the alternative 'boy or woman' occurs with perfect nonchalance in an erotic context, as if the two were functionally interchangeable."[15]  In fact, an instance of precisely such a nonchalant approach to matters of sexual object-choice can be found in the opening chapter of the *Erôtes*, in which one adult male speaker urges the other not to omit "mention of any of your passions, whether male or even female" (1).[16]  One question worth putting to the pseudo-Lucianic text, then, is this: how do exclusive sexual preferences on the part of men get conceptualized and represented in a culture generally so indifferent to men's sexual object-choices?  A second question springs immediately from the first: how can a modern interpreter of the *Erôtes* avoid reading modern sexual categories into the ancient text, thereby misconstruing it as a debate concerning the relative merits of "homosexual and heterosexual love"?[17]  How, after all, can we—the inheritors of the Kinsey scale—conceive of exclusive preference for male or female sexual contacts except in terms of sexual orientation?[18]

---

tual age; youths are customarily supposed to be desirable between the onset of puberty and the arrival of the beard: see K. J. Dover, *Greek Homosexuality* (London: Duckworth, 1978) 16, 85–87; Buffière 605–14. *Boy* refers, then, not to male children categorically but to adolescents or teenagers or to young men more generally in their capacity as objects of male erotic desire.

[15]David M. Halperin, *One Hundred Years of Homosexuality and Other Essays on Greek Love* (New York: Routledge, 1990) 34.

[16]All translations of the *Erôtes* included in this paper follow closely the text and translation of Macleod, though I have freely altered the translation where necessary.  The vehemence of Charicles and Callicratidas, the participants in the discussion about the relative sexual merits of women and boys that occupies the body of the text, is balanced by the disengagement of Lycinus and Theomnestus, the speakers in the framing dialogue, who are either indifferent to both women and boys (in the case of Lycinus: 4) or equally attracted to each (in the case of Theomnestus: 3, 4).  See Foucault 3:243.

[17]Macleod 147.

[18]For a recent example of the inability to conceive sexual preference in terms other than those of sexual orientation, and of the abuse to which such a rigid approach subjects the Kinsey scale (which Kinsey himself designed specifically in order to categorize sexual behavior without reference to the concepts of hetero- and homosexual identity), see John Boswell, "Categories,

It is with these questions in mind that I turn to the pseudo-Lucianic text. My reading will be an "engaged" one and, as such, it will have a limited scope. Its goal is not to provide a balanced description of the *Erôtes* or to convey much in the way of aesthetic appreciation of the work's admittedly numerous formal and stylistic perfections. Nor is it my intention to champion the ancients at the expense of the moderns or to promote a rhetoric of bodies and pleasures over a rhetoric of sexuality; it is not possible to reinstitute the ancient Greek sociosexual system, nor, if it were, would I wish to live under it. Finally, I am not about to undertake a critique (which it would be easy enough to do) of male sexual privilege as it permeates the world of the text or to analyze the operations of gendered, social power as it expresses itself in the adult male objectification of both women and boys. What I want to do, instead, is to bring the *Erôtes* into the arena of late twentieth-century ideological struggles over sexual definition and, in particular, to place its testimony at the service of various contemporary radical critiques of sexual identity.[19]  In particular, I want to exploit the text's cultural distance from the world of middle-class America in order to problematize some twentieth-century assumptions about sexual preference, erotic identity, and the linkages often made between them. By confronting the modern Western bourgeois distinction between hetero- and homosexuality with the Greek distinction between boys and women as objects of male sexual pleasure, and thereby calling attention to both thematic continuities and discursive rup-

Experience and Sexuality," *Forms of Desire: Sexual Orientation and the Social Constructionist Controversy*, ed. Edward Stein, Garland Gay and Lesbian Studies 1 (New York: Garland, 1990) 133–73; the abridged version of this essay, which appears in *differences* 2, n. 1 (Spring 1990): 67–87, under the title, "Concepts, Experience, and Sexuality," omits any mention of the Kinsey scale. For some current meditations on the use and abuse of the Kinsey scale, see David P. McWhirter, Stephanie A. Sanders, and June Machover Reinisch, eds., *Homosexuality/Heterosexuality: Concepts of Sexual Orientation*, The Kinsey Institute Series 2 (New York: Oxford, 1990).

[19]See, for example, Biddy Martin, "Lesbian Identity and Autobiographical Difference(s)," *Life/Lines: Theorizing Women's Autobiography*, ed. Bella Brodzki and Celeste Schenck (Ithaca: Cornell University Press, 1988) 77–103; Judith Butler, "Imitation and Gender Insubordination," *Inside/Out: Lesbian Theories, Gay Theories*, ed. Diana Fuss (New York: Routledge, 1991) 13–31.

tures in the history of sexuality, I aim to bring out the cultural specificity of ancient sexual experiences and at the same time to throw into sharper relief the ideological contingency of what we lightly call "our own" sexual practices and institutions.[20] The point is not to devise a popularity contest between the ancients and the moderns but to contrast them in order to distinguish more systematically the peculiar features of their respective sexual regimes. The ultimate effect of this stereoscopic—or dialectical—procedure, I hope, will be to defamiliarize current sexual behaviors and attitudes and, in particular, to destabilize the binary opposition between heterosexuality and homosexuality that so decisively structures contemporary discourses of homophobia.

The dialogue between Charicles and Callicratidas in the pseudo-Lucianic *Erôtes* sounds a number of themes that will be immediately familiar to modern readers from contemporary debates over the morality, or immorality, of homosexuality. Charicles argues, for example, that men should favor sex with women over sex with boys because it conduces to reproduction, renews life, and preserves the human race from annihilation (19). Callicratidas replies that the very instrumentality of cross-sex sexual intercourse for species reproduction is a mark of its unworthiness: "Anything cultivated for aesthetic reasons in the midst of abundance," he maintains, "is accompanied with greater honor than things which require for their existence immediate need, and beauty is in every way superior to necessity" (33). Connected to the argument about reproduction is another familiar one about the supposed naturalness of sex between men and women and the supposed unnaturalness of sex between men and boys, an argument borrowed in this case directly from Plato's *Laws* (835d-842a, esp. 836c, 839a).[21] Calling "luxury" (*trypshê*) what Callicratidas had called "beauty," Charicles associates boy-

---

[20] For a critique of such a procedure, emphasizing how historicizing accounts of past sexual formations normally have the effect of homogenizing contemporary sexual discourses, flattening out their crucial incoherences and contradictions, see Eve Kosofsky Sedgwick, *Epistemology of the Closet* (Berkeley: University of California Press, 1990) 44–48.

[21] On this genre of argument, see John J. Winkler, "Unnatural Acts: Erotic Protocols in Artemidoros' *Dream Analysis*," *The Constraints of Desire: The Anthropology of Sex and Gender in Ancient Greece* (New York: Routledge, 1990) 17–44, esp. 18–23.

love with eunuchs, with the surgical construction of gender,[22] and he goes on to appeal, in the Platonic manner, to animal behavior for a standard of alleged naturalness in matters of sex (20–22). Callicratidas, however, is unmoved by the analogy from animals; he claims that male animals eschew sex with one another and copulate with females precisely because they are mindless;[23] otherwise, he remarks, "they would not be satisfied with solitary lives in the wilderness, nor would they feed on one another, but just like us they would have built themselves temples and . . . would live as fellow citizens governed by common laws" (36). And to Charicles' assertion that anatomy is destiny, that sex between men and boys is necessarily one-sided in its distribution of sexual pleasure whereas sex between men and women is mutually enjoyable (27), Callicratidas retorts that true reciprocity consists in the shared erotic life of an ongoing, long-lasting relationship (48), not in who does what to whom.

Despite these points of correspondence between the pseudo-Lucianic debate and modern polemics, or between ancient misogyny and its twentieth-century gay male equivalent, a number of factors militate against interpreting the argument between Charicles and Callicratidas as a dispute over the relative merits of heterosexuality and homosexuality. Chief among these factors is the dialogue's focus on pederasty to the virtual exclusion of any mention of either female or adult male homosexuality. The text contains only one mention of female homosexuality, wholly negative in intent (if subversively potent in effect), and even it does not refer to lesbianism *per se* but rather to what the writer calls "tribadism"—that is, to the sexual penetration of women by other women.[24] "If males find intercourse with males accept-

---

[22]See the brilliant reflections of Marjorie Garber, "Spare Parts: The Surgical Construction of Gender," *differences* 1, n. 3 (Fall 1989): 137–59.

[23]See Plutarch, *Moralia* 750c–e, and the *Greek Anthology* 12.245, for similar arguments.

[24]See, now, Judith P. Hallett, "Female Homoeroticism and the Denial of Roman Reality in Latin Literature," *Yale Journal of Criticism* 3.1 (Fall 1989): 209–27, and compare George Chauncey, Jr., "From Sexual Inversion to Homosexuality: The Changing Medical Conceptualization of Female Deviance," *Passion and Power: Sexuality in History*, ed. Kathy Peiss and Christina Simmons (Philadelphia: Temple University Press, 1989) 87–117, esp. 99 and 113, n. 50. Further references to compilations of ancient evidence for the "tribad" can be found in Halperin, 166, n. 83; 180, n. 2; and in

able," exclaims Charicles (the partisan of women), playing what he clearly considers to be his trump card in the argument,

> henceforth let women too love one another. . . . Let them strap to themselves cunningly contrived instruments of wantonness, those mysterious monstrosities devoid of seed, and let woman lie with woman as does a man. Let wanton tribadism—that word seldom heard, which I feel ashamed even to utter—freely parade itself, and let our women's chambers . . . defile themselves with sexually indeterminate amours. (28)

Needless to say, Callicratidas (the partisan of boys) does not rise to his opponent's challenge and endorse such constructive and promising proposals.

Within the realm of male eroticism, correspondingly, the *Erôtes* makes absolutely no allowance for the possibility of sexual relations among adult men—for the possibility, that is, of "homosexual" rather than merely pederastic love. Both Charicles and Callicratidas seem to agree that adult males hold not the slightest sexual appeal to other men; and the terms in which they express that shared assumption reveal the distance that separates the aesthetic and sexual conventions of ancient Mediterranean pederasty from the canons of modern American middle-class gay male taste. "If a man makes attempts on a boy of twenty," Charicles (the partisan of women) remarks,

> he seems to me to be pursuing an equivocal love. For then the [boy's] limbs, being large and manly, are hard; the chins that once were soft are rough and covered with bristles, and the well-developed thighs are as it were sullied with hairs. And as for the parts less visible than these, I leave knowledge of them to you who have tried them. (26)[25]

---

Bernadette J. Brooten (Harvard Divinity School), "Women with Masculine Desires: Ancient Medical Treatments," paper delivered on October 16, 1991, at the Seminar in Lesbian/Gay Studies, Center for Literary and Cultural Studies, Harvard University.

[25]Cf. Saikaku 1:4: "It is said that, 'cherry blossoms forever bloom the same, but people change with every passing year.' This is especially true of

Each detail in this description of overripe boyhood is intended to evoke revulsion and disgust; it is telling that Charicles' opponent, Callicratidas, can say nothing to refute it.

A fuller description of the two rivals in the debate will help to illuminate their respective positions. Callicratidas, the partisan of boys, is an Athenian. He is a man of mature age, well established in life; his sexual taste bespeaks a stable and settled disposition, not a transition from one identity to another or a mere "phase" in his psychosexual development. Far from being socially marginalized by his openly acknowledged erotic preference, Callicratidas is a leading figure in Athenian public life. Far from being effeminized by his sexual predilection for boys, as the modern "inversion model" of homosexual desire would have it (whereby a man exclusively attracted to males has "a woman's soul in a man's body" or represents a "sexual intermediate" or member of a "third sex"),[26] Callicratidas' inclination renders him hypervirile: he excels at those activities traditionally marked in Greek culture as exclusively and characteristically masculine—namely, political life, public oratory, gymnastics (9, 29), and philosophy—and he takes as his role models the heroes and philosophers of old (46–49). Callicratidas' sexual desire for boys,

---

a boy in the bloom of youth. . . . When at last he comes of age, his blossom of youth falls cruelly to the ground. All told, loving a boy can be likened to a dream that we are not even given time to have" (69).

[26]The first phrase translates *anima muliebris virili corpore inclusa*, the notorious self-description of Karl Heinrich Ulrichs, the mid-nineteenth-century founder of the German movement for homosexual emancipation: see Hubert C. Kennedy, "The 'Third Sex' Theory of Karl Heinrich Ulrichs," *Historical Perspectives on Homosexuality*, ed. Salvatore J. Licata and Robert P. Petersen, *Journal of Homosexuality* 6, n. 1–2 (1980/81): 103–111; Hubert C. Kennedy, *Ulrichs: The Life and Works of Karl Heinrich Ulrichs, Pioneer of the Modern Gay Movement* (Boston: Alyson, 1988) 43–53. The second phrase refers to the theories of Magnus Hirschfeld and Edward Carpenter, two early writers and activists: Hirschfeld's journal (which began publication at the turn of the century) was entitled *Jahrbuch für sexuelle Zwischenstufen*; compare Carpenter, *The Intermediate Sex: A Study of Some Transitional Types of Men and Women* (2nd ed. 1909). For the best general account of the inversion model, see Chauncey; for the classic literary representation of male inversion, see Marcel Proust, *Cities of the Plain*, Part One.

then, does not weaken or subvert his male gender identity but rather consolidates it.[27]

By contrast, Charicles, the partisan of women, is young and handsome; he hails from Corinth, a city as traditionally renowned for its courtesans as Athens is renowned for political rhetoric and philosophy. He asserts that nature, in implanting in men and women a desire for one another, sought to polarize the sexes and to distinguish masculine from feminine styles, making males masculine and women feminine (19, 28), but his own comportment belies that claim. Just as Callicratidas' habit of consorting with boys represents either a symptom or a cause of his hypermasculinity, so Charicles' erotic preference for women seems to have had the corresponding effect of effeminizing him: when the reader first encounters him, for example, Charicles is described as exhibiting "a skillful use of cosmetics, so as to be attractive to women" (9); indeed, Greek women, if one is to credit the desires imputed to them by male authors, seem to have liked men who looked young[28] (no one in this world, apparently, would appear to find adult men sexually appealing). Now since cosmetic adornment is an indicatively feminine practice (38–41), Charicles would seem to have been infected by femininity from his long habit of associating with women.[29] His passionate encomium of women, moreover—his defense of their claims to be loved by men and his praise of their sexual attractiveness—signal to the jaundiced eye of Callicratidas that Charicles has simply enslaved himself to the cause of women: if he were a real man, the implication seems to be, he would not allow

[27]This is what Sedgwick (87–90) terms the "gender separatist" model.

[28]See, for example, *Homeric Hymn to Aphrodite* 225–36; Dio Chrysostom 7.117; Pausanias 7.23.1–2; Lucian, *Dialogues of the Courtesans* 7.2–3.

[29]See Chariton, *Chaereas and Callirhoe* 1.4, where a man who wishes to be mistaken for an adulterer makes a similarly lavish use of cosmetics: "his hair was gleaming and heavily scented; his eyes were made up; he had a soft cloak and fine shoes; heavy rings gleamed on his fingers" (trans. B. P. Reardon, *Collected Ancient Greek Novels*, ed. Reardon [Berkeley: University of California Press, 1989] 27). Compare the representations of Agathon in Old Comedy: commentary by Froma I. Zeitlin, "Travesties of Gender and Genre in Aristophanes' *Thesmophorizusae*," *Reflections of Women in Antiquity*, ed. Helene P. Foley (New York: Gordon and Breach Science Publishers, 1981) 169–217; Frances Muecke, "A Portrait of the Artist as a Young Woman," *Classical Quarterly* 32 (1982): 41–55.

himself to be so dominated by women as to be obliged to defend their interests in public. According to the terms of Greek misogynistic discourse, there would appear to be no distinction between being the champion of women and being their slave (30). Compared to Callicratidas, then, it is Charicles who is a traitor to his gender, having been led to betray his masculine identity by the very vehemence of his sexual preference for women: he has become woman-identified. In short, the sharply polarizing tendencies of Greek sexual discourse would seem to require that excessive liking for women on the part of a man be interpreted as a sign of deviant, specifically effeminate identity. Such an identity, in fact, closely approximates what a recent ethnographer of the American South has described as "a redneck queer," a Southern traitor to masculinity, whom she defines not as a male homosexual but, on the contrary, as "a boy from Alabama who laks girls better'n football."[30]

By Greek standards, then, neither Callicratidas nor Charicles is entirely conventional in the matter of his sexual tastes. Rather, each man is something of an extremist (5), a zealot whose fanatical attachment to his own erotic object-choice—and whose correspondingly violent revulsion against the sexual objects favored by his opponent—mark him out as peculiar and manifest themselves in his entire style of life. Each man's sexual inclination, if not exactly "written immodestly on his face and body" (as Foucault says of the nineteenth-century homosexual),[31] is at least visibly inscribed in his domestic arrangements. Callicratidas, the narrator points out, "was well provided with handsome slave-boys and all of his servants were pretty well beardless. They remained with him till the down first appeared on their faces, but, once any growth cast a shadow on their cheeks, they would be sent away to be stewards and overseers of his properties at Athens" (10). Charicles, by contrast,

---

[30]Rosemary Daniell, *Sleeping with Soldiers: In Search of the Macho Man* (New York: Holt, Rinehart, and Winston, 1984) 71. In the *Erôtes*, Lycinus' description of the erotically ambidexterous Theomnestus, whose life is given over to wrestling schools, fancy clothes, and elaborate hair-styles (3), similarly combines elements traditionally associated with the love of boys (outdoor physical exercise) and the love of women (personal adornment).

[31]Michel Foucault, *The History of Sexuality, Volume 1: An Introduction*, trans. Robert Hurley (New York: Pantheon, 1978) 43.

had in attendance a large band of dancing girls and singing girls and all his house was as full of women as if it were the Thesmophoria [a women's religious festival], with not the slightest trace of male presence except that here and there could be seen an infant boy or a superannuated old cook whose age could give even the jealous no cause for suspicion. (10)

Callicratidas and Charicles do not represent, then, spokesmen for abnormal and normal sexualities, respectively: rather, they are both a bit queer.

Nonetheless, each man demonstrates a certain connoisseurship in describing the good and bad features of the sexual objects favored by his rival, a knowingness that bespeaks a broader range of erotic sympathies or a wider sexual experience than one might initially have imputed to such self-styled sexual purists. I have already cited one instance: Charicles' vivid and sensuously precise evocation of the physical attributes of a boy past his prime. Charicles' taste in boys, his ability to judge when a boy is no longer desirable, his standards for discriminating smoothness and hairiness in youthful cheeks and thighs are confirmed in their inerrancy by the institutional arrangements of Callicratidas' household, which has well-established procedures for "graduating" overage, hirsute lads. Charicles evidently understands what Callicratidas likes and dislikes in a boy. Conversely, Callicratidas betrays an intimate knowledge of women. His violent denunciation of women's cosmetic practices (38–41) implies so extensive an acquaintance with them that one might imagine him to be a professional beautician—were it not that his accusations belong to the arsenal of traditional Greek misogyny.[32] Still, the very intensity of his disgust (he claims that "every man [who gets out of a woman's bed] is in immediate need of a bath" [42]) seems to indicate at least passing familiarity. And his acceptance, however reluctant, of the necessity of having sexual relations with women in order to beget offspring (38) demonstrates that he does not regard himself as incapable of consummating a sexual union with a woman, should the situation call for it.

On rare occasions, in fact, both Charicles and Callicratidas are able to agree on the attractiveness of a sexual object. Their

---

[32]See, for example, Achilles Tatius 2.38.2.

desires coincide in the case of the famous statue of Aphrodite at Cnidus, by the sculptor Praxiteles. Callicratidas, of course, is initially reluctant to view this world-renowned masterpiece because it has the form of a female figure (11), but even he is struck dumb by the sight of it, while Charicles raves over it and even kisses the statue (13). When the two men inspect the rear of the figure, however, it is Callicratidas' turn to rave, while Charicles stands transfixed with tears pouring from his eyes (14). "Heracles!" Callicratidas exclaims,

> what a well-proportioned back! What generous flanks she has! How satisfying an armful to embrace! How delicately moulded the flesh on the buttocks, neither too thin and close to the bone, nor yet revealing too great an expanse of fat! And as for those precious parts sealed in on either side by the hips, how inexpressibly sweetly they smile![33] How perfect the proportions of the thighs and the shins as they stretch down in a straight line to the feet! So that's what Ganymede looks like as he pours out the nectar in heaven for Zeus and makes it taste sweeter. For I'd never have taken the cup from Hebe if she served me. (14)

Charicles is hardly in a state to disagree. Such passages create the impression that what endears boys to Callicratidas and women to Charicles is not a preferred sex or gender but merely certain favorite parts of the human anatomy.

That impression is strengthened when the two men go on to discover that a discoloration of the marble they have noted on the back of the statue was caused by a young man who fell in love with it and who, having arranged to be locked up alone with the statue at night, had sex with it by stealth (15–16).[34] Charicles concludes that the feminine evokes love even when carved in stone. Callicratidas, however, observes that although the

---

[33]Could this phrase, *hōs hēdys ho gelōs*, be the source of Rilke's "Sonst ... im leisen Drehen / der Lenden könnte nicht ein Lächeln gehen / zu jener Mitte, die die Zeugung trug," in his famous sonnet (in the second part of the *Neue Gedichte*) on an "Archaic Torso of Apollo"?

[34]Discussion by David Freedberg, *The Power of Images: Studies in the History and Theory of Response* (Chicago: University of Chicago Press, 1989) 331–32, with notes.

amorous youth had the opportunity to glut his entire passion for
the goddess during an uninterrupted night of love, he chose to
make love to her "as if to a boy" (*paidikôs*)—that is, from the
rear—in order not to be confronted by the female part of her
(17). (Face-to-face intercourse would have been difficult to bring
off, in any case, even if the lover had desired it, since Praxiteles'
statue—in addition to being made of marble—was far from
anatomically correct. Callicratidas' rejoinder provides one more
indication of the highly sophistical tenor of the whole debate.)
These passages confirm that the quarrel between Charicles and
Callicratidas comes down not to a difference in sexual object-
choice, to differing sexual preferences or orientations, but rather
to a differential liking for particular human body parts, independent of the sex of the person who possesses them.

Furthermore, the specific arguments that the two men use
in order to establish the putative superiority of their preferred
sexual object display what modern middle-class readers may find
not only unpersuasive but positively bizarre styles of reasoning.
That is because most bourgeois Westerners nowadays tend to
think of sexual object-choice as an expression of individual
"sexuality," a fixed sexual disposition or orientation over which
no one has much (if any) control: any reasons one might give for
one's sexual object choice seem to be mere afterthoughts, adven-
titious rationalizations, late arrivals on the scene of sexual speci-
ation; reasons merely follow the fact of one's sexual being and do
not determine or constitute it.  Thus, sexual preference is not
something that one can be argued logically out of or into—least
of all by considerations of utility or convenience.  And yet those
are precisely the sorts of considerations that Charicles invokes in
order to demonstrate that women are superior vehicles of male
sexual pleasure.  For example, women have more sexual orifices
than do boys, Charicles observes; hence, it is possible for men to
make use of women in the same manner that they make use of
boys (*paidikôteron*), thereby availing themselves of "twin paths
to sexual pleasure," whereas "a male has no way of bestowing
the pleasure a woman gives" (27).  And here is yet another consideration of a practical nature: women, unlike boys, can be enjoyed for a protracted period of time.  "From maidenhood to middle age, before the time when the last wrinkles of old age spread
over her face, a woman is a pleasant armful for a man to embrace," Charicles points out (25), adding that a woman's body
(unlike a boy's) remains attractively hairless as she grows older

(26). Callicratidas does not dispute those assertions[35] but counters instead with a lengthy polemic about the superiority of art to nature (33-36: see the excerpt from it on p. 253 above).

What all this evidence indicates, finally, is that the anonymous author of the pseudo-Lucianic *Erôtes* approaches the question of male sexual object-choice not as a matter of sexual orientation but rather as a matter of taste—the sort of thing that, as everyone knows, there's no disputing and that everyone just loves to dispute. (As W. H. Auden wrote in 1936, "Who can ever praise enough / The world of his belief?")[36] The quarrel between Charicles and Callicratidas over the relative merits of women and boys as vehicles of male sexual pleasure is not an argument about the relative merits of heterosexuality and homosexuality in the modern sense but a disagreement over the respective advantages and disadvantages of different "avenues of sexual pleasure" (cf. 27) and different modes of styling personal life. The alternatives presented by the two disputants delineate sexual options apparently available, in principle at least, to any free adult Greek male such that anyone—no matter how set in his ways—might plausibly be thought at least capable of entertaining those options, if not necessarily eager to explore them.

To recapitulate: the text's emphasis on pederasty to the exclusion of homosexuality (whose existence, apparently, is not even recognized); the masculinization of the pederast and the effeminization of the lover of women; the pederast's lack of social marginalization; the shared queerness of both interlocutors; the ability of each interlocutor to put himself in the erotic subject position of the other; their common knowingness about both women

---

[35]A reply to the argument about the relative durability of women and boys as objects of male sexual enjoyment is provided by a character in Achilles Tatius 2.36 (trans. John J. Winkler, *Collected Ancient Greek Novels* 205-6):

Kleitophon, you don't know the principal fact about pleasure: to be unsatisfied is always a desirable state. Constant recourse to anything makes satisfaction shrivel into satiation. What can only be snatched is always fresh and blooming—its pleasure never grows old. And as much as beauty's span is diminished in time, so is it intensified in desire. The rose for this reason is lovelier than other plants: its beauty soon is gone.

[36]W. H. Auden, *Collected Poems*, ed. Edward Mendelson (New York: Random House, 1976) 129.

and boys; the pederast's capacity to eroticize elements of the human anatomy independently of the sex of the person whose anatomy is eroticized; the lover of women's utilitarian appeal to quantitative factors as a basis for calculating relative sexual value; and, finally, both men's treatment of sexual object-choice as a matter of taste—the conjunction of all of those considerations rules out the hypothesis that what one is dealing with in the *Erôtes* is a system of "sexuality," in the modern sense of that word.

In order to make sense of the quarrel between Charicles and Callicratidas in modern terms, it may be helpful to think of it somewhat along the lines of a passionate debate over dietary object-choice between a committed vegetarian and an unreconstructed omnivore—or, to be more exact, between someone who eats nothing but vegetables and someone who eats nothing but meat. It is a quarrel that springs not from fundamental differences in kind among human beings but from the dissimilar values, ideals, and preferred styles of life[37] that otherwise similar human beings happen (for whatever reason) to have espoused. It is therefore a dispute about the very sorts of things that people tend to argue about most heatedly—namely, their "basic commitments," to use a modern formulation. No matter how basic such commitments may be, however, they are susceptible of being criticized or debated precisely because they derive from what people believe and value, not from what or who they are. The probability of one disputant actually convincing another to alter his basic commitments, and to alter the behavior that follows from them, is admittedly slim, but by citing various reasons or adducing various considerations each disputant can nurture the (no doubt foredoomed) hope that his interlocutor may come one day to look at things from his own perspective. Without the conviction that the available options admit of right choices and wrong choices, that the choice is open to everyone to make, and that one's own choice is indeed the correct one, one has little motive to get worked up over the issue—and uncommitted onlookers

---

[37]See Foucault, 3:246–59, for a detailed elaboration of this point. Compare Saikaku, 5:2, in which a boy is held back momentarily from having sex with a beautiful girl who offers herself to him—not by his own lack of desire for her but by his personal commitments, specifically by his hitherto unswerving devotion to the way of boy-love (200–1).

have little cause to find the dispute amusing or entertaining. Such is not the case of sexuality nowadays. That is why modern debates over the respective merits of various sexual orientations tend to have an entirely different character: they are like debates over whether it is better to be a peasant or a king—matters possible to dispute in principle but impossible to alter in actual practice. Such debates have a distinctive tone to them, "forlorn / Yet pleasing," as Shelley puts it, "such as once, so poets tell, / The devils held within the dales of Hell, / Concerning God, freewill and destiny" ("Julian and Maddalo," 39–42).

These issues become clear when the *Erôtes* is situated in its wider generic context and compared to another text from an analogous cultural tradition, namely *The Great Mirror of Male Love* by the seventeenth-century Japanese writer Ihara Saikaku. Published in Osaka and Kyoto on New Year's Day, 1687, *The Great Mirror* contains forty tales of exemplary love between men and boys. Its opening chapter justifies the choice of subject by means of twenty-three comparisons of women to boys, each of them designed to champion the latter at the expense of the former and to establish the relative advantages of boys as vehicles of male pleasure. What sets off these alternatives from the arguments of Callicratidas is that they are couched entirely in negative terms. Instead of purporting to demonstrate straightforwardly that the love of boys is superior to the love of women, Saikaku's comparisons show that when affairs go badly, boy-love is on the whole less vexatious. Here is how Saikaku's argument begins:

> Which is to be preferred: A girl of eleven or twelve scrutinizing herself in a mirror, or a boy of the same age cleaning his teeth?
>
> Lying rejected next to a courtesan, or conversing intimately with a Kabuki boy who is suffering from hemorrhoids?
>
> Caring for a wife with tuberculosis, or keeping a youth who constantly demands spending money?
>
> Having lightning strike the room where you are enjoying a boy actor you bought, or being handed a razor by a courtesan you hardly know who asks you to die with her?

The choice is evidently not a difficult one: "In each case above," Saikaku concludes with a partisanship so extreme as to be ludicrous and therefore self-canceling, "even if the woman were a beauty of gentle disposition and the youth a repulsive pug-nosed fellow, it is a sacrilege to speak of female love in the same breath with boy love. . . . The only sensible choice is to dispense with women and turn instead to men."[38]

What the pseudo-Lucianic *Erôtes* shares with *The Great Mirror of Male Love*, besides its evident misogyny, is its combination of literary gamesmanship and sexual connoisseurship: it playfully explores various possibilities of sexual pleasure, presenting the (implied male) reader with specific sets of alternative options for achieving erotic enjoyment and personal satisfaction. Perhaps the final surprise that the *Erôtes* has to offer the modern historian of sexuality is its dramatization of the absurdity of the very notion of exclusive sexual object-choice, whether homo- or hetero-. It is not just that Greek males exhibited on the whole a different "sexuality" from modern American men of the professional classes, if one may judge solely on the basis of this one

---

[38]Saikaku 53, 56. Paul Gordon Schalow, the translator, explains in his introduction that

> In the first case, Saikaku is describing the age when boys and girls first become aware of themselves sexually. The girl fusses over her outward appearance in a mirror, whereas the boy is concerned about the less noticeable but in some ways more important cleanliness of his teeth. The preference implicit here is for the boy's more innocent and perhaps less calculating concern with hygiene than with superficial appearances. In the second case, neither situation with courtesan or actor allows sexual intercourse for the paying patron, but the 'intimate conversation' possible with the kabuki boy provides a recompense of sorts, suggesting a nonsexual satisfaction found in having an affair with an actor that is lacking with a courtesan. The third example juxtaposes two financially draining situations, supporting a sick wife versus supporting a spendthrift boy. Again the implication is that the sick wife represents a hopeless situation, whereas the boy, in spite of his spending habits, offers some pleasurable compensations. (12)

I wonder if a similarly earnest account could be given of the fourth example. For further arguments, see my review of Schalow's translation in the *Journal of Japanese Studies* 17 (1991): 398–403.

In the *Erôtes*, similarly, Callicratidas juxtaposes the image of a girl with a mirror and a comb to that of a boy with a book and a lyre (44).

text (which, of course, it would be extremely hazardous to do in the absence of corroborating documentation).[39] Rather, they exhibited no "sexuality" at all, in the modern sense. Not only are the very notions of "sexuality" and "sexual orientation" entirely foreign to the world of this text: to the extent that the text can even accommodate such notions—can represent human types who roughly approximate the modern hetero- and homosexual male—it treats them as outlandish and bizarre. Merely to have a fixed sexual object-choice of any kind is to be some sort of freak, apparently—a figure of fun whose foredoomed efforts at rationalizing his exclusive preference provide amusement and relaxation for one's fellow man (5, 29, 53).[40] Despite all the sound and fury of their polemics, then, Charicles and Callicratidas actually agree about the fundamentals. They certainly resemble each other more than either resembles a modern homosexual or heterosexual male (who, correspondingly, resembles his modern counterpart more than he resembles either Charicles or Callicratidas). Like the putative differences of gender that supposedly distinguish the two lovebirds represented on the United States "LOVE" stamp, the putative differences of sexual orientation that seem to distinguish Charicles and Callicratidas are largely an optical (that is, a semiotic) illusion—an effect of cultural perspective: the two disputants, like the two lovebirds, are mirror-opposites, which is to say that their basic outlook on the relation between sexual preference and erotic identity is pretty much the same.[41]

---

[39]For fuller documentation, see Dover; Winkler; Halperin; Halperin, Winkler, and Froma I. Zeitlin, eds., *Before Sexuality: The Construction of Erotic Experience in the Ancient Greek World* (Princeton: Princeton University Press, 1990); and the various studies cited in those works.

[40]Cf. Paul Gordon Schalow, "Male Love in Early Modern Japan: A Literary Depiction of the 'Youth'," *Hidden from History: Reclaiming the Gay and Lesbian Past*, ed. Martin Bauml Duberman, Martha Vicinus, and George Chauncey, Jr. (New York: NAL Books, 1989) 118-28, 506-09, esp. 120: "Those who pursued sexual relations exclusively with women or exclusively with youths were in a minority and were considered mildly eccentric for limiting their pleasurable options."

[41]Cf. Jacques Derrida, *The Truth in Painting*, trans. Geoff Bennington and Ian McLeod (Chicago: University of Chicago Press, 1987) esp. 332-35, 373-79, on the strange relations or irrelations among and within the terms *two, the pair, parity, the couple, the double, fetishism, homosexuality, heterosexu-*

If my interpretation of the pseudo-Lucianic *Erôtes* proves to be persuasive, it should provide some support for Foucault's proposition that sexuality is not lodged in our bodies, in our hormones, or in our genitals but resides in those discourses through which we gain access to ourselves as meaningful actors in our world and as the subjects of our desires. Bodies do not come with ready-made sexualities. Bodies are not even attracted to other bodies.[42] It is human subjects, rather, who are attracted to various objects, including bodies, and the features of bodies that render them desirable to human subjects are contingent upon the cultural codes, the social conventions, and the political institutions that structure and inform human subjectivity itself, thereby shaping our individual erotic ideals and defining the scope of what we find attractive. Modern cultural modes of interpellating European and American bourgeois subjects typically occlude that process of sexual subjectivation, prompting us to misrecognize it as a biophysical process—and thus to interpret the "sexuality ef-

---

ality, bisexuality. In a similar vein, it may be worth noting the various relations of resemblance, doubling, and difference that U.S. Postal Service Poster 669 (fig. 1) constructs by juxtaposing the philatelic series of four stamps to the quilt that presumably inspired their design. Like the mirror-opposite figures of the lovebirds on the stamp, each stamp in the series of repeated stamps resembles its counterparts exactly: they are all identical replicas of one another and, as such, indicate indexically the process of mechanical engraving or imaging, and the technology of industrial mass-production, that created them. The quilt, by contrast, is a unique, handmade, labor-intensive, and originally noncommodified artifact emanating from an indigenous folk tradition. The stamp is intended to glorify that tradition as a precious part of the national heritage of the United States. It does so by appropriating (supposedly) elements of the quilt's design and reproducing them in a new medium, thereby claiming for the products of impersonal mechanized industrial labor the aura of the artifactual and the homely. In that sense, the two opposites on the poster are not the paired lovebirds but the implicit couple constituted by the two featured modes of inscription or representation: quilting and engraving (computer graphics).

[42]For more elaborate philosophical arguments to this effect, see my essays, "Platonic Erôs and What Men Call Love," *Ancient Philosophy* 5 (1985): 161–204, esp. 182–87, and "Plato and the Metaphysics of Desire," *Proceedings of the Boston Area Colloquium in Ancient Philosophy* 5 (1989), ed. John J. Cleary and Daniel C. Shartin (Lanham, MD: University Press of America, 1991) 27–52.

fects" produced in our bodies as the collective sign of an intrinsically and irreducibly bodily event. As D. A. Miller remarks, "All the deployments of the 'biopower' that characterizes our modernity depend on the supposition that the most effective take on the subject is rooted in its body, insinuated within this body's 'naturally given' imperatives. Metaphorizing the body begins and ends with literalizing the meanings the body is thus made to bear."[43]

But just because the deployment of biopower we call sexuality uses our bodies as sites for the production of sexuality effects—in the form of literalized bodily meanings—we need not assume that sexuality itself is a literal, or natural, reality. Rather, sexuality is a mode of human subjectivation that operates in part by figuring the body *as* the literal, by pressing the body's supposed literality into the service of a metaphorical project. As such, sexuality represents a seizure of the body by an historically unique apparatus for producing historically specific forms of subjectivity. Through my reading of the pseudo-Lucianic *Erôtes* I have tried to confront the ancient discourses of erotic self-fashioning with the modern discourses of sexuality in order to dramatize the differences between them and to make visible the historical dimensions of that supposedly ahistorical and universal entity called "the body"—to historicize that discursive space in which modern biopower constructs "the body" as the "natural" ground of the subject. One aim, and (I hope) one effect, of my interpretative strategy is to contribute, insofar as scholarship can, to the task of reconstituting the body as a potential site of cultural activism and political resistance. If the sexual body is indeed historical—if there is, in short, no orgasm without ideology—perhaps ongoing inquiry into the politics of pleasure will serve to deepen the pleasures, as well as to widen the possibilities, of politics.

---

[43]D. A. Miller, "The Late Jane Austen," *Raritan* 10, n. 1 (Summer 1990): 55–79, quotation on 57. Much of the remainder of Miller's essay is taken up with adumbrating that fundamental insight.

# THE POETICS OF BIRTH

## Patricia Yaeger

David Byrne's "Little Creatures" offers an oasis of sexual simplicity in a world where sex is anything but simple. In an age infatuated with reproductive technologies and terrified by the unpredictability of AIDS, Byrne's song suggests a compensatory return to the old-fashioned pleasures of heterosexual reproduction:

> A woman made a man
> A man he made a house
> And when they lay together
> Little creatures all come out

> Well, I've seen sex and I think it's alright
> It makes those little creatures come to life
> I can laugh or I can turn away
> Well, I've seen sex and I think it's okay.[1]

---

Two years ago, in the midst of writing this essay, I adopted a baby girl from Brazil. I want to thank friends who helped me clarify my thoughts on this project by asking, "Why are you still writing about birth!? What kinds of pain are you inflicting upon yourself and other infertile women by writing about fertility? Why not write about adoption or reproductive technologies? Why not celebrate the pleasures of the nonreproductive body?"

These are hard questions, but after some thought, I can say that I've taken on this project for three reasons. First, my own alienation from the birth plot offers a wry point of contact, a strange rush of kinship, with men who experience women's reproductive prerogative as alienating. Reading *Dracula* or *Alice in Wonderland*—texts motivated by their authors' reproductive anxieties—I discover a wealth of literary symptoms that I both deplore and share. Second, as a feminist critic interested in emancipation, I'm drawn to a more bountiful side of the literary spectrum, to contemporary women writers like Sharon Olds or Margaret Atwood who have begun to revise and detheologize contemporary myths of reproduction.

Finally, I feel connected with this project because of the simple fact that I was born—and my daughter was born. As Sarah Ruddick says in *Maternal Thinking*, "all mothering depends on some woman's birthing labor"

Byrne's lyrics may try to comfort us with their illusion of symmetry between men's productive and women's reproductive labor, but in so doing they efface the complexity of women's reproductivity. In reducing the making of a child to the sexual act, to that moment when man and woman "come together," The Talking Heads have perpetuated one of our most persistent cultural myths; they have obliterated gestation and parturition from the story of the "little creatures" birth.[2]

The invisibility of gestation and parturition is a feminist dilemma. In this essay I will argue that we need to move beyond a copulative politics, beyond obsession with the-body-that-does-sex, in order to make these repressed stories visible. Feminist, poststructuralist, and even humanist critics are in need of a poetics of birth—a poetics that will suggest new directions not only for a textual, but for a reproductive politics.[3]

---

(Boston: Beacon, 1989) 211. My pleasures as a daughter and mother depend upon someone else's trauma and labor. While I cannot speak to these experiences directly, the unspoken and undervalued acts of gestation and parturition that all biological mothers endure have become part of my motive for metaphor.

[1]Talking Heads, "Creatures of Love," *Little Creatures*, Sire Records, 1985.

[2]I will argue that gestation and parturition are systematically overlooked as fundamental contributions—both to species continuity and to history. But their importance is growing harder to obliterate from consciousness—especially with the cases of "gestational surrogacy" (in which an "unrelated" mother carries and gives birth to someone else's genetic offspring) being debated in the media. If new technologies are controversial and potentially abusive to women, they also create an atmosphere in which the process of birth is becoming more dialectical. As technologies separate the discrete stages of insemination, gestation, and parturition into separate events, often involving separate actants, reproductive labor is inevitably reinvestigated and reinscribed. As a 1990 *New York Times* article urges: "the court will have to decide who is the legal mother: the woman who gives birth or the woman who provides the egg" (12 August 24). These up or down, either/or legalities are abusive to the women involved, but finally the value and the price of each stage of women's reproductive labor is receiving more space in our cultural debate.

[3]This work has already begun in Susan Stanford Friedman's brilliant, inclusive essay, "Creativity and the Childbirth Metaphor: Gender Difference

By a poetics of birth, I mean an investigation into the literary tropes and principles that preside over the presentation, deformation, or concealment of the story of reproduction in literary and cultural texts. In *The Politics of Reproduction*, Mary O'Brien argues that birth has been treated altogether differently from other biological necessities. Although philosophers and political theorists have invented complex theoretical systems to reinscribe our relation to our bodies, birth lacks a philosophy. Why has birth been ignored?[4]

---

in Literary Discourse" *Speaking of Gender* ed. Elaine Showalter (New York: Routledge, 1989) 73–100. Friedman investigates the connections between "artistic creativity and human procreativity" (73). She concludes that the childbirth metaphor works differently for male and female artists. While male artists offer praise for woman's powers of birth-giving, they also use the childbirth metaphor to exclude women from artistic process by reinforcing "the separation of creativities into mind and body, man and woman." In contrast, "the female childbirth metaphor challenges this covert concept of creativity by proposing a genuine bond between creation and procreation . . . a linguistic reunion of what culture has sundered" (94). See also Judith Wilt's probing explorations of abortion images in *Abortion, Choice, and Contemporary Fiction* (Chicago: University of Chicago Press, 1990), Cixous' celebration of pregnancy in "The Laugh of the Medusa," *New French Feminisms*, ed. Elaine Marks and Isabelle de Courtivron (Amherst: University of Massachusetts Press, 1980) 245–64, the explorations of afterbirth in Mary Kelly's *Post-partum Document* (London: Routledge and Kegan Paul, 1983), Emily Martin's *The Woman in the Body* (Boston: Beacon Press, 1987), and my essay, "The 'Language of Blood': Toward a Maternal Sublime," *Imag(in)ing Women*, ed. Juliet McMaster and Shirley Neumann (forthcoming).

[4]While many feminist thinkers have used the inequities of reproductive labor as the starting point for theories of sexual inequality, most notably Simone de Beauvoir in *The Second Sex* (New York: Knopf, 1952) and Shulameth Firestone in *The Dialectic of Sex* (New York: Morrow, 1970), only Mary O'Brien has attempted to create a complex and philosophic *theory* of birth. At the same time, contemporary feminists have begun to mount a systematic critique of patriarchal controls over reproduction. This critique has developed in response not only to the explosions of reproductive technologies and antiabortion movements but also to the recent prosecutions of "crack" mothers around the country. See Katha Pollitt, "A New Assault on Feminism," *The Nation*, 16 March 1990: 409–18; Jan Hoffman, "Pregnant, Addicted, and Guilty," *New York Times*, 19 August, 1990: sec. 6, 32; and

Postmodern America continues to view biological reproduction as a "natural" process that—while vulnerable to technological intervention—is primarily to be understood from the standpoint of the natural sciences.[5] To think about natality, Western thinkers have turned, O'Brien says

> to biology, anatomy and physiology, or, to the problematic wonders of genetics. What these sciences show us is that mammalian reproduction is but one class of animal reproduction. Anything specifically human in the process must await the appearance of the product of the process, the child, as a separate but dependent creature. The actual business of fertilization, parturition and birth, the anatomy and physiology of reproduction, we are told does not differ significantly between human females and, say, baboons.[6]

O'Brien responds to this naturalization of birth by redefining our relation to embodiment. Since we are creatures who delight in reinventing our bodies through elaborate social/epistemological rituals, what does it mean "to be trapped in a natural function"? Among the most socially charged of our "natural" functions—eating, sex, death, and birth—O'Brien suggests that only the first three have been explored, their meanings transformed by theoretical systems designed to remake our wishes and our bodies. That is, only the biological functions that men share with women—the need to eat, to satisfy sexual needs, and the inevitability of dying—have received extensive philosophical investigation. They have become the bases for major systems of thought that have changed our ideologies as well as our bodies.

---

Catharine R. Stimpson's "The Pure and the Impure, Again and Again, and Again," unpublished ms.

[5]Many feminist thinkers have challenged this objectification and medicalization of birth—most notably Emily Martin in *The Woman in the Body*. For a description of the genesis of theories that use biological fetishism to explain sexual difference, see Thomas Laqueur's "Female Orgasm, Generation and the Politics of Reproductive Biology," *Representations* 14 (1986): 1-82.

[6]Mary O'Brien, *The Politics of Reproduction* (Boston: Routledge, 1981) 19. Subsequent page references are incorporated in the text.

Only birth lacks a philosophy, a mode of epistemological elaboration.[7]

How have these biological necessities been "reontologized" by male philosophers? O'Brien's answer is quirky but brilliant. Just as eating and the modes of production necessary to provide for species continuity have been reinvented by Marx (since "Marx's theory of dialectical materialism takes as its fundamental postulate the need to eat"), so sexuality and the "lower" bodily functions have been reinvented by Freud, who uncovers the persistence of infantile sexuality within the adult (O'Brien 20). And death offers a central obsession for numerous philosophies, including Sartre's existential and Derrida's deconstructive nosologies.[8]

Of course, this does not mean that birth has been free of discursive embroideries. Instead, reproductive labor has been seized by theology "with a view to depreciating women's part, and rendering it passive and even virginal, while paternity took on divine trappings" (O'Brien 20–21). O'Brien explains that this appropriation has thrown women's reproductive labor into an abyss of unknowing. "Reproductive process is not a process which male-stream thought finds either ontologically or epistemologically interesting on the biological level. The human family

---

[7]In pursuit of this goal, feminists have begun to create knowledge systems that speak out against—and try to account for—the new technologies of birth. In addition to Gena Corea's *The Mother Machine* (New York: Harper & Row, 1985), see *Reproductive Technologies: Gender, Motherhood, and Medicine*, ed. Michelle Stanworth (Minneapolis: University of Minnesota Press, 1987). But these descriptions of technological crisis still turn away from the project of this essay, namely, to uncover our culture's reproductive unconscious and to explore the devaluations of reproductive labor in some of its myriad forms.

[8]As O'Brien says, "Death has haunted the male philosophical imagination since Man the Thinker first glimmered into action, and in our own time has become the stark reality which preoccupies existentialism, an untidy and passionately pessimistic body of thought in which lonely and heroic man attempts to defy the absurdity of the void which houses his consciousness and his world. The inevitability and necessity of these biological events has . . . not exempted them from historical force and theoretical significance" (20). For an elaboration of the Derridean body and death, see Henry Staten, *Wittgenstein and Derrida* (Lincoln: University of Nebraska Press, 1984).

is philosophically interesting, but its biological base is simply given" (21).

What are the implications of this absence of a philosophy or theory of birth for literary studies? If, as Muriel Rukeyser insists, "one is on the edge of the absurd the minute one tries to relate the experience of birth to the silence about it in poetry," we are also "on the edge of the absurd" when confronting a kindred silence in literary criticism.[9] We need to elaborate a poetics of birth under four different rubrics. First, I want to establish that until very recently literary texts have reenacted the silence around birth and gestation that dominates our culture's concept of reproduction.[10] The exceptions to this rule—texts like *A Winter's Tale*, *Tristram Shandy*, *A Room of One's Own*, *The Rainbow*, or Hemingway's "Indian Camp"— push reproductive labor into the foreground while still signaling the high cost of reproductive silence and envy.

Second, I want to suggest what this absent narrative of birth would look like if a poetics of birth were allowed into the apparatus of literary criticism. Constructing this absent narrative will require a dialogue with those feminist critics and theorists who argue that silence, absence, and the empty spaces outside the dominant language are the only places where women's voices can sound. Instead of claiming, with Claudine Herrmann, that "the void is . . . a respectable value,"[11] or assuming with Kristeva that women must seize their own "negative function" and "reject everything finite, definite, structured, loaded with meaning, in the existing state of society,"[12] we need to supply

---

[9]Muriel Rukeyser, "A Simple Theme," *Poetry* 74 (July 1949): 237. Friedman's "Creativity and the Childbirth Metaphor" is a notable exception to this generalization. Friedman quotes Rukeyser as a prelude to describing the "explosion of women's writing about pregnancy, childbirth, nursing, and motherhood" (86) during the second wave of feminism (1965 to the present).

[10]Numerous contemporary poets, from Sharon Olds to Lucille Clifton, have written lyrics about the traumas and pleasures of natality. The range of reproductive narratives in contemporary novels is even more divergent, from the mimetic realism of Margaret Drabble to the magical realism of Toni Morrison to the bizarre science fictions of Octavia Butler.

[11]Claudine Herrmann, "Women in Space and Time," trans. Marilyn R. Schuster, *New French Feminisms* 170.

[12]Julia Kristeva, "Oscillation between Power and Denial," trans. Marilyn A. August, *New French Feminisms* 166.

ourselves with new meanings, structures, codes, and other modes of symbolic power if we are to invent a story of birth with the power to supplement women's lost voices.

Third, as feminists invent a new rhetoric or "tropics" of birth, and as this project sends us in search of new narratives, we will see that the problem of renarrating birth is already a central preoccupation of Anglo-American literature. That is, this literature registers the incommensurability of reproductive politics as ideology and reproductive politics as experience. What I am positing (following Jameson's lead) is the complicating presence of a reproductive unconscious—of a series of tropes or thematic preoccupations that tilt a text "powerfully into the underside or *impensé* or *nondit*" of reproductivity.[13] Even when the bodily labor necessary to reproduce a child is elided or absent in the texts that we read, this absence may exert its own field of force—a field that may operate in one of two ways. Either a text can be understood as an illicit strategy, a symbolic move in an ideological confrontation between genders (or classes, or races) over who owns, or who legislates the meanings of, reproductivity. (Examples are almost too numerous to cite. Think, for example, of Frankenstein, or Adam and Eve, or Spenser's Garden of Adonis, where the power to bestow human life becomes a male principle.) Or a text may present the agon of birth as a more complicated site of cultural contestation and struggle. In Kleist's "Marquis von O," the Marquis' inability to name the father of her child accents the undecidability of paternity. But rather than dissolving this tale into a battle between the sexes for ownership of reproductive rights, Kleist suggests the problems that emerge when various modes of production and reproduction—birth and the ownership of children among them—become visibly antagonistic, "their contradictions moving to the very center of political, social and historical life" (Jameson 95).[14]

---

[13]Fredric Jameson, *The Political Unconscious: Narrative as Socially Symbolic Act* (Ithaca: Cornell University Press, 1981). Subsequent page references are incorporated in the text.

[14]Although Jameson makes room for feminist analysis within his system of symbolic readings (100), his own interest in class conflict works to exclude reproductive labor as a source of both class and gender antagonism. Jameson redefines the ways in which texts participate in ongoing "*cultural revolution*, that moment in which the coexistence of various modes of production becomes visibly antagonistic" (95), and the contradictions between

This reproductive anxiety may surface in a simple correspondence between the story-line and the laboring female body—as in Madeline's bloody entrance in Poe's "The Fall of the House of Usher" or the vampire women's hunger for baby's blood in *Dracula*. But the pattern of reproductive condensation and displacement can be more complex. In Byron's *Don Juan* the burial of a pregnant heroine offers a site of extraordinary turbulence for Byron's relation to older forms of Romanticism, and for his prosody itself—a turbulence worked out through obsessive changes in meter and rhyme.

Since a poetics must go beyond the description of particular texts to establish general laws "of which the particular text is the product,"[15] the fourth challenge for a poetics of birth will be to recognize the fluidity of these "laws." For if reproductive myths and anxieties are continuous, they are also temporal; they change over time. A poetics of birth will require a theory of the changing values and sociohistorical meanings of women's biological contribution (or refusal to contribute, or inability to contribute, or forced contribution) to the production of children. This theory is absent, missing, still being written—but its creation, especially in view of the antiabortion hysteria of the far right and the surrogacy anxiety of the new left—is a feminist imperative.

---

these modes of production become central for political and social life. But his analysis remains incomplete; he fails to recognize natality as one source of these contradictions. Attention to a reproductive unconscious will reshape notions of a "political" unconscious by initiating new models for understanding the "permanent struggles" that take place in every era "between the various coexisting modes of production" (97), with birth now among them. The class conflicts that have erupted in contemporary surrogacy battles offer one version of this antagonism; an interest in Baby "M" could open the door to analyses of more subterranean reproductive conflicts in other eras. For an analysis of how this works in Kleist, see Yaeger, "Kleist's 'Dialogic Midwifery'," *PMLA* 100 (1985): 812–13.

[15]See Tzvetan Todorov, *Introduction to Poetics* (Minneapolis: University of Minnesota Press, 1981) ix.

## *"The Grave"*


I want to begin with a reading of Katherine Anne Porter's "The Grave" (1934), a story that focuses on a homely and gravid image. While a brother and his younger sister are out hunting, the brother kills a rabbit and discovers, while skinning it, that the rabbit is pregnant. The children are horrified at the rabbit's death and fascinated with what they discover in the rabbit's interior. But while Porter focuses on her heroine's sorrow and vertigo in witnessing this event, we will see that not only Miranda, but Porter herself feels blocked by an absence of reproductive narrative.

The momentum of Porter's story depends on a little girl's loss of a discourse of birth. Miranda's psyche cries out for a story that explores—without theologizing—women's reproductive capacities and accounts for the violence of male control over these processes. The difficulty, terror, and beauty of what it means to be born and the mystery of what it means to nurture a child in one's animal-human belly are glimpsed and then repressed in "The Grave." The strength of Porter's story lies in its capacity to explore the ways in which birth and death have been narratively intermingled; her story suggests that insights about women's reproductive pleasures and dangers are continuously displaced in Western culture by images of male cultural productivity and death. That is, Porter's text swerves from an elegiac description of uneasiness about reproductive process into a domain of "delight without danger" in which Miranda focuses on the repressive gestures of male religion; the story celebrates—with terrible naivete—the impregnating fleshlessness of the holy ghost. This is, in short, a story about the construction and deformation of a modern reproductive unconscious.

To understand Porter's complicity in Miranda's dilemma, we will examine the ways in which the reproductive puzzle she traces for her heroine remains oddly unresolved. This half-made map will show the reproductive contradictions that "The Grave" seeks to control and finally represses. To put this in Jameson's terms, Porter's text allows the critic "to map out the inner limits" of her culture's ideology of birth. But where Jameson is interested in "nodal points implicit in the ideological system which . . . remain unrealized in the surface of the text, which have failed to become manifest in the logic of the narrative, and which we can therefore read as what the text represses" (48), what interests me about Porter's narrative is the way in which she teases out these repressed terms and keeps trying to make sense of them. Porter leaves a trail, a pattern of dispersed semes that point to the contradictions her "narrative pretext" attempts—and fails—to resolve. This is not to say that Porter's story is a failure. On the contrary, it is a brilliant success, and its efficient sublimations, its bizarre folding of reproductive anxiety back into the master tropes of Western theology, become one measure of this success. "The Grave" is at once an angry narrative about women and reproductive danger—a proto-feminist cry for help—and a reassertion of the Apostles' Creed. A text read as an imaginary resolution of real social contradictions, becomes, as Jameson suggests, a field of force "in which the . . . sign systems of several distinct modes of production can be registered and apprehended" (98). Adding reproductive labor to this catalogue of productive antagonisms uncovers a set of textual conflicts that Jameson's model ignores. Porter's "The Grave" offers the opportunity to inspect these conflicts in some detail.

"The Grave" begins with a quiet game of hide and seek. Two children entertain themselves in a summer landscape; they are leaping in and out of empty graves. The cemetery once belonged to the children's grandmother; this was the site where she buried those dear to her:

> The grandfather, dead for more than thirty years, had been twice disturbed in his long repose by the constancy and possessiveness of his widow. She removed his bones first to Louisiana and then to Texas as if she had set out to find her own burial place, knowing she would never return to the places she had left.[16]

The children's play in this dusty space becomes a haunting replica of their play with the dead rabbit later in the story; miming their grandmother's gesture, they will remove the bodies of the baby rabbits from the mother rabbit's belly, which has also become their grave. But while Porter's story begins with an ambivalence about woman as procreative source, in the second

---

[16]Katherine Anne Porter, "The Grave," *The Collected Stories of Katherine Anne Porter* (New York: Harcourt, Brace, Jovanovich, 1979) 362. Subsequent page references are incorporated in the text.

paragraph this ambivalence modulates into something more beautiful. The grandmother's gravesite refigures female fecundity; her body enters the text as a *locus amoenus*, a pleasant place.

> The family cemetery had been a pleasant small neglected garden of tangled rose bushes and ragged cedar trees and cypress, the simple flat stones rising out of uncropped sweet-smelling wild grass. The graves were lying open and empty one burning day when Miranda and her brother Paul, who often went together to hunt rabbits and doves, propped their twenty-two Winchester rifles carefully against the rail fence, climbed over and explored among the graves. She was nine years old and he was twelve. (362)

This gravesite is sexually charged; it becomes a site of openness, exploration, nonaggression, and sensuality, and yet, for the children, this is a landscape peculiarly without gender or name:

> They peered into the pits all shaped alike with such purposeful accuracy, and looking at each other with pleased adventurous eyes, they said in solemn tones: "These were graves!" trying by words to shape a special, suitable emotion in their minds, but they felt nothing except an agreeable thrill of wonder: they were seeing a new sight, doing something they had not done before. (362)

If this exploration is unprotected, unguarded (beyond the "no" or "name" of the phallus in the moment the children's rifles are set aside), this openness closes when the children discover a fixed set of cultural symbols.

> Miranda leaped into the pit that had held her grandfather's bones. Scratching around aimlessly and pleasurably as any young animal, she scooped up a lump of earth and weighed it in her palm. It had a pleasantly sweet, corrupt smell, resin mixed with cedar needles and small leaves, and as the crumbs fell apart, she saw a silver dove no larger than a hazel nut with spread wing and a neat fan-shaped tail. The breast had a deep round hollow in it. (363)

Porter's text is filled with reproductive metaphors. Odorous, evergreen, the earth, with unexpected fecundity, produces a dove. In this landscape where birth has no name, something comes out of the soil; Miranda discovers a mystery with a hole in it. Like the grave, like woman's body, like the reproductive center of the gravid rabbit, this dove contains "a hollow cut in little whorls." But the treasure quickly becomes Paul's property: "Paul had found a thin wide gold ring carved with intricate flowers and leaves. Miranda was smitten at sight of the ring and wished to have it. Paul seemed more impressed by the dove. They made a trade, with some little bickering." Before Miranda can delight too much in her discovery, Paul fits her dove into his world view. It must be "a screw head for a *coffin*! . . . I'll bet nobody else in the world has one like this" (363).

What follows is a meditation on the children's gender differences. "Waving her thumb gently and watching her gold ring glitter, Miranda lost interest in shooting." Although she is dressed comfortably in boys' clothing, the ring, "shining with the serene purity of fine gold on her rather grubby thumb," turns her against the lovely grime of her body (recalling, as it does, the "sweet, corrupt smell of resin" which released the dove). "She wanted to go back to the farmhouse, take a good cold bath, dust herself with plenty of Maria's violet talcum powder . . . put on the thinnest, most becoming dress she owned, with a big sash, and sit in a wicker chair under the trees" (365). Mixed with a little knowledge, the symbols of the dominant culture have reproductive power; they begin to replicate its sexual asymmetries.

What is forming in Porter's story is a picture of what it meant to be Southern, white, female, and lower middle class in the 1900s. But before this picture is complete, Paul shoots the mother rabbit, and in the wake of this violence, his differences with Miranda melt away:

> The children knelt facing each other over the dead animal. Miranda watched admiringly while her brother stripped the skin away as if he were taking off a glove. The flayed flesh emerged dark scarlet, sleek, firm; Miranda with thumb and finger felt the long fine muscles with the silvery flat strips binding them to the joints. Brother lifted the oddly bloated belly. "Look," he said in a very low amazed voice. "It was going to have young ones." (366)

Porter resists the temptation to be used by ordinary reproductive metaphors; she neither trivializes nor sentimentalizes what Miranda sees, and this becomes the difficulty of analyzing "The Grave" and its instructiveness. Absorbed by the pregnant rabbit's particularity, each child ceases to be difficult or particular. They kneel, as if in the presence of a sacrament, but neither child is sentimentalized. Instead, while their child-bodies mirror the vulnerability of the rabbit and its young, their busy minds are hushed by the knowledge that, even as children, they possess a power that can stop reproductive process altogether.

Porter describes the inside of the rabbit's flayed body with uncanny grace:

> Very carefully he slit the thin flesh from the center ribs to the flanks, and a scarlet bag appeared. He slit again and pulled the bag open, and there lay a bundle of tiny rabbits, each wrapped in a thin scarlet veil. The brother pulled these off and there they were, dark gray, their sleek wet down lying in minute even ripples, like a baby's head just washed, their unbelievably small delicate ears folded close, their little blind faces almost featureless.
>
> (366)

Porter places us at the center, the ompholos; in watching the dissection of the rabbit's body we hover between an anatomy lesson and the rippling of the mysterium tremendum. Caught between sacred and secular time, she shows us the site of that biological work that produces a baby out of a fetus.

And yet the rabbit's body is not meant to become the site of a new theology. Its mystery beckons toward a new way of knowing the world:

> Miranda said, "Oh, I want to *see*," under her breath. She looked and looked—excited but not frightened, for she was accustomed to the sight of animals killed in hunting—filled with pity and astonishment and a kind of shocked delight in the wonderful little creatures for their own sakes, they were so pretty. She touched one of them ever so carefully, "Ah, there's blood running over them," she said and began to tremble without knowing why. Yet she wanted most deeply to see and to know. (366)

Ordinarily impatient with Miranda's emotions, Paul responds to her voice

> cautiously, as if he were talking about something forbidden: "They were just about ready to be born." His voice dropped on the last word. "I know," said Miranda, "like kittens. I know, like babies." She was quietly and terribly agitated, standing again with her rifle under her arm, looking down at the bloody heap. (367)

For Miranda, it is not just the fact of the rabbit's labor—its impossible work of making the very young from the relatively old—that is fascinating, nor is it simply her terror of death. Miranda needs "to see, to know," and to put this knowledge into words. But the gift of language never comes. Stepping helplessly into his masculine role, Paul plunges the young rabbits back into their mother's body and carries them out of sight, insisting that Miranda be quiet about what she has seen:

> He came out again at once and said to Miranda, with . . . a confidential tone quite unusual in him. . . . "Listen now. Now you listen to me, and don't ever forget. Don't you ever tell a living soul that you saw this. Don't tell a soul. Don't tell Dad because I'll get into trouble. He'll say I'm leading you into things you ought not to do. . . . So now don't you go and forget and blab out sometime the way you're always doing. . . . Don't you tell." (367)

Does Miranda have a right to speak about reproduction, to seek knowledge about what she has seen? Not in this decade, not in Southern society. In linking Miranda's silence with the rabbit's death, Porter describes three forms of labor that cease to exist. First, the rabbit's gestational labor to reproduce itself is cut off. Second, as the children contemplate the rabbit's strange capacity to form, within its body, a bevy of dark creatures "with sleek wet down," they also recognize that the rabbit was about to embark on another stage of reproductive labor, that its babies were "just ready to be born." Third, Miranda's own struggle to understand what she's seen—her laborious desire to understand the mystery of reproduction—is cut short:

> Miranda never told, she did not even wish to tell anybody. She thought about the whole worrisome affair with confused unhappiness for a few days. Then it sank quietly into her mind and was heaped over by accumulated thousands of impressions, for nearly twenty years. (367)

Speech and knowledge are equally denied. But this "heap" of impressions—which replicates, in its shape, the "bloody heap" of rabbits that Paul buries—continues to do its work. Even in repression, this experience is trying to speak; the thoughts that accumulate around Miranda's lost memory only multiply the paths to this memory: what has been forgotten insists on repetition.

At this point the temporal structure of Porter's story goes haywire and, without warning, skips ahead twenty years. This leap is marked by a gap or caesura, an empty space on the page. After crossing this border, we find ourselves in India; Miranda is walking "among the puddles and crushed refuse of a market street in a strange city of a strange country" (367). As she picks her way through this alien space, she confronts an Indian vendor carrying

> a tray of dyed sugar sweets, in the shapes of all kinds of small creatures: birds, baby chicks, baby rabbits, lambs, baby pigs. There were in gay colors and smelled of vanilla, maybe. . . . It was a very hot day and the smell in the market, with its piles of raw flesh and wilting flowers, was like the mingled sweetness and corruption she had smelled that other day in the empty cemetery at home. (367)

With this odor, "the episode of that far-off day leaped from its burial place before her mind's eye" (367) and once again Miranda's work of deciphering her relation to reproductive labor can begin.[17] As she remembers the female rabbit's death and

---

[17]Here we encounter another detour in the construction of a "reproductive unconscious." Geographical displacement moves Miranda closer to a reading of her own latent thoughts as she encounters the psychic work of repression and displacement. Intriguingly, this reorienting or "orientalization" of the scene of birth takes place in India and suggests that the concepts of colonization and decolonization may be equally crucial in mapping a reproductive semiology.

the delicate young it was making, she is horrified and astounded that this event should have been buried so deeply. Until now, she remembered that day "vaguely as the time she and her brother had found treasure in the opened graves" (367).

And yet, under the impossible pressure of renarrativizing the tragedy of the rabbit's lost labor, Miranda's memory disappears once again, and "The Grave" comes to an end:

> Instantly upon this thought the dreadful vision faded, and she saw clearly her brother, whose childhood face she had forgotten, standing again in the blazing sunshine, again twelve years old, a pleased, sober smile in his eyes, turning the silver dove over and over in his hands.
>
> (367–68)

This image of Paul cradling the dove in his hands offers momentary redemption. But redemption from what? Exploring the rabbit's anatomy was not an act Miranda initially contemplated with horror. In fact, her investigation of the rabbit's pregnant body was accompanied by stirrings of beauty and curiosity, as well as sadness, and by a moment of insight about where babies come from. Miranda's forgetfulness is promulgated, then, as much by her brother's censorship as by her own revulsion. And this censorship is repeated at the end of the story, for as the image of the mother rabbit starts from its burial place, Paul's image covers it again. Why?

For years the ache of this final image dominated my reading of Porter's story. Under its sign, "The Grave" became a fable with a happy ending, a tale that transcended its morbid discovery that the womb is a tomb—a space as potentially dangerous for its female owner as for the young it produces. That is, I believed that Miranda found, in her backward-looking glance at her brother, an aesthetic that helped her transcend her knowledge of the womb's morbidity and get on with her life.

Of course the flaw in this reading lies in its political complicity, for Paul's image also works to restore Western culture's reproductive unconscious, just as his earlier censoring of Miranda's sadness and curiosity restores a silence about birth and male violence in the dominant discourse. While Paul means his sister no deliberate harm—the final image is, after all, the product of *Miranda's* unconscious—his imagined power over the silver dove lifts us, in its hypnotic spinning, away from a preoccupation with the fragility and power of feminine bios toward the transcendent powers of a masculine ethos. Contemplating her memory of Paul, Miranda escapes from the danger of reproductivity to the shadow of a fraternal theology. Instead of the "delicate" young the rabbit was making, the text focuses on the artifice of the silver dove and her brother's appropriation of this artifice. Paul's rhythmic turning of the dove in his hands elides its open belly. In this beautiful, violent gesture the dove is reasserted as an animal totem used to ward off animality; it resembles a traditional symbol of spirit and trinity: the holy ghost, a Biblical marker of masculine power that evades our relation to female flesh. By focusing on the apostolic radiance of still another "Paul," Porter is not simply refuting Miranda's knowledge of Paul's violence or the fact of the rabbit's death; she is also representing Miranda's, her own—and perhaps her reader's—inability to think about the female contribution to gestation/labor/birth, to the life of the human species, except through images of male appropriation and succession.[18]

Porter's story is obsessed with natality; it participates fully in her culture's terror of female reproductive labor. By dwelling on male transcendence rather than the female body, the ending avoids not only the danger but also the mysterious productivity Miranda discovers in the mother rabbit. What is neither articulated nor given a symbol system here is the particularly anxious, strange, and undertheorized experience of living in a woman's body that has a reproductive capacity—which means not only the capacity to die giving birth but also the capacity to reproduce society, to carry out the labor necessary for species continuity. Since the female body is the site of so much power, as well as

---

[18]A similar reading of "The Grave" emerges from Dorothy Dinnerstein's suggestion in *The Mermaid and the Minotaur* (New York: Harper & Row, 1976) that mothers come to represent, for the woman-raised child, both the indispensable animal source of the self and the dispensable enemy of the self—the menace to the child's burgeoning individuation. It is the male of the species, the father—or, here, the brother—who offers an alternative imago, a space where ambivalence dissipates in the promise of self-control and membership in a wider community. Dinnerstein adds another dimension to the concept of a modern reproductive unconscious. She argues that maternal closeness creates both a social and a psychological pressure to obliterate indebtedness to the maternal body.

such real and imagined trauma, it is effaced or "translated" in the covering gestures of male poetry and religion.[19]

"The Grave" shares with its culture the myth that female reproductive functions are inert, animalistic, a helpless reflex of the female body.  The typical scene of education about this body's powers is a violent one; the rabbit's blood is spilt in death rather than flowing toward the regenerative, blood-giving beauty of successful gestation.  However, in repeatedly discovering and then repressing the body of the mother rabbit, Porter shows us the rhythmic turns of reproductive repression.  Every time the mystery of birth hovers into view, it is briefly explored, goes in search of a story-line, and is then pushed away, as if Porter is searching for an alternative narrative, a story about reproductive labor that neither derides nor devalues the scope of this labor.  If, beyond the stirrings of technology or theology, there is neither story nor language that a child like Miranda can discover to talk about reproduction, the peculiar structure of Porter's story suggests that there should be; her culture lacks a secular theory of birth that would allow women to formulate a new relation to the difficulties and pleasures of natality.

### Beyond a Copulative Politics

The sexual and biological domains of reproduction need to be reconceptualized in a way that will allow moments of gestation and parturition, or of conception and abortion, or of refusal to conceive, to be renarrativized—to enter human time.  As O'Brien suggests:

> To insist upon the participation of fecund women in the conduct of communal life is to do more than seek strategies of female emancipation: it is to drag the process of reproduction, its objective contradictions and its historical mediations, from the dark corners of historiography and the hidden premises of political philosophy to its true sta-

---

[19]This is, of course, an old tropology.  See especially Kristeva's examination in "Stabat Mater," *The Female Body in Western Culture: Contemporary Perspectives*, ed. Susan Suleiman (Cambridge: Harvard University Press,

tus as a necessarily social and humanly valuable activity. It is also to claim for procreativity the capacity to transcend its natural roots and to 'make history' in a significant way. (167)[20]

How does procreativity "make history"? And can we make this history-making visible without assuming the stance of the pronatalist?

I want to begin to "drag the process of reproduction" into literary history by suggesting that, as literary scholars, we are overinvested in issues of copulative politics. That is, we are skilled at discovering sexual symbols in literary texts that tell us a great deal about the politics and history of love-making and foreplay; we are obsessed with the dirty joke, the bed trick, with textual hints about coitus. But if reproduction is the labor women do to make the social and biological beings a society needs "to survive humanly," then we must bring Marx into our analysis as well as Freud. Women's reproductive labor must be analyzed not only in terms of sexual but in terms of productive asymmetries. This means that feminists must refuse the simple dichotomies reflected in any reductionist analyses of reproductive labor. We must, for example, resist Catharine MacKinnon's tempting suggestion that "sexuality is to feminism what work is to Marxism."[21]

For MacKinnon, natality is an afterthought, a by-product of heterosexual desire rather than a fact of female labor. She argues that Marxist analysis must be distinguished from feminist

1985) 99–118, of the paradoxes in the Christian vision of Mary that still help to express and to contain anxieties about female reproductive power.

[20]While O'Brien invokes the grandeur of "History," she tends to collapse all theories of natality into one. In contrast, a number of cultural historians have begun the necessary work of differentiation; they have begun to investigate the wild variations among theories of conception and birth within different historical periods and cultures. See Laquer; Richard and Dorothy Wertz, *Lying-In: A History of Childbirth in America* (New Haven: Yale University Press, 1989); and Andrea Hendersen, "Doll Machines and Butcher Shop Meat: Models of Childbirth under Industrialization," *Genders* (forthcoming).

[21]Catharine A. MacKinnon, *Feminism Unmodified: Discourses on Life and Law* (Cambridge: Harvard University Press, 1987) 48. Subsequent page references are incorporated in the text.

analysis because Marxism describes a dialectic of labor whereas feminist analysis offers an account of the ways in which sexuality "organizes, expresses, and directs desire." While Marxist definitions of work describe both "the social process of shaping and transforming the material and social worlds" and the process that creates people as social beings, "work" is not a term that describes the biological process of creating children (MacKinnon 48).

Thus MacKinnon finds herself embroiled in the same epistemological impasse as The Talking Heads. If reproduction is simply the consequence of sexuality and must be analyzed under sexuality's banner, then we have no categories to describe the tragedy of misappropriated female labor. Where The Talking Heads insist that sex makes the child, that when man and woman lie "together / Little creatures all come out," MacKinnon argues that "theorists sometimes forget that in order to reproduce one must first, usually, have had sex" (49). When the politics of heterosexual copulation becomes the model for a reproductive politics, the dialectical interaction among reproductive desire, reproductive labor, and the production of the child may remain hidden in the "dark corners" of feminist theory. I will argue, in contrast, that—as in class analysis—reproductive analysis must examine the striking inequities involving modes of production—namely, when women have labored, men have appropriated both this labor and the children it has produced.

To suggest some of the ways in which these reproductive asymmetries should influence literary analysis, we will turn to Eudora Welty's "The Wide Net" (1943), a story in which a gang of young men drag a river—searching for the body of a pregnant woman. Although "The Wide Net" begins with the declaration that "William Wallace Jameson's wife Hazel was going to have a baby," Hazel's body disappears from the story, and instead of her reproductive adventures the narrative focuses on her husband's phallic escapades. Peeved with his wife's new bodiliness, William Wallace takes an overnight jaunt with his friends and returns to find a letter announcing that Hazel "was going to the river to drown herself."[22] Although the story's ostensible subject is a fight between parents-to-be, its enduring focus becomes

---

[22]Eudora Welty, "The Wide Net" in *The Wide Net and Other Stories* (New York: Harcourt, Brace, Jovanovich, 1971) 34. Subsequent page references are incorporated in the text.

William Wallace's search for a playful band of men who drag the river for Hazel's body while forming male friendships above the encumbrances of race, class, and age. As Eve Kosofsky Sedgwick predicts in *Between Men*, this bonding is mediated through the body of an abjected woman.[23] Can "The Wide Net" be described, then, as a story in which women's reproductive labor enters history?

At first, Welty's story seems all too comfortable claiming kin with a venerable tradition of stories about companionate men. William Wallace's best friend on this trip to the water world is even named "Virgil." But as Welty tells a story of triangular desire, she lets the reader in on its secret. This particular saturnalia of male bonding happens because a new child-to-be threatens to square an old triangularity. And if this child-to-be squares an old desire, then "The Wide Net" also offers an intriguing site for tracing a reproductive politics.

Welty's story is extravagantly concerned with the self-multiplication of families:

> "I'll bring the Malones, and you bring the Doyles," said William Wallace, and they separated at the spring.
> When William Wallace came back, with a string of Malones just showing behind him . . . he found Virgil with the two little Rippen boys . . . solemn little towheads. . . .
> "Here come all the Malones," cried William Wallace. "I asked four of them would they come, but the rest of the family invited themselves." . . .
> "If two little niggers would come along now" . . . And the words were hardly out of his mouth when two little Negro boys came long, going somewhere . . . as though they waded in honeydew to the waist. (41–42)

This superfluity of Doyles and Rippens and Malones announces Welty's glee about some woman's reproductivity. And yet everyone who joins this group—with the exception of the two African-American children—is identified by his patronym.

As these father-named children cluster around William Wallace, he becomes preoccupied with the inadequacies of

---

23Eve Kosofsky Sedgwick, *Between Men: English Literature and Male Homosocial Desire* (New York: Columbia University Press, 1985).

names. "'What is the name of this river?' . . . 'Everybody knows Pearl River is named the Pearl River,' said Doc" (49). But for William Wallace, meaning is more evasive; in this world where neither the verb "to be" nor the proper name can lend certainty to paternity, only the wide net offers assurance. The net operates as an enormous placenta—golden, ageless, heaped with life. "'Don't let her get too heavy, boys,' Doc intoned regularly . . . 'she won't let nothing through'" (51).

The first thing these young men catch in their net ("so old and so long-used, it too looked golden, strung and tied with golden threads") is a baby alligator—its scales burnished by the net's golden veins:

> "He ain't nothing but a little-old baby," said William Wallace.
> The Malones only scoffed, as if he might be only a baby but he looked like the oldest and worst lizard.
> "What are you going to do with him?" asked Virgil.
> "Keep him."
> "I'd be more careful what I took out of this net," said Doc. (53)

When the net has done its work and the men settle down for a fishy feast, William Wallace "took a big catfish and hooked it to his belt buckle and went up and down so that they all hollered, and the tears of laughter streaming down his cheeks made him put his hand up, and the two days' growth of beard began to jump out, bright red" (59). As if on signal "the King of Snakes" raises his "old hoary head" (60) out of the water, dazzling the revelers with his copulative glory.

In response to this weird phallic splendor, a storm comes up, and the great tree hovering above the revelers splits open, as if to expose the perils of parturition itself. The river turns a new shade of purple; it fills "with sudden currents and whirlpools . . . a great current of wet leaves was borne along before a blast of wind, and every human being was covered. 'Now us got scales,' wailed Sam. 'Us is the fishes'" (63). As the boys and men are layered with scales, another reproductive anxiety intrudes in their story. Ontogeny recapitulates phylogeny, and, as their sense of phallic control dissipates, what begins to assert itself is not the abstract identity of male biology and animal splendor but the anxious eruption of the male animal's relationship to other fauna. Just when William Wallace seems to have mastered an abstract and safely androgynous mode of reproductivity, Welty insists on his uneasy tie to bios and the animal kingdom.

This knowledge redoubles as William Wallace cuts his foot open on a rock, and we see the stirrings of male couvade; William Wallace's recuperation of reproductive potency is disturbed in an accidental mimesis of Hazel's future passage of baby and blood. Hazel, of course, is waiting at home for her husband, and the cut on his body becomes the space where they meet. "'You ought to have been more careful,' she said. 'Supper's ready. . . . Go and make yourself fit to be seen,' she said, and ran away from him" (71)

Welty begins to drag the story of men's complex relation to reproductive labor into Southern history. She locates a severe male anxiety at each of the humorous turns in her story—from William Wallace's imitation of gestation and parturition when he drags the river with his wide net to his forthright assertion of his phallic connectedness to all of creation in that wild scene where he hooks the catfish to his belt buckle and dances by the shore. William Wallace feels a need to assimilate the fish-babies he has just eaten to a masculine system of bios. He asserts the continuity between phallus and child via the phallic fish he hooks to his belt.[24] Despite Welty's comic hijinks, "The Wide Net" tells a serious story. In believing that his pregnant wife has drowned, in searching for Hazel at the bottom of the river and appropriating her gestational tasks, William Wallace is constructing a patriarchal counter-narrative, a workable story that will help him mediate his own anxieties about female fecundity.

Earlier, I defined the poetics of birth as an investigation into the principles that preside over the presentation or deformation of the stories of reproduction in literary and cultural texts. I will now argue that there are natal principles driving these deformations and that they can be read systematically. By analyzing the relation between reproductive asymmetries and Welty's fiction-making, we may begin to trace, in a general way, the residues and betrayals of a Western reproductive unconscious.

How to begin? First, the biological dimensions of reproduction need to be taken more seriously—that is, with a seriousness

---

[24]Welty capitalizes on this equation between fish and human babies throughout her story. See, for example, her references to the "string of Malones" that William Wallace captures for his adventure (42).

that will reilluminate our vision of biology. This is O'Brien's tack in *The Politics of Reproduction*, when she faults male philosophers for ignoring (1) the "alienation" of men's sperm in the moment of coitus; (2) women's contributions to reproductive process as a form of transformative "labor"; (3) the unequal division of this reproductive labor between the sexes; and (4) the fact that the child is, at least potentially, "a value" produced by reproductive labor. These reproductive asymmetries provide a preliminary map for tracing the nocturnal obsessions with reproductive labor that pervade Western literature. Any of these asymmetries can become the site of textual anxiety; together, they make up the core of a modern reproductive unconscious.

1. *Alienation of the male seed in the copulative act.*

While a man's genetic material is essential for the creation of a child, the temporal distance between insemination and parturition is immense. The conceptual distance is even greater, as suggested by the old adage: "Mama's baby, Papa's maybe." Since only the biological mother nurtures the child-to-be in her belly, and since it is she alone who labors to release the child from her body into the world, paternity is marked with uncertainty.[25]

Although no child is born in "The Wide Net" or claimed by William Wallace, the protagonist's relation to his child-to-be is driven by a need to overcome alienation. What William Wallace appropriates is the right to make masculine history. While "The Wide Net" ends with a comic return to home and hearth, this return is premised on the construction of a community of men who delight in constructing extra-uterine stories, for in Welty's story, it is not Hazel's pregnancy but the wide net that produces history. The fishermen parade into town:

> following behind and pointing authoritatively at the ones
> in front strolled Doc, with Sam and Robbie Bell still

---

[25]In the last decade, biological maternity has become a source of equal uncertainty. In theory this is promising since it forces renegotiation of at least one of the gendered asymmetries of reproductive labor. At the same time, this new form of maternal alienation gives rise to greater class antagonisms, since middle-class women are exploiting the labor power of poorer women to make babies.

chanting in his wake. In and out of the whole little line Grady and Brucie jerked about. . . . Brucie . . . was darting rapidly everywhere at once, delighted and tantalized, running in circles around William Wallace, pointing to his fish. . . .

"Did you ever see so many fish?" said the people in Dover.

"How much are your fish, mister?"

"Would you sell your fish?"

"Is that all the fish in Pearl River?" (66)

The annals of the Pearl River will not reflect upon "women as bearers and nurturers of children" (O'Brien 174). Instead, the townspeople come out to celebrate the bearers of the wide net, local heroes with the power to create their own placental politics.

### 2. *Maternal alienation of the child through labor.*

Marx and Hegel have explained that labor is essential to establish connections between human beings and the natural world. In labor both working women and men as well as the worked-for world are mutually transformed. But while neither Marx nor Hegel grants women's reproductivity the status of labor, an honor reserved for the "work" of copulation alone, the birth of a child also represents an act of labor in which the world is transformed.

The young men who drag the river in "The Wide Net" intuit that their reenactment of female reproduction must be laborious. The river becomes the site of self-replication in which one's double can only be wrested from the water with hard work. When William Wallace glimpses an image of his father in the water, he dives deep, and when he comes up, "it was in an agony from submersion, which seemed an agony of the blood and of the very heart, so woeful he looked." Although he brings up only "a little green ribbon of plant," his labors give rise to a feast where the "King of Snakes" appears "in the center of three light-gold rings across the water" (57). This phallic/umbilical fantasy is comically appropriative, but in "Flowers for Marjorie," another of Welty's stories from the 1940s, the fantasy becomes tragic. Down on his luck and out of work, the hero murders his pregnant wife because the success of her gestational labors mocks his own productive failures in a form too painful to bear.

## 3. *The sexual division of labor.*

Marx suggests that antagonisms are created historically between those who labor and those who do not. And yet he does not recognize that this agon extends to the childbearing process. "The fact that as material process, biological reproduction necessarily also sets up an opposition between those who labour reproductively (women), and those who do not (men) does not command Marx's attention" (O'Brien 36).

This reproductive asymmetry informs "The Wide Net" from its very beginning. William Wallace and Hazel find themselves set in angry opposition by Hazel's pregnancy: "When he came in the room she would not speak to him, but would look as straight at nothing as she could, with her eyes glowing.  If he only touched her she stuck out her tongue or ran around the table" (34).  What is a game in this story becomes gothic in "Flowers for Marjorie."  This story insists that the unequal division of reproductive labor can have bitter consequences: it enforces a tension between genders equal in force and fury to Marx's class conflict.[26]

---

[26]In looking for "true universals, experiences common to all," O'Brien notes, Marx excludes female reproductive labor from his analysis of productivity.  "He translates *male* experience of the separation of sexuality and reproduction into a priori universal truth.  Thus the labour of reproduction is excluded from the analysis, and children seem to appear spontaneously or perhaps magically.  Reproductive labour, thus sterilized, does not produce value, does not produce needs and therefore does not make history nor make men" (174).  Jameson's rendition of the "political unconscious" is equally exclusive.  He argues for textual analysis within three concentric frameworks: 1) the text as political history (in the narrow, punctual sense of contemporary events); 2) the text as mirror of diachronic social struggles among classes; and 3) the text as ongoing cultural revolution, as a response to a "vast" succession of modes of production (75).  In adding reproductive events to his first category, gender antagonisms to his second, and successive modes of birth control and reproduction to his third, we stretch this frame and make it more adequate to feminist theorizing about reproductive labor.

288     *Discourses of Sexuality*

## 4. *The child as value.*

O'Brien suggests that the child is "a value produced by re-productive labor" (39). But a value in what sort of economy? While male productivity is glorified in Anglo-American literature, female reproductive labor is rarely represented in its difficulty or splendor. When we find scenes describing women's contributions to reproduction, they often take the form of an elegy; for exam-ple, a poem written to mourn the death of a mother who has lost her life in childbirth.[27]

Until the modern era, direct literary representations of suc-cessful parturition have been few and far between. When these scenes do appear, even in protomodernist texts like Kate Chopin's *The Awakening*, they become the occasion for medita-tions upon women's abjection. In *The Awakening*, Madame Ratignolle does not die in childbirth, but her labors are the pre-lude to Edna's suicide. As Edna tries to ease Madame Ratig-nolle's pain and exhaustion in childbed, Edna, recalling her own painful labors, moves closer to death. Why does reproductive labor always move us toward the margins of a dominant dis-course? Perhaps it is not simply custom nor delicacy nor fright-eningly high rates of infant mortality that have impeded repre-sentations of female natality. These scenes may also be missing from Western literature because of a more general devalua-tion—the exclusion from consciousness of the value of reproduc-tive labor as labor.[28]

The inestimable value of reproductive labor becomes a focus for the bearers of Welty's wide net. The laborers in Welty's story recognize an economic problem at the heart of their labor; they find themselves caught between contradictory modes of ex-change:

"Is that all the fish in Pearl River?"

---

[27]Milton's "Epitaph on the Marchioness of Windsor" is the most beau-tiful of these elegies: "This rich Marble doth inter / The honor'd Wife of Winchester / . . . The hapless Babe before his birth / Had burial, yet not laid in earth, / And the languisht Mother's Womb / Was not long a living Tomb." *John Milton Complete Poems and Major Prose*, ed. Merritt Y. Hughes (New York: Bobbs-Merrill Co., 1957) 65–66, 11, 1–2, 31–34.

[28]For an argument against "labor" as a productive category for re-thinking birth, see Emily Martin's *The Woman in the Body*.

"How much you sell them for? Everybody's?"
"Take 'em free," said William Wallace suddenly and
loud. The Malones were upon him and shouting, but it
was too late. "I don't want no more of 'em. I want my
wife!"   he yelled, just at the moment when Hazel's
mother walked out of her front door.
      "What have you done with my child?" Hazel's
mother shouted. (66–67)

William Wallace feels a need to establish his relation to procreativity in a different economy. He settles for a form of conspicuous generosity, a gesture resembling the noblesse oblige of a
Kwakiutl potlatch.

      How should writers and critics value the children that
women produce and conceptualize the reproductive labor that
produces these children? First, we must continue to work past
our investment in a copulative politics, a macho poetics, and begin to explore reproduction in a more analytic key. Second, we
need to create narratives of birth—both critical and literary—that break new ground, that refuse to perpetuate the dis-
placements and deformations of woman's reproductive capacity.

      This work is already being done by contemporary women
poets with a restlessness, a bloody beauty, that takes my breath
away.[29]  And yet even as contemporary poets and critics construct a more progressive story of reproduction that focuses on
new origin myths, on maternal rather than paternal histories,
this natalism may also recall old forms of complicity. As Peggy
Kamuf argues in "Replacing Feminist Criticism":

      if feminist theory lets itself be guided by questions such
      as what is women's language, literature, style or experi-
      ence from where does feminist theory get its faith in the
      form of these questions to get at truth, if not from the
      same central store that supplies humanism with its faith
      in the universal truth of man?  And what if notions such
      as "getting-at-the-truth-of-the-object" represented a prin-

---

[29]For an analysis of this new work, see Yaeger, "The 'Language of
Blood'."

cipal means by which the power of power structures are sustained and even extended?[30]

Within a poststructuralist world, any faith in clear origins and clean endings, any construction of a totalizing world view with the birthing mother at center, contributes to this store of bad faith. After such knowledge, what forgiveness? Perhaps very little, and yet the invisibility of gestation and parturition remains a feminist dilemma.[31]

In *The Political Unconscious*, Jameson suggests that foundational arguments tempt us because "such master narratives have inscribed themselves in . . . texts as well as in our thinking about them. . . . They reflect a fundamental dimension of our collective thinking and our collective fantasies about history and reality" (34). To initiate new counter-narratives of birth means to seek out these collective fantasies. For example, in *Alice in Wonderland* and *Water Babies*, Dodgson and Kingsley construct incredible fantasies that mingle the life of the child as separate being with the dependent life of the fetus. In these dreamy visions of the mature child as fetus, the Darwinian anxieties about human bestiality that erupt in the mid-nineteenth century are assuaged: the fetus can consort safely with other animals without losing its human identity. The problem of what it means to have come from a womb is provisionally controlled by an obsessive imaging of the child's separateness and maturity, while the anxiety about what it means to evolve in the womb from blastocyte to embryo to baby is allowed to run wild.

---

[30]Peggy Kamuf, "Replacing Feminist Criticism," *Diacritics* 12 (1982): 42–47.

[31]The recent "More Demi Moore" cover of *Vanity Fair* (August 1991) is a case in point. Here a pregnant woman poses nude on the cover of a national magazine, her body brazen and beautiful. "I let my belly out all the time, so why not on the cover of Vanity Fair? It's glamorous being pregnant" (*Newsweek* 22 July 1991: 51). This is genuinely exciting—a new narrative of birth making waves in the national press. But the public's reaction has been oddly reactionary; the magazine's vendors demanded censorship, and *Vanity Fair*'s publishers were "compelled to cover the issue in white paper in most of the nation. Now staffers fear it looks like a naughty-nurses magazine" (*Newsweek*, 51). Once again, we move a reproductive to a copulative politics, and censorship reigns.

In these texts, anxieties about reproductive labor take on historical specificity. And yet this specificity suggests a more general problem: the mystery, worry, and aggravation of what it means to come from a womb require continual re-elaboration. Reproduction must be tamed or tampered with to fit within an era's ideology, to acquire appropriate meaning. One reason to set forth a reproductive philosophy as new "master" narrative would be to rekindle the problem of natality in our imaginations—in part, by revealing the constancy, as well as the transformations, of these collective fantasies about birth.[32]

But the suggestion that the politics of birth may require foundational or "quasimetanarrative" arguments to help us rethink reproductive praxis is risky. With the advent of postmodernism, multiculturalism, and feminist heterodoxy, we have grown suspicious of grand metanarratives that use the words of a few to account for the lives of the many. Within feminism, theories of motherhood and sexuality have become especially vulnerable to such overgeneralizations. In "Social Criticism without Philosophy" Nancy Fraser and Linda Nicholson describe the foibles of theorists like Nancy Chodorow or Catharine MacKinnon who construct "a quasi metanarrative around a putatively cross-cultural, female-associated activity." "Each claims to have identified a basic kind of human practice found in all societies that has cross-cultural explanatory power. In each case the practice in question is associated with a biological or quasibi-

---

[32]The emphasis on constancy rather than transformation, on metanarrative rather than history, presents a problem for those interested in O'Brien's work on reproduction. For O'Brien, reproductive labor becomes the fundamental narrative of Western culture, and paternal alienation offers an allegorical "key" for unlocking the secrets of Western politics. She asserts that "women do not, like men, have to take further action to annul their alienation from the race, for their labour confirms their integration" (32). These assertions seem not just dogmatic but wrong—one has only to think about Mary Shelley's postpartum despair and the genesis of *Frankenstein* or Sylvia Plath's unhappy "Morning Song," in *Ariel* (New York: Harper & Row, 1966) 1, to refute the notion of women's lack of reproductive alienation. And yet, stripped of this insistence on expressive causality, O'Brien's ideas are stimulating; they offer a wealth of new categories for thinking about reproduction and reinventing its history.

ological need and is construed as functionally necessary to the reproduction of society."[33]

For Fraser and Nicholson, "quasi metanarratives hamper, rather than promote, sisterhood, since they elide differences among women and among the forms of sexism" (99–100). This seems indisputable; it's echoed in "The Ethics of Linguistics," where Julia Kristeva also redefines the bonds of postmodern communities: "ethics used to be a coercive, customary manner of ensuring the cohesiveness of a particular group through the repetition of a code. . . . Now, however, the issue of ethics crops up wherever a code (mores, social contract) must be shattered."[34] This endeavor to rupture ethical imperatives may be persuasive from the perspective of a postmodern skepticism about the legitimating metanarratives of Western culture, but what about those arenas of thought and action that lack metanarratives? Aren't there stories that will benefit from reformulation as well as deconstruction—that is, from some new grandiosity? Aren't there norms so phallocentric that to recast them in feminist terms—however limiting those terms may be—can prove useful to feminist debate?

Generalizing about birth means risking this melodrama. According to Mary O'Brien, human society has as its inescapably necessary substructure the process of human reproduction. However, since male and female contributions to reproductive labor are unequal—and since the male of the species has sustained this inequality by grounding "reproductive" value in cultural or economic activity alone—society still lacks an epistemology that would allow us to frame, to recreate, and therefore to begin to control the meanings of reproductive pleasure and

---

[33]Nancy Fraser and Linda Nicholson, "Social Criticism without Philosophy: An Encounter between Feminism and Postmodernism" *Universal Abandon: The Politics of Postmodernism,* ed. Andrew Ross (Minneapolis: University of Minnesota Press, 1988) 97. Subsequent page references are incorporated in the text.

[34]Julia Kristeva, *Desire in Language: A Semiotic Approach to Literature and Art* (New York: Columbia University Press, 1980) 23. Kristeva suggests that this new ethics demands the repudiation of all norms and myths designed to maintain the status quo. It involves its actants in "the free play of negativity"—in acts of deconstruction and negation that challenge norms even as these norms are "being put together again, although temporarily and with full knowledge of what is involved" (23).

danger in women's lives. This is not to say that diverse cultures will share the same epistemologies. A poetics of birth should help define crosscultural reproductive differences by inviting comparisons. Nella Larsen's *Quicksand* (1928) and Buchi Emecheta's *The Joys of Motherhood* (1979) ask frightening questions about women's roles in economies where they are only valued for the babies they produce. But while these African-American and West African economies are related, they are also utterly dissimilar, and Emecheta's and Larsen's tales of reproductive despair invite us to reflect upon these differences.[35]

There is an additional impetus for constructing a poetics of birth. If feminist theorists have reified or essentialized motherhood in order to reclaim stolen territory, there has been an equal impulse to turn away from mothering and its metaphors in order to purge femininity of its victimizing rituals. This reflex can be just as destructive as the metanarrative turn—especially when it dominates the writings of Simone de Beauvoir or Shulameth Firestone; this antireproductive impulse also informs Donna Haraway's exemplary "Manifesto for Cyborgs":

> Every story that begins with original innocence and privileges the return to wholeness imagines the drama of life to be individuation, separation, the birth of the self. . . . These plots are ruled by a reproductive politics—rebirth without flaw, perfection, abstraction. In this plot women . . . have less selfhood, weaker individuation, more fusion to the oral, to Mother, less at stake in masculine autonomy. But there is another route to having less at stake in masculine autonomy, a route that . . . passes through women and other present-tense, illegitimate cyborgs, not of Woman born, who refuse the ideological resources of victimization so as to have a real life.

> One last image: organisms and organismic, holistic politics depend on metaphors of rebirth and invariably call on the resources of reproductive sex. I would suggest that cyborgs have more to do with regeneration and are suspicious of the reproductive matrix and of most birthing. . . .

[35]Nella Larsen, *Quicksand and Passing*, ed. Deborah McDowell (New Brunswick: Rutgers University Press, 1986) and Buchi Emecheta, *The Joys of*

> We require regeneration, not rebirth, and the possibilities
> for our reconstitution include the utopian dream of the
> hope for a monstrous world without gender.[36]

Is the facticity of the birthing body really so dangerous?
Why not reimagine pregnant women as cyborgian ciphers rather
than tossing out gestation and parturition—as if these biological
events were responsible for the dreams of Cartesian man? If the
cyborg becomes one site where the boundaries among humans,
animals, and machines can be "thoroughly breached" (Haraway
68), might not the pregnant woman's body offer another site of
utopian monstrousness?

Kristeva begins to reinvent this body in "Stabat Mater";
here the pregnant woman becomes the perfect simulacrum for a
split subjectivity:

> a mother-woman is rather a strange "fold" (*pli*) which
> turns nature into culture, and the "speaking subject" (*le
> parlant*) into biology. Although it affects each woman's
> body, this heterogeneity, which cannot be subsumed by
> the signifier, literally explodes with pregnancy—the di-
> viding line between nature and culture—and with the ar-
> rival of the child—which frees a woman from uniqueness
> and gives her a chance, albeit not a certainty, of access
> to the other, to the ethical. These peculiarities of the ma-
> ternal body make a woman a creature of folds, a catas-
> trophe of being that cannot be subsumed by the dialectic
> of the trinity or its supplements.[37]

Kristeva's woman-of-folds may not tell the story of every-
woman's reproductivity. But her attempt to reinvent pregnancy,
to exaggerate both its monstrosity and sacredness, opens the
birthing body to much-needed reinscription.

Barbara Johnson confronts this necessity in "Apostrophe,
Animation, Abortion." Describing the limits of male tradition,
she argues that, for writers like Thoreau, "pregnancy was not

---

*Motherhood* (New York: Braziller, 1979).

[36]Donna Haraway, "A Manifesto for Cyborgs: Science, Technology, and
Socialist Feminism in the 1980's," *Socialist Review* 15 (1985): 65–105, quotations from 96, 100. Subsequent page references are incorporated in the text.

[37]Julia Kristeva, "Stabat Mater" 114.

an essential fact of life. Yet for him as well as for every human being that has yet existed, someone else's pregnancy is the very first fact of life. How might the plot of human subjectivity be reconceived (so to speak) if pregnancy rather than autonomy is what raises the question of deliberateness?"[38]   In this essay I have begun to explore some of the literary repercussions of this reproductive repression by asking what difference it makes that we have all emerged from someone else's body — and that Western culture has chosen to ignore or to enslave women's contributions to bodiliness, to species being.

Faced with this storylessness, feminists have rewritten the mother's story in the last decade. Not only Nancy Chodorow but Hélène Cixous, Dorothy Dinnerstein, Carol Gilligan, Luce Irigaray, and Julia Kristeva (among others) have protested the marginalization of mothering in Western myth systems and rewritten oedipal myths as preoedipal stories. As their numerous critics have charged, these mother-centered narratives are fraught with empirical and epistemological peril. But the foregrounding of birthing mothers' stories — as well as the thoughtful resistance to these stories from within feminist ranks — has been essential for the development of a woman-centered consciousness in the last decade.   Without the worn-out tropes, blotched Freudianisms, and colonizing assumptions that continue to speak in Dinnerstein's and Chodorow's narratives, the discourse of paternity (or of the woman-in-effect) might still be the only discourse available, and maternal stories could still be invisible.

While these theorists have helped reveal the mother or mother-child dyad as the repressed content of numerous cultural texts, the reproductive dyad — meaning women's contributions to gestation and parturition — has hovered on the horizon, just outside our narrative consciousness. This is to insist that while history-making has its dangers, silence is more dangerous still. As Hayden White explains, the desire to write history arises from a fantasy, a desire to have real events display the coherence, integrity, and closure that can only be displayed in an imaginary world — in "the formal attributes of the stories we tell

---

[38]Barbara Johnson, "Apostrophe, Animation, Abortion," *A World of Difference* (Baltimore: Johns Hopkins University Press, 1987) 184–199, quotations on 190.

about imaginary events."[39]   Nevertheless feminists must devote themselves to the construction of new reproductive narratives so that motherhood, birth, and the unspoken dramas of gestation and parturition will enter the real, will enter history, will be seen as important, or "true," or at least somewhat true, because they possess the character of narrativity.

A reproductive poetics should follow.   And if 1) the "alienation" of men's sperm, 2) the importance of gestation and parturition as labor power, 3) the unequal division of reproductive labor between the sexes, and 4) the importance of the child as value do not become the ultimate terms of this poetics, then other categories will emerge.   We still need an abundance of terms to help unearth the reproductive unconscious of Western literatures. In inventing these terms, we must also work to prevent a theory and poetry of natality from turning into a poetics of natalism—the demand that women prove themselves through, and limit themselves to, the act of giving birth.

---

[39]Hayden White, "The Value of Narrativity," *Critical Inquiry* 7 (1980): 5–27, quotation on 27.

# MISCARRIAGE/MS. CARNAGE AND OTHER STORIES: A VISUAL ESSAY

*Joanne Leonard*

"Poems are like dreams. In them you put what you don't know you know."[1] In many of the works gathered here, which were originally part of three separate collage series, there are resting and dreaming figures. These dreamers knew things I had yet to acknowledge. From the vantage of 1991, I look at these older works, which date from the early 1970s, and see in them concerns that I did not recognize when the images were made. Arising from particular moments in my own life story and bound by the common thread of autobiography, the collages here are linked, as I now see it, by a set of themes acted out on the body: struggle and violence, victimization and power, conjunctions and severances, and the tensions between inner and outer worlds.

---

[1]Adrienne Rich, *On Lies, Secrets, and Silence: Selected Prose, 1967–1978* (New York: Norton, 1979) 40.

## Of Things Masculine

Figure 1, from *Of Things Masculine and Related Works, c. 1970*, 12" x 16", gelatin silver print photograph and collage on three layers of plex in frame, collection of the artist. Above my photograph of the nude, sleeping figure of my husband, I placed a  starry sky (actually sperm under a microscope) and below, war-wounded  bodies. I understood that I was contrasting an intimate view in our bedroom with forces of life and death in the world beyond but only later realized the extent to which I had tried to describe my relation to power and vulnerability.

## Death for a Wife

Figure 2, from *Dreams and Nightmares, 1971–72*, 9 3/4"
x 9 3/4", photocollage with selectively opaqued positive
black and white transparency and collage, private collection.   Here I sought to express the painful story of my
husband's departure and my marriage's end by looking
at the violent destruction of my romantic dream.   I had
believed in the myth that our lives had become one
through marriage, and the separation was akin to physical annihilation.   At that time, I did not ask where the
myth of romantic union had come from.   I had not yet
adopted Carolyn Heilbrun's view that "if marriage is
seen without its romantic aspects, it ceases to be attractive to its female half and, hence, is no longer useful to
its patriarchal supporters."[2]

---

[2]Carolyn Heilbrun, *Writing a Woman's Life* (New York: Norton, 1988) 87.

## Woman and Snail

Figure 3, from *Journal, 1973*, 11" x 17", collage and pencil on paper, collection of the artist. This ambivalent image expressed a tension surrounding sexual inter-course. The woman is at once an object of desire, a de-siring sexual subject, and a female self that desires a child. The receptive flower and the predatory snail that I made repelled me, and I did not exhibit or reproduce this image for nearly twenty years. Many of the images in *Journal, 1973* have been censored from exhibition or publication by others. But in this case, and a few others, I had internalized the prohibitions and become my own censor.

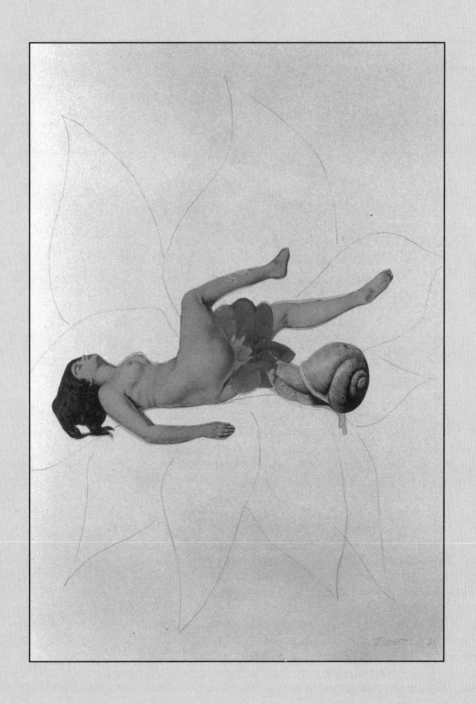

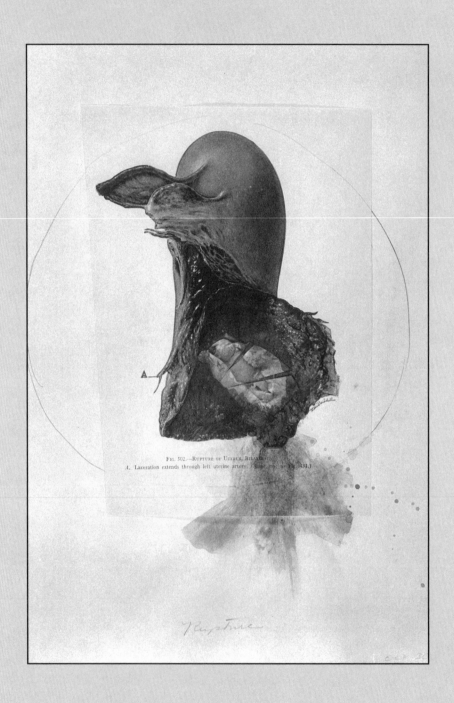

FIG. 302.—RUPTURE OF UTERUS, BILATERAL.

A. Laceration extends through left uterine artery. (Same case as FIG. 431.)

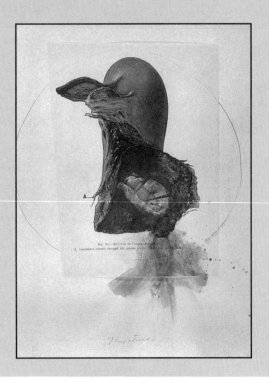

## Rupture and Miscarriage/Ms. Carnage

Figures 4 and 5, both from *Journal, 1973: Rupture*, 1973, 11" x 17", collage with blood and pencil on paper, collection of Jeremy Stone, San Francisco; *Miscarriage/Ms. Carnage*, 1973, 11" x 17", collage with blood, paint, and tissue paper, collection of Jeremy Stone, San Francisco. I had begun a journal in collage form during the early weeks of pregnancy. Then the bleeding began, and I put the blood on the journal's pages. After the miscarriage, I made one image representing the frightening, damaging bleeding. In the next image, the blood was associated with the loss of a baby, shown as destroyed. My dreams of having a baby had ruptured, but the shock and loss empowered me to represent my experience and to make images of subjects deemed taboo.

James Dickey's comment on Anne Sexton's work in 1963 represents a typical response to the breaking of taboos by women: "It would be hard to find a writer who dwells more insistently on the pathetic and disgusting aspects of bodily experience."[3] With the first showing of *The Journal of a Miscarriage* (thirty works created in fifty-three days during 1973 and shown later that year at the San Francisco Art Institute, my work began to find a distinct female audience, and I began to understand the difference having such an audience made. With a few exceptions, men found the specifics of this female experience disgusting. Women, however, seemed to see their own experiences validated and, like the critic Lucy Lippard, viewed the work with enthusiasm.

**Woman and Frog**

Figure 6, from *Journal, 1973*, 11" x 17", silver print photograph and collage on paper, collection of Jeremy Stone, San Francisco. "The frog, in her supine posture," I wrote of this collage, "seemed brazenly receptive. This self portrait reflects a time of desire for insemination and maternity."[4]    A colleague, Ruth Behar, recently suggested that this almost mirrorlike image of female/frog might represent the dream of a woman complete unto herself, not needing a sexual partner to become pregnant. Even though I still thought of myself as passive and receptive, my dream image figures a woman in control of her own reproductive destiny.

---

[4]*In/Sights: Self-Portraits by Women*, ed. Joyce Tenneson Cohen (Boston: Godine, 1978) 124.

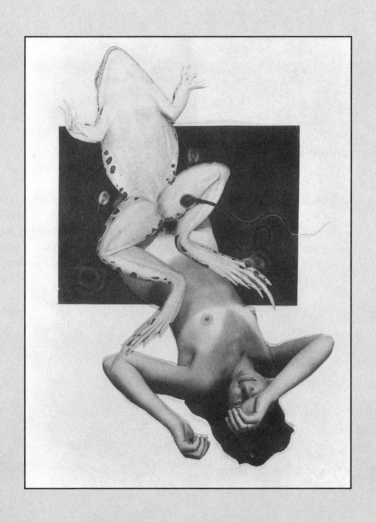

**Baby and Sea Shell**

Figure 7, *Journal, 1973*, 11" x 17", collage on paper, collection of Jeremy Stone, San Francisco.  The birdlike form, actually a sea shell, represents the mother's body during birth, struggling for possession of her infant against the world, symbolized here by the pulling hands of the doctor and the medical management of birth.

# TONI MORRISON'S BELOVED:
## RE-MEMBERING THE BODY AS HISTORICAL TEXT

### Mae G. Henderson

> Now, women forget all those things they don't want to remember. The dream is the truth. Then they act and do things accordingly. . . . So the beginning of this was a woman and she had come back from burying the dead.
> —Zora Neale Hurston, *Their Eyes Were Watching God*

> We tell stories because in the last analysis human lives need and merit being narrated. This remark takes on its full force when we refer to the necessity to save the history of the defeated and the lost. The whole history of suffering cries out for vengeance and calls for narrative.
> —Paul Ricoeur, *Time and Narrative*

> Upon the death of the other we are given to memory, and thus to interiorization . . . since Freud, this is how the "normal" "work of mourning" is often described. It entails a movement in which an interiorizing idealization takes in itself or upon itself the body and voice of the other, the other's visage and person, ideally *and* quasi-literally devouring them. This mimetic interiorization is not fictive; it is the origin of fiction, of apocryphal figuration. It takes place in a body. Or rather, it makes for a body, voice, and a soul which, although "ours," did not exist and had no meaning *before* this possibility that one *must* always begin by remembering, and whose trace must be followed.
> —Jacques Derrida, *Memories for Paul de Man*

> . . . I had brought not a child but suffering into the world and it, suffering, refused to leave me, insisted on coming back, on haunting me, permanently. One does not bear children in pain, it's pain that one bears: the child is pain's representative and once it is delivered moves in for good. . . . [A] mother is . . . marked by pain, she succumbs to it.
> —Julia Kristeva, "Stabat Mater"

312

There is an "uncanniness" about his past that a present
occupant has expelled (or thinks it has) in an effort to
take its place. The dead haunt the living. The past: it
"re-bites" [il remord] (it is a secret and repeated biting).
History is "cannibalistic," and memory becomes the
closed arena of conflict between two contradictory operations: forgetting, which is not something passive, a loss,
but an action directed against the past, and the mnemic
trace, the return of what was forgotten . . . . More generally speaking, an autonomous order is founded upon
what it eliminates; it produces a "residue" condemned to
be forgotten. But what was excluded . . . re-infiltrates
the place of its origin—It resurfaces, it troubles, it turns
the present's feeling of being "at home" into an illusion,
it lurks—this "wild," this "obscene," this "filth," this
"resistance" of "superstition"—within the walls of the
residence, and behind the back of the owner (the *ego),* or
over its objections, it inscribes there the law of the other.
   —Michel de Certeau, *Heterologies: The Discourse of*
   *the Other*

Describing nineteenth-century slave narratives, Toni Morrison observes, "No slave society in the history of the world wrote
more—or more thoughtfully—about its own enslavement." Yet,
for Morrison, the narratives, with their "instructive" and
"moral" force are incomplete:

Over and over, the writers pull the narrative up short
with a phrase such as, "but let us drop a veil over these
proceedings too terrible to relate." In shaping the experience to make it palatable to those who were in a position to alleviate it, they were silent about many things,
and they "forgot" many other things.[1]

---

A slightly different version of this essay has appeared in *Comparative
American Identities: Race, Sex, and Nationalities in the Modern Text,* ed. Hortense Spillers (New York: Routledge, 1991).

[1]Toni Morrison, "Site of Memory," *Inventing the Truth: The Art and
Craft of Memoir,* ed. William Zinsser (Boston: Houghton-Mifflin, 1987)
109–10.

"Things too terrible to relate" were most often the sexual exploitation of slave women by white men. Convention allowed, indeed almost demanded, that these violations be named but not described. Morrison continues, "But most importantly—at least for me—there was no mention of their *interior life*" (my emphasis). The writer's "job"—as Morrison sees it—"becomes how to rip that veil drawn over proceedings too terrible to relate," to "find and expose a truth about the interior life of people who didn't write it," to "fill in the blanks that the slave narratives left, to part the veil that was so frequently drawn," and, finally, "to implement the stories that [she has] heard" (110–13).

Morrison's image of the veil revises a DuBoisian metaphor that was originally intended to suggest the division between blacks and whites in American society.[2] Rather than measuring a division *between* the races, however, Morrison's veil measures a division *within* the race—a psychic and expressive boundary separating the *speakable* from the *unspeakable* and the *unspoken*.[3] Her task as a writer, therefore, is to transgress these discursive boundaries by setting up a complementary and dialogic relationship between the "interiority" of her own work and the "exteriority" of the slave narrative.

Morrison, then, aims to restore a dimension of the repressed personal in a manifestly political discourse. In some ways, the texts of the slave narratives can be regarded as classic examples of the "return of the repressed," primarily because the events relating to violence and violation (which are self-censored or edited out) return again and again in "veiled allusions." To the degree that her work is intended to *resurrect* stories *buried* and *express* stories *repressed*, Morrison's relation to the slave narrators, as well as the relation of her text to its precursor narratives, can be profitably compared not only to the relation of historian to informant but also of analyst to analysand.

Dedicating her novel *Beloved* to the "Sixty Million and more" who failed to survive the Middle Passage, Morrison sets out to give voice to the "disremembered and unaccounted for"—the women and children who left no written records. The

---

[2]See W. E. B. Du Bois, "The Forethought," *The Souls of Black Folk* (Chicago: A. C. McClurg, 1903) viii.

[3]See Toni Morrison's "Unspeakable Things Unspoken," *Michigan Quarterly Review* 28 (Winter 1989): 1–34.

epigraph from Romans 9:25 prefigures the writer's purpose of reclaiming this "lost tribe":

> *I will call them my people,*
> *which were not my people;*
> *and her beloved,*
> *which was not beloved.*

By citing a New Testament passage that echoes a passage from the Old Testament, the author not only problematizes the nature of the relation between the past and the present but also thematizes the importance of historical reclamation and repossession. As Jehovah reclaimed the Israelites after their apostasy (figured in Hosea as spiritual adultery), so Morrison seeks to repossess the African and slave ancestors after their historic violation (figured in *Beloved* as physical rape). Further, Morrison reinscribes the tension between Old Testament law and New Testament spirit. Significantly, it is the epistles of Paul (Romans and Galatians, in particular) which announce that the doctrine of justification by deeds under the Old Dispensation of the Law is revised through justification by grace under the New Dispensation of the Spirit.[4] Engaging the Scriptures as a kind of intertext, Morrison enacts in her novel an opposition between the law and the spirit, redeeming her characters from the "curse of the law" as figured in the master's discourse. In her rewriting of Scripture, Morrison ushers in an ironic new dispensation figured not by the law of the (white) Father but by the spirit of the (black and female) child, Beloved. Thus, Morrison challenges the hegemonic status of the (primarily male) slave narratives as well as the "canonical" history embodied in the master('s) narratives in a project that holds both more accountable to the "disremembered and unaccounted for."

Like several of her contemporaries, Morrison seeks to achieve these ends in a novel that both historicizes fiction and

---

[4]"Therefore we conclude that a man is justified by faith without the deeds of the law" (Romans 3:28); "But that no man is justified by the law in the sight of God, *it is* evident: for, The just shall live by faith" (Galatians 3:11).

fictionalizes history.[5]    In following passage she recollects the events on which the novel was based:

> I . . . remember being obsessed by two or three little fragments of stories that I heard from different places. One was a newspaper clipping about a woman named Margaret Garner in 1851. It said that the Abolitionists made a great deal out of her case because she had escaped from Kentucky . . . with her four children. She lived in a little neighborhood just outside of Cincinnati and she had killed her children. She succeeded in killing one; she tried to kill two others. The interesting thing, in addition to that, was the interviews that she gave. She was a young woman. In the inked pictures of her she seemed a very quiet, very serene-looking woman and everyone who interviewed her remarked about her serenity and tranquility. She said, "I will not let those children live how I have lived." She had run off into a little woodshed right outside her house to kill them because she had been caught as a fugitive. And she made up her mind that they would not suffer the way that she had and it was better for them to die. They put her in jail for a little while and I'm not even sure what the denouement is of her story. But that moment, that decision was a piece, a tail of something that was always around.[6]

Morrison links the above story fragment to another related in James Van der Zee's *The Harlem Book of the Dead:*

> In one picture, there was a young girl lying in a coffin and he says that she was eighteen years old and she had gone to a party and that she was dancing and suddenly she slumped and they noticed there was blood on her and they said, "what happened to you?" And she said, "I'll

---

[5]Contemporary black writers whose work fictionalizes history include, among others, Margaret Walker *(Jubilee)*, Ernest Gaines *(The Autobiography of Miss Jane Pittman)*, David Bradley *(The Chaneysville Incident)*, Alice Walker *(The Color Purple)*, Sherley Anne Williams *(Dessa Rose)*, and Barbara Chase Riboud *(Sally Hemings* and *The Echo of Lions).*

[6]Gloria Naylor and Toni Morrison, "A Conversation," *The Southern Review* 21 (Summer 1985): 583–84.

tell you tomorrow. I'll tell you tomorrow. . . ." That's all she would say. And apparently her ex-boyfriend or somebody who was jealous had come to the party with a gun and a silencer and shot her. And she kept saying, "I'll tell you tomorrow" because she wanted him to get away. And he did, I guess; anyway she died. (584)

These newspaper clippings and Van der Zee's photostory provided the historical or "real-life" bases for the novel. "Now what made those stories connect, I can't explain," says Morrison, "but I do know that, in both instances, something seemed clear to me. A woman loved something other than herself so much, she had placed all of the value of her life in something outside herself." Morrison's project, then, is twofold: the exploration of the black woman's sense of self and the imaginative recovery of black women's history.

Describing her narrative strategy as a "kind of literary archeology," Morrison explains that, for her, "the approach that's most productive and most trustworthy . . . is the recollection that moves from the image to . . . text." Her task, as she defines it, is to "[move] that veil aside" in order to penetrate the "memories within." Although these memories—personal and collective—constitute the "subsoil of [her] work," she believes that these alone cannot give "total access to the unwritten interior life." For Morrison, "only the act of the imagination" can provide such access:

> on the basis of some information and a little bit of guesswork you journey to a site to see what remains were left behind and to reconstruct the world that these remains imply. What makes it fiction is the nature of the imaginative act: my reliance on the image—on the remains—in addition to recollection, to yield up a kind of truth. By "image," of course, I don't mean "symbol"; I simply mean "picture" and the feelings that accompany the picture.[7]

Elaborating on the relationship between picture and meaning, Morrison contrasts her own literary method (to move from image to text) to that of writers who move "from event to the image

---

[7]Morrison, "Site of Memory" 111-12.

that it left": "My route is the reverse: the image comes first and tells me what the 'memory' is about."[8]

The notion of "literary archeology"—the imaginative and reconstructive recovery of the past that characterizes Morrison's fictive process—can be usefully compared with R. G. Collingwood's description of the historical process: If the novelist relies upon the *a priori* imagination to construct the *possible* story in which characters and incidents develop "in a manner determined by a necessity internal to themselves," the historian relies upon the same inferential process to construct "his" story of the *past*. In the following passage, Collingwood demonstrates that "as works of imagination, the historian's work and novelist's do not differ":

> Each of them makes it his business to construct a picture which is partly a narrative of events, partly a description of situations, exhibition of motives, analysis of characters. Each aims at making his picture a coherent whole, where every character and every situation is so bound up with the rest that this character in this situation cannot but act in this way, and we cannot imagine him as acting otherwise. The novel and the history must both of them make sense; nothing is admissible in either except what is necessary and the judge of this necessity is in both cases the imagination. Both the novel and the history are self-explanatory, self-justifying, the product of an autonomous or self-authorizing activity; and in both cases this activity is the *a priori* imagination.[9]

The present essay will examine Morrison's novel in the context of contemporary historical theory on discourse and narrativity,

---

[8]Morrison, "Site of Memory" 113–14.

[9]Collingwood argues that, like the novelist, the historian "constructs an imaginary picture consistent with the historical data, testimony, memory, documentation, etc." In an attempt to explain a fragmentary or incomplete record of the historical past, Collingwood further argues, the historian must employ what he calls "the constructive imagination" to create a "coherent and continuous picture" consistent with the available historical data. R. G. Collingwood, *The Idea of History* (London: Oxford University Press, 1946) 245–46.

and suggest a reading that links historiography and psychoanalysis.

Like Morrison, the principal character in *Beloved* struggles with a past that is part of white/male historical discourse. Lacking a discourse of her own, Sethe must transform the residual images ("rememories") of her past into an historical discourse shaped by narrativity. These images, however, remain for a time disembodied—without form, sequence, or meaning. The challenge of the illiterate slave is similar to that of the highly literate contemporary historian or novelist: to discover a way of organizing memory, of contriving a narrative configuration in the absence of written records. If it is true, as Henry Louis Gates, Jr. argues, that the sense of self as defined in the West since the Enlightenment, "turns in part upon written records," if "our idea of the self. . . is . . . inextricably interwoven with our ideas . . . of [writing]," then what are the consequences of an absence of written records? Quite simply and perhaps startlingly, as a slave "one's sense of one's existence . . . depended upon memory." "It was memory, above all else," according to Gates, "that gave shape to being itself."[10] What these remarks do not address, however, is how one formally shapes and derives meaning from disparate memories. In other words, how does one extract a configuration from a cluster of images or diversity of events? How does one, finally, transpose memories from a visual to a diegetic, or narrative, register? Like Morrison, Sethe must learn to represent the unspeakable and unspoken in language—and more precisely, as narrative.

Morrison figures both the interiority and the exteriority of memory, that is, memory as thought and memory as material inscription.[11] In the novel, "Beloved" is the public inscription of a private memorial—seven letters chiseled into the pink headstone of a child-victim of "mother-love," a word Sethe had remembered from the preacher's funeral eulogy. If the inscription of Beloved is the trace ("the mark left behind") that initiates the novel's plot, it is also an image that haunts the text in the multiple guises of the character Beloved. Besides designating an object of affection, the term *beloved* occurs in matrimonial and eu-

---

[10]Henry Louis Gates, Jr., "Frederick Douglass and the Language of Self," *The Yale Review* 70 (July 1981): 592–611.

[11]See Jacques Derrida's *Memoires for Paul de Man* (New York: Columbia University Press, 1986) 102–50 passim.

logistic discourse.   Both are commemorative, linguistic events:
the former prefiguring the future, the latter refiguring the past.
The action of the novel, however, attends to the novelistic present—a present problematized by an unresolved past and an
unanticipated future, a present that the past does not prefigure
nor the future refigure.

At the outset of the novel, Sethe's "future was a matter of
keeping the past at bay" (42).[12]  Her aim has been to protect her
children from "rememory," which she describes as follows:

> Someday you be walking down the road and you hear
> something or see something going on.  So clear. . . . It's
> when you bump into a rememory that belongs to some-
> body else.   Where I was before I came here, that place
> [Sweet Home] is real.  It's never going away.  Even if the
> whole farm—every tree and grass blade of it dies.   The
> picture is still there and what's more, if you go
> there—you who never was there—if you go there and
> stand in the place where it was, it will happen again; it
> will be there for you, waiting for you. (36)

"Rememory," it seems, is something that possesses (or haunts)
one rather than something that one possesses.  It is, in fact, that
which makes the past part of one's present.   Yet, despite her
best efforts to "[beat] back the past," Sethe remains, in her
words, "full of it."  "Every mention of her past life hurt.  Everything in it was painful or lost"(58).  Hayden White's description
of Ibsen's Hedda Gabler also seems apt for Morrison's Sethe:
She "suffers [from] the incubus [or, in this case, the succubus] of
the past—a surfeit of history compounded by, or reflected in, a
pervasive fear of the future."[13]

Thus, unable to contrive a meaningful or appropriate
configuration for her memories, Sethe finds herself tyrannized by
unconfigured and literally disfiguring images.   As a consequence
of an attempted escape, she receives a savage beating, which
leaves her back "a clump of scars."   These scars function as
signs of ownership inscribing her as property, while the mutila-

---

[12]Toni Morrison, *Beloved* (New York: Alfred Knopf, 1987).  Page references to this work are given in the text.

[13]Hayden White, *Tropics of Discourse: Essays in Cultural Criticism*
(Baltimore: Johns Hopkins University Press, 1979) 33–34.

tion signifies her diminishment to a less-than-human status. Traces of the past that Sethe represses (but can neither remember nor forget) have been gouged onto her back by the master's whip and bear the potential burden of both *history* and *her*story. Like the inscription of Beloved and the pictorial images of the past, the scars function as an archaeological site or memory trace.

If the master has inscribed the master('s) code on Sethe's back, a white woman and a black man offer her alternative readings of it. Although initially "struck dumb" at the sight of Sethe's scars, Amy, a runaway white girl who saves the fugitive's life and midwifes the delivery of her second daughter, sees Sethe's back as a "chokecherry tree":

> See, here's the trunk—it's red and split wide open, full of sap, and this here's the parting for the branches. . . . Leaves, too, look like, and dern if these ain't blossoms. Tiny little cherry blossoms, just as white. Your back got a whole tree on it. In bloom. (79)

Amy describes an image that prompts her to wonder "what God have in mind." In her reverie, Sethe's back remains the trace of an event whose meaning, motivation, and consequence are largely unreadable.

Alternative readings are provided by Baby Suggs, Sethe's mother-in-law, and by Paul D, the last survivor of the men from Sweet Home, the Kentucky plantation where he and Sethe had met before the war. Baby Suggs perceives her daughter-in-law's back as a pattern of "roses of blood," stenciled onto the bedsheet and blanket. Paul D, who arrives after the open wounds have healed, remarks on "the sculpture [Sethe's] back had become, like the decorative work of an ironsmith too passionate for display." The distance between these suggestively gendered readings—the chokecherry tree and blood roses, on the one hand, and the wrought-iron maze, on the other—signifies the distance between so-called "natural" and culturally inscribed meanings attributed to the sign.

It is the white man who inscribes; the white woman, the black man, and the black woman may variously read but not write. Because it is her back (symbolizing the *presence* of her *past*) that is marked, Sethe has only been able to read herself through the gaze of others. Her challenge is to learn to read herself—that is, to configure the history of her body's text. If, as Paul Ricoeur contends, "the past survives by leaving its trace," then Sethe must learn how to link these traces (marks of her passage through slavery) to the construction of a personal and historical discourse.[14] Her dilemma is that as an illiterate female slave, she finds herself the written object of a white male discourse and the spoken subject of a black male and white female discourse. Significantly, Baby Suggs does *not* speak of the wounds on Sethe's back. "Baby Suggs hid her mouth with her hand" (93). Instead, she concentrates on the ritual of healing: *"[W]ordlessly*, the older woman greased the flowering back and pinned a double thickness of cloth to the inside of the newly stitched dress" (93; my emphasis). The presumption is, of course, that black women have no voice, no text, and consequently no history. They can be written and written upon precisely because they exist as the ultimate Other, whose absence or (non)being only serves to define the being or presence of the white or male subject. The black woman, symbolizing a kind of double negativity, becomes a *tabula rasa* upon which the racial/sexual identity of the other(s) can be positively inscribed.

Sethe's back is numb ("the skin on her back had been dead for years"), signifying her attempts to repress the past. (But the return of Paul D, as later of Beloved, signals the return of the repressed.) For Sethe, these scars constitute traces of past deeds too horrible and violent either to forget or to remember, a situation that Morrison describes elsewhere as "a perfect dilemma." The brutal whipping she received as punishment for her attempt to run away is only part of a cluster of events that Sethe vainly seeks to forget.

If Morrison formalizes and thematizes the operation of imaginative construction, she also dramatizes, in the character of "schoolteacher" (as he is called by the slaves), the consequences of an alternative approach. The scenes with schoolteacher are a paradigm for reading the methodology of the white male as scholar and master. Arriving at Sweet Home after the death of its previous owner, schoolteacher announces himself "with a big hat and spectacles and a coach full of paper" and begins to "watch" his subjects. His methodology—based on numbering, weighing, dividing—suggests the role of the cultural historian (or

[14]Paul Ricoeur, *The Reality of the Historical Past* (Milwaukee: Marquette University Press, 1984) 11.

ethnologist) who is concerned with sizes, densities, details, appearances, externalities, and visible properties ("Schoolteacher'd wrap that string all over my head, 'cross my nose, around my behind. Number my teeth").[15]

Schoolteacher possesses the master('s) text, and as a data collector, cataloguer, classifier, and taxonomist concerned with matters of materiality and empiricism, he divides or dismembers the indivisibility of the slaves' humanity to reconstruct (or perhaps deconstruct) the slave in his text. His physical measurements recall those of Hawthorne's Custom's House Surveyor, whose careful and accurate measurements disclose little except that "each limb [of the letter A] proved to be precisely three inches and a quarter in length." In both cases, putatively scientific techniques prove altogether inadequate. Yet, unlike Hawthorne's Surveyor, who discovers himself confronted with a "riddle which . . . [he] sees little hope of resolving," Morrison's historical investigator remains hopelessly unconscious "of his own infirmity."[16] Sethe tells us,

> He was talking to one of his pupils and I heard him say, "Which one are you doing?" And one of the boys said, "Sethe." That's when I stopped because I heard my name, and then I took a few steps to where I could see what they was doing. Schoolteacher was standing over one of them with one hand behind his back. He licked a forefinger a couple of times and turned a few pages. Slow. I was about to turn around and keep on my way . . . when I heard him say, "No, no. That's not the way. I told you to put her human characteristics on the left; her *animal* ones on the right. And don't forget to line them up." (193; my emphasis)

---

[15]See Waldo E. Martin, Jr., *The Mind of Frederick Douglass* (Chapel Hill: University of North Carolina Press, 1984) for a discussion of the relation between the ethnologist and the cultural historian in the context of nineteenth-century practice: "Practitioners of a broad and allegedly scientific discipline, ethnologists . . . attempted to uncover stages and meanings of human developments primarily in cultural and related physical and secondarily in historical terms" (225).

[16]Nathaniel Hawthorne, *The Scarlet Letter* (New York: E. P. Dutton & Co. Inc., 1938) 42, 51.

Schoolteacher's historiography encodes the notion and forms of "wildness" and "animality." As Hayden White explains, this notion is a "culturally self-authenticating device" intended to "confirm the value of [the] dialectical antithesis between 'civilization' . . . and 'humanity.'" [17] Like Nehemiah Adams, the historical investigator in Sherley Anne Williams' *Dessa Rose*, Morrison's schoolteacher espouses a concept of "otherness" as a form of subhumanity that serves, through a process of negative self-identification, to confirm his own sense of superiority. Sethe's "savagery" confirms schoolteacher's "civilization"; her "bestiality" assures his "humanity." Schoolteacher's sense of history is defined by the struggle between culture and nature, and questions of meaning and interpretation turn upon this opposition. [18]

The dismemberment of schoolteacher's method is the discursive analog to the dismemberment of slavery. Just as his pupils measure and divide Sethe according to schoolteacher's instructions, so schoolteacher himself, speaking with the slave catchers, reveals to Paul D "his worth." Overhearing the men talking, Paul D, who "has always known, or believed he did, his value—as a hand, a laborer who could make profit on a farm . . . now [discovers] his worth, which is to say he learns his price. The dollar value of his weight, his strength, his heart, his brain,

---

[17]See White 151. Unlike the notion of historical reconstruction which seeks to account for otherness by questioning the normative model, this method seeks to identify difference with deviance and/or diminishment.

[18]Cf. Sherley Anne Williams' unnamed narrator in "Meditations on History" and Adam Nehemiah in *Dessa Rose*. Williams and Morrison share reservations concerning disciplinary behaviors. Their works constitute a critique of certain aspects of both the praxis and the practitioners of these activities. Like Williams' characters, Morrison's investigator (who might as appropriately be designated ethnographer-as-historian) represents the author's indictment of the kind of "scholarly" and "scientific" discourse in which the preconceptions of the inquirer lead to gross distortions. For critical treatments of Williams' work from this perspective, see my "(W)Riting The Work and Working The Rites," *Feminism and Institutions: Dialogues on Feminist Theory*, ed. Linda Kauffman (London: Basil Blackwell, 1989) 10–43, and "Speaking in Tongues: Dialogics, Dialectics, the Black Woman Writer's Literary Tradition," *Changing Our Own Words: Essays on Criticism, Theory and Writing by Black Women*, ed. Cheryl Wall (New Brunswick: Rutgers University Press, 1989) 16–37.

his penis, and his future" (226).    As both slaveholder and scholar, schoolteacher is involved with the *dis-membering* of slaves from their families, their labor, their selves.    Against these forms of physical, social, and scholarly dismemberment the act of (re)memory initiates a reconstitutive process in the novel. If dismemberment deconstitutes and fragments the whole, then rememory functions to re-çollect, reassemble, and organize the various discrete and heterogeneous parts into a meaningful sequential whole through the process of narrativization discussed below.

The scenes of Paul D's figurative dismemberment both refigure the earlier scene of schoolteacher's anatomical dismemberment of Sethe and prefigure a later scene that Sethe vainly attempts to forget: "I am full God damn it of two boys with mossy teeth, one sucking on my breast the other holding me down, their book-reading teacher watching and writing it up" (70).    Like Paul D, who is forced to go around with a horse's "bit" in his mouth, Sethe is forced to submit to the bovine-like humiliation of "being milked."    In this grotesque parody of Madonna and child, Sethe's milk, like her labor and the fruits of her womb, is expropriated.    But the theft of her "mother's milk" suggests the expropriation of her future—her ability to nurture and ensure the survival of the next generation.

Ironically, Sethe herself has mixed schoolteacher's ink,

> [Schoolteacher liked] how [she] mixed it and it was important to him because at night he sat down to write in his book.    It was a book about [the slaves]. . . . He commenced to carry round a notebook and write down what we said. (37)

The image of schoolteacher's ink converges with the expropriation of Sethe's milk in a symbol that evokes Hélène Cixous' metaphor for "écriture féminine"—women writing a language of the body in the white ink of the mother's milk.    Not only the pages of his notebook but also the literal inscription of Sethe's back with schoolteacher's whip(pen) constitute the perverse fulfillment of Cixous' call.[19]    Appropriating Sethe's "milk"

---

[19]See Hélène Cixous, "The Laugh of the Medusa," *New French Feminisms: An Anthology,* ed. Elaine Marks and Isabelle de Courtivron (Amherst: University of Massachusetts Press, 1980) 251.

through a process of phallic substitution, schoolteacher uses the pen—for Sandra Gilbert and Susan Gruber the symbol and instrument of masculine "authority"—to "re-mark" the slave woman with the signature of his paternity.[20] Sethe must discover some way of regaining control of her story, her body, her progeny, her milk, her ability to nurture the future.

Schoolteacher's association with "the prison- house of language," figured not only in his private ledger but in the public slave codes as well, refigures the New Testament's personification of the Decalogue. St. Paul tells the churches in Galatia that "the law was our schoolmaster," or (alternatively translated) "we were held prisoners by the law."[21] It is this white/male construction of the law according to the authority of the master discourse that Sethe must first dismantle in order to construct her own story.

For schoolteacher, history is a confining activity; for Sethe, it must become a liberating one. She must accomplish precisely what Morrison does in the act of historicizing fiction—namely, "to free retrospectively, certain possibilities that were not actualized in the historical past," and to detect "possibilities buried in the . . . past."[22] As historian, Sethe must liberate her present from the "burden of the past" constructed in *history*. She must learn to remap the past so that it becomes a blueprint for her future. Her job is to reconstitute the past through personal narrative, or storytelling. Collingwood has argued that the historian is primarily "a story teller," suggesting that "historical sensibility is manifested in the capacity to make a plausible story out of congeries of 'facts' which, in their unprocessed form, made no sense at all."[23] Like Morrison, Sethe uses the memory of personal experience and what Collingwood calls the "constructive imagination" as a means of re-membering a dis-membered past, family, and community.

If Morrison moves "from image to text," Sethe, too, begins with the image and shapes "rememories" of the past, endowing

---

[20]See Sandra Gilbert and Susan Gubar, *Madwoman in the Attic: The Woman Writer and the Nineteenth-Century Literary Imagination* (New Haven: Yale University Press, 1970).

[21]These are alternative translations of Galatians 3:24.

[22]See Paul Ricoeur, *Time and Narrative* (Chicago: University of Chicago Press, 1988) 3:191–92.

[23]See White on Collingwood 83.

them with form, drama, and meaning through a process of narrativization described by Ricoeur as *configuration* and White as *emplotment*.  Narrativization enables Sethe to construct a meaningful life story from a cluster of images, to transform separate and disparate events into a coherent story.[24]

For Sethe, the past has the power to make her either captive or free.  Her feelings, hopes, desires, perceptions—all colored by past incidents and events—culminate in what remain for her unspeakable acts and actions: physical violation and infanticide. "Freeing yourself was one thing;" Sethe thinks, "claiming ownership of that freed self was another" (95).  Her preoccupation with the past makes it impossible for her to process new experiences except through the distant lens of the particular events in question.  What Gates describes as "this brilliant substructure of the system of slavery"—the dependence of the slave upon her memory—had the potential to make the slave [and later the ex-slave], in some respects, "a slave to [her]self, a prisoner of [her] own power to recall."[25]

If certain events remain unconfigured, others are overly and inappropriately configured.  Thus, an alternative reading of Sethe's dilemma, based on White's model, might be that she has "overemplotted" the events of her past; she has "charged them with a meaning so intense that . . . they continue to shape both [her] perceptions and [her] responses to the world long after they should have become 'past history.'"  The problem for Sethe, then, is to configure or emplot, on the one hand, but to *re*configure or *re*emplot on the other.  She must imaginatively reconstitute, or re-member, her history "in such a way as to change the *meaning* of those events for [her] and their *significance* for the economy of the whole set of events that make up [her] life."[26]  If Gates can

---

[24]According to Ricoeur, emplotment "brings together diverse and heterogeneous story elements . . . agents, goals, means, interactions, [and] circumstances. . . . [A]n event must be more than just a singular occurrence. It gets its definition from its contribution to the development of the plot.  A story, too, must be more than just an enumeration of events in serial order; it must organize them into an intelligible whole, of a sort such that we can always ask what is the thought of this story.  In short, emplotment is the operation that draws a configuration out of a simple succession."  See Ricoeur, *Time and Narrative* (1984) 1:65.

[25]Gates 593.

[26]See White 87.

assert that "the act of writing for the slave [narrator] constitute[s] the act of creating a public . . . self," then the act of
remembering, for the unlettered slave, constitutes the act of
constructing a private self.[27]    As Ricoeur argues, the (re)con-
figuration of the past enables one to refigure the future; such is
Sethe's task.

If memory is *materialized* in Beloved's reappearance, it *is
maternalized* in Sethe's (re)configuration. Sethe gives *birth to her
past and to her future:* first to the baby with no name whose sad
and angry spirit comes back to haunt 124 Bluestone Road and
later to the incarnate Beloved, the young woman with "flawless
skin and feet and hands soft and new." The return of Beloved,
therefore, becomes not only a psychological projection but also a
physical (rather than spiritual) manifestation.    Her "rebirth"
represents, as it were, the uncanny return of the dead to haunt
the living, the return of the past to shadow the present.

Yet it is the notion of "self-distanciation" that intrigues
Morrison in this as in other works: "What is it that really compels a good woman to displace the self, her self?" asks Morrison.
What interests her is not only the nobility and generosity of
these actions but also the fact that such love ("the best thing
that is in us") "is . . . the thing that makes us [as women] sabotage ourselves, sabotage in the sense [of perceiving] that our life
['the best part of ourselves'] is not as worthy." Her method of
characterization is intended to suggest this process of displacement—"to project the self not into the way we say 'yourself' but
to put a space between those words, as though the self were really a *twin* or a thirst or a friend or something that sits right
next to you and watches you." Morrison has "[projected] the
dead out into the earth" in the character of Beloved, so that
Beloved becomes the twin self or mirror of Sethe and other
women in the novel.[28] The author's critical reflections, however,
point to another dimension of Sethe's dilemma, a dilemma that
combines the private and public functions of "rememory." If the
individual is defined as a conduit of communal consciousness,
then (drawing on Teresa de Lauretis) the events of Sethe's life
can be emplotted through historiography; conversely, if the
community is defined as a conduit of individual consciousness,

[27]Gates 599.
[28]Naylor and Morrison, "A Conversation" 585.

then the events of Sethe's psychic life can be encoded in psycho-analytic discourse.[29]

At the point of this intersection between the personal and the social, the psychic and the historical begin to merge. What I have been describing as social subjectivity emplotted by historiography can also be figured in terms of psychic subjectivity and represented in the discourse of psychoanalysis. Speaking to the relation between psychoanalytical and historical consciousness, Norman Brown observes that "the method of psychoanalytical therapy is to deepen the historical consciousness of the individual ('fill up the memory-gaps') till [she] awakens from [her] own history." Interpreting Freud's notion of "archaic heritage," Brown further develops the link between history and psychoanalysis by recalling that humankind is a "prisoner of the past in the same sense as [quoting Freud] 'our hysterical patients are suffering from reminiscences' and neurotics 'cannot escape from the past'." He concludes that not only are all cultures bound to the past but individuals are likewise bound to what Freud describes as "the memory-traces of the experiences of former generations."[30]

---

[29]Teresa de Lauretis, *Alice Doesn't: Feminism, Semiotics, Cinema* (Bloomington: Indiana University Press, 1984).

[30]Freud, according to Brown's reading, extends this to recapitulation theory (ontogeny recapitulates phylogeny), in which "each individual recapitulates the history of the race. . . . From this it follows that the theory of neurosis must embrace a theory of history; and conversely a theory of history must embrace a theory of neurosis." See Norman O. Brown, *Life against Death: The Psychoanalytical Meaning of History* (Middletown: Wesleyan University Press, 1959) 19, 12–13. Robert Guthrie elaborates further: "The recapitulation theory held that an individual organism, in the process of growth and development, passes through a series of stages representing those in the evolutionary development of the species. G. Stanley Hall, for example, believed 'that in its play activity the child exhibits a series of phases corresponding to cultural phases of human society, a hunting period, a building period, and so on.' Hall's attempt to mold individual development (ontogeny) with racial characteristics (phylogeny) was supported by many leading behavioral scientists of this time [early twentieth century]. (John Mark Baldwin's *Mental Development in the Child and the Race*, for example, was a frequently quoted source.)" Robert V. Guthrie, *Even the Rat Was White: A Historical View of Psychology* (New York: Harper & Row, 1976) 82.

This link between history and psychoanalysis, then, permits the events in Sethe's life to be encoded in an alternate plot structure. The sources of her "complex" or dis-ease manifest themselves in her endless efforts to avoid the past and avert the future. The events in her past—namely, her own violation and the ensuing decision to take her daughter's life—have become sources of both repression and obsession. Sethe must "conjure up" her past—symbolized by Beloved—and confront it as an antagonist. As in Freud's "recommendations on the technique of psychoanalysis," Sethe must learn to regard her problematic past as an "enemy worthy of [her] mettle, a piece of [her] personality, which has solid ground for its existence and out of which things of value for [her] future life have to be derived." Her communication with Beloved—and the events of the past that Beloved both symbolizes and evokes—affords Sethe the opportunity "to become . . . conversant with this resistance over which [she] has now become acquainted, to *work through* it, to overcome it, by continuing, in defiance of it, the analytic work."[31] Thus, the psychoanalytic process becomes the means by which Sethe must free herself from the burden of her past and from the burden of *hi*story.

In fact, as Michel de Certeau points out, psychoanalysis is based on the theme that dominates Morrison's novel: the return of the repressed. "This 'mechanism,' " writes de Certeau, "is linked to a certain conception of time and memory, according to which consciousness is both the deceptive *mask* and the operative *trace* of events that organize the present." "If the past . . . is *repressed*," he continues, "it *returns* in the present from which it was excluded." The figuration of this "detour-return," and its consequences in the lives of individual characters as well as the community as a whole, structures Morrison's novel.[32]

In the "poetic" chapters of the novel the reader senses the full implications of Beloved (and the younger daughter, Denver) for Sethe. The retreat of Sethe and her daughters behind the closed doors of 124 Bluestone represents a familial figuration of

---

[31]Sigmund Freud, "Remembering, Repeating and Working-Through," *Standard Edition of the Works of Sigmund Freud*, ed. James Strachey (London: Hogarth Press, 1914) 12:146–57.

[32]Michel de Certeau, *Heterologies: Discourse on the Other*, Theory and History of Literature 17 (Minneapolis: University of Minnesota Press, 1986) 3.

what Alfred Schutz calls "the succession of generations: contemporaries, predecessors, and successors,"[33] associated with the present, past, and future, respectively. The connection of Sethe's present with her past is embodied in her relationship to Beloved, while the connection with her future is embodied in her relationship with Denver. The family thus becomes the site at which to explore notions of "time and being." As an historical field, it represents the complex and intimate interdependence of past, present, and future; as an ontological field, it represents the complexity of the relation between Self and Other. The family, in other words, becomes an historically constituted social site where individual subjectivity is constructed.

Further, Beloved symbolizes women in both the contemporaneous and historical black communities. She represents the unsuccessfully repressed "Other" of Sethe as well as other women in and associated with the community: Ella, whose "puberty was spent in a house where she was abused by a father and son"; Vashti, who was forced into concubinage by her young master; and the girl reportedly locked up by a "whiteman" who had used her to his own purpose "since she was a pup." Beyond this, however, Beloved is associated with her maternal and paternal grandmothers and the generation of slave women who failed to survive the "middle passage." As trace of "the disremembered and unaccounted for," Beloved's symbolic function of otherness connects the individual to repressed aspects of the self as well as to contemporaneous and historical others. In fact, Beloved's implication in the lives of the collectivity of women makes it necessary that all the women in the community later participate in the ritual to exorcise her.

The reconstitution of self and other through rememory in the act of storytelling is central to Morrison's vision. It is an act that imposes sequence and meaning on the welter of images that shape and define one's sense of self. Yet Sethe must not only narrativize her life in White's sense of formulating her past into a coherent story; she must also be able to continue the process of metamorphosis by "metaphorizing" her experiences within narrative.[34] Morrison uses the metaphor of maternity to establish

---

[33]Alfred Schutz as quoted in Ricoeur 3:109.

[34]Although White's work speaks eloquently to a "classification of discourses based on tropology" (22), Philip Stambovsky's work on metaphor and historical writing addresses my concerns more specifically in this in-

an alternative to the metaphor of paternity common in white/male historical discourse. This recurrent structuring metaphor complements and amplifies the images of the female body encoded in the text. In "Site of Memory," Morrison provides a *cognitive* metaphor for representing her reconstructive methods as a novelist. The images of interiority that she privileges are specifically female, associated with the "interior" rather than the "exterior" life, with the personal rather than the public representation of experience. Ultimately, such a metaphor suggests that the object of our understanding is *inside* rather than *outside*, and can be reached only by what Morrison describes as "literary archeology."[35]

Moreover, Sethe's birthing of the past and future appropriately figures Morrison's use of *depictive* metaphor. If the act of birthing represents Sethe's life story in a metaphor of maternity, then the womb functions as an image of corporeal interiority, the counterpart to Sethe's psychic interiority and Morrison's diegetic interiority. As a narrative metaphor, maternity privileges interiority and marks Sethe's entry into subjectivity. Perhaps the best example of this function is found in the scene describing Sethe's reaction upon seeing the incarnate Beloved for the first time:

> for some reason she could not immediately account for, the moment she got close enough to see [Beloved's face], Sethe's bladder filled to capacity. . . . She never made the outhouse. Right in front of its door she had to lift her skirts, and the water she voided was endless. Like a horse, she thought, but as it went on and on she thought, No, more like flooding the boat when Denver was born. So much water Amy said, "Hold on . . . You going to sink us you keep that up." But there was no stopping water

---

stance. Using Maurice Mandelbaum's "three historical forms—explanatory, sequential, and interpretive" as a "context for determining the functioning . . . of . . . metaphor in historical discourse," Stambovsky identifies three functions of metaphor: heuristic, depictive, and cognitive. See Philip Stambovsky, "Metaphor and Historical Understanding," *History and Theory* 27 (1988): 125–34.

[35]See Kaja Silverman, *The Acoustic Mirror: The Female Voice in Psychoanalysis and Cinema* (Bloomington: Indiana University Press, 1988) for an interesting discussion of the notions of interiority and exteriority.

breaking from a breaking womb and there was no stopping now. (51)

Sethe rejects the equine metaphor on second thought. In a radical reconception of history and culture, her ritual of birthing figures motherhood as a primary metaphor of history and culture. The postdeluvian connotation of "breaking of the water" historicizes the event and, at the same time, signifies a maternal delivery that becomes a means of "deliverance" from the dominant conception of history as a white/paternal metaphor. Morrison seems to depict here a second immaculate conception, as it were, in which black motherhood becomes self-generative—a process that reconstitutes black womanhood. By shifting the dominant metaphor from white to black and from paternity (embodied in the slavemaster) to maternity (embodied in the black female slave), Morrison has shifted meaning and value. Through this process of destructuring and restructuring, of decoding and recoding, the author redefines notions of genesis and meaning as they have constituted black womanhood in the dominant discourse.

The images of motherhood function *heuristically* to explain or "trace" Sethe's history and that of the community along "motherlines." Her past, birthed from a womblike matrix, is read back through motherlines tracked through four generations of marked slave women. Beloved's "thirst" for these stories gives her mother "an unexpected pleasure" in *speaking* things that "she and Baby Suggs had agreed without saying so . . . [were] *unspeakable*" (my emphasis). In speaking, that is, in storytelling, Sethe is able to construct an alternate text of black womanhood. This power to fashion a counter-narrative, thereby rejecting the definitions imposed by the dominant other(s), finally provides Sethe with a self—a past, present, and future.

Beloved's persistent questions enable Sethe to re-member long-forgotten traces of her own mother, traces carried through memory as well as through the body. Sethe remembers that her own mother bore a mark, "a circle and a cross burnt right in the skin" on her rib. It was the mark of ownership by the master who had as much as written "property" under her breast. Yet like Sethe (as well as Hawthorne's Hester Prynne), her mother had transformed a mark of mutilation, a sign of diminished humanity, into a sign of recognition and identity. Sethe recalls her mother's words: "This is your ma'am. . . . I am the only one got this mark now. The rest dead. If something happens to me and you can't tell me by my face, you can know me by this mark" (61). Indeed, her own markings help her to decode the meaning of her mother's remarks. Sethe tells her own daughters, Denver and Beloved, "I didn't understand it then. Not till I had a mark of my own."

Constructed and metaphorized along motherlines, Sethe's retelling of her childhood story also enables her to decipher and pass on to her own daughter meaning encoded in a long-forgotten "mother tongue." Equally important, Sethe's story enables her to reread or reemplot her own experiences in the context of sacrifice, resistance, and mother-love. Although Sethe knows that the "language her ma'am spoke . . . would never come back," she begins to recognize "the message—that was and had been there all along," and she begins "picking meaning out of a code she no longer understood." Like the historian who seeks to configure a probable story out of a plethora of documents, Sethe seeks to reconfigure events based on "words. Words Sethe understood then but could neither recall nor repeat now" (62). Remembering the story told her by Nan—"the one she knew best, who was around all day, who nursed babies, cooked, had one good arm and half of another"—Nan, who spoke "the same language her ma'am spoke," Sethe is able to reconstruct her own story:

> Nighttime. Nan holding her with her good arm, waving the stump of the other in the air. "Telling you. I am telling you, small girl Sethe," and she did that. She told Sethe that her mother and Nan were together from the sea. Both were taken up many times by the crew. "She threw them all away but you. The one from the crew she threw away on the island. The others from more whites she also threw away. Without names, she threw them. You she gave the name of the black man. She put her arms around him. The others she did not put her arms around. Never. Never. Telling you. I am telling you, small girl Sethe." (62)

Sethe's name recalls the Old Testament Hebrew name "Seth," meaning "granted" or "appointed." (Eve named her third-born Seth, saying, "God has granted me another child in the place of

Abel.")[36]    In this instance, Sethe seems to signify the child
whose life was spared or "granted" by her mother, who did not
keep the offspring of her white rapists.   The story about her own
mother that she hears as a child from Nan, another mutilated
mother, ironically prefigures Sethe's own actions but at the same
time challenges her to some accountability.    For although
Beloved, like Sethe and her mother, bears a mark of mutilation,
the scar across Beloved's throat is the mark of Sethe's own
hand.   And it is the fingerprints on Beloved's forehead as well as
the scar under her chin ("the little curved shadow of a smile in
the kootchy-koochy-coo place") that enables Sethe to recognize
her daughter returned from "the other side."

In light of her recognition Sethe reconstitutes a family story
of infanticide, a story of repetition but repetition with a marked
difference.   Sethe's story of mother-love seems to overwrite a
story of rejection, and her task as historian is to find a narrative
form that speaks to that difference.   But it is her mother's story
that refamiliarizes her own story.   She receives from her mother
that which she had hoped to discover with Paul D: "Her story
was   bearable"—*not*   because   it   was   Paul   D's   but   *her
mother's*—"to tell, to refine and tell again" (99).   The maternal
discourse becomes a testimonial for Sethe.   Mother and daughter
share protection of their own children—the one by saving a life
and the other by taking a life.

But there are competing configurations as well.   The first
full representation of the events surrounding the infanticide
comes from a collective white/male perspective, represented by
schoolteacher and the sheriff:

> Inside [the shed], two boys bled in the sawdust and dirt
> at the feet of a nigger woman holding a blood-soaked
> child to her chest with one hand and an infant by the
> heels in the other.   She did not look at them; she simply
> swung the baby toward the wall planks, missed and tried
> to connect a second time. . . . Right off it was clear, to
> schoolteacher especially, that there was nothing there to

---

[36]Genesis 5:25. Seth was also the name of the Egyptian god of confusion, described as a trickster-like marginal figure located "beyond or between the boundaries of social definition . . . [who] gleefully breaks taboos
and violates the limits that preserve order."   See Anna K. Nardo, "Fool and
Trickster," *Mosaic* 22 (Winter 1989): 2.

claim. The three (now four—because she'd had the one coming when she cut) pickaninnies they had hoped were alive and well enough to take back to Kentucky, take back and raise properly to do the work Sweet Home desperately needed, were not. . . . He could claim the baby struggling in the arms of the mewing old man, but who'd tend her? Because the woman—something was wrong with her. She was looking at him now, and if his other nephew could see that look he would learn the lesson for sure: you just can't mishandle *creatures* and expect success. (149-50; my emphasis)

In schoolteacher's narrative, Sethe is "the woman [who] . . . made fine ink, damn good soup, pressed his collars the way he liked besides having at least ten breeding years left." In his words, "she's gone wild, due to mishandling of the nephew" (149). The white sheriff reads these events as a cautionary tale on "the results of a little so-called freedom imposed on people who needed every care and guidance in the world to keep them from the cannibal life they preferred" (151). Granting authority to the white newspaper's account, Stamp Paid concludes that "while he and Baby Suggs were looking the wrong way, a pretty little slavegirl had recognized [her former master's hat], and split to the woodshed to kill her children" (158). Paul D, who suddenly "saw what Stamp Paid wanted him to see," summarizes events by insisting, "You got two feet, Sethe, not four" (164-65).

Sethe must compete with the dominant metaphors of the master('s) narrative—wildness, cannibalism, animality, destructiveness. In radical opposition to these constructions is Sethe's reconceptualized metaphor of self based on motherhood, motherlines, and mother-love—a love described by Paul D as "too thick." Convinced that "the best thing she was, was her children," Sethe wants simply to stop schoolteacher:

Because the truth was . . . [s]imple: she was squatting in the garden and when she saw them coming and recognized schoolteacher's hat, she heard wings. Little hummingbirds stuck their needle beaks right through her headcloth into her hair and beat their wings. And if she thought anything, it was No. No. Nono. Nonono. Simple. She just flew. Collected every bit of life she had made, all the parts of her that were precious and fine and beautiful, and carried, pushed, dragged them through the veil, out, away, over there where no one could hurt them. (163)

"I took and put my babies where they'd be safe," she tells Paul D (164). And in this way, she explains to Beloved, "[N]o one, nobody on this earth, would list her daughter's characteristics on the animal side of the paper" (251).

In effect, Sethe creates a counter-narrative that reconstitutes her humanity and demonstrates the requirements of mother-love. By shifting the dominant white male metaphor to a black maternal metaphor for self and history, Sethe changes the plot and meaning of the story—and finally, the story itself. A story of oppression becomes a story of liberation; a story of inhumanity has been overwritten as a story of higher humanity. This process of destructuring and restructuring the dominant discourse and its organizing tropes enables Sethe (and Morrison) to subvert the master code of the master('s) text. By privileging specifically female tropes in her narrative, Sethe is able to reconstitute her self and herstory within the context of intergenerational black women's experiences as represented in memory and narrative. By placing her life history within a maternal family history and, by implication, placing her family history within a broader tradition of racial history, Morrison demonstrates both the strength of motherlines in the slave community and the ways in which ontogeny followed black female phylogeny. (The absence of Sethe's two runaway sons leaves Denver as sole heir and guarantor of the family's future.)

In accordance with Collingwood's notion of "history as reenactment" of past experience, Sethe is able, finally, to "reenact" a critical moment in her life. Collingwood describes this process, in which knowledge of the self is recovered:

> In thus re-thinking my past thought I am not merely remembering it. I am constructing the history of a certain phase of my life: and the difference between memory and history is that whereas in memory the past is a mere spectacle, in history it is re-enacted in present thought. So far as this thought is mere thought, the past is merely re-enacted; so far as it is thought about thought [or the thought underlying an action], this past is thought of as

being re-enacted, and my knowledge of myself is historical knowledge.[37]

Like the historian, Sethe is able to "re-enact" or "re-think" a
critical moment from the past and is consequently able to
demonstrate her possession of rather than by the past and to alter her own life history. Sethe's actions, moreover, show that
the present is bound to the past and the past to the future, and it
is precisely the (re)configuration of the past that enables her to
refigure the future.[38]

What has been enacted in the psychic field in the past is
dramatically and therapeutically reworked, in the social field.
The bonds of the past are broken in a climactic scene in which,
unable to "countenance the possibility of sin moving on in the
house," thirty neighborhood women perform a ritual of exorcism, which "frees" Sethe from the burden of her past:

> Instantly the kneelers and the standers joined [Sethe].
> They stopped praying and took a step back to the begin-
> ning. *In the beginning there were no words. In the begin-
> ning was the sound,* and they all knew what that sound
> sounded like. (259; my emphasis)

---

[37]Continuing, Collingwood writes, "The history of myself is thus not
memory as such, but a peculiar case of memory. Certainly a mind which
could not remember could not have historical knowledge. But memory as
such is only the present thought of past experience as such, be that experience what it may; historical knowledge is that special case of memory where
the object of present thought is past thought, the gap between present and
past being bridged not only by the power of past thought to think of the
past, but also by the power to reawaken itself in the present" (293–94).

[38]I use Collingwood's term advisedly, heeding the admonitions of Ricoeur that although the "re-enactment" of the past in the present operates
under the sign of the same, "to re-enact does not consist in reliving what
happened," primarily because it involves the notion of "rethinking." And
according to Ricoeur, "rethinking already contains the critical moment that
requires us to detour by way of the historical imagination" (Ricoeur
3:144–45). Rather than locate this process under the sign of the same, which
implies repetition, I would rather locate it under both the same and the
other—repetition with a difference.

Evoking "the beginning" in which there were "no words"—only "the sound"—black women's voices revise Scripture ("In the beginning was the word") in a way that associates the semiotic (rather than the symbolic) with creation and creativity. In its revision of Scripture, this "key," this "code," this "sound that broke the back of words" represents a challenge to the dominant white male discourse in which the text of black womanhood is constructed. Sethe is, moreover, "born again" in her reclamation by the community ("[The voices] broke over Sethe and she trembled like baptized in its wash") as much as by the community's exorcism of Beloved. The communal voice of black women, then, possesses the power not only to destroy but also to create. In fact, Sethe's "re-birth" is predicated upon the rupture of the master('s) discourse. Thus, not only is Sethe "delivered" from the "errors" of her past, but her discourse is "delivered" from the constraints of the master('s) discourse.

During the communal exorcism Sethe espies the "black hat wide-brimmed enough to hide [Schoolteacher's] face but not his purpose. He is coming into her yard and he is coming for her best thing. She hears wings. Little hummingbirds stick needle beaks right through her headcloth into her hair and beat their wings. And if she thinks anything, it is no. Nŏ no. Nonono. She flies. The ice pick is not in her hand; it is her hand" (262). Sethe, in effect, re-enacts the original event—"remembering, repeating, and working-through" the "primal scene" in a process that emblematizes the psychoanalytic process. This time, however, Sethe directs her response to the threatening Other rather than to "her best thing"—her children. Yet it is not only Sethe but the community itself that re-enacts the earlier scene. Because the community had failed to send warning of the slave captors' approach the first time, its "sin of omission" makes it no less responsible for Beloved's death than Sethe's "sin of commission." In a scene of collective re-enactment, the women of the community intervene at a critical juncture, saving not Beloved but Sethe. Thus, by revising her actions, Sethe is able to preserve the community, and the community, in turn, is able to protect one of its own.

According to Ricoeur's model, prefiguration denotes the temporality of the world of human action; configuration the world of the narrative emplotment of these events; and refiguration the moment at which these two worlds interact and affect each other. Sethe's actions constitute the prefigurative aspect; her storytelling the configurative aspect; and finally, the re-enactment constitutes the refigurative aspect.[39]  Moreover, Morrison enables the reader to connect with the otherness of these past generations—especially as it relates to the experiences of the slave women—in a process made possible by "the intersection of the world of the text with the world of the reader."  Just as Nan's story of the generational mother enables Sethe to (re)configure her past, so Morrison's story of the historical m(other) enables the reader to do likewise.  The reader, like Sethe, learns that she must claim and surrender the past in order to refigure the future.[40]

The question of Sethe's accountability, however, remains. Does Morrison, finally, indict or defend Sethe's "too thick" mother-love?  Is Sethe truly redeemed from an unspeakable past?  If so, by what means?  Where does Sethe's "redemption" from the "sins" of her past lie—both those perpetuated *upon* her and *by* her?  Is grace achieved through the spirit of Beloved (the past generations she symbolizes) or by its exorcism?  Characteristically, Morrison draws out the paradoxes and the ambiguities of this "perfect" dilemma.  I suggest, in fact, that she neither condemns nor condones but rather "delivers" her protagonist. For Sethe achieves redemption through *possession* by the spirit as well as *exorcism* of the spirit.  Significantly, for Morrison, it is not through the law ("Because the Law worketh wrath") but the

---

[39]Ricoeur designates these modes alternatively as mimesis 1, mimesis 2, and mimesis 3.  His formulation of mimesis includes what we normally (after Aristotle) call diegesis—thus expanding the notion of the imitation of an action to include description.  Ricoeur makes it clear that refiguration (or mimesis 3) is a stage that "marks the intersection of the world of the text and the world of the hearer or reader," thereby relating the world configured by the text to the world of "real action."  I have modified and extended his model by using the term to describe both the intersection of the inner world of the character and the outer world of her actions as well as the intersection of the world of the text and the world of the reader.  See Ricoeur 1:54–76.

[40]"The basic thesis [of refiguration] from which all the others are derived holds that the meaning of a literary work rests upon the dialogical relation established between the work and its public in each age.  This thesis, similar to Collingwood's notion that history is but a reenactment of the past in the mind of the historian, amounts to including the effect produced by the work—in other words, the meaning the public attributes to it—within the boundaries of the work itself" (Ricoeur 3:171).

spirit (its reclamation and relinquishment) that the individual achieves "deliverance" from the "sins" of the past.[41] *Beloved,* then, (re)inscribes the conditions of the promise in the New Testament. What is important for Morrison, however, is the mediation between remembering (possession) and forgetting (exorcism). It is the process of "working-through" that the author finally affirms. As in previous novels, Morrison focuses less on "what" and "why" and more on "how." She privileges the journey rather than the destination, the means rather than the end—a process that enables Sethe to achieve redemption by creating a cohesive psychoanalytical and historical narrative.

Like Sethe, Morrison herself seeks to achieve some mediation between "resurrecting" the past and "burying" it. Expressing her desire to provide a proper and artistic burial for the historical ancestors figured by Beloved Morrison says:

> There's a lot of danger for me writing. . . . The effort, the responsibility as well as the effort, the effort of being worth it. . . . The responsibility that I feel for . . . all these people; these unburied, or at least unceremoniously buried, people made literate in art. But the inner tension, the artistic inner tension those people create in me, the fear of not properly, artistically, burying them, is extraordinary.[42]

She apparently intends to pay the historian's debt to the past, in Ricoeur's sense of rendering the past its due and, in the process, to put it to rest.

What, then, is Morrison's final legacy to readers, and what is her own relation to the past? Does Sethe become for the reader what Beloved is for Sethe—an embodiment of the past and the experiences of previous generations? What of the haunting injunction at the end of the novel that this is NOT a story to "be passed on"—that is, to be remembered, to be retold? Must Morrison's story, along with Sethe's past, be put behind? Must the reader rid herself of the burden of the past by exorcising from historical consciousness the violence and violation experienced by her ancestors? If this injunction is taken seriously, how can Morrison's own commitment to a project of recovery and

---

[41]See Romans 4:15.

[42]Naylor and Morrison, "A Conversation" 585.

"rememory" be explained? Clearly, such an injunction would threaten to contradict the motive and sense of the entire novel.

In a 1989 interview, Morrison called *Beloved* a book "about something that the characters don't want to remember, I don't want to remember, black people don't want to remember, white people don't want to remember."[43] The author's remarks speak to the public desire to repress the personal aspects of the story of slavery. Morrison's accomplishment as historian and analyst in this novel, however, is precisely *not* to allow for the continuation of a "national amnesia" regarding this chapter in America's history. For her, the absent (like the historical) is only the "other" of the present—just as the repressed is only the "other" of the conscious. Read in this context, the narrator's final and thrice-repeated enjoinder resonates with ambivalence and ambiguity. Suggesting that what is absent is not necessarily "gone" (leaving behind no "name," no "print," no "trace"), the narrator's closing reflections ensure the novel's open-endedness and subvert any monologic reading of the final injunction. Is it possible that the narrator means, indeed must she mean, that this is not a story to be PASSED ON—not in the sense of being retold but in the sense of being forgotten, repressed, or ignored? For if Richard Hofstadter is correct when he says that "Memory is the thread of personal identity, history of public identity," then it would follow that the importance of our private memories becomes, ultimately, the basis for a reconstructed public history.[44]

---

[43]Toni Morrison, "The Pain of Being Black," *Time* 22 May 1989: 120.

[44]Richard Hofstadter, *The Progressive Historians* (New York: Alfred A. Knopf, 1968) 3.

# PART FOUR.  AIDS AND THE CRISIS OF MODERNITY

# SEXUAL INVERSIONS

## Judith Butler

*In honor and memory of Linda Singer*

Some might say that the scandal of the first volume of Foucault's *History of Sexuality* consists in the claim that we did not always have a sex. What can such a notion mean? Foucault proposes that there was a decisive historical break between a socio-political regime in which sex existed as an attribute, an activity, a dimension of human life, and a more recent regime in which sex became established as an identity. This particularly modern scandal suggests that for the first time sex is not a contingent or arbitrary feature of identity but, rather, that there can be no identity without sex and that it is precisely through being sexed that we become intelligible as humans. So it is not exactly right to claim we did not always *have* a sex. Perhaps the historical scandal is that we *were* not always our sex, that sex did not always have the power to characterize and constitute identity with such thoroughgoing power (later, there will be occasion to ask after the exclusions that condition and sustain the Foucaultian "we," but for now we will try on this "we," if only to see where it does not fit). As Foucault points out, sex has come to characterize and unify not only biological functions and anatomical traits but sexual activities as well as a kind of psychic core that gives clues to an essential, or final meaning to, identity. Not only is one one's sex, but one has sex, and in the having, is supposed to show the sex one "is" even as the sex one "is" is psychically deeper and more unfathomable than the "I" who lives it can ever know. Hence, this "sex" requires and secures a set of sciences that can meditate endlessly on that pervasive indecipherability.

What conditioned the introduction into history of this notion of sex that totalizes identity? Foucault argues that during the course of the eighteenth century in Europe, famines and epidemics start to disappear and that power, which had previously been governed by the need to ward off death, now becomes occupied with the production, maintenance, and regulation of *life*. It is in the course of this regulatory cultivation of life that the category of sex is established. Naturalized as heterosexual, it is designed to regulate and secure the reproduction of life. Having a true sex with a biological destiny and natural heterosexuality thus becomes essential to the aim of power, now understood as the disciplinary reproduction of life. Foucault characterizes early modern Europe as governed by *juridical* power. As juridical, power operates negatively to impose limits, restrictions, and prohibitions; power reacts defensively, as it were, to preserve life and social harmony over and against the threat of violence or natural death. Once the threat of death is ameliorated, as he claims it is in the eighteenth century, those juridical laws are transformed into instances of *productive* power, in which power effectively *generates* objects to control, in which power elaborates all sorts of objects and identities that guarantee the augmentation of regulatory scientific regimes.[1] The category of "sex" is constructed as an "object" of study and control, which assists in the elaboration and justification of productive power regimes. It is as if once the threat of death is overcome, power turns its idle attention to the construction of objects to control. Or, rather, power exerts and articulates its control through the formation and proliferation of objects that concern the continuation of life. (Later I will briefly examine the way in which the term "power" operates in Foucault's text, its susceptibility to personification and the interrelations of the juridical and productive modalities.

I want to raise two kinds of questions in this essay, one concerning the problematic history Foucault tries to tell, and why it cannot work in light of the challenge of the recent emergence of the epidemic of AIDS, and a second, subordinate here, concerning the category of sex and its suppression of sexual difference. To be sure, Foucault could not have known in 1976 when he published the first volume of *The History of Sexuality* that an epidemic would emerge within the very terms of late modern power that would call the terms of his analysis into question. "Sex" is not only constructed in the service of life or reproduction but, what might turn out to be a logical corollary, in the service of the regulation and apportionment of death. In some recent medico-juridical discursive efforts to produce sex, death is installed as a formative and essential feature of that sex. In some recent dis-

---

[1]See Michel Foucault, *The History of Sexuality, Volume 1: An Introduction*, trans. Robert Hurley (New York: Pantheon, 1978) 85–91. This text was originally published as *La Volonté de savoir* (Paris: Editions Gallimard, 1976).

course, the male homosexual is figured time and again as one whose desire is somehow structured by death, either as the desire to die or as one whose desire is inherently punishable by death (Mapplethorpe); paradoxically and painfully, this has also been the case in the postmortem figuration of Foucault himself. Within the medico-juridical discourse that has emerged to manage and reproduce the epidemic of AIDS, the juridical and productive forms of power *converge* to effect a production of the homosexual subject as a bearer of death. This is a matrix of discursive and institutional power that adjudicates matters of life and death through the construction of homosexuality as a category of sex. Within this matrix, homosexual sex is "inverted" into death, and a death-bound desire becomes the figure for the sexual invert. One might ask here whether lesbian sexuality even qualifies as *sex* within hegemonic public discourse. "What is it that they do" might be read as "Can we be sure they do anything at all?"

For the most part, I will concentrate on the question of how Foucault's historical account of the shift in power calls now to be rewritten in light of the power/discourse regime that regulates AIDS. For Foucault, the category of "sex" emerges only on the condition that epidemics are over. So how are we now, via Foucault, to understand the elaboration of the category of sex within the very matrix of this epidemic?

Along the way, I will ask about the adequacy of this notion of "sex" in the singular. Is it true that "sex" as an historical category can be understood apart from the sexes or a notion of sexual difference? Are notions of "male" and "female" similarly subjected to a monolithic notion of sex, or is there here an erasure of difference that precludes a Foucaultian understanding of "the sex which is not one."[2]

## Life, Death, and Power

In the final section of the first volume, the "Right of Death and Power over Life," Foucault describes a cataclysmic "event" which he attributes to the eighteenth century: "nothing less than

[2]See Luce Irigaray, *The Sex Which is Not One*, trans. Catherine Porter with Carolyn Burke (Ithaca: Cornell University Press, 1985).

the entry of life into history" (1:141). What he means, it seems, is that the study and regulation of life becomes an object of historical concern, that is, that life becomes the site for the elaboration of power. Before this unprecedented "entry" of life into history, it seems that history and, more important, power were concerned with combatting death. Foucault writes:

> the pressure exerted by the biological on the historical had remained very strong for thousands of years; epidemics and famine were the two great dramatic forms of this relationship that was always dominated by the menace of death. *But through a circular process*, the economic—and primarily agricultural—development of the 18th century, and an increase in productivity and resources even more rapid than the demographic growth it encouraged, allowed a measure of relief from those profound threats: despite some renewed outbreaks, the period of great ravages from starvation and plague had come to a close before the *French Revolution*; death was ceasing to torment life so directly. But at the same time, the development of the different fields of knowledge concerned with life in general, the improvement of agricultural techniques, and the observations and measures relative to man's life and survival contributed to this relaxation: a relative control over life averted some of the imminent risks of death. (1:142)

There are of course several reasons to be suspicious of this kind of epoch-making narrativizing. It appears that Foucault wants to mark an historical shift from a notion of politics and history that is always threatened by death, and guided by the aim of negotiating that threat, to a politics that can to some extent *presume* the continuation of life and, hence, direct its attention to the regulation, control, and cultivation of life. Foucault notes the Eurocentrism in his account, but it alters nothing. He writes,

> it is not that life has been totally integrated into techniques that govern and administer it; it constantly escapes them. Outside the Western world, famine exists, on a greater scale than ever; and the biological risks confronting the species are perhaps greater, and certainly

more serious, than before the birth of microbiology.
(1:143)

Foucault's historical account can perhaps be read only as a wishful construction: death is effectively expelled from Western modernity, cast *behind* it as an historical possibility, surpassed or cast *outside* it as a non-Western phenomenon. Can these exclusions hold? To what extent does his characterization of later modernity require and institute an exclusion of the threat of death? It seems clear that Foucault must tell a phantasmatic history in order to keep modernity and productive power free of death and full of sex. Insofar as the category of sex is elaborated within the context of productive power, a story is being told in which sex, it seems, surpasses and displaces death.

If we accept the historically problematic character of this narration, can we accept it on logical grounds? Can one even defend against death without also promoting a certain version of life? Does juridical power in this way entail productive power as its logical correlate? "Death," whether figured as *prior* to modernity as that which is warded off and left behind or as a threat *within* premodern nations *elsewhere*, must always be the death, the end of a specific way of life; and the life to be safeguarded is always already a normatively construed *way* of life, not life and death pure and simple. Does it make sense, then, to reject the notion that life entered into history as death took its exit from history? On the one hand, neither one ever entered or departed, since the one can only appear as the immanent possibility of the other; on the other hand, life and death might be construed as the incessant entering and departing that characterizes any field of power. Perhaps we are referring neither to an historical shift nor to a logical shift in the formation of power. For even when power is in the business of warding off death, that can only be in the name of some specific form of life and through the insistence on the right to produce and reproduce that way of life. At this point, the distinction between juridical and productive power appears to collapse.

And yet this shift must make sense for Foucault to argue convincingly that "sex" enters history in later modernity and becomes an object that productive power formulates, regulates, and produces. When sex becomes a site of power, it becomes an object of legal and regulatory discourses; it becomes that which power in its various discourses and institutions *cultivates* in the image of its own normative construction. There is no "sex" to which a supervening law attends; in attending to sex, in monitoring sex, sex itself is constructed, produced as that which calls to be monitored and *is* inherently regulatable. There is a normative development to sex, laws that inhere in sex itself, and the inquiry that attends to that lawlike development postures as if it merely discovers in sex the very laws that it has itself installed at the site of sex. In this sense, the regulation of "sex" finds no sex there, external to its own regulation; regulation produces the object it comes to regulate; regulation has regulated in advance what it will only disingenuously attend to as the object of regulation. In order to exercise and elaborate its own power, a regulatory regime will generate the very object it seeks to control.

And here is the crucial point: it is not as if a regulatory regime first controls its object and then produces it or first produces it in order then to control it; there is no temporary lag between the production and the regulation of sex; they occur at once, for regulation is always generative, producing the object it claims merely to discover or to find in the social field in which it operates. Concretely, this means that we are not, as it were, (merely) discriminated against on the basis of our sex; power is more *insidious* than that: either discrimination is built into the very formulation of our sex, or enfranchisement is precisely the formative and generative principle of some one else's sex. And this is why, for Foucault, sex can never be liberated *from power*: the formation of sex is an enactment of power. In a sense, power works on sex more deeply than we can know, not only as an external constraint or repression but as the formative principle of its intelligibility.

Here we can locate a shift or inversion at the center of power, in the very structure of power, for what appears at first to be a law that imposes itself upon "sex" as a ready-made object, a juridical view of power as constraint or *external* control, turns out to be—all along—performing a fully different ruse of power; silently, it is *already productive* power, forming the very object that will be suitable for control and then, in an act that effectively disavows that production, claiming to discover that "sex" outside of power. Hence, the category of "sex" will be precisely what power produces in order to have an object of control.

What this suggests, of course, is that there is no historical shift from juridical to productive power but that juridical power is a kind of dissimulated or concealed productive power from the start and that the shift, the inversion, is within power, not between two historically or logically distinct forms of power.

The category of "sex," which Foucault claims is understandable only as the result of an historical shift, is actually, as it were, produced in the midst of this shift, this very shiftiness of power that produces in advance that which it will come to subordinate. This is not a shift from a version of power as constraint or restriction to a version of power as productive but a production that is *at the same time* constraint, a constraining in advance of what will and will not qualify as a properly sexed being. This constraining production works through linking the category of sex with that of identity; there will be two sexes, discrete and uniform, and they will be expressed and evidenced in gender and sexuality, so that any social displays of nonidentity, discontinuity, or sexual incoherence will be punished, controlled, ostracized, reformed. Hence, by producing sex as a category of identity, that is, by defining sex as one sex or another, the discursive regulation of sex begins to take place. It is only after this procedure of definition and production has taken place that power comes to posture as that which is external to the object—"sex"—that it finds. In effect, it has already installed control in the object by defining the object as a self-identical object; its self-identity, presumed to be immanent to sex itself, is precisely the trace of this installation of power, a trace that is simultaneously erased, covered over, by the posturing of power as that which is external to its object.

What propels power? It cannot be human subjects, precisely because they are one of the occasions, enactments, and effects of power. It seems, for Foucault, that power seeks to augment itself within modernity just as life sought to augment itself prior to modernity. Power acts as life's proxy, as it were, taking over its function, reproducing itself always in excess of any need, luxuriating in a kind of self-elaboration that is no longer hindered by the immanent threat of death. Power thus becomes the locus of a certain displaced vitalism in Foucault; power, conceived as productive, is the form life takes when it no longer needs to guard itself against death.

## Sex and Sexuality

How does this inversion from early to late modern power affect Foucault's discussion of yet another inversion, that between *sex and sexuality*? Within ordinary language we sometimes speak, for instance, of being a given sex, and having a certain sexuality, and we even presume for the most part that our sexuality in some way *issues* from that sex, is perhaps an *expression* of that sex, or is even partially or fully *caused* by that sex. Sexuality is understood to come from sex, which is to say that the biological locus of "sex" in and on the body is somehow conjured as the originating source of a sexuality that, as it were, flows out from that locus, remains inhibited within that locus, or somehow takes its bearings with respect to that locus. In any case, "sex" is understood logically and temporally to *precede* sexuality and to function, if not as its primary cause, then at least as its necessary precondition.

However, Foucault performs an *inversion* of this relation and claims that this inversion is correlated with the shift from early to late modern power. For Foucault, "it is apparent that the deployment of sexuality, with its different strategies, was what established this notion of 'sex'" (1:154). Sexuality is here viewed as a discursively constructed and highly regulated network of pleasures and bodily exchanges, produced through prohibitions and sanctions that quite literally give form and directionality to pleasure and sensation. As such a network or regime, sexuality does not emerge from bodies as their prior causes; sexuality takes bodies as its instrument and its object, the site at which it consolidates, networks, and extends its power. As a regulatory regime sexuality operates primarily by *investing bodies with the category of sex*, that is, making bodies into the *bearers of a principle of identity*. To claim that bodies are one sex or the other appears at first to be a purely *descriptive* claim. For Foucault, however, this claim is itself a *legislation* and a *production* of bodies, a discursive demand, as it were, that bodies become produced according to principles of heterosexualizing coherence and integrity, unproblematically as either female or male. Where sex is taken as a principle of identity, it is always positioned within a field of two mutually exclusive and fully exhaustive identities; one is either male or female, never both at once, and never neither one of them.

the notion of sex brought about a fundamental reversal;
it made it possible to invert the representation of the relationships of power to sexuality, causing the latter to
appear, not in its essential and positive relation to power,
but as being rooted in a specific and irreducible urgency
which power tries as best it can to dominate; thus the
idea of "sex" makes it possible to evade what gives
"power" its power; it enables one to conceive power
solely as law and taboo. (1:155)

For Foucault, sex, whether male or female, operates as a principle of identity that imposes a fiction of coherence and unity on an
otherwise random or unrelated set of biological functions, sensations, pleasures.   Under the regime of sex, every pleasure becomes symptomatic of "sex," and "sex" itself functions not
merely as the biological ground or cause of pleasure but as that
which determines its directionality, a principle of teleology or
destiny, and as that repressed, psychical core which furnishes
clues to the interpretation of its ultimate meaning. As a fictional
imposition of uniformity, sex is "an imaginary point" and an
"artificial unity," but as fictional and as artificial, the category
wields enormous power.[3]   Although Foucault does not quite claim
it, the science of reproduction produces intelligible "sex" by imposing a compulsory heterosexuality on the description of bodies.
One might claim that sex is here produced according to a heterosexual morphology.

The category of "sex" thus establishes a principle of intelligibility for human beings, which is to say that no human being
can be taken to be human, can be recognized *as* human unless
that human being is fully and coherently marked by sex.   And
yet it would not capture Foucault's meaning merely to claim that
there are humans who are marked by sex and thereby become
intelligible; the point is stronger: to qualify as legitimately human, one must be coherently sexed.   The incoherence of sex is

---

[3]"It is through sex," Foucault writes, "—in fact an imaginary point determined by the deployment of sexuality—that each individual has to pass
in order to have access to his own intelligibility, (seeing that it is both the
hidden aspect and the generative principle of meaning), to the whole of his
body (since it is a real and threatened part of it, while symbolically constituting the whole), to his identity (since it joins the force of a drive to the
singularity of a history)" (1:155–56).

precisely what marks off the abject and the dehumanized from the recognizably human.

Luce Irigaray would clearly take this point further and turn it against Foucault. She would, I think, argue that the only sex that qualifies as a sex is a masculine one, which is not marked as masculine but parades as the universal and thereby silently extends its dominion. To refer to a sex which is not one is to refer to a sex which cannot be designated univocally as sex but is outside identity from the start. Are we not right to ask, which sex is it that renders the figure of the human intelligible, and within such an economy, is it not the case that the feminine functions as a figure for unintelligibility? When one speaks of the "one" in language—as I do now—one makes reference to a neuter term, a purely human term. And whereas Foucault and Irigaray would agree that sex is a necessary precondition for human intelligibility, Foucault appears to think that any sanctioned sex will do, but Irigaray would argue that the only sanctioned sex is the masculine one; that is, the masculine that is reworked as a "one," a neuter, a universal. If the coherent subject is always sexed as masculine, then it is constructed through the abjection and erasure of the feminine. For Irigaray, masculine and feminine sexes are not similarly constructed as sexes or as principles of intelligible identity; in fact, she argues that the masculine sex is constructed as the only "one," and that it figures the feminine other as a reflection only of itself; within that model, then, both masculine and feminine reduce to the masculine, and the feminine, left outside this male autoerotic economy, is not even designatable within its terms or is, rather, designatable as a radically disfigured masculine projection, which is yet a different kind of erasure.[4]

---

[4]In this sense, the category of sex constitutes and regulates what will and will not be an intelligible and recognizable human existence, what will and will not be a citizen capable of rights or speech, an individual protected by law against violence or injury.

The political question for Foucault, and for those of us who read him now is *not* whether "improperly sexed" beings should or should not be treated fairly or with justice or with tolerance. The question is whether, if improperly sexed, such a being can even be a being, a human being, a subject, one whom the law can condone or condemn. For Foucault has outlined a region that is, as it were, outside of the purview of the law, one that excludes certain kinds of improperly sexed beings from the very category of the

This hypothetical critique from an Irigarayan perspective suggests something problematic about Foucault's constructivism. Within the terms of productive power, regulation and control work through the discursive articulation of identities. But those discursive articulations effect certain exclusions and erasures; oppression works not merely through the mechanism of regulation and production but by foreclosing the very possibility of articulation. If Foucault claims that regulation and control operate as the formative principles of identity, Irigaray in a somewhat more Derridean vein would argue that oppression works through other means as well, through the *exclusion* and *erasure* effected by any discursive formation, and that here the feminine is precisely what is erased and excluded in order for intelligible identities to be produced.[5]

## Contemporary Identity in the Age of Epidemic

This is a limitation of Foucault's analysis. And yet he offers a counterwarning, I think, to those who might be tempted to treat femaleness or the feminine as an identity to be liberated. To attempt that would be to repeat the gesture of the regulatory regime, taking some aspect of "sex" and making it stand synecdochally for the entirety of the body and its psychic manifestations. Similarly, Foucault did not embrace an identity politics that might in the name of homosexuality combat the regulatory effort to produce the symptomatic homosexual or to erase the homosexual from the domain of intelligible subjects. To take identity as a rallying point for liberation would be to subject oneself at the very moment that one calls for a release from subjec-

human subject. The journals of Herculine Barbin, the hermaphrodite (ed: Michel Foucault, *Herculine Barbin, Being the Recently Discovered Memoirs of a Nineteenth Century Hermaphrodite*, trans. Richard MacDougall (New York: Colophon, 1980), demonstrate the violence of the law that would legislate identity on a body that resists it. But Herculine is to some extent a *figure* for a sexual ambiguity or inconsistency that emerges at the site of bodies and that contests the category of subject and its univocal or self-identical "sex."

[5]This gives some clues to what a deconstructive critique of Foucault might look like.

tion. For the point is not to claim, "yes, I am fully totalized by the category of homosexuality, just as you say, but only that the meaning of that totalization will be different from the one that you attribute to me." If identity imposes a fictive coherence and consistency on the body or, better, if identity is a regulatory principle that produces bodies in conformity with that principle, then it is no more liberatory to embrace an unproblematized gay identity than it is to embrace the diagnostic category of homosexuality devised by juridico-medical regimes. The political challenge Foucault poses here is whether a resistance to the diagnostic category can be effected that does not reduplicate the very mechanism of that subjection, this time—painfully, paradoxically—under the sign of liberation. The task for Foucault is to refuse the totalizing category under either guise, which is why Foucault will not confess or "come out" in the *History of Sexuality* as a homosexual or privilege homosexuality as a site of heightened regulation. But perhaps Foucault remains significantly and politically linked to this problematic of homosexuality all the same.

Is Foucault's strategic *inversion* of identity perhaps a redeployment of the medicalized category of the invert? The diagnostic category "invert" presumes that someone with a given sex somehow acquired a set of sexual dispositions and desires that do not travel in the appropriate directions; sexual desire is "inverted" when it misses its aim and object and travels wrongheadedly to its opposite or when it takes itself as the object of its desire and then projects and recovers that "self" in a homosexual object. Clearly, Foucault gives us a way to laugh at this construction of the proper relation between "sex" and "sexuality," to appreciate its contingency, and to question the causal and expressive lines that are said to run from sex to sexuality. Ironically, or perhaps tactically, Foucault engages a certain activity of "inversion" here but reworks that term from a noun to a verb. His theoretical practice is, in a sense, marked by a series of inversions: in the shift to modern power, an inversion is performed; in the relation of sex and sexuality, another inversion is performed. And with respect to the category of the "invert," yet another inversion is performed, one that might be understood to stand as a strategy of refiguration according to which the various other inversions of the text can be read.[6]

The traditional invert gets its name because the *aim* of its desire has run off the rails of heterosexuality. According to the construction of homosexuality as narcissism, the aim has turned back against itself or exchanged its position of identification for

---

[6]If sexuality takes sex as its instrument and object, then sexuality is by definition more diffuse and less uniform than the category of sex; through the category of sex, sexuality performs a kind of self-reduction. Sexuality will always exceed sex, even as sex sets itself up as a category that accounts for sexuality *in toto* by posturing as its primary cause. In order to claim that one is a given sex, a certain radical reduction must take place, for "sex" functions to describe not only certain relatively stable biological or anatomical traits but also an activity, what one does, and a state of mind or psychic disposition. The ambiguities of the term are temporarily overcome when "sex" is understood as the biological basis for a psychic disposition, which then manifests itself in a set of acts. In this sense, the category of "sex" functions to establish a fictive causality among these dimensions of bodily existence, so that to be female is to be disposed sexually in a certain way, namely, heterosexually, and to be positioned within sexual exchange such that the biological and psychic dimensions of "sex" are consummated, integrated, and demonstrated. On the one hand, the category of sex works to blur the distinctions among biology, psychic reality, and sexual practice, for sex is all of these things, even as it proceeds through a certain force of teleology to relate each of these terms. But once the teleology is disrupted, shown to be disruptible, then the very discreteness of terms like biology and psyche becomes contestable. For if sex proves no longer to be as encompassing as it seems, then what in biology is "sex," and what contests the univocity of that term, and where, if at all, is sex to be found in the psyche, if sex can no longer be placed within that heterosexualizing teleology? These terms become disjoined and internally destabilized when a biological female is perhaps psychically disposed in nonheterosexual ways or is positioned in sexual exchanges in ways that the categories of heterosexuality cannot quite describe. Then what Foucault has called "the fictive unity of sex" is no longer secure. This disunity or disaggregation of "sex" suggests that the category only works to the extent that it describes a hyperbolic heterosexuality, a normative heterosexuality, one that, in its idealized coherence, is uninhabitable by practicing heterosexuals and as such is bound to oppress in its status as an impossible idealization. This is an idealization before which everyone is bound to fail and which of course is a failure, for clear political reasons, to be savored and safeguarded.

the position of the object desired, an exchange that constitutes a kind of psychic mistake. But to locate inversion as an exchange between psychic disposition and aim, or between an identification and an object, or as a return of an aim upon itself is still to operate within the heterosexualizing norm and its teleological explanations. Foucault calls this kind of explanation into question, however, through an explanatory inversion which establishes sexuality as a regulatory regime that dissimulates itself by setting up the category of "sex" as a quasi-naturalistic fictive unity. Exposed as a fiction, the body becomes a site for unregulated pleasures, sensations, practices, convergences and refigurations of masculine and feminine such that the naturalizing status of those terms is called radically into question.

Hence, the task for Foucault is not to claim the category of invert or of homosexual and to rework that term to signify something less pathological, mistaken, or deviant. The task is to call into question the explanatory gesture that requires a true identity and, hence, a mistaken one as well. If diagnostic discourse would make of Foucault an "invert," then he will invert the very logic that makes something like "inversion" possible. And he will do this by inverting the relation between sex and sexuality. This is an intensification and redoubling of inversion, one that is perhaps mobilized by the diagnosis but that has as its effect the disruption of the very vocabulary of diagnosis and cure, true and mistaken identity. This is as if to say: "Yes, an invert, but I will show you what inversion can do; I can invert and subvert the categories of identity such that you will no longer be able to call me that and know what it is you mean."

The pathologization of homosexuality was to have a future that Foucault could not have foreseen in 1976. For if homosexuality is pathological from the start, then any disease that homosexuals may sometimes contract will be uneasily conflated with the disease that they already are. Foucault's effort to delineate a modern epoch and to claim a break between the era of epidemics and that of recent modernity must now become subject to an inversion, which he himself did not perform but which in a sense he taught us how to perform. For Foucault claims that the epidemic is over, and yet he may well have been one of its hosts at the time he made that claim, a silent carrier who could not know the historical future that arrived to defeat his claim. Death is the limit to power, he argued, but there is something that he missed here, namely, that in the maintenance of death

358 Discourses of Sexuality

and of the dying, power is still at work and that death is and has its own discursive industry.

When Foucault gives his grand narrative of epidemiology, he can only be mistaken, for to believe that technological advance forecloses the possibility of an age of epidemic, as Linda Singer has called the contemporary sexual regime,[7] is finally evidence of a phantasmatic projection and a vainly utopian faith. For it not only presumes that technology will ward off death, or already has, but that it will preserve life (a highly questionable presumption). And it fails to account for the way in which technology is differentially deployed to save some lives and to condemn others. When we consider which technology receives federal funding, and we note that recent AIDS appropriations bills have been drastically cut, it becomes clear that inasmuch as AIDS is understood to afflict marginalized communities and is itself taken as a further token of their marginalization, technology can be precisely what is withheld from a life-preserving deployment.

On the Senate floor one hears quite specific references to AIDS as that which is somehow *caused* by gay sexual practices. Here homosexuality is itself made into a death-bearing practice, but this is hardly new. Jeff Nunokawa argues that a long-standing discursive tradition figures the male homosexual as always already dying, as one whose desire is a kind of incipient and protracted dying.[8] The discourse that attributes AIDS to homosexuality is an intensification and reconsolidation of that same tradition.

On Sunday, October 21, 1990, the *New York Times*[9] ran a memorial story on Leonard Bernstein who had recently died

---

[7]See Linda Singer, "Bodies—Powers—Pleasures," *differences* 1 (1989): 45–66; see also her forthcoming manuscript, *Erotic Welfare: Sexual Theory and Politics in the Age of Epidemic* (Routledge).

[8]Jeff Nunokawa, *"In Memoriam* and the Extinction of the Homosexual," *English Literary History*, forthcoming.

[9]Donal Henahan (H:1, 25). Later Henahan remarks that "It struck some who knew him as contradictory that the conductor who struggled to reveal himself in every performance, faithful to the great romantic tradition, nevertheless kept his private life out of the public eye. His homosexuality, never a secret in musical circles, became more overt after the death of his wife, but, perhaps, out of his concern for his carefully cultivated image, he was not eager to disillusion the straight-arrow public that had adopted him as the all-American boy of music." Here the romantic tradition of self-

from lung disease. Although this appears not to be a death from AIDS or from AIDS-related complications, a journalistic effort is nevertheless made to link his death with his homosexuality and to figure his homosexuality as a death drive. The essay tacitly constructs the scene of his death as the logical consequence of a life which, even in the romantic music he liked, seemed to know that "death was always standing in the wings." It is usually friends, admirers, lovers who stand in the wings when a conductor performs, but here it is somehow death who is uneasily collapsed into the homosexual phantasm. Immediately following this statement comes another: "his compulsive smoking and other personal excesses certainly could be interpreted in classic death-wish terms. In the Romantically committed mind, for every plus there must be a minus, for every blessing of love, a compensating curse." Here death is understood as a necessary compensation for homosexual desire, as the *telos* of male homosexuality, its genesis and its demise, the principle of its intelligibility.

In 1976, Foucault sought to disjoin the category of sex from the struggle against death; in this way, he sought, it seems, to make of sex a life-affirming and perpetuating activity. Even as an effect of power, "sex" is precisely that which is said to reproduce itself, augment and intensify itself, and pervade mundane life. Foucault sought to separate sex from death by announcing the end of the era in which death reigns; but what kind of radical hopefulness would consign the constitutive power of death to an irrecoverable historical past? What promise did Foucault see in sex, and in sexuality, to overcome death, such that sex is precisely what marks the overcoming of death, the end to the strug-

---

disclosure would appear to demand that he disclose his homosexuality, which suggests that his homosexuality is at the heart of his romanticism and, hence, his commitment to being cursed by love. The use of "straight-arrow" for straight imports the sense of "straight as an arrow," a phrase used to connote honesty. The association here suggests that to be straight is to be honest, and to be gay is to be dishonest. This links back to the question of disclosure suggesting that the author takes Bernstein's insistence on privacy as an act of deceit, and at the same time, that homosexuality itself, that is, the content of what is concealed, is a kind of necessary deceitfulness. This culminates the moralistic circle of the story, which now constructs the homosexual as one who, by virtue of his essential deceitfulness, is cursed by his own love to death.

gle against it? He did not consider that the regulatory discourse on sex could itself produce death, pronounce death, even proliferate it. And that, insofar as "sex" as a category was supposed to secure reproduction and life, those instances of "sex" that are not directly reproductive might then take on the valence of death.

He warned us, wisely, that "we must not think that by saying yes to sex, one says no to power; on the contrary, one tracks along the course laid out by the general deployment of sexuality. It is the agency of sex that we must break away from" (?). And that is right, for sex does not cause AIDS. There are discursive and institutional regimes that regulate and punish sexuality, laying down tracks that will not save us, indeed, that may lead rather quickly to our demise.

One ought not to think that by saying yes to power, one says no to death, for death can be not the limit of power but its very aim.

Foucault clearly saw that death could become an aim of politics, for he argued that war itself had become sublimated into politics: "the force relationships that for a long time had found expression in war, in every form of warfare, gradually became invested in the order of political power" (1:102). He wrote in the *History of Sexuality* "One might say that the ancient right to *take* life or *let* live was replaced by a power to *foster* life or *disallow* it to the point of death" (1:138).

When he claims that "sex is worth dying for," he means that preserving the regime of "sex" is worth dying for and that political wars are waged so that populations and their reproduction can be secured. "Wars are no longer waged in the name of a sovereign who must be defended; they are waged on behalf of the existence of everyone; entire populations are mobilized for the purpose of wholesale slaughter in the name of life necessity: massacres," he writes, "have become vital" (1:137). He then adds,

> the principle underlying the tactics of battle—that one has to be capable of killing in order to go on living—has become the principle that defines the strategy of the states. But the existence in question is no longer the juridical existence of sovereignty; at stake is the biological existence of a population. If genocide is indeed the dream of modern powers, this is not because of a recent return

of the ancient right to kill; it is because power is situated
and exercised at the level of life, the species, the race,
and the large-scale phenomena of population. (1:137)

It is not only that modern states have the capacity to destroy
one another through nuclear arsenals but that "populations"
have become the objects of war, and it is in the name of whole
"populations" that ostensibly defensive wars are waged.

In a sense, Foucault knew full well that death had not
ceased to be the goal of "modern" states but only that the aim of
annihilation is achieved through more subtle means. In the political decisions that administer the scientific, technological, and
social resources to respond to the epidemic of AIDS, the parameters of that crisis are insidiously circumscribed; the lives to be
saved are insidiously demarcated from those who will be left to
die; "innocent" victims are separated from those who "deserve
it." But this demarcation is, of course, largely implicit, for modern power "administers" life in part through the silent withdrawal of its resources. In this way, politics can achieve the goal
of death, can target its own population, under the very sign of
the administration of life. This "inversion" of power performs
the work of death under the signs of life, scientific progress,
technological advance, that is, under the signs that ostensibly
promise the preservation of life. And because this kind of dissimulated killing takes place through the public, discursive production of a scientific community in competition to find a cure,
working under difficult conditions, victims of economic scarcity,
the question of how little is allocated and how poorly it is directed
can hardly be heard. The technological aim to preserve life,
then, becomes the silent sanction by which this dissimulated
killing silently proceeds. We must not think that by saying yes
to technology, we say no to death, for there is always the question of how and for what aim that technology is produced. The
deeper offense is surely to be found in the claim that it is neither
the failure of government nor of science but "sex" itself that continues this unfathomable procession of death.

# PORTRAITS OF PEOPLE WITH AIDS

## Douglas Crimp

In the fall of 1988, the Museum of Modern Art in New York presented an exhibition of Nicholas Nixon's photographs called "Pictures of People." Among the people pictured by Nixon are people with AIDS (PWAs), each portrayed in a series of images taken at intervals of about a week or a month. The photographs form part of a larger work-in-progress, undertaken by Nixon and his wife, a science journalist, to, as they explain it, "tell the story of AIDS: to show what this disease truly is, how it affects those who have it, their lovers, families and friends, and that it is both the most devastating and the most important social and medical issue of our time."[1] These photographs were highly praised by reviewers, who saw in them an unsentimental, honest, and committed portrayal of the effects of this devastating illness. One photography critic wrote:

> Nixon literally and figuratively moves in so close we're convinced that his subjects hold nothing back. The viewer marvels at the trust between photographer and subject. Gradually one's own feelings about AIDS melt away and one feels both vulnerable and privileged to share the life and (impending) death of a few individuals.[2]

Andy Grundberg, photography critic for the *New York Times*, concurred:

> The result is overwhelming, since one sees not only the wasting away of the flesh (in photographs, emaciation has become emblematic of AIDS) but also the gradual dimming of the subjects' ability to compose themselves for the camera. What each series begins as a conventional effort to pose for a picture ends in a kind of abandon; as the subjects' self-consciousness disappears, the

---

[1]Nick and Bebe Nixon, "AIDS Portrait Project Update," 1 January 1988, quoted in the press release for "People with AIDS: Work in Progress," New York, Zabriskie Gallery, 1988 (this exhibition was shown at the same time as the MOMA show).

camera seems to become invisible, and consequently there is almost no boundary between the image and ourselves.[3]

In his catalogue introduction for the show, MOMA curator Peter Galassi also mentions the relationship between Nixon and his sitters:

> Any portrait is a collaboration between subject and photographer. Extended over time, the relationship can become richer and more intimate. Nixon has said that most of the people with AIDS he has photographed are, perhaps because stripped of so many of their hopes, less masked than others, more open to collaboration.[4]

And, after explaining that there can be no representative portrait of a person with AIDS, given the diversity of those affected, he concludes, "Beside and against this fact is the irreducible fact of the individual, made present to us in body and spirit. The life and death of Tom Moran [one of Nixon's subjects] were his own."[5]

Such mainstream photography criticism exhibits curious contradictions. All these writers agree that there is a consensual relationship between photographer and subject that results in the portraits' effects on the viewer. But is this relationship one of growing intimacy? or is it one of the subjects' gradual tuning out, their abandonment of a sense of self? And is the result to accord the subjects the individuality of their lives and deaths? or do their lives and deaths become, through some process of identification, one with the viewer's?

[2]Robert Atkins, "Nicholas Nixon," 7 Days 5 October 1988.

[3]Andy Grundberg, "Nicholas Nixon Seeks a Path to the Heart," New York Times 11 September 1988: H37.

[4]Peter Galassi, "Introduction," Nicholas Nixon: Pictures of People (New York: Museum of Modern Art, 1988) 26.

[5]Galassi 27.

Figure 1. Nicholas Nixon, "Tony and
Anna Mastrorilli" (Mansfield, MA,
July 1987)

Figure 2. "Tony Mastrorilli"
(Mansfield, MA, December 1987)

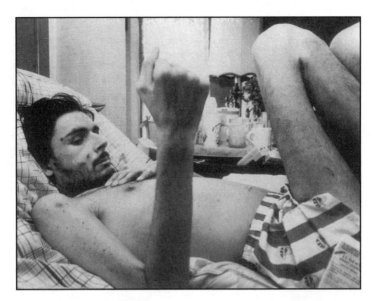

Figure 3.  "Tony Mastrorilli"
(Mansfield, MA, April 1988)

Figure 4.  "Tony Mastrorilli"
(Mansfield, MA, May 1988)

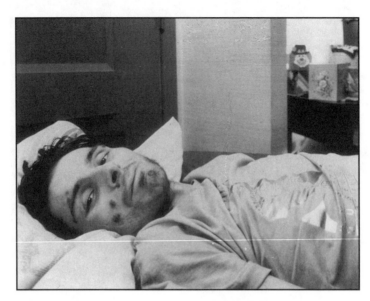

Figure 5. "Tony Mastrorilli"
(Mansfield, MA, June 1988)

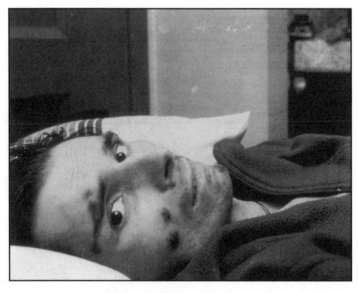

Figure 6. "Tony Mastrorilli"
(Mansfield, MA, June 1988)

For those who have paid careful attention to media representations of AIDS, none of this appears to matter, because first
and foremost Nixon's photographs reiterate media truisms about
people with AIDS: that they are ravaged, disfigured, and debili-
tated by the syndrome; they are generally alone, desperate, but
resigned to their "inevitable" deaths.

During the time of the MOMA exhibition, a small group from
ACT UP, the AIDS Coalition to Unleash Power, staged an
uncharacteristically quiet protest of Nixon's portraits. Sitting on
a bench in the gallery where the photographs of PWAs were
hung, a young lesbian held a snapshot of a smiling middle-aged
man. It bore the caption, "This is a picture of my father taken
when he'd been living with AIDS for three years." Another
woman held a photograph of PWA Coalition cofounder David
Summers, shown speaking into a bank of microphones. Its caption read, "My friend David Summers living with AIDS." They
and a small support group spoke with museum visitors about
pictures of PWAs and handed out a flier that read, in part:

NO MORE PICTURES WITHOUT CONTEXT

> We believe that the representation of people with AIDS
> affects not only how viewers will perceive PWAs outside
> the museum, but, ultimately, crucial issues of AIDS
> funding, legislation, and education.

> In portraying PWAs as people to be pitied or feared, as
> people alone and lonely, we believe that this show per-
> petuates general misconceptions about AIDS without ad-
> dressing the realities of those of us living every day with
> this crisis as PWAs and people who love PWAs.

> FACT: Many PWAs now live longer after diagnosis due to
> experimental drug treatments, better information about
> nutrition and health care, and due to the efforts of PWAs
> engaged in a continuing battle to define and save their
> lives.

> FACT: The majority of AIDS cases in New York City are
> among people of color, including women. Typically,
> women do not live long after diagnosis because of lack of
> access to affordable health care, a primary care physi-

cian, or even basic information about what to do if you have AIDS.

The PWA is a human being whose health has deteriorated not simply due to a virus, but due to government inaction, the inaccessibility of affordable health care, and institutionalized neglect in the forms of heterosexism, racism, and sexism.

We demand the visibility of PWAs who are vibrant, angry, loving, sexy, beautiful, acting up and fighting back.

STOP LOOKING AT US; START LISTENING TO US.

As against this demand—stop looking at us—the typical liberal position has held, from very early in the epidemic, that one of the central problems of AIDS needing to be combatted was bureaucratic abstraction. What was needed was to "give AIDS a face," to "bring AIDS home." And thus the portrait of the person with AIDS had become something of a genre long before a famous photographer like Nicholas Nixon entered the field. In the catalogue for an exhibition of another well-known photographer's efforts to give AIDS a human face—Rosalind Solomon's *Portraits in the Time of AIDS*—Grey Art Gallery director Thomas Sokolowski wrote of their perceived necessity: "As our awareness of [AIDS] grew through the accumulation of vast amounts of numerically derived evidence, we still had not seen its face. We could count it, but not truly describe it. Our picture of AIDS was a totally conceptual one."[6]   Sokolowski's catalogue essay is entitled "Looking in a Mirror," and it begins with an epigraph from the late George Whitmore, which reads, "I see Jim—and that could be me. It's a mirror. It's not a victim-savior relationship. We're the same person. We're just on different sides of the fence."   Sokolowski's appropriation of these sentences from a man who himself had AIDS once again creates—as with the texts written in response to the Nixon photographs—a defense mechanism, that denies the difference, the obvious sense of oth-

---

[6]Thomas Sokolowski, preface to *Rosalind Solomon: Portraits in the Time of AIDS* (New York: Grey Art Gallery and Study Center, New York University, 1988) n.p.

erness, shown in the photographs by insisting that what viewers really see is themselves.

A remarkably similar statement begins a CBS *Sixty Minutes* newsmagazine devoted to AIDS, in which a service organization director says, "We know the individuals, and they look a lot like you, they look a lot like me." The program, narrated by CBS news anchor Dan Rather, is titled "AIDS Hits Home." Resonating with the assertion that PWAs look like "you and me," the "home" of the show's title is intended to stand in for other designations: white, middle-class, middle-American, but primarily *heterosexual*. For this program was made in 1986, when, as Paula Treichler has written, "the big news—what the major U.S. news magazines were running cover stories on—was the grave danger of AIDS to heterosexuals."[7]

"AIDS Hits Home" nevertheless consists of a veritable catalogue of broadcast television's by-then typical portraits of people with AIDS, for example, the generic or collective portraits, portraits of so-called risk groups: gay men in their tight 501s walking arm in arm in the Castro district of San Francisco; impoverished Africans; prostitutes, who apparently always work on streets; and drug addicts, generally shown only metonymically as an arm with a spike seeking its vein. Also included in this category of the generically portrayed in "AIDS Hits Home," however, are "ordinary" heterosexuals—ordinary in the sense that they are white and don't shoot drugs—since they are the ostensible subject of the show. But the heterosexual in AIDS reportage is not quite "you and me." Since television routinely assumes its audience as heterosexual and therefore unnecessary to define or explain, it had to invent what might be called the heterosexual of AIDS. As seen on *Sixty Minutes*, the heterosexual of AIDS appears to inhabit only aerobics classes, discos, and singles bars and is understood, as *all* gay men are understood, to be always ready for, or readying for, sex. In addition, in spite of the proportionately much higher rate of heterosexually transmitted AIDS among people of color, the heterosexuals portrayed on *Sixty Minutes* are, with one exception, white.

The gallery of portraits in "AIDS Hits Home" also includes individuals, of course. These are the portraits that Dan Rather

---

[7]Paula Treichler, "AIDS, Homophobia, and Biomedical Discourse: An Epidemic of Signification," *AIDS: Cultural Analysis/Cultural Activism*, ed. Douglas Crimp (Cambridge, Massachusetts: MIT Press, 1988) 39.

warns of in the beginning of the program, when he says, "The images we have found are brutal and heartbreaking, but if America is to come to terms with this killer, they must be seen." For the most part, though, they are not seen, or only partially seen, for these are portraits of the ashamed and dying. As they are subjected to callous interviews and voice-overs about the particularities of their illnesses and their emotions, they are obscured by television's inventive techniques. Most often they appear, like terrorists, drug kingpins, and child molesters, in shadowy silhouette, backlit with light from their hospital room windows. Sometimes the PWA is partially revealed, as doctors and nurses manipulate his body while his face remains off-camera, although in some cases *only* the face is shown, but in such extreme close-up that the whole visage cannot be seen. And in the most technologically dehumanizing instance, the portrait of the PWA is digitized. This is the case of the feared and loathed bisexual, whose unsuspecting suburbanite wife has died of AIDS. He is shown—or rather not shown—responding to an interlocutor who says, "Forgive me asking you this question, it's not easy, but do you feel in some way as if you murdered your wife?"

The *Sixty Minutes* portrait gallery moves eventually to those whose faces can see the light of day. Among these are a few gay men, but most are women. They are less ashamed for they are "innocent." They or the narrator explain how these perfectly normal women came to be infected with HIV: one had a boyfriend who used drugs, another had a brief affair with a bisexual, and another had a bisexual husband; none of them suspected the sins of their partners. And finally there are the most innocent of all, the white, middle-class hemophiliac children. They are so innocent that they can even be shown being comforted, hugged, and played with.

Among the gay men who dare to show their faces, one is particularly useful for the purposes of *Sixty Minutes*, and interestingly he has a counterpart in an ABC *20/20* segment of a few years earlier. He is the identical twin whose brother is straight. The double portrait of the sick gay man and his healthy straight brother makes its moral lesson so clear that it needs no elaboration.[8]

---

[8]For both *Sixty Minutes* and *20/20*, the ostensible reason for showing the twins is to discuss an experimental bone marrow transplant therapy,

Indeed, the intended messages of "AIDS Hits Home" are so obvious that I do not want to belabor them but only to make two further points about the program.   First, there is the reinforcement of hopelessness.   Whenever a person with AIDS is allowed to utter words of optimism, a voice-over adds a caveat such as: "Six weeks after she said this, she was dead."   Following this logic, the program ends with a standard device.   Dan Rather mentions the "little victories and the *inevitable* defeats" and then proceeds to reveal what has happened to each PWA since the taping of the show.   This coda ends with a sequence showing a priest—his hand on a PWA's head covered with Kaposi's sarcoma lesions—administering last rites.  Rather interrupts to say, "Bill died last Sunday," and the voice of the priest returns: "Amen."

Secondly, the privacy of the people portrayed is both brutally invaded and brutally maintained.   Invaded, in the obvious sense that the subjects' difficult personal circumstances have been exploited for public spectacle, their most private thoughts and emotions exposed.   But at the same time, maintained: The portrayal of these personal circumstances never includes an articulation of the public dimension of the crisis, the social conditions that made AIDS a crisis and continue to perpetuate it as a crisis.  People with AIDS are kept safely within the boundaries of their private tragedies.   No one utters a word about the politics of AIDS, the mostly deliberate failure of public policy at every level of government to stem the course of the epidemic, to fund biomedical research into effective treatments, provide adequate health care and housing, and conduct massive and ongoing preventive education campaigns.   Even when the issue of discrimination is raised—in the case of children expelled from school—this too is presented as a problem of individual fears, prejudices, and misunderstandings.  The role of broadcast television in creating and maintaining those fears, prejudices, and misunderstandings is, needless to say, not addressed.

It is, then, not merely faceless statistics that have prevented a sympathetic response to people with AIDS.   The  media has, from very early in the epidemic, provided faces. Sokolowski acknowledges this fact in his preface to the Rosalind Solomon catalogue:

---

which requires an identical twin donor.  It does not, of course, require that the donor twin be straight.

Popular representations of AIDS have been devoid of depictions of people living with AIDS, save for the lurid journalistic images of patients *in extremis*, published in the popular press where the subjects are depicted as decidedly *not* persons *living* with AIDS, but as victims. The portraits in this exhibition have a different focus. They are, by definition, portraits of individuals with AIDS, not archetypes of some abstract notion of the syndrome. Rosalind Solomon's photographs are portraits of the human condition; vignettes of the intense personal encounters she had with over seventy-five people over a ten-month period. "I photographed everyone who would let me, who was HIV-positive, or had ARC, or AIDS . . . they talked to me about their lives."

The resulting seventy-five images that comprise this exhibition provide a unique portrait gallery of the faces of AIDS.[9]

The brute contradiction in this statement, in which "portraits of individuals with AIDS, not archetypes of some abstract notion" is immediately conflated with "portraits of the human condition"—as if that were not an abstract notion—is exacerbated in Sokolowski's introductory text, where his interpretations of the photographs read as if they were contrived as parodies of the art historian's formal descriptions and source mongering. In one image, which reminds Sokolowski of Watteau's *Gilles*, the viewer is asked to "contemplate the formal differences between the haphazard pattern of facial lesions and the thoughtful placement of buttons fastened to the man's pullover."[10] He completes his analysis of this photograph by comparing it with an "early fifteenth-century *Imago Pietatis* of the scourged Christ." Other photographs suggest to him the medieval *Ostentatio Vulneris*, the *Momento Mori*, the *Imago Clipeata*, and the image of the *Maja* or Venus.

Clearly most viewers of Solomon's photographs will not seek to place them within art historical categories. Nor will they be struck by their formal or compositional interest. Rather, many of us will see in these images, once again, and in spite of Sokolowski's insistence to the contrary, the very representations

---

[9]Sokolowski, preface to *Rosalind Solomon*.
[10]Thomas W. Sokolowski, "Looking in a Mirror," *Rosalind Solomon*.

made familiar by the mass media. William Olander, a curator at New York's New Museum of Contemporary Art who died of AIDS on March 18, 1989, saw precisely what I saw:

> The majority of the sitters are shown alone; many are in the hospital; or at home, sick, in bed. Over 90% are men. Some are photographed with their parents, or at least their mothers. Only four are shown with male lovers or friends. For the photographer, "The thing that became very compelling was knowing the people—knowing them as individuals. . . ." For the viewer, however, there is little to know other than their illness. The majority of sitters are clearly ravaged by the disease. (No fewer than half of those portrayed bear the most visible signs of AIDS—the skin lesions associated with Kaposi's Sarcoma. Not one is shown in a work environment; only a fraction are depicted outside. None of the sitters is identified. They have no identities other than as victims of AIDS.[11]

But giving the person with AIDS an identity as well as a face can also be a dangerous enterprise, as is clear from the most extended, and the most vicious, story of a person with AIDS that American television has thus far presented: the notorious episode of PBS *Frontline*, "AIDS: A National Inquiry." "This is Fabian's story," host Judy Woodruff explains, "and I must warn you it contains graphic descriptions of sexual behavior." One curious aspect of this program, given its ruthlessness, is its unabashed self-reflexivity. It begins with the TV crew narrating about itself, apparently roaming the country in search of a good AIDS story: "When we came to Houston, we didn't know Fabian Bridges. He was just one of the faceless victims." After seeing the show, viewers might conclude that Fabian would have been better off if he had remained so. "AIDS: A National Inquiry" is the story of the degradation of a homeless black gay man with AIDS at the hands of virtually every institution he encountered, certainly including PBS. Fabian Bridges was first diagnosed

[11]William Olander, "'I Undertook this Project as a Personal Exploration of the Human Components of an *Alarming Situation*' 3 Vignettes (2)," *New Observations* n. 61 (October 1988): 5. (The quote used as a title is Rosalind Solomon's.)

with AIDS in a public hospital in Houston, treated, released, and given a one-way ticket out of town—to Indianapolis, where his sister and brother-in-law live. They refuse to take him in because they are afraid for their young child, about whom the brother-in-law says, "He doesn't know what AIDS is. He doesn't know what homosexuality is. He's innocent." Arrested for stealing a bicycle, Fabian is harassed and humiliated by the local police, who are also under the illusion that they might "catch" AIDS from him. After a prosecutor drops the charges against him, Fabian is once again provided with a one-way ticket out of town, this time to Cleveland, where his mother lives. But in Indianapolis, a police reporter has picked up the story, and, as the *Frontline* crew informs us, "It was Kyle Niederpreun's story that first led us to Fabian. It was a story about the alienation and rejection that many AIDS victims suffer"—an alienation and rejection that the crew seems all too happy to perpetuate.

*Frontline* finally locates its "AIDS victim" in a cheap hotel room in Cleveland. "We spent several days with Fabian," the narrator reports, "and he agreed to let us tell his story." Cut to Fabian phoning his mother in order that her refusal to let him come home can be reenacted for the video camera. "He said he had no money," the crew goes on, "so sometimes we bought him meals, and we had his laundry done. One day Fabian saw a small portable radio he liked, so we bought it for him." The narration continues, "He spent time in adult bookstores and movie houses, and he admitted it was a way he helped support himself." Then, in what is surely the most degrading invasion of privacy ever shown on TV, Fabian describes, on camera, one of his tricks, ending with the confession, "I came inside him . . . accident . . . as I was pulling out, I was coming." "After Fabian told us he was having unsafe sex, we faced a dilemma," the narrator explains. "Should we report him to authorities or keep his story confidential, knowing that he could be infecting others? We decided to tell health officials what we knew." At this point begins the story *Frontline* has really set out to tell, that of the supposed conflict between individual rights and the public welfare.[12]

---

[12]The fascination of the media with the supposed threat of "AIDS carriers" was most dramatically revealed in the response to Randy Shilts' *And the Band Played On*, which focused almost exclusively on Shilts' story of the so-called Patient Zero (see my essay "How to Have Promiscuity in an Epidemic," *AIDS: Cultural Analysis/Cultural Activism*, esp. 237–46. The fascina-

It is a story of the futile attempts of health officials, policemen, and the vice squad to lock Fabian up, protected as he is by troublesome civil rights. A city council member in Cleveland poses the problem: "The bottom line is we've got a guy on the street here. The guy's got a gun and he's out shootin' people. . . . What do we say collectively as a group of people representing this society?" But while the city council contemplates its draconian options, the disability benefits Fabian had applied for several months earlier arrive, and after a nasty sequence involving his sadly ill-counseled mother, who has momentarily confiscated the money in order to put it aside for Fabian's funeral, Fabian takes the money and runs.

By now *Time* magazine has published a story on what it calls this "pitiful nomad," and the local media in Houston, where Fabian has reappeared, have a sensational story for the evening news. The *Frontline* crew finds him, homeless and still supporting himself as a hustler, so, they report, "We gave him $15 a night for three nights to buy a cheap hotel room. We gave him the money on the condition that he not practice unsafe sex and that he stay away from the bathhouses." Pocketing the generous gift of $45, Fabian continues to hustle, and the vice squad moves in to enforce an order by the Houston health department, issued in a letter to Fabian, that he refrain from exchanging bodily fluids. But now the vice squad, too, faces a dilemma. "Catch 22," one of the officers says. How do you entrap someone into exchanging bodily fluids without endangering themselves? They decide to get Fabian on a simple solicitation charge instead, to "get him to hit on one of us," as they put it, but Fabian doesn't take the bait.

Ultimately a leader of the gay community decides on his own to try to help Fabian, and a lawyer from the Houston AIDS Foundation offers him a home—developments about which the Houston health commissioner blandly remarks, "It would never have occurred to me to turn to the gay community for help."

---

tion has clearly not abated. At the Sixth International Conference on AIDS in San Francisco, June 20–24, 1990, members of the media took part in a panel addressing "AIDS and the Media: A Hypothetical Case Study." The hypothetical case was that of an American soldier stationed in the Philippines accused of infecting forty prostitutes. The soldier's "past" had him frequenting prostitutes in Uganda and bathhouses in the Castro district of San Francisco.

But *Frontline* has now lost its story.   As the narrator admits,
"The gay community was protecting him from the local press
and from us."   There is, nevertheless, the usual coda: "The inevitable happened.   Fabian's AIDS symptoms returned.   Just one
week after he moved into his new home, he went back into the
hospital.   This time, he stayed just over a month.   Fabian died
on November 17.   His family had no money to bury him, so after
a week he was given a pauper's funeral and buried in a county
grave."

Judy Woodruff had introduced this program by saying, "The
film you are about to see is controversial; that's because it's a
portrait of a man with AIDS who continued to be promiscuous.   In
San Francisco and other cities, the organized gay community is
protesting the film, because they say it is unfair to persons with
AIDS."   This strikes me as a very ambiguous reason to protest,
and I have no doubt that the organized gay community's position
against the film was articulated more broadly.   How is it unfair
to persons with AIDS?   What persons with AIDS?   Isn't the film
unfair, first and foremost, to Fabian Bridges?   The true grounds
on which I imagine the gay community protested are the
dangerous insinuations of the film: that the public health is endangered by the free movement within society of people with
AIDS; that gay people with AIDS irresponsibly spread HIV to
unsuspecting victims.   They might also have protested the film's
racist presumptions and class biases, its exploitation not only of
Fabian Bridges but of his entire family.   In addition, it seems
hard to imagine a knowledgeable person seeing the film who
would not be appalled at the failure of PBS to inform its audience
of the extraordinary misinformation about AIDS conveyed by
virtually every bureaucratic official in the film.   And finally I
imagine the gay community protested the film because it is so
clear that the filmmakers were more interested in getting their
footage than in the psychological and physical welfare of their
protagonist, that instead of leading him to social service agencies
or AIDS service organizations that could have helped him and his
family, they lured him with small bribes, made him dependent
upon them, and then betrayed him to various authorities.   A
particularly revealing sequence intercut toward the end of the
film returns to Fabian's hotel room in Cleveland.   "We remembered something he'd said to us earlier," the narrator says, and
Fabian then intones in his affectless voice, "Let me go down in
history as being . . . I am somebody, you know, somebody that'll

be respected, somebody who's appreciated, and somebody who can be related to, because a whole lot of people just go, they're not even on the map, they just go."

Here we have explicitly the terms of the contract between the *Frontline* crew and Fabian Bridges. *Frontline* found in Fabian, indeed, the "alienation and rejection" that many people with AIDS suffer and offered him the false means by which our society sometimes pretends to grant transcendence of that condition, a moment of glory in the mass media. They said to this lonely, ill, and scared young man, in effect, "We're gonna make you a star."

Such a contract sheds new light on the various claims that the work of photographers Nicholas Nixon and Rosalind Solomon differs from ordinary photojournalism's exploitation of people with AIDS because of the pact they have made with their sitters. "The rather unique situation of Rosalind Solomon's portraits, done in the time of AIDS," writes Thomas Sokolowski, "is that the subjects have been asked."[13]  The claim for Nixon is made less directly by his curatorial apologist.  When introducing Nixon for a lecture at the Museum of Modern Art, Peter Galassi said,

> Mr. Nixon was born in Detroit in 1947.  It seems to me that's all you really need to know, and the part about Detroit isn't absolutely essential.  What is relevant is that Nixon has been on the planet for about forty years and has been a photographer for about half of that time. It's also relevant that for about the past fifteen years he as worked with a large, old-fashioned view camera which stands on a tripod and makes negatives measuring eight by ten inches.[14]

The point about the size of Nixon's equipment, of course, is that it is so obtrusive that he could never be accused of catching his subjects unawares; he has to win their confidence. According to a friend of Nixon quoted in the *Boston Globe*, "The reason people trust him is that he has no misgivings about his own motivations

---

[13]Sokolowski, preface to *Rosalind Solomon*.

[14]This introduction by Peter Galassi and the following statements by Nicholas Nixon are transcribed from Nixon's talk at the Museum of Modern Art, 11 October 1988.

Discourses of Sexuality

or actions."[15]  Or, as Nixon himself put it in his talk at MOMA, "I know how cruel I am, and I'm comfortable with it."

My initial reaction upon seeing both the Nixon and Solomon exhibitions was incredulity. I had naively assumed that the critique of this sort of photography, articulated over and again during the past decade, might have had some effect. A single paragraph from a founding text of this criticism, written in 1976, indicates the lessons not learned:

> At the heart of [the] fetishistic cultivation and promotion of the artist's humanity is a certain disdain for the "ordinary" humanity of those who have been photographed. They become the "other," exotic creatures, objects of contemplation. . . . The most intimate, human-scale relationship to suffer mystification in all this is the specific social engagement that results in the image; the negotiation between photographer and subject in the making of a portrait, the seduction, coercion, collaboration, or rip off.[16]

Here is one indication of the photographer's disdain while negotiating with his sitter: Showing one of his serial PWA portraits, Nixon explained,

> I started taking his picture in June of '87, and he was so resistant to the process—even though he kept saying "Oh no, I love it, I want to do it"—every other part of him was so resistant that after three times I kind of kicked him out and said, "When you really want to do this, call me up, you don't really want to do this." Then one day in December he called me up and said, "I'm ready now," and so I went, of course, and this picture doesn't kill me, but, I'll tell you, it's miles better than anything I'd gotten from him before. I really felt like he was ready when I saw it. He was paralyzed from the waist down. That was part of the challenge, I guess.

---

[15]Neil Miller, "The Compassionate Eye," *Boston Globe Magazine*, 29 January 1989: 36.

[16]Allan Sekula, "Dismantling Modernism, Reinventing Documentary (Notes on the Politics of Representation)," *Photography against the Grain* (Halifax: Press of the Nova Scotia College of Art and Design, 1984) 59.

An audience member asked Nixon to explain what he meant when he said the subject was resistant, and he replied,

> He wasn't interested. He was giving me a blank wall. He was saying, "Yes, I think this is something I'm interested in, but I don't like this process, I don't like this big camera, I don't like it close to me, I don't like cooperating with you, I don't like the fact that your being here reminds me of my illness, I'm uncomfortable." But at the same time he kept on going through the motions. I had to drive forty minutes to his house. I'm not interested in somebody just going through the motions. Life's too short.

How, then, might this intimate, human-scale relationship that Sekula cautions about be constructed differently?

It can perhaps be agreed that images of people with AIDS created by the media and art photographers alike are demeaning, and that they are overdetermined by a number of prejudices that precede them about the majority of the people who have AIDS—about gay men, IV drug users, people of color, poor people. Not only do journalism's (and art's) images create false stereotypes of people with AIDS; they depend upon already existing false stereotypes about the groups most significantly affected by AIDS. Much of the PBS discussion with "experts" that followed its airing of Fabian's story focused on the fear that Fabian would be seen as the stereotype of the homosexual with AIDS. When we see homosexuality portrayed in the media, many of us respond by saying, "That's not true. We're not like that" or "I'm not like that" or "we're not all like that." But what are we like? What portrait of a gay person, or of a PWA, would we feel comfortable with? Which one would be representative? how could it be? and why should it be? One problem of opposing a stereotype, a stereotype that Fabian Bridges was indeed intended to convey, is that we tacitly side with those who would distance themselves from the image portrayed, we tacitly agree that it is other, whereas our foremost responsibility in this case is to *defend* Fabian Bridges, to acknowledge that he is one of us. To say that it is unfair to represent a gay man or a PWA as a hustler is tacitly to collaborate in the media's ready condemnation of hustlers, to pretend along with the media that prostitution is a moral failing rather than a choice based on economic and other factors limiting autonomy. Or, to take another example, do we really wish to claim that the photographs by Nicholas Nixon are untrue? Do we want to find ourselves in the position of denying the horrible suffering of people with AIDS, the fact that very many PWAs become disfigured and helpless, and that they die? Certainly we can say that these representations do not help us, and that they probably hinder us, in our struggle because at best they elicit pity, and pity is not solidarity. We must continue to demand and create our own counter-images, images of PWA self-empowerment, of the organized PWA movement and of the larger AIDS activist movement, as the ACT UP demonstrators insisted at MOMA. But we must also recognize that every image of a PWA is a *representation* and formulate our activist demands not in relation to the "truth" of the image but in relation to the conditions of its construction and to its social effects.

I want to conclude, therefore, with a work that does not seek to displace negative images with positive ones, that does not substitute the good PWA for the bad, the apparently healthy for the visibly ill, the active for the passive, the exceptional for the ordinary. My interest in the videotape *Danny*, made by Stashu Kybartas,[17] does not derive from its creation of a countertype but rather from its insistence upon a particular stereotype, one that is referred to among gay men, whether endearingly or deprecatingly, as the clone.

Without doing so deliberately or programmatically, I think, *Danny* constitutes one of the most powerful critiques of media images of PWAs. This is in part because many of its features duplicate the stereotypes of PWA portraiture but at the same time reclaim the portrait for the community from which it emerges, the community of gay men, who have thus far been the population most drastically affected by AIDS in the United States. *Danny* accomplishes this through one overriding difference: the formulation of the relationship between artist and subject not as one of empathy or identification but as one of explicit sexual desire, a desire that simultaneously accounts for Kybartas' subjective investment in the project and celebrates Danny's own sense of gay identity and hard-won sexual freedom.

---

[17]*Danny*, 1987, is distributed by Video Data Bank, Chicago.

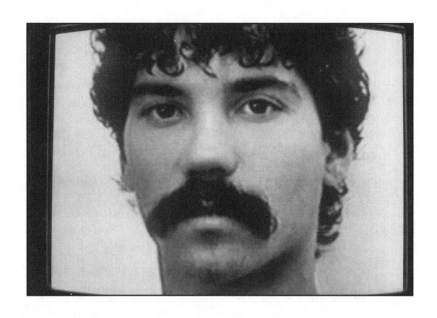

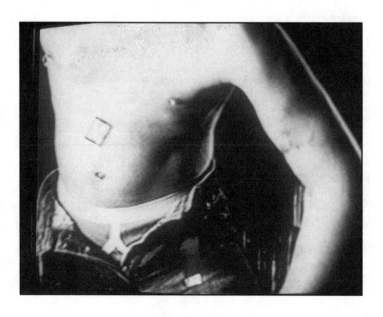

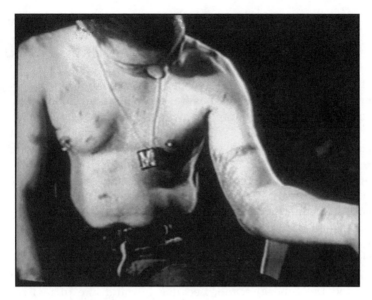

Figures 7–11.   Stashu Kybartas,
"Danny"

A great many of the conventions of media portraits of the
PWA appear in *Danny*, but their meanings are reinvested or reversed. *Danny* begins, for example, where virtually every other
television portrait ends: with the information about the death of
the video's subject, here matter-of-factly announced in a rolling
text before any image has appeared.   Thus, although the video
ends at the second recounting of Danny's death, it does not come
as a coda revealing what has happened to the subject after the
tape was made.   Indeed, as the apostrophizing voice-over makes
clear, the tape was made as a work of mourning, the artist's
working through of his loss of a friend in the AIDS movement.
The retrospective voice is reinforced by a refusal of the live video
image's movement.   Using videotape that he shot with Danny
during their brief friendship, Kybartas compiled it as a series of
stills, which also serves to make it equivalent to the still photographs taken of Danny prior to his illness, when he lived in
Miami.

In a voice that is somewhat difficult to understand, Danny
opens with these words: "He doesn't refer to me as his son. Instead of saying, 'My son'll be up to get it,' 'The boy'll be up to
get it.'   Whadaya mean the boy?   It makes me feel like Tarzan

and the jungle. Me boy." The statement remains opaque until we come to those fragments of dialogue in which Kybartas queries Danny further about his father. When Danny talks of his decision to return to his parents' home in Steubenville, Ohio, at the moment when he learned he would have to begin chemotherapy for his Kaposi's sarcoma, he mentions the difficulty of telling his mother, who nevertheless accepted the fact. Kybartas asks, "Were you worried about your dad?" "Yeah," says Danny, "I was wondering how he was going to take having a gay son, and one with AIDS on top of it, but she never told him. I have to watch what I say around him, or if anything about AIDS is on television, my mom flicks it off. She doesn't want him to hear about it."

Viewers are left to imagine Danny's home life, as his father watches his son die and never bothers to ask why. Then, in the final conversation between the two friends before the tape ends, Danny says, "What I should have done this week was to have contacted the funeral home, because I would like to feel secure knowing that I could be buried there, instead of their getting the body and saying, 'No, we can't handle that body,' and my father saying, 'Why?' 'Because he has AIDS.' That's not a time that he needs to be faced with that, not after my dying." Kybartas probes, "Why are you concerned about his reaction to that?" and Danny answers, "Trying to spare his feelings, I guess." "Why?" Kybartas persists. "I guess as much as I dislike him, I don't want to hurt him either." "Why not?" Kybartas chides, and the dialogue fades out.

It is this gruesome family scene, so typical—perhaps even stereotypical—of gay men's relations with their fathers, that is denied in sentimental media stories of gay men going home to die in the caring fold of the family, something they often do as a last resort when medical insurance has run out or disability benefits won't cover the rent. In the mainstream media, though, this scenario tells of the abandonment of gay men by their friends in the dark and sinful cities they inhabit and the return to comfort and normality in some small town in the Midwest. But in Kybartas' tape it is the small hometown, a steel town near Pittsburgh, that is dark and sinister, "slowly dying," as Danny puts it, whereas the metropolis to which Danny fled to find his sexual freedom is the very opposite of dark, though it may, in conventional moralizing terms, be sinful—that, of course, is its appeal.

This reversal of mainstream media pieties about hometown USA and the biological family serves to delimit the space of the sexual for gay men, for if Danny's father has not discerned that his son is gay and dying of AIDS, it is because Danny's identity as a sexual being must be disavowed.  Kybartas articulates this in the tape by saying, "I wanted you to come and live with us. We'd take care of you.  We could go to the gay bars in Pittsburgh, dance, and watch the go-go boys."

Danny's image as a kid who lived for sex is complicated in the video by another subtle reversal.  Mainstream coverage of AIDS is padded with portentous pictures of medical procedures—IV needles being inserted, doctors listening through stethoscopes, tinkering in laboratories.   Parallel imagery in *Danny* refers not to Danny's disease but to his profession as a medical technician, showing the carotid angiogram that he performed.  Although a full human being with a respectable profession, Danny is not heroicized by Kybartas.  Immediately following his reminiscence about his job is the "Miami Vice" sequence, in which Kybartas uses footage from that program's credits as Danny talks about shooting cocaine with shared needles back in 1981, before anyone knew the transmission risks.  This sequence interferes with still another media myth: the one that makes gay men (always presumed to be white and middle-class) and IV drug users (presumed to be poor people of color) separate "risk groups."

A standard media device for constructing AIDS as a morality tale uses before-and-after images of people with AIDS.   Stuart Marshall's *Bright Eyes*, made for Britain's Channel 4 in 1984, performed a brilliant analysis on the British tabloid *Sunday People*'s use of PWA Kenny Ramsaur to that end.   In 1983, ABC's *20/20* also used Kenny Ramsaur to show the effects of AIDS in one of the earliest and most lurid television newsmagazine stories on the subject, narrated by none other than Geraldo Rivera.  ABC's camera first shows Ramsaur's face, horribly swollen and disfigured; then snapshots of the handsome, healthy Kenny as hedonistic homosexual appear, after which the live image returns as the camera pans down to Kenny's arm to show him pulling up his sleeve to reveal his sarcoma lesions. Kybartas reworks this ploy in *Danny*. Snapshots of a young and healthy hedonist in Miami appear as Danny talks with relish of his life, of how he would spend the day on the beach, return home and let the suntan oil sink in, and then shower.  After douching in the shower, he tells us, he would shave his balls and the side of his cock, put on his tight 501s, and go out and cruise. Close-ups of Danny putting in his nipple ring are intercut with a close-up of the nipple surrounded by lesions, taken in Kybartas' studio in Pittsburgh during Danny's illness. And when a second series of early snapshots of Danny changes to the video images of his face, shot after he has returned to Steubenville, it is bloated from chemotherapy. He is nevertheless still fully sexualized. Kybartas, narrating over the image of the face, laments, "Danny, when I look at all these pictures of you, I can see that the chemotherapy caused your appearance to change from week to week. One day when you walked into the studio, I thought you looked like a longshoreman who had just been in a fight.[18] [pause]  The only time I saw you cry was on Christmas Eve, when your doctor told you that the chemotherapy was no longer working." This movement back and forth from the tough to the tender, from desiring to grieving in relation to the whole series of images constitutes the major text of the tape, and it may be said to encompass something of the range of gay men's sexuality as well as our present condition. The thematic is most often shown in the revelation of the sarcoma lesions, as stop-motion footage of Danny removing his shirt repeats time and again, or as still images show fragments of his chest and arms covered with lesions. But, like scars or tattoos, the lesions are always seen as marking the body as sexually attractive, a sexiness that Kybartas indicates in the following way: "Danny, do you remember the first night we were shooting the film at my studio?  You'd taken off your shirt and we were looking at all your lesions.  Later, as I was rubbing your back and you were telling me about the problems you were having with relationships and sex, something happened.  It was suddenly very quiet in the studio, and my heart was beating fast.  I don't know what it was . . . the heat, your body.  The only sound was the steam hissing out of the radiator."

After seeing *Danny*, it occurred to me that there is a deeper explanation for portrayals of PWAs, and especially of gay male PWAs, as desperately ill, as either grotesquely disfigured or as having wasted to fleshless, ethereal bodies.  These are not im-

---

[18]The sexual attractiveness of the gay clone was constructed through stylistic reference to cliched hyper-masculine professions such as the cowboy, policeman, sailor, and, indeed, the longshoreman.

ages intended to overcome the fear of disease and death, as is sometimes claimed. Nor are they meant only to reinforce the status of the PWA as victim or pariah, as often charged. Rather, they are, precisely, *phobic* images, images of the terror at imagining the person with AIDS as still sexual. In the *Frontline* special the Houston public health commissioner says, with patent fear and loathing, "Fabian was only diagnosed last April. He might live another two years, and furthermore this person is in remission now. He's not demonstrating any *signs* of illness!" The unwillingness to show PWAs as active, as in control of their lives, as acting up and fighting back, is the fear that they might also still be sexual, or as Judy Woodruff said of Fabian Bridges, that "he was a man with AIDS who continued to be promiscuous."

The comfortable fantasy that AIDS would spell the end of gay promiscuity, or perhaps of gay sex altogether, has pervaded American and Western European culture for a decade now. But anyone who thinks it only preoccupies the minds of the likes of Jesse Helms and Patrick Buchanan will fail to understand its pervasiveness. I want to end, therefore, by bringing this phobic fantasy close to home. In an interview published in the German art magazine *Kunstforum*, Jean Baudrillard appears sanguine about William Burroughs's (and Laurie Anderson's) dictum that "language is a virus":

> Language, particularly in all areas of information, is used in a more and more formulaic way, and thereby gets sicker and sicker from its own formulas. One should no longer speak of sickness, however, but of virality, which is a form of mutation. . . . Perhaps the new pathology of virality is the last remedy against the total disintegration of language and of the body. I don't know, for example, whether a stock market crash such as that of 1987 should be understood as a terrorist process of economy or as a form of viral catharsis of the economic system. Possibly, though, it is like AIDS, if we understand AIDS as a remedy against total sexual liberation, which is sometimes more dangerous than an epidemic, because the latter always ends. Thus AIDS could be un-

derstood as a counterforce against the total elimination of structure and the total unfolding of sexuality.[19]

---

[19]"Virtuelle Katastrophen" (interview with Jean Baudrillard by Florian Rotzer), *Kunstforum*, January-February 1990: 266. Thanks to Hans Haacke for bringing this interview to my attention.

# VALUES IN AN AGE OF UNCERTAINTY

## Jeffrey Weeks

We live in an age of uncertainty, when firm guarantees seem in short supply and our cultural goals are clouded and indeterminate. Nowhere is this uncertainty more acute than in the domain of sexuality, which has been the focus of so many recent moral panics and controversies. Is it still possible, then, to elaborate a coherent set of values and principles without surrendering to absolutism or fundamentalist beliefs of one sort or another? I believe the answer is yes, but I want to reach this tentative conclusion by first exploring some of the dilemmas that face us. And as an introduction to those dilemmas I shall begin with a particular crisis that confronts us all, a crisis that must dominate our thinking about sexuality today: the health crisis generated by HIV infection, summed up in the powerful and symbolic term "AIDS."

I agree fully with those who refuse to see "AIDS" as a metaphor for anything. It is, as AIDS activists have put it, "a natural disaster," though one helped along by prejudice, discrimination, and less than benign neglect. It is not a judgment from God, not "nature's revenge" on any group of people, not a symbol of a culture gone wrong. HIV disease is an illness like any other, and it should be confronted with all the compassion, empathy, and resources that other major health crises demand. But that is not, of course, how it has been seen. As the baroque language and the proliferation of metaphors surrounding it suggest, the response to HIV has not been like the response to any other virus.[1] During the 1980s AIDS became a symbol of a culture at odds with itself, a global issue that evoked a multitude of

---

This is a substantially revised version of an essay originally published as "Invented Moralities" in *History Workshop Journal* 32 (Autumn 1991): 151–66. I am grateful to the editors of the journal and to Oxford University Press for permission to republish. The essay originated in a paper given at the Institute for the Humanities, University of Michigan, 28 March 1991. I wish to record my thanks to those who commented on the paper on that occasion.

[1]See, for example, Susan Sontag, *AIDS and its Metaphors* (London: Allen Lane, 1989).

389

local passions, moralities, and prejudices, the epitome of a civilization whose values were uncertain. The AIDS crisis throws into relief many contemporary discontents and dilemmas, exposing many a dark and murky corner of our collective unconscious. Any discussion of sexual values as we approach the end of the millennium must therefore confront the challenge of AIDS.[2]

Of course, the person with HIV or AIDS must live with uncertainty all the time: the uncertainty of diagnosis, of prognosis, of reactions of friends, families, loved ones, of anonymous and fearful or hate-filled others. Everyone else must live with uncertainty too: the uncertainty bred of risk, of possible infection, of *not* knowing, of loss. Uncertainty breeds anxiety and fear: about the past and for the present and future. For the impact of AIDS is not predetermined but haphazard. Despite efforts to prove the contrary, there is no straightforward correlation between lifestyle and HIV infection. The virus itself, though potentially devastating in its effects, is relatively weak and is not easily transmitted except through interchange of bodily fluids. People who "do risky things" do not necessarily fall ill. As yet ill-understood cofactors (way of life, general health, incidence of poverty and other diseases) may ease the way; but a high element of chance determines who will get HIV and then who among these will succumb to opportunistic diseases. "Contingency" is a hallmark of the AIDS crisis.

Chance, accident, contingency: these are more than characteristics of a particular set of diseases. They appear as markers of the present, when things happen to us without apparent rationale or justification. The hope of modernity, that we could control nature, become the masters of all we survey, may be brought to naught by a stray assassin's bullet, by the fluttering of a butterfly in the jungles of Asia—or by a microscopic organism unknown until the 1980s.

Yet though the event may be random and unexpected, the ways in which we respond are not. AIDS may be a modern phenomenon, *the* disease of the *fin de millennium*, but it is already a remarkably historicized phenomenon, framed by histories that burden people living with HIV and AIDS with a weight they should not have to bear. There are histories of previous

---

[2]For a more detailed discussion of this theme see Jeffrey Weeks, "Postmodern AIDS?," *Ecstatic Antibodies: Resisting the AIDS Mythology*, ed. Tessa Boffin and Sunil Gupta (London: Rivers Oram Press, 1990) 133–41.

diseases and response to diseases. There are histories of sexuality, especially the unorthodox sexualities, and histories of the ways in which sexuality has been regulated. There are histories of racial categorization, of development and undevelopment. There are histories of moral panics, of punitive interventions, of various forms of oppression, and of resistance. We are overwhelmed with histories, and with the lessons they could, but usually do not, teach us. But they have one thing in common. They are histories of difference and diversity. So with AIDS. Despite the common viral and immunological factors, HIV and AIDS are experienced differently by different groups of people. The suffering and loss felt by gay men in the urban communities of large Western cities is no less nor greater than the suffering or loss of the poor in the black and Hispanic communities of New York or in the cities and villages of East Africa; but it is different.

AIDS is a syndrome that can threaten catastrophe on an unprecedented scale, but it is experienced, directly or empathetically, as a particular, historically and culturally organized series of diseases. AIDS is both global and local in its impact, and this reveals something vital about the historic present. It reminds us, first of all, about our interdependence. Migrations across countries and continents, from country to town, from "traditional" ways of life to "modern," in flight from persecution, poverty, or sexual repression, made the spread of HIV possible. The modern information society, global programs, international consultations and conferences also make possible a worldwide response to threatening disaster. Yet the very scale and speed of this internationalization of experience force us to seek localized or specialized identities, to resurrect or create particularist traditions, to invent moralities. Part of the shock of AIDS, as Paula A. Treichler has put it, was "the shock of identity."[3] In becoming aware of the global village, we seem to need to affirm and reaffirm our local loyalties, our different identities.

HIV and AIDS have also provided the challenge and opportunities for creating new identities and communities, forged in the furnace of suffering, loss, and survival: a testimony to the possibilities of realizing human bonds across the chasms of an unforgiving culture. One among innumerable examples is this

[3]Paula A. Treichler, "AIDS, Homophobia and Bio-Medical Discourse," *Cultural Studies* 1 (October 1987): 3.

testimony from the historian of homosexuality in the military, the historian Joseph Interrante, who lost his partner to the epidemic:

> Paul's illness and death condensed our life experience, and we grew and changed through it as we would through any experience, albeit at a greatly accelerated pace. But Paul's death, and AIDS generally, was not a good thing. It was not romantic, it was not heroic, it was not kind. We shared it, and I discovered, to quote Gerda Lerner, that it is "like life—untidy, tangled, tormented, transcendent. And we accept it finally because we must. Because we are human."[4]

I thus see in the AIDS crisis, and in the response it has engendered, three elements that cast a sharp light on wider currents and concerns. First, many regard AIDS as reinforcing a general sense of crisis, a "sense of an ending," generated by rapid cultural change. This is the crisis of modernity, the herald of the controversial concept of "postmodernity." Secondly, AIDS exposes the complexities and interdependence of the world, a globalization that produces, as if by a necessary reflex, a burgeoning of new identities, new communities, and conflicting demands and obligations. This is the site of many of the most acute political, social, and cultural debates today. But thirdly, these very changes, which seem to many to illustrate the final collapse of the enlightened hopes of modernity, have produced new solidarities as people grapple with the challenges of "postmodernity" in humane ways. Here, I believe, lie the real possibilities of what I shall call "radical humanism." This is a perspective that rejects the essentialism and limitations of traditional humanism and recognizes the contingency of truth—claiming systems of belief while at the same time reaffirming some of the more enduring values of the Enlightenment tradition. This is a humanism, moreover, that is grounded in people's struggles, experiences, and particular histories.

These three tendencies, illuminated by the AIDS crisis but having a wider significance, provide the unifying strands for the rest of my essay. In exploring them my purpose is to demon-

---

[4]Joseph Interrante, "To Have without Holding: Memories of Life with a Person with AIDS," *Radical America* 20, n. 6 (1987): 61.

strate that we have the opportunity to reinvent or rediscover values that help us to live with what seems to me the only irreducible truth of the contemporary world: the fact of human and social diversity, including sexual diversity. This is the real challenge of living with uncertainty.

### On Approaches To Sexuality

My work on sexuality has been shaped by a rejection of what have come to be known as essentialist arguments and an attempt to elaborate what has generally, though inadequately, been called "social constructionism." Over the past twenty years theories of sexuality as a purely natural phenomenon, of human drives as fixed and inherent, of our identities as dictated by that nature and those drives, and thus of a history of sexuality merely as an account of reactions to those basic biological givens, have been profoundly challenged, building on a century of challenges to essentialist modes of thought. Through anthropology and social analysis we have strengthened our awareness of the relativity and complexity of sexual norms. From Freud we can derive (though sadly most interpreters have not) insights into the tentative and always provisional nature of gender and sexual identities. From the new social history we have become aware of the multiple narratives of sexual life. Since feminism, lesbian and gay politics, and the theoretical work of Michel Foucault we are increasingly sensitive to the subtle forms of power that invest the body and make us simultaneously subjected to and subjects of sex. And we have recognized that ideology works precisely by making us believe that what is socially created and therefore subjected to change is really natural and therefore immutable. We no longer believe that of all social phenomena sexuality is the least changeable but, on the contrary, that it is probably the most sensitive to social influence, a conductor of the subtlest of changes in social mores and power relations. All these influences in turn feed into the deconstructionist project, which questions the fixities and certainties of post-Enlightenment humanism, rationalism, and progressivism.[5]

---

[5]For a discussion of all these themes see Jeffrey Weeks, *Sexuality and Its Discontents: Meanings, Myths and Modern Sexualities* (London: Routledge

As a result we increasingly recognize that sexuality can only be understood in its specific historical and cultural context. There cannot be an all-embracing history of sexuality, only local histories, contextual meanings, specific analyses. Instead of universalistic arguments which assume a common experience throughout time and history we need, to use Eve Sedgwick's distinction, particularist arguments that strive to understand the specifics of any sexual phenomenon: the histories that organize it, the power structures that shape it, and the struggles that attempt to define it.[6]

My own work has been concerned with three interlocked issues. First, I have questioned the sexual identities such as lesbian and gay identities, but certainly not only these, which are taken for granted as given and fixed but which any careful historical reading shows to be culturally specific, as the dominant, heterosexual forms are. Secondly, I have attempted to examine the social regulation of sexuality: the forms of control, the patterns of domination, subordination, and resistance that shape the sexual. Finally, I have explored the sexual discourses that organize meanings, and especially the discourse of sexology, which has been so central, if not alone, in proclaiming the "truth" of sex. I believe that it is only possible to understand sexuality through uncovering the cultural meanings that construct it. This does not make biology irrelevant, nor individuals merely blank

---

and Kegan Paul, 1985); and *Against Nature: Essays on History, Sexuality and Identity* (London: Rivers Oram Press, 1991). The attempt to recover the radicalism of Freud, particularly by emphasizing his disruption of identity, is perhaps the most controversial of these themes. On this see Jacqueline Rose, *Sexuality in the Field of Vision* (London: Verso, 1986). For the new social history, particularly as inspired by feminist scholarship, see, as examples, Carroll Smith-Rosenberg, *Disorderly Conduct: Visions of Gender in Victorian America* (Oxford and New York: Oxford University Press, 1985); and John D'Emilio, *Sexual Politics, Sexual Communities: The Making of a Homosexual Minority in the United States, 1940–1970* (Chicago and London: University of Chicago Press, 1983).

[6]Eve Sedgwick has usefully suggested that rather than speak any longer about essentialism versus constructionism, which has led to a tired and repetitive (and perhaps incomprehensible) internal debate among students of sexuality, we should think in terms of universalistic and particularist positions: Eve Kosovsky Sedgwick, *The Epistemology of the Closet* (Berkeley: University of California Press, 1990).

pieces of paper on which society writes its preferred meanings. To say that lesbian and gay identities have a history, have not always existed and may not always exist, does not mean that they are not important. Nor should it necessarily be taken to imply that homosexual feelings are not deeply rooted. The real question is not whether homosexuality is inborn or learned but rather: what are the meanings this particular culture gives to homosexual behavior, however it may be caused, and what are the effects of those meanings on the ways in which individuals organize their sexual lives? That historical and political question forces us to analyze the power relations that determine why those meanings are hegemonic and to investigate how those meanings can be changed.

In tracing the genealogy of our present sexual arrangements and identities, in seeking the elements that order our current discontents and political aspirations, and in surveying the sexual battlefields that make the current situation so morally and politically fraught, I have concluded that oppositional sexual identities of the present, such as the gay and lesbian identities that challenge discrimination and oppression, are historically contingent but politically essential. They may be social inventions but they also seem to be "necessary fictions," which provide the basis for an affirmative sense of self and a communal belonging.

And yet many people fear that if identities are conceived of as historically contingent, then they will lose all solidity and meaning. This points to a real problem. Social constructionism does not carry with it any obvious political program. It can be used as much by sexual conservatives as by sexual progressives. In the attempt to ban the "promotion" of homosexuality in Britain in 1987–88, culminating in the passing into law of the notorious Clause 28 of the Local Government Act, the bill's proponents explicitly argued that homosexuality could be promoted and learned—hence the bill's justification.[7] Of course, the logical corollary is that heterosexuality could equally well be learned, and is in fact promoted all the time by the institutions of our culture. But by and large heterosexuality has not been subjected to

---

[7]Clause 28, passed into law in 1988, sought to outlaw the promotion by local authorities of homosexuality as a "pretended family relationship." For a discussion of its implications see my essay, "Pretended Family Relationships," *Against Nature*.

the same vigorous inquiry as homosexuality.[8]   Very few people
are interested in tracing its social construction.   It is still regarded as the natural norm from which all else is an unfortunate
perversion.

Against the uncertainties of constructionism, then, many
seek the certainty of nature.   Isn't it better, the argument seems
to go, to define lesbians and gays as a permanent and fixed minority of the population, like a racial minority, and to claim their
place as a legitimate minority on that basis?   Early campaigners
for gay rights used precisely that justification.   From pioneers
such as Ulrichs and Hirschfeld through to the early Mattachine
Society, the idea that homosexuals constituted a third or intermediate sex, or a permanent minority, has shaped sexual politics.[9]   But it did not prevent the Nazis from using precisely the
same argument to persecute homosexuals and to send them to
die in concentration camps.

The reality is that theoretical perspectives alone cannot
promote a particular outcome.   Their effectiveness is dictated by
the meanings they glue together in specific power relations.
Sexual identities, as I have suggested, are important not because
they are either "natural" or "social," but because they provide a
basis of positive social identification.   Such an identification is
important for the sense of security and belonging that is necessary for a productive social life.   It also makes possible the
achievement of that sense of common cause with others which is
indispensable for political struggle against those who would deny
the validity of a chosen way of life.   For this reason many writers closely identified with both feminist sexual politics and the
deconstructionist approach have recently argued for what they

---

[8]Carole S. Vance, "Social Constructionist Theory: Problems in the His-
tory of Sexuality," *Homosexuality, Which Homosexuality?*, ed. Anja van
Kooten Niekerk and Theo van der Meer (Amsterdam: Uitgeverij An
Dekker/Schorer; London: GMP Publishers, 1989) 13–34.

[9]Karl Heinrich Ulrichs was a German theorist of homosexuality in the
1860s and 1870s. Magnus Hirschfeld was a giant in the German sexology
and sex reform movements from the 1890s onwards. The Mattachine Society
was established in the USA in the late 1940s and was the pioneering ho-
mophile organization there.

call a "strategic essentialism," based not in nature or truth but the political field of force—in my terms, a necessary fiction.[10]

The crucial factor, then, is not the truthful or mythic nature of sexual identities but their effectiveness and political relevance. Sexuality, as Foucault put it, is not a fatality; it is a possibility for creative life.[11] And in creating that life, we need to be clearer than ever before about the values that motivate us and to be able to affirm and validate them in a convincing way.

## A Sense of an Ending

In his influential book of that title, published in the mid-1960s, Frank Kermode wrote of "the sense of an ending" that has shadowed Western thought and its fictions.[12] That looming sense does appear to haunt much of our thought as we approach not only the culmination of the century but also the end of the millennium. As Susan Sontag has said, in the countdown to the millennium, a rise in apocalyptic thinking may be inevitable.[13] Old certainties disappear or lose their meaning; new ones clash as we attempt to reconstruct a common value system. "Panic-culture," it has been argued, dominated by a sense of loss, cancellation, and exterminism, may be one characteristic result.[14] Many writers seem to want to give up the struggle altogether as they assert the impossibility of agreeing on any values whatsoever.

---

[10]See Diana Fuss, *Essentially Speaking: Feminism, Nature and Difference* (New York and London: Routledge, 1990). For a a wide-ranging discussion of the complexities of the essentialist/constructionist debates see Jonathan Dollimore, *Sexual Dissidence: Augustine to Wilde, Freud to Foucault* (Oxford: Clarendon Press, 1991).

[11]Michel Foucault, "Sex, Power and the Politics of Identity" (interview by Bob Gallagher and Alexander Wilson), *The Advocate* n. 400 (1984): 29.

[12]Frank Kermode, *The Sense of an Ending: Studies in the Theory of Fiction* (London and Oxford: Oxford University Press, 1968).

[13]Susan Sontag, *AIDS and its Metaphors* (New York: Farrar, Straus, Giroux, 1989).

[14]Arthur and Marilouise Kroker, *Body Invaders: Sexuality and the Postmodern Condition* (London: Macmillan, 1988) 13.

"Endings" are of course largely fictions, attempts to impose some sort of order on the chaos of events. A century, after all, is only an arbitrary time frame. But the imminence of a new period, however invented, may dramatize a sense of impending change and even portend disaster. The crises of the *fin de siècle*, Showalter argues, "are more intensely experienced, more emotionally fraught, more weighted with symbolic and historic meaning, because we invest them with the metaphors of death and rebirth that we project onto the final decades and years of a century."[15] It is, perhaps, no accident then that our contemporary sensibility produces an intense interest in the political, cultural, and philosophical movements of the turn of the last century.[16]

Myths, metaphors, and images of sexual crisis and apocalypse have marked both the nineteenth-century *fin de siècle* and our own. Just as the decades since the 1960s have been attacked for their endorsement of sexual permissiveness and license, so the 1880s and 1890s were seen by the novelist George Gissing as decades of "sexual anarchy."[17] In both periods, all the laws governing sexual identity and behavior seemed to be undergoing rapid transformation, as the boundaries between men and women were challenged and stretched, as family life seemed to be under threat, as male and female homosexuality achieved an unparalleled verbosity, as the sexually "perverse" invaded the arts and literature, and as the fear of sexual disease taunted the imaginary of private and public life. Like AIDS today, syphilis haunted sex, marriage, and the family in the nineteenth-century. The child sex abuse scandals of the 1980s and 1990s immediately evoke memories of the discovery of "the maiden tribute of modern Babylon," child exploitation and prostitution, in the 1880s. Divisions in the feminist movement today about pornography echo the late nineteenth century splits over prostitution and moral purity. Fears of racial diversity today play on themes of racial superiority and racial decline prevalent in the last century. Anxieties about the sexual habits of the young and the poor (often also the black) and overpopulation in the Third

---

[15]Elaine Showalter, *Sexual Anarchy: Gender and Culture at the Fin de Siecle* (London: Bloomsbury, 1991) 2.

[16]David Harvey, *The Condition of Postmodernity* (Oxford: Blackwell, 1989) 285.

[17]Cited in Showalter 3.

World recirculate anxieties from the last century about the promiscuous sexuality of the newly urbanized masses.

All these anxieties revolve around questions of boundaries that separate one group of people from another and identities that merge them: the boundaries between men and women, the normal and the abnormal, adults and children, the civilized and the uncivilized, the rich and the poor, the enlightened and the masses. In periods of flux and unprecedented change the boundaries begin to dissolve, and identities are undermined and reformed. And in sexuality, above all, these dissolutions and mergings are most acute. Oscar Wilde in the 1890s not only breached the codes of sexual respectability by leading an increasingly dangerous homosexual life; he also broke the barriers of class by pursuing working-class youths. And sexual abuse of children in the 1980s, beyond the imposition of unwelcome adult power over children, also meant a fundamental undermining of the boundaries between, and responsibilities of, (usually) male parents for their offspring. Sexually transmitted diseases, above all, are the most radical dissolvers of boundaries: they do not admit of barriers of class, race, gender, or age.

Still, to see the late nineteenth century as a mirror image of the twentieth would be a mistake. There are common elements ("identities") but also important differences. In a brilliant essay, *Who Was That Man? A Present for Mr. Oscar Wilde*, the playwright and novelist Neil Bartlett attempted to forge connections between his generation of gay men, those of the embattled but self-conscious and confident urban subcultures of the 1980s, and that of Wilde and his contemporaries in the 1880s and 1890s.[18] He discovered that certain languages, rituals ("camp," cruising for sexual partners, the disruption of sexual orthodoxy) unite the different generations. But more fundamental are the distance and the differences: the possibilities of living an openly gay lifestyle have been radically transformed, whatever the hazards that still exist. We live in a different world, which for want of a better term I shall call *postmodern*.

There are striking parallels between recent debates on sexuality and the wider debates about the nature of postmodernity, not least in the challenge to essentialism and the opening up of

---

[18]Neil Bartlett, *Who Was That Man? A Present for Mr. Oscar Wilde* (London: Serpent's Tail, 1988).

value debates that are central to both.[19]    Postmodernity is clearly a relational term defined by a "modernity" that came before or at least is passing.   It carries with it the sense of an ending, as already noted.   We can debate its implications.   Are we, as the sociologist Anthony Giddens argues, simply witnessing the juggernaut of modernity gathering speed, causing a radicalization of modernity, sweeping away the barriers to change?[20] Or, as another sociologist Zygmunt Bauman suggests, are we watching the sleek ship of modernity finally receding into the distance, its mission achieved, but leaving us adrift in its wake?[21] However we characterize the age, there can be no doubt of its sense of radical change and, yes, uncertainty.

One of the most discussed features of postmodernity, the challenge to the "grand narratives" that characterized high modernity, highlights one of the sources of that uncertainty.[22] The "Enlightenment project" of the triumph of reason, progress, and humanity, the sense that science and history were leading us inexorably to a more glorious future, has been subjected to searching challenge.   Reason has been seen as a rationalization of power, progress as the tool of white, Western expansionism, and humanity as the cloak for a male-dominated culture.   Inevitably, this affects the discourses of sexual progressivism.   A number of feminists have seen the science of sex as a tattered cover for reaffirming male power, imposing a male-oriented "sexual liberation" on women.   Foucault has famously undermined our illusions concerning the very notion of sexual

---

[19]There is a crucial distinction to be drawn between concepts of *postmodernism* and *postmodernity*. The first term, in my view, should be limited to a series of interventions in debates on aesthetics—in architecture, literature, cinema, the visual arts—and subsequently social and cultural theory more generally. Associated with the term are a host of others, such as pastiche, eclecticism, frivolity, pleasure, nostalgia, diversity, play, amorality, nihilism, deconstruction, and so on. This must be distinguished from *postmodernity*, clearly a relational term, which refers to something—an era or epoch—that is fading.

[20]Anthony Giddens, *The Consequences of Modernity* (Cambridge: Polity Press, 1990).

[21]Zigmunt Bauman, "From Pillars to Post," *Marxism Today* (February 1990): 20–25.

[22]Compare Jean-François Lyotard, *The Postmodern Condition: A Report on Knowledge* (Manchester: Manchester University Press, 1984).

"liberation"; and many others have denounced sexual liberalism or enlightenment as a new garb for the incessant process of sexual regulation and control.[23]

In the process the original bases for the enlightened hopes of the pioneers of sexual reform at the end of the nineteenth century have disappeared. In his presidential address to the 1929 Congress of the World League for Sexual Reform, the pioneering sexologist Magnus Hirschfeld declared that: "A sexual impulse based on science is the only sound system of ethics." He proclaimed on the portals of his Institute for Sexual Science the words, "Through Science to Justice."[24] Part of that hope died as the institute burned under the Nazi torch. Much of the rest faded in the succeeding decades as the sexual scientists squabbled over their inheritance and disagreed over everything from the nature of sexual difference, female sexual needs, and homosexuality to the social consequences of disease. Behind this lay the more subtle undermining of the sexual tradition that had been defined in the nineteenth-century, in sexology, medico-moral practice, legal enactments, and personal life. A single narrative was challenged, to be replaced by a number of new narratives, many by those hitherto disqualified by the would-be science of sex. As Gayle Rubin has observed, a veritable catalogue of types from the pages of Krafft-Ebing marched onto the stage of social history, each new sexual subject claiming its legitimacy.[25] If the hallmark of the nineteenth-century pioneers of sex reform and sexology was a belief in the efficacy of science and the revelation of the laws of nature, the characteristic note of modern sexual activists is self activity, self making, the questioning of received truths, and the contestation of laws that elevate some and exclude others. Scientific sexology has been challenged by a grassroots sexology; reform from above by community organiza-

---

[23]See Sheila Jeffreys, *The Spinster and her Enemies: Feminism and Sexuality 1880–1930* (London and Boston: Pandora Press, 1985); Michel Foucault, *The History of Sexuality, Volume 1: An Introduction* (London: Allen Lane, 1979); Stephen Heath, *The Sexual Fix* (London and Basingstoke: Macmillan, 1982).

[24]See Jeffrey Weeks, *Sexuality* (Chichester and London: Ellis Horwood and Tavistock, 1986) 111.

[25]Gayle Rubin, "Thinking Sex: Notes for a Radical Theory of the Politics of Sexuality," *Pleasure and Danger: Exploring Female Sexuality*, ed. Carole S. Vance (Boston and London: Routledge and Kegan Paul, 1984).

tion from below; and a single narrative of sexual enlightenment by a host of separate histories from women, lesbians and gays, racial minorities, and others.

## *Identity and Community Again*

The contestation of the narratives of the Enlightenment co-exists with a continuing desire for certainty, for a common value system. The roots of that desire may have been undermined, but the desire is constantly reaffirmed, most dramatically in recent times in the revival of fundamentalisms of various sorts. Yet those fundamentalisms are the "truths" of distinct groups, specific traditions, which have little hope of generalizing their belief systems over unbelievers, whatever the depth of their faith, the violence of their rhetoric, or the local effects of their communal or legislative powers. The increasing complexity of the social world, the growing intermingling of experiences—and hence the proliferation of possible social belongings and identities—constantly work to undermine the idea that there can be a single truth that must be revealed, whether this is the truth of the body, of gender, of sexuality, of race or nation, or anything else. There are, it appears, only local and partial truths, relative positions, relational identities. Is it possible, then, to inhabit any identity, sexual, racial, or political, without a feeling of being arbitrarily trapped within contingent and limiting categories, pinned like butterflies to the table? The British feminist writer Denise Riley wonders whether it is even possible to inhabit a gender without a feeling of horror.[26]

The question of identity is made even more problematic because of the existence of conflicting values, both among different communities and within our own heads. Debates over values are particularly fraught and delicate because they are not simply speculations about the world and our place in it. They touch on fundamental and deeply felt issues about who we are and what we want to be or become. They also pose what increasingly can be seen as a key question in late twentieth-century politics: how to reconcile our collective needs as human beings with our

---

[26]Denise Riley, *"Am I That Name?": Feminism and the Category of "Women" in History* (London: Macmillan, 1988).

specific needs as individuals and members of diverse communities.

As the black British sociologist Paul Gilroy has put it, unable to control the social relations in which they find themselves, people have shrunk the world to the size of their communities and begun to act politically on that basis.[27]  The result has been the development of a variety of pseudopluralisms, in which difference became a substitute for any wider moral strategy, and a "category politics," which prefers a militant particularism to the finding of a common language.  But without a sense of the limits of particularist communities and in the absence of some sense of common purpose, the results have often been politically nugatory, where they were not disastrous.[28]  The danger lies not in commitments to community and difference but in their exclusive nature.  Community all too often becomes the focus of retreat from the challenges of modernity, while identity becomes a fixed attribute to hold on to at all costs.  Yet, as the political theorist Michael Sandel writes:

> Each of us moves in an indefinite number of communities, some more inclusive than others, each making different claims on our allegiance, and there is no saying in advance which is *the* society or community whose purpose should govern the disposition of any particular set of our attributes and endowments.[29]

Difference can never be absolute nor identities finally fixed in the modern world.  In a brilliant essay on "Cultural Identity and Diaspora," Stuart Hall rethinks the positioning and repositioning of Caribbean cultural identities in terms of three presences: *Présence Africaine*, the site of the repressed, apparently silenced by the burden of slavery and colonization but present everywhere in Caribbean life; *Présence Européenne*, the site of

---

[27]Paul Gilroy, *There Ain't No Black in the Union Jack* (London: Hutchinson, 1987) 245.

[28]On this see Kobena Mercer, "Welcome to the Jungle: Identity and Diversity in Postmodern Politics," and other essays in *Identity: Community, Culture, Difference*, ed. Jonathan Rutherford (London: Lawrence and Wishart, 1990).

[29]Michael J. Sandel, *Liberalism and the Limits of Justice* (Cambridge: Cambridge University Press, 1982) 146.

power, exclusion, imposition, and expropriation but which has become a constitutive element in Caribbean identities; and finally, the *Présence Américaine*, the ground, place, and territory of identity, the site of diaspora, what makes Afro-Caribbean people a people of difference. The Afro-Caribbean identity cannot be defined as essence or purity but, as Hall puts it, "by the recognition of a necessary heterogeneity and diversity; by a concept of 'identity' which lives with and through, not despite, difference; by *hybridity*."[30]

Hybridity, however, is not simply the characteristic of diaspora peoples, but, it can be argued, a marked feature of all identities in the contemporary world, despite the historically organized differences and inequalities among peoples. For identity is not a finished product but a continuing process, which is never finally achieved or completed, of shaping and reshaping into a viable narrative the fragments and diverse experiences of personal and social life, organized as they are through "violent hierarchies" of power and difference. Essentialist views of identity offer a final closure which can never be true to the experience of people living through various communities. Hence the paradox: identities are invented in complex histories but apparently essential in negotiating the hazards of everyday life. They provide the sense of belonging that makes social life possible; but they are constantly subject to reassessment and change. They seem to make us whole, but in their variety they signal our allegiances to diverse communities.

The fluidity of identities, and the diversity they reflect, provides the terrain of modern politics in general and sexual politics in particular. To see identity and community as multiple and open creates a space in which political change becomes possible. Benedict Anderson has argued that communities must be distinguished not by their falsity or genuineness but by the style in which they are imagined.[31] How to achieve a new style of debate about values, and in the context of this essay, sexual values, is the supreme challenge of the recognition of difference.

---

[30]Stuart Hall, "Cultural Identity and Diaspora," *Identity* 235.

[31]Benedict Anderson, *Imagined Communities: Reflections on the Origin and Rise of Nationalism* (London: Verso, 1982) 15.

## *For an Ethics of Moral Pluralism*

Is it possible, then, to construct a common normative standard by which we can affirm different identities and ways of life? Can we balance relativism and some sense of minimal universal values? For would-be reformers of sexual life in earlier periods the answer lay in science and history. But these provide an inadequate basis for a common standard of values today. We no longer fully trust "Science" with a capital S; and we sense that history lacks a hidden dynamic pressing toward enlightenment.

In the absence of a common language for dealing with the dilemma of difference, two types of arguments have emerged. The first is the "discourse of rights," probably still the most powerful mobilizing force in politics and ethics and the one around which most struggles over sexuality focus. Unfortunately, the claim to right does not easily reveal whose rights are to be respected. The rights of lesbians and gay men are denied as often as they are recognized. "The rights of women" are highly contested, even among women. And in the case of abortion, the conflict between "the rights of the unborn child" and the right of a woman to control her own fertility is unresolvable because two value systems pull in violently different directions. The problem is that rights do not spring fully armed from nature and cannot find a justification simply because they are claimed. Rights are products of human association, social organization, historical definitions of needs and obligations, and traditions of struggles. Whatever their assumption of universality, they are limited by the philosophical traditions to which they belong and by the social and political contexts in which they are asserted.

The second major argument, the "discourse of emancipation," assumes that difference will be transcended by "liberation." However, there are conflicts over the meaning of emancipation and the "emancipatory potential" of different social movements. Many feminists regarded the sexual liberationists of the 1960s as having increased the burden of sexual oppression on women. And not many people have been prepared to support the emancipatory potential of the pedophile movement. More often than not, the social movements claiming an emancipatory potential tend to represent the militant particularism of some rather than a social emancipation for all. The politics of emancipation, however appealing, have been no more able than the discourse of rights to provide a common set of values for coping with difference.

Against this uncertainty, it is, I believe, important to develop a language of politics that recognizes the positive value of diversity. The starting point for this is an emphasis on the "good" as a human creation, not a gift from heaven, a revelation from science, or an imposition from without, but something we all are involved in developing and defining. "The good," Foucault said, "is defined by us, it is practised, it is invented. And this is a collective work."[32] This collective work in turn relies on the elaboration, invention even, of traditions of values that provide meaning and context.

One thinks, as Ernesto Laclau has put it, from a tradition.[33] Traditions are the context of any truth. As arguments continue over time, they embody their own principles for demarcating the appropriate from the inappropriate, right from wrong. Which traditions we align ourselves with depends on a host of contingencies of birth and location, as much as on conscious choice. We have no absolute grounds for saying one tradition is better than another. But I personally want to align myself with those traditions that prefer tolerance to intolerance, choice to authoritarianism, individual autonomy to group uniformity, and pluralism to absolutism. This is the terrain of what I call *radical pluralism*. It is a tradition like any other. It has roots and points of departure, drawing on the principles of the democratic revolution, of popular struggles for rights and autonomy, of humanism. It is a tradition still in evolution that does not claim to have "truth" on its side. Indeed, if it became a dominant way of seeing the world, many truths would flourish.

In many ways, of course, radical pluralism draws on central values in the liberal tradition: its commitment to toleration and individual autonomy above all. The argument is not against liberalism *per se* nor, certainly, against the achievements of liberal democracy. The problem lies, rather, in the limitations of those achievements. The aim of a *radical* pluralism is to realize the possibilities of liberalism by identifying and combatting the forces

---

[32]Michel Foucault, "Power, Moral Values, and the Intellectual" (interview with Michel Foucault conducted by Michael Bess, 3 November 1980), *History of the Present*, n. 4 (Spring 1988): 13.

[33]Ernesto Laclau, *New Reflections on the Revolution of Our Time* (London: Verso, 1990) 219.

that limit its full potentiality: above all, institutionalized inequalities and structures of domination and subordination. It therefore simultaneously draws on traditions other than the liberal one: traditions of feminist analysis, antiracist struggle, democratic and humanist socialism. To put it another way, the achievement of a radical and plural democracy is a project to be constructed, a set of values to be worked for against the institutional barriers that inhibit the possibilities of its realization. Radical pluralism is an argument for a more open and democratic culture which does not assume any historic inevitability nor any *a priori* justification in "the nature of humankind." Its success will not be measured by the attainment of an ideal society but by its ability to respond to individual and collective needs as these evolve and change over time. Like every other, it is an "invented tradition," whose merits can only be demonstrated pragmatically, in concrete historical circumstances.

The guiding principles of this radical pluralism, and in my view the indispensable starting point for thinking about values in a diverse world, are freedom and life. In their book the *Postmodern Political Condition*, Agnes Heller and Ferenc Feher see these as the two minimum universal values, fundamental to a range of systems of thought and ethics.[34] Social systems and forms of regulation can be regarded as just, they suggest, insofar as they share common institutions, maximize the opportunities for communication and discourse, and are controlled by the conditional value of equality: "equal freedom" and "equal life chances" for all. In a pluralistic cultural universe, writes Heller elsewhere, there are "good lives":

> Different ways of life can be good, and can be equally good. Yet a lifestyle good for one person may not be good for another person. The authentic plurality of ways of life is the condition under which the life of each and every person can be good.[35]

It follows that the radically different life goals and cultural patterns of different people should be beyond formal regulation to

---

[34]Agnes Heller and Ferenc Feher, *The Postmodern Political Condition* (Cambridge: Polity Press, 1988).

[35]Agnes Heller, *Beyond Justice* (Oxford: Basil Blackwell, 1987) 323.

the extent that they are based on the conditions of equal freedom and equal life chances.

There are clearly problems with this claim to universality. It apparently conflicts with the reality of different, and clashing, value systems. I would argue, however, that the claim to universality lies not in the actual current acceptance of these "minimum common values," but in their potentiality for acceptance. They provide the minimum basis for the elaboration of a universalistic set of values that can tolerate difference. These abstract values, of course, need to be further elaborated; this is precisely the project of what we can best call a radical humanism.

I want now to explore three key ideas, which in my view provide ways of developing values around sexuality in the context of this wider inquiry: the idea of morals as pluralistic, situational, and relative; a commitment to the continuing democratization of everyday life; and the setting out of certain rights of everyday life, the necessary guarantee for the protection of individuals. I want to look at each in turn.

The central idea of radical pluralism involves respect for different ways of life, different ways of being human and of achieving self-determined ends. Since values are relative and context-bound, no act in itself can be either good or bad. We can make judgments only by attempting to understand the internal meanings of any action, the power relations at play, the subtle coercions of daily life that limit autonomy, and the formal structures of domination and subordination. But this simple idea is difficult to apply. Radical pluralism requires a set of values that can make pluralism and choice meaningful.

This suggests, as a second key theme, the application of the principle of democracy to the personal sphere. Our concepts are rightly shaped by a commitment to formal democracy at the level of national government and to vaguer notions of participation in other spheres of life. Democratic values in everyday life would judge acts by the way people deal with one another, the absence of coercion, the degree of pleasure and of needs they can satisfy. This suggests in turn a notion of reciprocity that does not calculate benefits or costs but is sustained over time and acts as a moral cement of involvement. This is often present in the obligations of family life. It is also a key characteristic of many of the alternative foci of daily life. A sense of moral involvement with others, of common belonging sustained over time without expectation of direct or immediate reward except that of mutual support, is .characteristic of what Ann Ferguson has called "chosen families," whether of lesbians and gays or others who choose to live outside conventional domestic arrangements.[36] It is also a marked feature of the support systems built up as a response to the AIDS crisis. The idea of reciprocity assumes a sense of common need and common involvement, a compassion and solidarity based on care and responsibility for others. A situational ethic is necessarily an ethic of responsibility because it is about the responsibility of choice: choice about how to live, with whom, under what circumstances. It is concerned with respect for, and the enhancement of, human dignity.

These values provide a context for asking whether there are any distinctive rights of everyday life. One present throughout this discussion is the right to difference. The recognition of diversity and acceptance of individual differences grow out of and facilitate a solidarity based on mutual respect. Indeed, it has been well argued that the right to equality, under whose banner all modern revolutions have been fought, is being replaced by an appeal to the right to difference.[37]

A second claim hovering over this discussion of personal life is the right to space. I use this idea as a metaphor for freedom for people to determine the needs and conditions of their lives. The space for individual self-determination and autonomy is constrained and limited by a host of factors, from economic deprivation and endemic poverty to the structured inequalities along lines of race, gender, sexuality, age, and culture. Calling for freedom of space does not, therefore, mean that we can take for granted that individuals have the necessary means of attaining autonomy. On the contrary, it is establishing an ethical principle against which the limits of freedom can be measured. It offers an objective to be achieved, against all the barriers that inhibit its attainment.

Freedom and autonomy are of course conditional on the acceptance of the principle that these values do not involve the treatment of another person or group of people as mere means. Radical pluralism can only work if individuals and groups are prepared to accept that a condition of freedom or space for their

---

[36]Ann Ferguson, *Blood at the Root: Motherhood, Sexuality and Male Dominance* (London: Pandora, 1989).

[37]Bauman, "From Pillars to Post."

way of life is a tolerance of the space of others. Protection of minorities must be a principle of a plural society on the condition that the minorities themselves guarantee the freedom of individuals and thus variety or autonomy for all their members, including the right of exit. In turn, the freedom of exit must be accompanied by the public freedom of voice, which at bottom is the guarantee of all the freedoms and rights of everyday life.

Morality, as Michael Walzer has written, is something we have to argue about.[38] There is no final end, no final proof of what is right or wrong—only the possibility of continuing debate about it. The idea that the condition for a good life is continuous dialogue provides a yardstick by which the degree of tolerance of a culture (or a way of life within the culture) can be measured. It directs attention to the forces that inhibit free communication. It is also the necessary condition for changing the conditions of the debate and for effecting change in intimate as well as public life, individual and collective life.

The new elective communities that have emerged in the past generation, particularly around sexuality, have been described as laboratories of social life. These "experiments in living," as Mill described them over a century ago in his essay on liberty,[39] set forth new ways of seeing and describing everyday life and hence put forward new ways of life. Only through a radical tolerance of experimentation and continuous dialogue can new ways of life be properly tested.

Ernesto Laclau has argued that "the first condition of a radically democratic society is to accept the contingent and radically open character of all its values—and in that sense, to abandon the aspiration to a single foundation.'"[40] That means that the obligation is simply transferred to us to create, choose, and clarify our values. In the end we must choose where our alignments must lie. My position, which I have described as radical pluralism, is clearly located in a certain tradition of humanist thought, and I am aware of the dubious origins of some of that

---

[38]Michael Walzer, *Interpretation and Social Criticism* (Cambridge, Mass. and London: Harvard University Press, 1987).

[39]John Stuart Mill, "On Liberty," *Three Essays: On Liberty, Representative Government, The Subjection of Women,* intro. Richard Wollheim (Oxford and New York: Oxford University Press, 1975).

[40]Laclau 125.

thinking.[41] But I believe it nonetheless contains elements for understanding and learning how to live with the irreducible and irreversible variety and diversity of modern life. Radical pluralism is not a position to be imposed, but it is one that can be argued for and argued above all in the domain of sexuality.

In an interview in 1980 Foucault offered three principles for his morals:

> (1) the refusal to accept as self-evident the things that are proposed to us; (2) the need to analyze and to know, since we can understand nothing without reflection and understanding—thus the principle of curiosity; and (3) the principle of innovation: to seek out in our reflection those things that have never been thought or imagined. Thus: refusal, curiosity, innovation.[42]

Foucault's skepticism about received wisdoms, combined with a willingness to confront the challenges of change, seems to me a good position from which to measure the transformations of personal life in general and sexual life in particular. In my view the arguments for a radical pluralism I have put forward here are rooted in those transformations. That does not mean that we are living in a world that is yet willing to accept the positive merits of diversity. The barriers to the full realization of diversity are still high. But we can measure how far we still have to go only by exploring the spaces of personal life and the conflicts around sexuality within them. That seems an appropriate way for us to learn to live with uncertainty.

---

[41]On the exclusion of women from the liberal humanist tradition see Carole Pateman, *The Sexual Contract* (Cambridge: Polity Press, 1988).

[42]Foucault, "Power, Moral Values, and the Intellectual" 1.

# Notes on Contributors

**Judith Butler** is Professor of Humanities at Johns Hopkins University. She is the author of *Gender Trouble: Feminism and the Subversion of Identity* (1990) and coeditor with Joan W. Scott of *Feminists Theorize the Political* (Routledge, 1992).

**Douglas Crimp** teaches gay and lesbian studies at Sarah Lawrence College and contemporary art theory at the Cooper Union. He is the editor of *AIDS: Cultural Analysis/Cultural Activism* (1988); the coauthor, with Adam Rolson, of *AIDS Demo Graphics* (1990); and the author of *On the Museum's Ruins*, a forthcoming collection of essays on contemporary art.

**Lesley Dean-Jones** has published articles and reviews on Greek history and literature, ancient medicine, and women in antiquity. Her book, *Women's Bodies in Classical Greek Science*, will appear in 1992. She is Assistant Professor of Classics at the University of Texas, Austin.

**Teresa de Lauretis** is Professor of the History of Consciousness at the University of California, Santa Cruz. Her books have been translated into seven languages and include: *Alice Doesn't* (1984) and *Technologies of Gender* (1987). She is currently working on *The Practice of Love*, a book on lesbian subjectivity, sexual structuring, and fantasy.

**David M. Halperin** is the author of *Before Pastoral: Theocritus and the Ancient Tradition of Bucolic Poetry* (1983) and *One Hundred Years of Homosexuality and Other Essays on Greek Love* (1990). He has prepared *The Lesbian/Gay Studies Reader* (1992) and is now at work on *Queering the Canon*, a collection of oppositional readings of classical texts. Halperin is Professor of Literature at MIT.

**Mae G. Henderson** is Associate Professor of English and African-American Studies at the University of Illinois in Chicago. The author of several articles on black/women's literature, she is the coeditor of the five-volume *Antislavery Newspapers and Periodicals: An Annotated Index of Letters, 1817-1871* (1980). Her monograph on black expatriate writers is forthcoming.

**Lynn Hunt** is the author of *Politics, Culture, and Class in the French Revolution* (1984) and *The Family Romance of the French Revolution* (1992). She has also edited *The New Cultural History* (1989) and *Eroticism and the Body Politic* (1991). Hunt is Annenberg Professor of History at the University of Pennsylvania.

**Abdul R. JanMohamed**, Associate Professor of English at the University of California, Berkeley, is currently completing a study of Richard Wright. He is the author of *Manichean Aesthetics: The Politics of Literature in Colonial Africa* (1983); the editor, with David Lloyd, of *The Nature and Context of Minority Discourse* (1990); and Associate Editor of *Cultural Critique*.

**Thomas W. Laqueur** is the author, most recently, of *Making Sex: Body and Gender from the Greeks to Freud* (1991). Professor of History at the University of California, Berkeley, Laqueur is now writing on the commemorations of the dead of the Great War and preparing a series of studies on desire in commercial society.

**Joanne Leonard** is Professor of Art at the School of Art, University of Michigan. Her work has been exhibited and reproduced widely, notably in *Time Life's Library of Photography* (1970), Lucy Lippard's *From the Center* (1976), H. W. Janson's *History of Art* (1986), and Helen Gardner's *Art through the Ages* (1991).

**Catharine A. MacKinnon** is Professor of Law at the University of Michigan Law School and a writer, lawyer, and activist who focuses on issues of sex inequality and sexual abuse. She pioneered the legal claim for sexual harassment and, with Andrea Dworkin, she coauthored ordinances recognizing pornography as a violation of civil rights. Her most recent book is *Toward a Feminist Theory of the State* (1989).

**Louis Montrose** has published on Elizabethan cultural practices and on theory and method in the historical analysis of literature. His essay in this volume will form part of a book on *The Subject of Elizabeth*. Montrose is Professor of English Literature and Chairman of the Literature Department at the University of California, San Diego.

**Jeffrey Weeks**, Professor of Social Relations at Bristol Polytechnic, England, is the author of articles and books on the social regulation of sexuality. His most recent books are: *Between the Acts: Lives of Homosexual Men 1885-1967* (with Kevin Porter, 1991), and *Against Nature: Essays on History, Sexuality and Identity* (1991). Weeks is currently working on a book about sexual values.

**Patricia Yaeger** is the author of *Honey-Mad Women: Emancipatory Strategies in Women's Writing* (1988) and coeditor of *Nationalisms and Sexualities* (1992). Associate Professor of English at the University of Michigan, Ann Arbor, Yaeger is currently at work on *Dirt and Desire: The Grotesque in Southern Women's Writing*.